The Prairie People

. . . .

Published in cooperation with

the Center for American Places,

Santa Fe, New Mexico, and

Harrisonburg, Virginia

Frontispiece. Young Prairieleut women at Langham, Saskatchewan, 1915. Photograph courtesy of Catherine Masuk.

The Prairie People

. . . .

Forgotten Anabaptists

Rod Janzen

University Press of New England

HANOVER AND LONDON

University Press of New England, Hanover, NH 03755

Printed in the United States of America

5 4 3 2 1

CIP data appear at the end of the book

. . . .

"Fats said, 'Yeh, bo, this is quite a town. Quite a town.
Everybody in it is related. Full a Hofers and Kleinsassers
and Tschetters.' Fats cleared his nose with a gurgling
sniff. "Yeh, an' when the Hofers get t'huffin,' an' the
Kleinsassers t'sassin,' an' the Tschetters t'spittin' seeds,
you got somethin." Fats allowed himself a chuckle at his
own wit. But Elof said nothing. People had laughed at his
name too. Elof scowled. How could one laugh after
having seen the lonely stones of the Tschetters and
Kleinsassers in the country graveyard?"

Frederick Manfred, *The Chokecherry Tree*

Contents

. . . .

Tables and Illustrations

. . . .

Tables

Maps

Figures

Acknowledgments

. . . .

Numerous people require thanks for their assistance in the completion of this book. The author is particularly grateful to Arnold M. Hofer and Norman Hofer, and their work with the Hutterian Centennial Committee. These individuals represent the two primary pathways (Mennonite Brethren and General Conference Mennonite) taken by noncommunal Hutterians in the Mennonite world at-large. Norman Hofer was particularly helpful in securing numerous photographs documenting the experience of the Prairie People. Arnold M. Hofer graciously fielded thousands of questions from the author over the course of the past decade. And Donald B. Kraybill and John A. Hostetler provided expert advice during the peer review process, for which I am most grateful.

The maps included in this volume were created by Bill Slusser, a cartographer at California State University, Fresno. Assistance on graphics was provided by Jeff Janzen, son of the author, who knows the inner workings of the computer much better than his father. Editorial assistance and continual encouragement came from George F. Thompson, president of the Center for American Places, Harrisonburg, Virginia. At the University Press of New England, my editor and copy editor provided numerous insightful suggestions.

With regard to Hutterian surnames, the author received significant assistance from geneticist and Hutterite descendent Evan Eichler. Reuben Goertz, from the East Freeman (South Dakota) Swiss Mennonite community, was extremely helpful in identifying individuals, social issues, and movements that required additional research. Historians John D. Unruh and Paul Toews were also valuable resources, as was American religious studies specialist Timothy Miller. Archivist Kevin Enns-Rempel, as well, provided invaluable assistance, as did Jerald Hiebert, Catherine Masuk, Lesley Masuk, Marie Waldner, Edna Wurtz, and the Reverend Terry Miller, an old friend.

The author would also like to thank all members of his immediate family (Deborah, Chris, Jeff, Annika) for patient acquiescence in this project, particularly recalling those many "vacation" excursions, which were almost always combined with research interests.

The Prairie People

I

· ·

Introduction: The Prairie People (Prairieleut)

We are brothers who love God and His truth, we are witnesses of our Lord Jesus Christ, and we have been driven out of many countries for the sake of God's name.
Jacob Hutter, 1535

So they had no place to stay and no house to live in . . . They were as worthless rubbish to everybody, continually on the move.
The Chronicle of the Hutterian Brethren, **1549**

If there is no private property in heaven, there should be none either among God's people here on earth.
Hutterite minister Hans Decker, 1988

A Forgotten People

In the late 1990s nearly 40,000 Hutterites lived in 400 communal colonies located primarily in the plains states and prairie provinces of the United States and Canada. The Hutterites were a much-studied, analyzed, and visited group because of their unique economic system and social practices and the fact that they had sustained a communal way of life for over 450 years, ever since it had been established by a group of radical Austrian Anabaptists in the sixteenth century. Sociologists studied the Hutterites because of their historic success at living communally; theologians, because of their unique anti-individualistic understanding of the Christian faith; geneticists, because of Hutterite inbreeding and one of the highest birthrates on record.[1]

North American Hutterites are descendents of about 425 people who emigrated to southeastern Dakota Territory from Ukrainian Russia in the 1870s. At that time, almost every ethnic Hutterian left his or her home north of the Black Sea and came to North America. The mass migration was undertaken in response to restrictive government policies (Russification), which threatened to destroy traditional Hutterian religious beliefs and cultural practices.

Today the communal Hutterites are well known for establishing successful agricultural colonies across the American and Canadian West. In the 1870s, however, only one-third of the Hutterian immigrants had decided to live communally. The other two-thirds—the Prairie People, or Prairieleut —maintained Hutterian social and theological traditions, as did friends and relatives in the colonies, but without community of goods.

By the time of the 1880 census, 443 Hutterians were living in colonies, but another 822, including the Rev. Paul Tschetter and his uncle Lohrentz, the delegated "scouts" who had convinced the Hutterian people to settle in the Dakotas in the first place, expressed no interest in Christian communism and had settled instead on private farms. The noncommunal Hutterians chose to live outside the *Gutergemeinschaft* (the Hutterian term for full community of goods) on the glacial outwash, the undeveloped yet fertile prairie lands of southeastern Dakota Territory.

Since they had established homes on the rolling plains instead of on the river-bottom land preferred by the communitarians, the colony Hutterites called them "Prairie People" or "Prairieleut," a designation that stuck. The noncommunal Hutterians put down roots in private soil, taking advantage of the Homestead Act or purchasing property from settlers who had given up on the Dakotas for one reason or another. Others bought land from railroad companies.

The Prairie People then carried on a noncommunal rendition of Anabaptist Christianity to which the Hutterian majority had adhered since the early 1800s. In the Dakotas these "independent Hutterites" established their own churches and religious organizations, under the leadership of many of the same individuals who had provided wisdom and guidance in the old world. There was nothing novel about any of this.

Perhaps this is why the Prairieleut Hutterians have been almost completely overlooked by scholars, and why they are relatively unknown to the general public. Academicians specializing in Anabaptist, Hutterian, Mennonite, and American religious studies have devoted much time, money, and effort to explaining the history and traditions of the distinctive and exotic Hutterites. Yet, conversely, they have given little attention to the Prairie People. The most prestigious Anabaptist journal, the *Mennonite Quarterly Review*, for example, has published only two articles, since its inception, related to the noncommunal Hutterians, and one of those was Prairieleut leader Paul Tschetter's 1873 diary account.[2] The recently completed four-volume historical series *The Mennonite Experience in America* also includes very little mention of the Prairie People.[3]

Complicating factors have resulted from the following reality: In the late nineteenth century, many Hutterians had a difficult time choosing between communal life and private property. Families did not always maintain a commitment for a lifetime to one worldview. They experimented with both, testing each with regard to economic, social, and spiritual expectations. Each Hutterian group—communal and noncommunal—experienced continuous alteration of demographic composition.

In response to the internal Hutterian division, historians and sociologists were pushed to make a determination about what constituted the "authentic" Hutterian identity. Their general response was to embrace the communal Hutterites but rarely to study or to write about the noncommunal Prairieleut.

The eventual association of the Prairie People with Mennonite churches created further confusion. Though many Prairieleut retained distinctive Hutterian social and ideological patterns in churches with Hutterian ethnic majorities, most had become—by the 1950s—"Mennonites" in terms of denominational affiliation. It was hard to avoid being swallowed whole by the large Mennonite conferences that noncommunal Hutterian congregations had joined. Significantly, in works with titles such as *Why I Am a Mennonite*, and *Women Among the Brethren*, not a single "Mennonite" of Hutterian background was featured.[4]

Detailed studies of American Mennonite history have not even discussed the influential impact of the Prairie People on the Krimmer Mennonite Brethren Conference, within which noncommunal Hutterians had at one time constituted nearly 50 percent of the membership.[5] To all appearances, the Prairie People had vanished in a Mennonite fog.

Since most noncommunal Hutterian congregations had eventually associated with different branches of the Mennonite Church, ethnic Prairie People were in the course of time called "Hutterite-Mennonites" to distinguish them both from the communal Hutterites and from Swiss and Low-German Mennonites. They were also, at times, referred to as "Hutterisch" after the Austrian dialect that most spoke, or "Hutters," a shortened form of the word "Hutterite."

In this book, the term "Prairieleut"—German for "Prairie People"—is employed most often, since it is the appellation with which noncommunal Hutterian contemporaries are most accustomed. The German word "Prairieleut" ("leut" is pronounced "loit"), is used more than its English counterpart, "Prairie People," because of the term's widespread use and its relative simplicity. It is also the designation most often employed by communal Hutterites, as well as by specialists in Hutterian studies.

Though the word "Prairieleut" is a pluralized expression in German, this work, at times, employs the term as a singular idiom, akin to the word "Hutterite" (as compared to "Hutterite people"). This is the way the word is used by Hutterians, whether spoken or written, in English or Hutterisch (where the term is spelled "Prairieleit," "leit" pronounced as "light"). Thus the phrase "I'm Prairieleut" means "I'm one of the noncommunal Hutterian people." This is similar in nature to saying something like "I'm Swedish."

The term "Hutter" is also occasionally used in this book. It came into fashion in the Dakotas as a way of distinguishing the noncommunal Hutterian community—via an easier-to-pronounce slang expression—from that of neighboring communal Hutterites and from local Low German and Swiss Mennonites. The term "Hutter" is not heard as often outside the Dakotas, however, and holds negative connotations in some contexts.[6] The designation is thus generally employed only when dealing with South Dakota Prairie People.

Noncommunal Hutterians accepted the appellation "Prairieleut" in order to distinguish themselves from communitarian friends and relatives. They were not communal Hutterites, but neither were they Mennonites until a generation or two later, and even then they continued to think of themselves first as "Hutterians" and only secondarily as "Mennonites."

The Prairie People found themselves in an identificational no-man's land and were sometimes misdefined as "Hutterites" but more often categorized as "Mennonites." Though the latter description was accurate with regard to denominational affiliation and Anabaptist ideological roots, it did not faithfully reflect unique ethnic, cultural, and, in many ways, theological traditions.

The Hutterians were one of the only new ethnic groups to have arisen in the late modern historical period. Shared unique religious beliefs led to marriages limited almost exclusively to other members of that group. The resulting small size of the community and its historic longevity created a social environment in which a few "founding" families provided the physical, cultural, and religious code for what became an increasingly inbred ethno-religious assemblage. From the early 1800s on, scarcely more than nineteen extended families had been part of the whole of the Hutterian ethnic enclave. At the time of settlement in North America, the average Hutterian husband and wife were more closely related than second cousins.

The Prairie People, furthermore, were descendents of Hutterian families, which had embraced community of goods only sporadically from the late seventeenth century on. The Prairieleut felt they represented, therefore, a valid form of Hutterian Christianity, much as members of the Reorganized Church of Jesus Christ of the Latter Day Saints considered themselves true Latter Day Saints.

It is important to note that, in this work, the terms "communal" and "noncommunal" refer, in general, to positions taken with regard to economic structures. "Communal" indicates the organizational arrangement that requires adherents to keep possessions in common. "Noncommunal" defines the viewpoint that suggests that supporters hold property privately.

The chosen terminology should not imply that elements of private ownership were completely absent among communal Hutterites. One found some difference with regard to personal possessions, even within the Hutterite system of general equality. Neither should the term "noncommunal" imply that persons thus designated thought only in terms of the individual or, perhaps, limited their focus to the nuclear family. The noncommunal Prairie People placed major emphasis on multilateral social accountability.

With regard to the North American scene, this work employs the term "Hutterite" only to describe those Hutterians who decided to live communally. The word "Hutterian," alternatively, is used as a more inclusive designation, referring to all persons of European "Hutterite" ethno-religious background, whether or not they had decided to live communally. The term "Hutterian" is also used adjectivally with reference to traditional Anabaptist beliefs and practices—as they were filtered through a distinctive ethno-religious culture—to which both communal and noncommunal groups had adhered historically.

A Corrupted Hutterianism?

The Hutterians established themselves as a separate religious society in the sixteenth century as part of the Anabaptist movement, which suggested an interpretation of Christianity different from that professed by Catholics and Protestants. Anabaptists did not accept the hierarchical governing and interpretive structures of the Catholic Church; neither did they give assent to more individualistic and biblicist, yet state-dominated, Protestant religious understandings.

The appellation "Anabaptist" simply meant one who is rebaptized, a heretical and criminal offense in the sixteenth century. The Anabaptists maintained that individuals could not become true followers of Jesus unless they made carefully reasoned and emotionally mature decisions to act in accordance with New Testament teachings. They believed in the collective democratic discernment of Christian assumptions within the context of congregations composed of adult devotees.

Anabaptists insisted that personal and social implications of church membership should be fully understood before baptism. They did not, therefore, recognize the validity of infant baptisms conducted in Catholic or Protestant churches. Anabaptists were also pacifists, who had refused to serve in any country's armed forces. They believed in simplicity of lifestyle, and they practiced strict church discipline.

The Hutterians, who represented the wing of the Anabaptist movement that originated in Austria, accepted one additional precept, which set them apart from sister Anabaptists. The Hutterians—named after early leader Jacob Hutter—maintained that all Christians should live communally, as they believed Jesus and his community of disciples had exemplified in various gospel accounts. The early church in Jerusalem had also been portrayed as a communal organization in the New Testament Book of Acts.

Although the communal ideal had been discussed frequently in various Anabaptist communities, "only the Hutterites," as Werner Packull put it, "retained and institutionalized the Jerusalem model, laying claim to the original communitarian vision."[7] Over the years the Hutterians also developed a devotion to distinctive sermons, hymns, worship styles, and other idiosyncratic traditions.

For a number of reasons, including changes in theological interpretation, economic disappointments, and religious persecution, noncommunal forms of Anabaptism had been established at different points in Hutterian history. Noncommunal Hutterianism was the only structure in existence from 1690 to 1757, for example, and again from 1821 to 1859. From 1859 into the years of emigration from Russia, furthermore, it was the majority movement within Hutterianism as a whole.

A major issue discussed in this work is whether or not the historic commitment to community of goods was essential—ideologically and structurally —for the successful preservation of a unique sense of Hutterian peoplehood. Did one have to live communally to be Hutterian? The dilemma of Prairieleut identity is intricately connected to that question.

In the late nineteenth century, the Prairie People established independent churches in the Dakotas and elsewhere, hoping to maintain their unique noncommunal understanding of Hutterian teaching. To have done anything different would have meant accepting an institutionalized Christian communism that the majority of Hutterians in the 1870s had not experienced personally and did not accept theoretically, even though they knew their ancestors had once lived that way.

Most published works on Hutterians, however, associated the Prairieleut with a debased interpretation of Hutterianism, one which had disavowed orthodox communal traditions. That view was exemplified by the following statement from seventeenth-century Hutterite "Servant of the Word," Andreas Ehrenpreis: "The truth is more dangerous the closer one comes to it. Menno Simons [the sixteenth century Anabaptist leader after whom Mennonites were named] himself slid past very carefully a little to one side of the truth."[8]

If one "slid" a bit to the side of the communal expression of Anabaptism, as the Mennonites did—and, similarly, the Prairie People—one would not be recognized as Hutterian at all, regardless of one's ethno-religious background.

An interesting irony related to the Prairieleut dilemma is the fact that most communes in North America had not experienced long-term social and economic success. The communal Hutterites were markedly different, showing both longevity and demographic ascendance. Eighteenth- and nineteenth-century America saw an explosion of both religious and secular renditions of communalism, from the Ephrata, Icarian and Oneida communities, to the Harmonists, Owenites, Brook Farm Transcendentalists, and the various Fourierist phalanxes. None of those experiments, however, have been ongoing. The early Latter Day Saints also practiced community of goods but have not—with a few exceptions—carried on the tradition. The United Society of Shakers continue to exist as a community in the 1990s but with only a handful of members.

In the 1960s, North America saw a rebirth of interest in communal life, from both religious and secular perspectives. Some sixties-era attempts were successful enough to be still functioning in the 1990s, offering an alternative to the American tradition of individual private ownership. One notes, for example, the continuing vitality of Jesus People U.S.A., the Family, the Skinnerian Twin Oaks community, the Farm, Padanaram and many others. From 1958 to 1991 more than 25,000 persons had been members of the California-based Synanon community. The 1995 *Communities Directory*, furthermore, listed more than 500 operating communities in North America.[9] Most American communal experiments have been unsuccessful, however, and even those named above have not been in existence very long.

The typically transient nature of North American communal ventures provides a striking contrast to the venerable triumph of the Hutterites. Their phenomenal success has intrigued academicians, journalists, and movie directors, simultaneously placing a shroud over the story of their noncommunal kinfolk.

Yet nineteenth-century Prairie People held a vision, which was in many ways similar to that advocated by modern Christian-oriented intentional communities. In addition, they maintained a unique ethno-religious identity with peculiar social and ecclesiastical traditions. These traditions were intertwined with a singular Carinthian/Tyrolean culture and a genetically inbred population. The Prairie People believed they were preserving an authentic historic Hutterian way of life. But they did not live communally. Therefore the Hutterites, as well as scholars in general, did not accept them as "true Hutterians." Their experience was written off as inconsequential.

As defined and practiced by communal Hutterites, community of goods required an all-embracing social, economic, and religious institutional structure. The fundamental question in this book is whether or not such a communal arrangement was so central to what it meant to be Hutterian that survival in North America as a separate and distinct people was unachievable without it. Though this was not the perspective of the Hutterian majority in the nineteenth century, the collectivist assemblage did not believe the noncommunal Prairieleut could legitimately call themselves "Hutterians" without living communally.

In the 1870s the Prairieleut Hutterians had no doubt about the ongoing success of their venture. They were sincerely committed to maintaining ethnic and religious traditions, expected to do so without community of goods, and were convinced it would be easier to sustain the Hutterian ethos in

North America than it had been in mother Russia. And though they allowed members of their churches to own private property, the Prairie People were not without a sense of social obligation, nor did they pursue an intensely individualistic way of life. Prairieleut ministers were selected by collective discernment, followed by the casting of lots. Mutual aid, service to others, personal humility, and a life of suffering had all received significant attention in the sermons read on Sunday mornings.

The Prairie People adhered to a noncommunal interpretive framework, one that was first accepted by a majority of Hutterians in 1685, when a significant number were living in Slovakia. Though noncommunal Hutterianism had been a short-lived, eighty-two year experiment motivated by religious persecution, the Hutterites gave up community of goods once again in 1819, for reasons totally unrelated to societal discrimination. The noncommunal Prairie People believed their understanding of Hutterianism was in fact the most likely to preserve correct Christian teaching. They followed the example of the majority of Anabaptist Christians—the Mennonites and Amish, for example—who did not believe that Jesus had called the faithful to practice full community of goods.

In North America, the Prairie People sustained Hutterian traditions, most particularly, by continuing to read the historic sermons (*Lehren*), which were considered spiritually inspired interpretations of the Bible, and by singing the martyr hymns of the Hutterian songbook, the *Gesangbuch*. The noncommunal Hutterians married within the ethno-religious enclave, ate traditional foods, and spoke a Carinthian/Tyrolean dialect they called Hutterisch. In addition, the Prairieleut preached and practiced religious doctrines which demanded that members accept a sense of collective concern for the economic and spiritual well-being of the community.

The Prairie People thus preserved what they considered to be the most significant elements of traditional Hutterian cultural and religious practice. They embarked on that experiment, however, while acclimating themselves to an altogether strange set of surroundings. Especially during the early settlement years in North America, issues related to basic economic survival received constant attention in a more privatized and capitalistic environment than that to which they had grown accustomed.

Though the Prairieleut community tried to recreate semi-communal institutional forms in the Dakotas, they had been unable to purchase connected sections of land, forcing individuals to live in greater physical isolation than had been the case in Russia. The Prairie People were, therefore, unsuccessful in structurally duplicating the eastern European village pattern of existence.

In the Dakotas, younger Prairieleut generations also attended public schools, where they studied, played with, and were directed by persons of diverse cultural and religious backgrounds. Young Prairieleut were introduced to non-Hutterian ways of being and thinking. In Russia, no comparable interethnic social and ideological mix had existed. The Prairie People had to contend, in ways not experienced by communal Hutterites, both with the critical judgment of a traditional past—that is, with the communal aspect which they had rejected—and with direct persuasion from Protestant Christians and other patriotic citizens living nearby.

North American Hutterite colonies, conversely, established their own schools—eventually authorized by state and provincial governments—which shielded the young from intercultural and interreligious exchanges. The Prairie People followed suit at the secondary and college levels, but they did so only after being pushed by Mennonite neighbors who desired that such schools be inter-Anabaptist endeavors.

On the northern Great Plains of North America, the Prairieleut had to deal with the seductive attraction of an individualistic American way of life while being constantly reminded by Hutterites, in colonies nearby, that a noncommunal existence was "sinful" and spiritually "incomplete." The physical presence of relatives in the Hutterite agricultural collectives represented a living indictment of the Prairieleut decision to reside "on the outside." This caused early noncommunal settlers to reflect deeply on the direction in which their church communities were heading.

As the Prairie People sought social acceptance from non-Hutterian friends and neighbors in the post–World War I period, however, communitarian relatives became an embarrassment. Hutterites not only practiced community of goods, but they also retained an archaic mode of dress, spoke with thick accents, and were ridiculed by Prairieleut acquaintances, making it increasingly difficult for members of the noncommunal group to desire substantive connection with the Hutterian past. This was particularly true of third and fourth generation Prairieleut-Americans.

Though most retained membership in the noncommunal Hutterian congregations (which had themselves moved in evangelical Protestant directions), many ethnic Prairie People sought disassociation from all remnants of Hutterianism. Some left the Prairieleut churches completely, joining congregations unconnected to particular ethnic traditions. A marker event, one that revealed the influence of assimilationist forces on even those who had remained in the ethnic church communities, was the decision taken by many to volunteer for military service during World War II, thereby turning their backs on the historic Anabaptist peace position.

The communal Hutterites, in contrast, continued to uphold their traditions, regardless of how such beliefs and practices were perceived by "outsiders." Reflecting on that manifestation, many scholars speculated that communal life must have been the key to the establishment of boundary maintenance structures strong enough to keep "the world" out.[10] Positive numerical growth and a dynamic yet traditional religious faith had been the public outcomes of that social, economic and ideological system.

This book deals with a number of questions related to that thesis. Was communalism indispensable for the retention of a unique ethno-religious

Hutterian identity? Or did the noncommunal Prairieleut, as well, experience some measure of success in their endeavor to preserve the traditions? In that regard this book also deals with the question of what really constitutes the essence of Hutterian belief.

During the first thirty years of life in North America, families had a difficult time choosing between communal and noncommunal interpretations of the Hutterian faith. Entire families and parts of other families moved back and forth between "colony" and "prairie" forms of existence. Stories of family division, anxious decision making, joy, and regret abound but are relatively unknown outside of the Prairieleut community. Many are told in this book.

This movement between colony and prairie was not so much in evidence after the turn of the twentieth century, however. Ultimately, the Prairieleut choice in favor of private ownership of property turned out to be an endorsement of a slow but progressive movement away from other Hutterian traditions, as well. It did not completely destroy a sense of ethno-religious uniqueness; the Prairie People were still committed to many Hutterian folkways. But the Prairieleut had no communal structural device and, thus, in a sense, no historic spiritual mechanism with which to guard their initially isolated ethnic community from the non-Hutterian world around them.

Third and fourth generation Prairieleut were strongly attracted to evangelical Protestantism, to its general acceptance of patriotic American traditions, and to its more individualistic understanding of the Christian faith. Many also discovered a greater sense of foundational security by accepting the fundamentalist teaching of "assurance of salvation" combined with a more definitive and emotional "salvation experience." A new, more individualistic way of experiencing God proved to be as comforting and tension-releasing for many Prairie People as life within the restricted boundaries of the colony might have been. Many Prairieleut Hutterians were financially successful, became politically active, and sought closer identification with the dominant Anglicized culture around them.

However, other Prairie People had remained committed to traditional Hutterian customs and theological principles. A process of "Mennonitization" both assisted and hindered those who held that position. On the one hand, the Mennonitization of the Prairieleut provided strong support for the maintenance of an Anabaptist theological identity. As Prairie People joined together with Mennonites institutionally, they were given a unique opportunity to preserve many Hutterian theological traditions within a kindred religious enclave.

On the other hand, Mennonitization also subverted traditional Hutterianism by denigrating historic social conventions and ecclesiastical forms. Most Mennonites were not interested in the sermons, hymns, folkways, and other ethno-religious traditions that had most clearly distinguished the Prairieleut as an autonomous Hutterian group. Association with Mennonites was, therefore, a curse as well as a blessing. It brought greater respect and social status to the Prairieleut, since Mennonites were, in general, more open to North American ideological, social, and economic trends. And in some ways, it helped preserve the Anabaptist theological heritage. But it also pushed the Prairie People to surrender the very customs—both social and religious—that had given them a separate identity.

Ultimately, during the twentieth century, the communal Hutterites experienced numerical growth far greater than the noncommunal Prairieleut. While the Hutterites presently number some 40,000 persons, there are currently only 3,500 Prairie People who are members of churches that have affiliated with Mennonite conferences. Since 1952, when the last Prairieleut congregation merged with a Mennonite district, no Prairieleut churches operated independently until the mid-1990s.

While contemporary Hutterites are part of a vibrant, growing assembly, which is gradually becoming as well known as the Old Order Amish, the Prairie People have struggled to preserve a separate public identity. Their communities, however, have sustained a number of distinctive folk customs and relational structures, which continue to identify the Prairieleut as a unique and separate Hutterian people.

In addition, since the early 1970s, a growing number of Prairie People have established direct relationships with colony members. Some have even supported reintroduction of Hutterian theological viewpoints in the congregations they attend. A new-found interest in Hutterian roots has resulted not only in the resurrection of a more positive ethnic identity, but also in a certain openness to religious communion with the Hutterites. Traditional Hutterian positions on war and peace, on church discipline, and on the social and economic nature and implications of the Christian faith are being discussed and reassessed.

The Prairie People thus present a unique case. Descendents of communal Austrian Anabaptists, they had sought to defend and preserve the Hutterian heritage by taking a noncommunal economic and ideological pathway. The story of that endeavor—the primary players, the major social influences —is the focus of this book. After an introductory review and analysis of the Hutterian experience in Europe, primary attention is given to the history of Prairieleut Hutterians in the United States. Though a number of narrative excursions to places of settlement in Canada do take place, the great majority of Prairie People did not settle there. The glossary at the end of the book provides explanation of various terms related to Hutterian life and thought.

The historical context within which the Prairie People and the Hutterites have emerged is described and evaluated, as is the relationship between Prairie People, Hutterites, and Mennonites. Although the Prairieleut immigrant experience bears a certain similarity to that which many ethnic groups have encountered in American and Canadian history, in few other situations does one find an ethno-religious enclave split apart over the issue of community of goods.

2

. . . .

Across the Great World Ocean

The door to the community stands wide open. Come out of
your private nests. Out of your private houses. Stop looking
after your own affairs. Away with self-will.
Andreas Ehrenpreis, Hutterite Servant of the Word, 1650

For those who believed were together, not dispersed and
separated, one here and the other there, separated in property,
like all those Christians and apparent Brotherhoods of today—
those who consider themselves separated from the world, and
are also separated from their fellow-believers.
Hutterite sermon on Acts 2, circa 1650

The Hutterians

The Hutterians are a unique Christian assemblage with
roots in the Anabaptist movement of the sixteenth century. The Anabaptists,
who emerged in various parts of Switzerland, Austria, Germany, and the
Netherlands, had disagreed with both Catholic and Protestant Christians
in emphasizing a literal following of the teachings of Jesus. They believed,
therefore, that no Christian should kill anyone for any reason.

The Hutterites, who became the predominant religious faction in the
Austrian Anabaptist community, were named after early leader Jakob Hutter, a former gun-carrying Peasant War sympathizer from the Tyrol, who
had become a gifted evangelist and organizer.[1] Hutter, a hatter by trade,
had been chosen as *Prediger* (minister) in the Anabaptist community in 1533,
and was executed for heresy three years later.[2] The Hutterite *Chronicle* described Hutter's death in the following manner:

They put him in ice-cold water and then took him into a warm room and had him beaten with rods. They lacerated his body, poured brandy into the wounds, and set it on fire. . . . Putting a tuft of feathers on his head, they led him into the house of their idols and in every way made a laughing-stock of him.[3]

Hutter was then burned alive at the stake.

Though essentially Anabaptist with regard to other theological positions, the Hutterian insistence that Christians not own private property set them apart from other groups. It set them apart, for example, from Mennonites, who originated in the Netherlands and were named after early leader and former Catholic priest Menno Simons.

The Hutterites believed that the second, fourth, fifth and sixth chapters of the Book of Acts, were eminently clear in their description of an early Christian assemblage which had practiced community of goods. Further-more, they believed the injunction to live communally was closely related to the Pentecost experience and had thus been empowered, as nineteenth-century Hutterite Peter Janzen put it, "through the influence of the Holy Spirit."[4] The Hutterians believed that Jesus himself had lived communally, together with his small assemblage of followers, as had the apostles in the early church. As one of the Hutterite sermons put it: "Christ himself ob-served community [of possessions] with his disciples."[5] For these reasons, Hutterites had established colonies which were strictly regimented and which, in many ways, resembled noncelibate Catholic monasteries more than they resembled other Anabaptist and/or Protestant churches.

Hutterians, like other Anabaptist groups, preached the importance of church discipline, believers' baptism, pacifism, humility, and the priesthood of all members, but their commitment to communal life made the social and eco-nomic structure of their communities radically dissimilar. The Hutterians had developed a unique theology, therefore, which brought together the teaching of *gelassenheit*—complete surrender of the will to God—with community of goods.[6] In the Hutterian view, a Christian could not consider himself in a position of complete submission to the will of God unless he lived communally.

Hutterian beliefs and practices were set forth in great detail in Servant of the Word Peter Rideman's *Account of Our Religion, Doctrine and Faith*, pub-lished in 1540, a confessional statement, still honored and given adherence.[7] The Hutterians also valued the preservation of history and assigned promi-nent individuals to continually update their story in the *Chronicle of the Hut-terian Brethren.*[8] This significant document makes it possible for us to know a great deal more about the Hutterites than is known about many socio-religious organizations of much greater size. Preserving the memory of im-portant past events provided enormous emotional support to the Hutterian people during times of persecution and hardship.

Hutterites patterned their lives after the description of the early Chris-tian church, delineated in Acts 4:32:

> Now the company of those who believed were of one heart and soul, and
> no one said that any of the things which he possessed was his own, but they
> had everything in common.

Peter Rideman's two-hundred-page document placed great emphasis on
that first-century entreaty. The confessional statement also incorporated
commentary on and interpretation of the Bible and included specific instruction with regard to prayer, singing, swearing, taxation, and even "standing drinks" and "innkeepers."[9]

To give a sense of the blunt outspokenness of some early Austrian leaders, note that in a farewell address to Carinthian Anabaptists, Antonius Erfordter—who joined the Hutterites in Moravia—had once described the
Catholic clergy as "bags full of maggots."[10] Hutterians did not mince words
when describing the "godless" around them, who were indeed hunting Hutterites down and killing them. The outspoken Erfordter was also reputed
to be "one of the best poets among the Hutterites."[11] Six of his songs were
included in the Hutterian songbook, the *Gesangbuch*, which contained lengthy
accounts of early Hutterian martyrs.

Though some Bavarian, Hessian, and other south and central Germans
joined the Hutterites—as did a few Italians—a large majority of the Hutterian Anabaptists were Tyrolean Austrian in ethnic background. Their ethnicity helped to set them apart from Mennonite Anabaptists who were predominately Swiss/South German and Dutch/Low-German. Because of intense
persecution in Austria and southern Germany, the Hutterians fled to Moravia
and Slovakia in successive waves in the late 1520s, 1530s, and 1540s, creating
a "new Tyrol" that was, as James Stayer noted, "statistically more impres-
sive than the early English and French colonies (in North America)."[12]

A short "golden" period in the middle to late sixteenth century followed
as the Hutterian population grew to as many as 40,000, with continued
large-scale emigration from Tyrol, the promotion of active evangelism
throughout Germany and Austria, and continued protection from local nobility, who were impressed by the economic vitality of the Hutterian communities.[13] During the period, the Hutterites established many still-surviving
communal structures and practices. Work assignment and material distribution models were developed and ecclesiastical forms were solidified.

Sixteenth-century Hutterian craftsmen engaged in numerous trades, from
bookbinding, saddlery, and watchmaking, to the production of pottery, for
which they became well known. In later centuries, Hutterite ceramic work
found its way to the national museums of Vienna, Prague, and Budapest,
and the sale of replicas has turned into a profitable business, particularly in
postcommunist Hungary and Slovakia.[14]

The Hutterites also placed major emphasis both on education and on
missions. They established, for example, the first "kindergartens" in Europe
to provide moral and academic training for their children. They also de-

Table 1.
Hutterian Lineage in and from Europe[a]

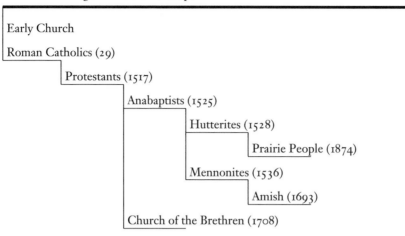

Early Church

Roman Catholics (29)

    Protestants (1517)

        Anabaptists (1525)

             Hutterites (1528)

                  Prairie People (1874)

           Mennonites (1536)

              Amish (1693)

        Church of the Brethren (1708)

Note:
  [a]This table charts the Hutterian lineage in relationship to other Christian groups in Western Europe and North America.

veloped model elementary schools, which were sometimes attended by local non-Hutterites.[15] To establish missions, *Sendboten* (evangelists) were sent across the European continent in search of converts. It is said that 80 percent of those missionaries suffered martyrdom along the way.[16] Many missionaries wrote "epistles" enroute, which were preserved and subsequently read by members of the community. The experiences of the *Sendboten* also provided the lyrical content for many Hutterite hymns.

    The era of Hutterian prosperity was followed by a period of extensive persecution and harassment at the hands of both Catholics and Protestants, particularly during the Thirty Years War (1618–1648). Thousands of Hutterians were killed, and numerous others recanted their commitment to the Anabaptist "apostasy," rejoining one of the state churches. Thousands of Hutterites went underground, literally, in survival endeavors reminiscent of the early Christians in Rome. Many lived for years in still-existent subterranean cave dwellings, with secret entrances and passages, hiding out from brother Christian persecutors. Those Hutterians who refused to compromise their faith but had survived were expelled in total from Moravia in 1622. Most fled to Hutterite communities in neighboring Slovakia, where conditions were somewhat more favorable. By 1631, however, there were only 1000 Hutterites left in existence.[17]

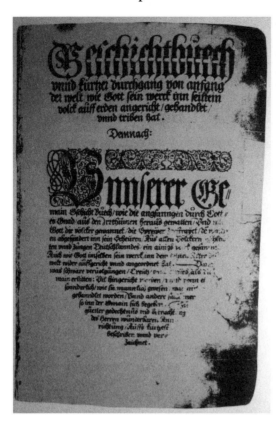

Fig. 2.1. Title page of the 1581 codex of the *Chronicle of the Hutterian Brethren.* Photograph courtesy of Hutterian Centennial Committee.

Experiments in noncommunal Hutterianism

Only a small Hutterite remnant came out of the wood-work after the Thirty Years War and the various plagues and famines that had ensued. Those several hundred that emerged gradually lost commitment to full communal life, despite the strong pastoral leadership of Andreas Ehrenpreis from 1630 to 1662.[18] The mid-seventeenth century was also the time period when Hans Friedrich Kuentsche (a minister in the Kesselsdorf, Slovakia, community) composed many sermons that continued to be read in Hutterite colonies hundreds of years later.

After the Thirty Years War the Hutterites found refuge both in Slovakia and in Transylvania. It was during that time period that the German writer H. J. C. von Grimmelshausen discovered what he called "a paradise on earth" and glorified the Hutterites in his book *Adventures of a Simpleton.*[19] Shortly thereafter, however, the Hutterites discontinued their commitment to a fully communal social order.

As a result of unrelenting oppression and heavy-handed pressure from governing authorities of the Austro-Hungarian Empire, large numbers of

Table 2.
Hutterians in Europe[a]

Date	Place	Economy	Identity
1525–1540[b]	Austria	Noncommunal	Anabaptists
1528–1621	Moravia	Communal	Hutterites
1546–1685	Slovakia	Communal	Hutterites
1621–	Slovakia	Noncommunal	Habaner
1621–1690; 1767	Transylvania	Communal	Hutterites
1685–1800[b]	Slovakia	Noncommunal	Hutterites
1690–1800[b]	Transylvania	Noncommunal	Hutterites
1767–1770	Wallachia	Communal	Hutterites
1770–1802	Ukraine (Wischenka)	Communal	Hutterites
1802–1819	Ukraine (Raditschewa)	Communal	Hutterites
1819–1842	Ukraine (Raditschewa)	Noncommunal	Hutterites
1842–1879	Ukraine (in Mennonite Chortitza and Molotschna Colony areas)	Noncommunal	Hutterites
1859–1879	Ukraine (in Mennonite Chortitza and Molotschna Colony areas)	Communal	Hutterites

Notes:
[a]This table shows the general outline of Hutterian history in Europe up until the time of the mass emigration to America in the 1870s, with corresponding information on places of residence and community economic structures.
[b]denotes approximate date of disbanding.

Hutterites also converted to the Catholic faith. Conversion can be attributed to extensive persecution that included constant raids on property and individuals, torture, rape, famine, and the billeting of troops in Hutterite homes.[20] Contributing, as well, to the number of conversions were the many children who were taken away from their parents to be raised by Catholic families in order to save their souls from eternal damnation and to put an end to the Hutterian apostasy. As the Hutterites put it (in Hutterisch): "Unsra lait hom in sendra rasn fil dingan durchcleibt." (Our people experienced many things in their pilgrimage).

Unexpectedly, those Hutterians who converted to Catholicism retained a unique Hutterian cultural identity, within the boundaries of the Slovakian Catholic community, into the twentieth century. This group of expert craftsmen and successful farmers continued to live in ethnically exclusive villages and to speak the Tyrolean—Hutterisch—dialect into the mid-twentieth

Fig. 2.2. Habaner pottery replica, 1690. Photograph by the author.

century. They were known locally as Habaner, the Slovakian peasant nickname for Hutterians, perhaps derived from the Hebrew *Ha-banim*, meaning "the true children of God." They continue to be recognized especially for the quality of their ceramic products.

Those Hutterians who had not recanted and joined the Catholic Church came to believe that legal recognition as individual property owners might at least make them less of a target for official and unofficial harassment. Communal life was, therefore, discontinued in the Slovakian villages, as, for example, at Sabatisch, in 1685. The Transylvanian colonies, centered at Alwinz, gave up communal life five years later.[21]

The discontinuation of communal life in the late seventeenth century led ultimately to a disassociation from Anabaptist Christianity for all but five Hutterian communities. Members of every other community had either converted to Catholicism, been imprisoned, or fled to Protestant enclaves within the empire. The numerous sermons *(Lehren)* written in the seventeenth century, before communalism was abandoned, served an influential prophetic function, however, by continuing to emphasize the importance of communal life even during those years when none existed. It is also true that, even after community of goods was discontinued, the Hutterites, as well as the Habaner, lived in villages with semi-communal economic and institutional characteristics.

The seventeenth-century Hutterian sermons, which were eventually recognized as specially blessed and inspired by the Holy Spirit, continued to be read in the now noncommunal Hutterite church services, although the most direct and specific references to communal life were, at times, deleted by ministers. The *Lehren* offered biblical commentary on a variety of social, economic, and political issues, as well as on those questions more specifically related to theological exegesis. In the course of time, these sermons, which began to take on the character of holy writ, were virtually the only homilies delivered by Hutterite ministers at worship services. They became almost as important as the Bible itself.

In 1757 an unexpected influx of former Lutheran converts, crypto-Protestants exiled from the Austrian province of Carinthia, provided the motivational force that led forty-six Hutterites to readopt communal life ten years later in Alwinz, Transylvania.[22] Led by Johannes Kleinsasser, the highly committed and active Carinthian converts had found the sermons, which emphasized communal life, too powerful to overlook. They led the few traditional ethnic "old" Hutterites willing to follow back to community of goods, *Gutergemeinschaft*, in 1767. One, Susanna Zilch, even left her husband and two children in order to join the newly established colony.[23] Martin Glanzer did the same, leaving a wife and one-year-old daughter behind in Aich, Carinthia.[24]

The Carinthian converts played a seminal role in re-establishing communal living in concert with the small group of "old" Hutterites who had joined them. These "new" communal Hutterians suffered harassment, for many years, from Catholic authorities in Carinthia's Spittal District. For example, a document secured in the early 1980s by geneticist Evan Eichler from Catholic Church authorities in Klagenfurt, Austria confirmed that ancestor, Peter Miller, one of the refugees, had at one time been put on trial for having a Bible in his possession.[25]

With the resurrection of communalism, however, there came a concurrent and renewed effort by the Jesuit monastic order to forcibly convert all Protestants in the Austrian Empire to the Catholic Church. In that same year, 1767, a group of sixty-seven communal Hutterites fled Transylvania. The assemblage included a number of new adherents from the Slovakian Hutterian settlements who had not personally experienced communal life but were attracted to it. The refugees had first moved to Wallachia (in present-day Romania) and eventually to Ukrainian Russia, where, in 1770, they established a full-fledged communal society at Wischenka, northeast of Kiev, on the estate of a nobleman, Count Rumiantsev. There they were joined by forty-six additional Hutterites, most of whom had come from the traditional and noncommunal Slovakian Hutterian communities.

One observer noted that food was so scarce during the mass escape via Romania that the fugitives had "scraped the bark from the trees and ate that, also many weeds."[26] Along with young children, who were tied to the refugees' backs, the escapees managed to carry with them copies of the *Chronicle*, the

Gesangbuch, and the *Lehren*. These sacred works helped provide the theological foundation for the development of a new communal social order in the Ukraine.

In 1802, the communal Hutterians were forced to leave Wischenka when Count Rumiantsev's heirs attempted to reduce them to the status of serfs. The Hutterites appealed to the Russian government, which allowed them to settle on crown lands, eight miles to the northeast, at Raditschewa, on the Desna River. By that time, there were 202 persons living in the community.[27]

At Raditschewa, the Hutterites re-established the craft industries for which they were well known in Moravia, Slovakia, and Transylvania, and they had constructed two whiskey distilleries, which produced "over twelve thousand liters of whiskey annually."[28] Internal conflicts, however, led the revived communal experiment to die in 1819.

An investigation conducted by the Russian Government the previous year (1818) documented just how much distance existed between theoretical communalism and practical individualism in the Raditschewa community. Individual Hutterians had been accused of holding back earnings for their own private use, for example, instead of transferring the money to the common fund.[29] By 1819, the colony economy was in recession. Though Hutterians had invented the "kindergarten" while living in Moravia, the educational vision at Raditschewa was also in decline. Ideological differences had emerged, and, in addition to all of these problems, a devastating fire destroyed most of the colony buildings.

In 1819, the various difficulties led members of a noncommunal faction, under the leadership of Jacob Walter, to relocate, temporarily, to the Chortitza Mennonite Colony area, 350 miles to the south. Though most members of that group returned to Raditschewa that same year, two young men, Mathias and Andreas Miller, remained and joined the Mennonite Church.[30]

Factional contentions at Raditschewa were caused in part by personal clashes between influential leaders Johannes Waldner (Carinthian) and Jacob Walter ("old Hutterite"), who had taken opposing positions on the issue of communal life. In this regard, it is important to note that many older Hutterians living at Wishenka and Raditschewa had not lived communally in Transylvania and Slovakia. No communal organizations had existed there since the late seventeenth century, with the exception of the small Carinthian-dominated group.

Some "old" Hutterians found it hard, therefore, to accept communal regulations at Wishenka and Raditschewa. They were part of an entire generation that was unfamiliar with community of goods. Leader Jacob Walter, for example, did not leave Sabatisch (Slovakia) for the Ukraine until 1784 and was referred to as a "foreigner" when he did arrive. It is also important to note that the new Carinthian majority (after 1767) spoke a different idiom than that used by the Tyrolean "old Hutterites." What became the Hutterisch dialect in subsequent years now included many more Carinthian than Tryolean words.

According to the Hutterite *Chronicle*, in 1818 Jacob Walter had "openly confessed his backsliding from the faith" and insisted on owning private property, in opposition to the communal position of Johannes Waldner.[31] The Hutterites, therefore, traditionally blamed Walter for "wrecking" communal life. That was, indeed, the way the *Chronicle* described the series of events. It is also interesting to note that Walter's father, Zacharias, had been chosen as Hutterite Elder in 1746 but had ultimately recanted and joined the Catholic Church, becoming one of the Habaner.

Hutterite baptismal records also contained the comment, added at a later date, that four baptisms conducted by Jacob Walter in 1820 had occurred "after community living ceased and through him [was] destroyed."[32] Still, when Jacob Walter died in 1855 at age eighty-six, official Hutterian death records noted that "he carried the cares of the congregation for thirty years."[33] Walter's supporters (some of whose descendents were Prairieleut) believed his noncommunal vision was a good one.

Among the Mennonites

In 1842, now in considerable poverty and having experienced much social disorganization, the Hutterians had resettled north of the Black Sea, near the Ukrainian Molotschna and Chortitza Mennonite districts. At the invitation of Catherine the Great and her successors, thousands of Mennonites had settled in that area, beginning in the late eighteenth century. Here the Hutterites had established five villages: Hutterthal, Neu Hutterthal, Hutterdorf, Johannesruh and Scheromet. Mennonite Johann Cornies, chair of the powerful Agricultural Society which controlled land allocation and economic development, had personally supervised the planning and construction of two of the villages (Hutterthal and Johannesruh), which had been named, respectively, by him and for him.

Cornies, who had once hosted Tsar Alexander I, had been the beneficiary of semi-dictatorial powers granted him by the Russian Government as its Mennonite "trustee." Though Cornies generally wielded that authority in a benevolent manner, he experienced occasional conflicts with Mennonite religious leaders, which caused him to be known in some circles as the "Mennonite Tsar," and in others as "the forest devil."[34]

With regard to the Hutterian immigrants, Cornies pushed hard for adoption of Mennonite social and religious practices, hoping for the general assimilation of the entire Hutterite population into Mennonite society.[35] Cornies had no interest in Hutterian social or theological distinctives. He demanded, for example, that the Hutterian practice of congregational involvement in marital selection cease immediately. But he had also provided jobs and housing for the destitute Hutterians, and he introduced them to successful Mennonite agricultural practices.

Map 1. Hutterian settlements in Europe. Map by Bill Slusser.

The communal dream lived on, however. In 1859, Hutterites Michael Waldner and Jacob Hofer reinstituted communal life at Hutterdorf village. Before his return to community, Waldner said that God had sent him an illness so severe "that he lay like a dead man," "felt like he was flying," and had eventually been "enraptured," seeing "heaven and hell and the damned."[36] Influenced by "visions" from a "spirit" of God, and highly cognizant of communal traditions, Waldner had been instructed to restore community of goods, as had Jacob Hutter before him, and he did so.

The following year, Darius Walter, another Hutterian minister, started an additional communal group at the other end of Hutterdorf. Amazingly enough, the two groups could not agree on organizational issues. Four years later, in 1864, communal advocates within the village of Johannesruh, under the leadership of Jacob Wipf, engaged in yet a third social experiment. They converted one of their homes "into a meetinghouse, another into a dining room for men, a third one for women, a fourth for a children's home."[37] All work responsibilities were reallocated communally. All of these events showed the continuing attraction of community of goods for the Hutterian people, yet they also showed much internal conflict.

Karl Peter has ascribed the continuous alternation between community of goods and private property in Hutterian history to "an irreconcilable struggle between the Hutterite community and the Hutterite family."[38] According to Peter's analysis, private property had won out during times when religious ideology was not vital enough to supercede family issues. This had first occurred among Hutterians in the seventeenth century, when people began keeping money and goods received for outside services for their families instead of turning them over to the common treasury.

According to Peter, this was accompanied by parents insisting on more time with their children and a greater influence over selecting their mate, traditionally superintended by ministers. Similar noncommunal displays had then occurred periodically throughout the eighteenth, nineteenth, and twentieth centuries.

Peter's nuclear family–based explanation for anticommunal tendencies is helpful. But other influences, theological, socio-economic, and political, were also significant. Beginning in the late seventeenth century, for example, the Hutterite majority developed a solid theological rationale for a non-communitarian yet uniquely Hutterian Anabaptism. Hutterite communalists disliked the interpretation, but it was very popular with segments of the Hutterian community and often represented mainstream opinion.

In any case, in the 1860s, two groups in Ukrainian Russia called themselves "Hutterites," as had been the case previously in Transylvania and Slovakia. One gathering practiced communal life; the other did not. The noncommunal group was by far the larger. The communalists, furthermore, experienced internal organizational schisms that were never eradicated. All Hutterian groups, however, continued to observe similar social and religious customs.

Everything changed in 1870, when Tsar Alexander II, seeking to Russify the diverse ethnic groups within the empire, dictated new laws that threatened the numerous social, political, and religious liberties enjoyed by the Hutterians, Mennonites, and other Germans who had settled in the Russian Empire. Hutterians and Mennonites were particularly concerned about the loss of complete exemption from military service. As Krimmer Mennonite Brethren leader Jacob A. Wiebe put it: "Dann kames, wie ein Blitz aus klar em Himmel: Das Privilegium ist aus keine Militar-Freiheit mehr fur die Mennoniten." (Then it came, like lightning out of clear sky: the privileges were gone, no freedom from military service for Mennonites any longer.)[39]

An offer of noncombatant alternative service, even service in forestry divisions, did not satisfy most Hutterians as it did two-thirds of the Russian Mennonites. Hutterians, communal and noncommunal, viewed this possibility as an unacceptable compromise, as indirect assistance to whatever military engagement the Tsar might decide to start or join.

Hutterians were also concerned about losing control of schools to teachers appointed by the Russian Government, the introduction of the Russian language in those schools, and the loss of self-government in their villages. Therefore, in 1873 communal and noncommunal Hutterian assemblages commissioned thirty-one-year-old Paul Tschetter, a minister, and his fifty-

four-year-old uncle, Lohrentz, to join a delegation of Mennonite representatives in exploring the possibilities offered by the North American continent for settlement.

Previous attempts to petition the Tsar for legal exemptions to new government mandates were unsuccessful. Paul Tschetter had represented noncommunal Hutterians in one such venture of entreaty to St. Petersburg, in
January 1873.[40] Another endeavor, involving George Hofer, Darius Walter,
and Joseph "Yos" Hofer, representing one of the communal groups, had also
been unsuccessful.[41]

America as Refuge

Enroute to America in the summer of 1873, the Tschetters
experienced the cosmopolitan life of the modern West for the first time in
their lives. Paul Tschetter kept a journal providing a personal account of the
adventure for later generations, and it clearly delineated the Hutterian mindset of that age.[42]

Before leaving for America, the Tschetters had first visited the city of
Hamburg, where Paul had "purchased a book on Menno Simons," the sixteenth-century Dutch Anabaptist leader but had refused an invitation to attend services at the Altona Mennonite Church. Tschetter said he feared he
"might get into an argument," believing the pastor to be "an unsound Mennonite."[43] Although Tschetter experienced the usual seasickness and often
had to "throw up,"[44] his primary focus during the entire Atlantic crossing
was "the godless rabble" with whom he was "obligated to spend such a long
time."[45] An isolated existence in small eastern European villages had not
prepared the Rev. Tschetter for what he encountered aboard ship.

In the United States, the delegates initially spent time in Pennsylvania
and Indiana, conversing with American Mennonites and Amish, some of
whom had been in North America since the early eighteenth century. In his
diary Tschetter complained a great deal about those encounters, particularly about the Mennonite use of tobacco, to which Tschetter was strongly
opposed. Later, as leader of the Neu Hutterthaler Church in Dakota Territory, he once refused to accept a donation from parishioner, John Hofer
(who grew tobacco in his garden), until Hofer agreed to quit smoking.[46]
Tschetter also criticized Mennonites for using musical instruments, something that Hutterites opposed. When asked if he had enjoyed a particular
religious service that had included instrumental accompaniment, Tschetter
had responded with a simple "no."[47]

Tschetter himself composed many songs during the course of his trav-
els. One hymn, entitled "The New Jerusalem," was inspired by the natural
beauty of the Red River valley. One assumes, however, that if Tschetter's
hymns were sung upon his return to Russia, they were sung a capella.

Among the North American Anabaptists, Tschetter felt comfortable only with the Amish. The Amish, who observed a very conservative set of *Ordnungen* (church rules and regulations), had established a separate denomination in 1693, as the result of a split in the Swiss Mennonite Church, led by Jacob Ammann. Tschetter was particularly impressed by the Amish style of dress, which, he noted, was similar to Hutterian garb.

The Mennonite/Hutterian delegation visited the territories, provinces, and states of the United States and Canada, using passes freely distributed by railroad, steamship, and land companies actively promoting settlement on North America's central plains.[48] Some of the delegates preferred to settle in Manitoba, others in Kansas and Nebraska. The Tschetters chose Dakota Territory.

Because they were concerned that the United States might not guarantee the religious privileges they had traditionally been granted in Russia, the two Hutterian delegates (along with Tobias Unruh, who represented Low-German Mennonites from Polish Volhynia), had requested an appointment with President Ulysses S. Grant. Amazingly, they were granted one, on August 8, 1873.[49] They had also drafted a petition to the President, which included their various requests. The Hutterian/Mennonite delegation was interested in securing the following privileges: freedom from military service; permission to live in separated, self-governed communities; freedom to operate schools in the German language; exemption from jury duty and public office; exemption from taking the oath in legal proceedings; and freedom to leave the United States at any time, if they desired to do so.[50]

In their letter of petition, the three delegates made it very clear that their primary reason for seeking emigration from Russia was the loss of the military service exemption, which was, as they put it, "against our conscience and religious faith." The delegates, who had referred to themselves as Grant's "obedient servants," insisted on temporary immunity, as well, from paying the fines that were then used to hire military service substitutes, fines which had been imposed on American Mennonites during the recent Civil War.

That a meeting between three unsophisticated German-speaking foreigners and the President of the United States could ever have been arranged showed the importance with which railroad company executives viewed Hutterian and Mennonite settlement on the sparsely populated plains. The influence of well-known banker, financier, Republican Party fundraiser, and Northern Pacific Railroad trustee Jay Cooke had been particularly important in arranging this meeting with the President. Cooke's company owned land that it wanted to sell to the potential immigrants.

When the Tschetters arrived in Philadelphia, enroute to meet the President, they went immediately to Jay Cooke's office, where they were greeted by his German-speaking assistant, Michael Hiller, head of the railroad company's land settlement department.[51] Hiller served as interpreter, guide, and host for the Tschetters during the days that followed as they negotiated with

Fig. 2.3. The Rev. Paul Tschetter, the spiritual leader of the Prairie People during the early settlement years, circa 1873. Photograph courtesy of Hutterian Centennial Committee.

land office agents and met with the President. A few days before gaining an audience with Grant, the delegates sampled "some very excellent wine" with Mr. Cooke himself and discussed their plight.[52] Cooke had, subsequently, written a letter of introduction to present to the President.[53]

The delegates met America's Civil War hero at 8:00 P.M. on August 8, at his Long Beach summer home, on Long Island. According to Tschetter, the President received them "in the most pleasing manner," listened to their requests (as they were interpreted by the bilingual Hiller, since Grant could not speak German) and agreed to respond to their petition as soon as possible.[54] Jay Cooke then intervened personally, but unsuccessfully, in an attempt to get an answer from President Grant by mid-August before the delegates returned to Russia.[55]

Responding for Grant in September 1873, Secretary of State Hamilton Fish notified the delegates straightforwardly that the federal government did not have the constitutional authority to grant their requests. Fish also suggested that if military service was required in the future there was little likelihood Congress would "free" Hutterians from "all" defense obligations.[56] He concluded, however, by saying that "for the next fifty years we will not be entangled in another war in which military service will be necessary," a rather optimistic and, as it turned out, inaccurate prediction.

Others, however, pursued a different political angle. In early, 1874, for example, the United States Senate began debate on a measure referred to as the "Mennonite Bill." This legislation had been introduced by Senator

Simon Cameron of Pennsylvania, at the request of American Mennonite leaders Amos Herr and John F. Funk, who had intervened on behalf of the prospective immigrants. The bill asked the government to set aside 500,000 acres of coterminous Red River valley land—allowing railroad property and government tracts to be sold together—for the specific purpose of encouraging Mennonite/Hutterian settlement in what is now the state of North Dakota.[57]

One of the strongest advocates of the Mennonite Bill was Secretary of the Interior Columbus Delano. President Grant, as well, in his annual message to Congress, on December 1, 1873, had advocated "concessions" which would enable "a large colony of citizens of Russia . . . to settle in a compact colony."[58] In his address, Grant described the "colonists" as "industrious, intelligent and wealthy," as well as "desirous of enjoying civil and religious liberty."[59]

Unfortunately for the Mennonites and Hutterians, Secretary Delano had been connected with various land speculation schemes and was associated with the infamous Whiskey Ring. His support for the bill had, therefore, lent no credibility to the Hutterite/Mennonite request. Secretary of State Fish had also opposed the bill because of his interest in continuing good relations with Russia, which was opposed to large-scale emigration. President Grant and his secretary of state were thus on opposite sides of the issue.

In the Senate itself, concerns had been raised regarding Mennonite/Hutterian pacifism and the anticipated refusal of Anabaptists to defend the United States militarily in the event of war. Questions continued to be asked about the specific request for military exemption. The fear that land speculators like Jay Cooke, Columbus Delano, and other Grant cronies might surreptitiously benefit, via semi-legal procedures, from such a large sale of land in one area was another behind-the-scenes issue affecting legislative opinion.

Senators in opposition to the bill had placed additional emphasis on the long-term implications of granting special advantages to a particular ethno-religious group. Other immigrants, for example, might seek similar privileges. What impact might this have on the development of a unified national culture? Various issues were discussed, and many amendments added to the original "Mennonite Bill." But in the end, the legislation was rejected. In April 1874, after much debate, the Senate decided against encouraging a semi-autonomous Anabaptist culture to develop, as it had been allowed to flourish in various parts of eastern Europe, in the American Midwest.

Liberal Republicans, interested in cleaning up the image of their party, which was at the time tainted by the worst corruption in United States history, had opposed the bill from the outset. For example, some of the senators advocating for the bill were railroad company stockholders. Contemporaneously, nativist factions within the party feared that a large influx of eastern Europeans might lead to the destruction of a traditionally northern and western European way of life. Others, like Senator Edmonds from Vermont, simply did not like the idea of a closed ethnic enclave with constituents protected by special privileges. As Edmonds put it, "Let us have no exclusions, let us have no boundaries, let us be a nation and a people where every man everywhere stands on an equality with his fellow man . . ."[60]

Still, many senators made strong supporting comments. Senator Thomas Tipton from Nebraska, for example, noted: "Look to Arkansas today, where the people are never happy unless they are in a fight . . . send us a few advocates of peace . . . let us bid them welcome."[61] Senator Pratt of Indiana agreed: "There is no worthier class of people upon the face of the globe," he noted.

The decision of the Senate to turn its back on the Mennonite/Hutterian request ensured that Hutterians and Mennonites would settle in scattered communities across the Canadian and American plains. It made it difficult to purchase acreages large enough to accommodate the establishment of eastern European–style villages with strip farming possibilities and common pastures. Since the Hutterians did not want to live in immediate proximity to persons of other ethnic and/or religious backgrounds, the land that most interested them was alternating railroad and government-owned land, available for original purchase or resale. To secure large connected properties within this real estate context was an extremely difficult assignment.

The first group of communal Hutterite immigrants (what became Bon Homme Colony) were successful in securing 2500 acres from a private landowner near the town of Tabor. A second communal assemblage (Wolf Creek Colony) purchased 5400 acres of land on the James River near the town of Olivet. Members of the first noncommunal group to arrive in the Dakotas bought smaller, unconnected, properties in nearby Hutchinson County.

Once the "Mennonite Bill" failed, the noncommunal Hutterian community evidently had not delegated anyone to negotiate with land agents for the purchase of large alternating property sections. If they had, a less individualistic social structure might have ensued, at least temporarily. Why they did not is a mystery, in light of the fact that semi-communal configurations had been emphasized by all Hutterians in Russia. In the Dakotas, however, each noncommunal Hutterian family fended for itself, and no villages were ever established.

In reviewing railroad land company records and various government files, Ernst Correll came to the conclusion that the power of the railroad companies in a highly competitive market was extremely influential in determining who would settle where. He concluded: "The keen competition between the land departments of the various railroad companies resulted in rapid contractual arrangements with the Mennonite pioneers. As a result the original plans for compact settlements were more or less abandoned."[62]

A major reason for the heated rivalry between a number of railroad company land offices had been their own overexpansion into sparsely populated regions, which had contributed to investor wariness, in turn helping to bring on the Panic of 1873, a major nationwide economic downturn.

Jay Cooke's Northern Pacific Railroad, for example, declared bankruptcy on September 18, 1873, shortly after the Tschetters returned to Europe.[63] The declaration of bankruptcy caused the stock market to close for ten days and helped precipitate a six-year economic depression. Whether or not the Hutterians knew about any of this at the time is difficult to determine. American Mennonite businessmen, however, must have been aware of it.

Economic conditions in the United States in the 1870s presented a mixed blessing for Hutterian immigrants. On the one hand, the national financial panic meant low land prices. But on the other hand, economic contraction, combined with intense competition, worked against large purchases from single companies (or via consolidated company arrangements) and also made it difficult to secure good prices for harvested agricultural products during the early settlement years.

In any case, the Canadian Government had been much more sympathetic to Mennonite and Hutterian requests, providing written guarantees of military exemption, protection of language rights, and the possibility of purchasing large coterminous sections of land. In Canada, the noncommunal Hutterians might have lived in villages, as did early Mennonite settlers, instead of on isolated homesteads. But no Hutterian leaders made the decision to go north. Certainly the limited growing season had been a significant factor in that judgment, but it did not in itself provide sufficient justification for the decision to settle, instead, in the United States. Rather, negative impressions of Manitoba secured during the 1873 visit had also been influential. As Theron Schlabach put it, "Just about everything that could go wrong did go wrong."[64]

In the Winnipeg area, for example, the Tschetters discovered large groups of unwelcoming residents, and some of the delegates had been treated rather badly. According to a contemporary newspaper account, mixed-race Manitobans (Metis) were "opposed to all immigration ideas" and seemed "bent on resisting them, even with violence."[65] The delegates had hesitated to publicize their discomfort, but "ill usage" of the representatives on board a Manitoba steamer in June of 1873 and a life-threatening incident faced by three Mennonites after the other delegates had continued south probably left a bad taste in the Tschetters' mouths.

Note the following newspaper account of what happened to three of the Mennonite delegates a few days after the Tschetters left for the United States: On the 25th of June,

> A difficulty occurred between the teamsters and residents, in which the latter were worsted and retired. They returned with reinforcements, drove the delegates (the Mennonites, who were at a tavern) upstairs, whereupon

they defended the staircase as well as they could, and ultimately retreated to their own room which they secured inside. After a time the assailants went downstairs to consult, and gave Mr. Hespeler (the Canadian Government agent accompanying the delegates, who was wielding a revolver) the opportunity to go amongst them to persuade them to desist from the attack, pointing out at the same time the risk they were incurring by their infraction of the laws of the country. They consented to leave . . . (but) posted pickets a little distance off on all the roads leading to the tavern. Fortunately for the Mennonites, their imprisonment terminated at about half-past five, on Thursday morning, through the prompt action of the Lieutenant Governor, who directed a troop of fifty men, under Col. Smith, to be sent down at once to their relief."[66]

One suspects that accounts of such experiences got back to the Tschetters, solidifying their hesitancy to settle in Canada. And conversely, the Hutterian delegates had been impressed by the unpretentious demeanor of Ulysses S. Grant and had evidently been under the impression that the Hutterians would be allowed to settle in what is now the state of North Dakota. Sixty years ago, Ernst Correll reminded us that many state governments in the United States had a record of granting conscientious objector status to those requesting it.[67] Correll also noted that, contrary to common opinion at the time (an opinion still expressed by many Mennonite historians), some of the most "conservative" of the Russian immigrants had decided not to settle in Canada.

Not conversant with democratic political traditions, and notwithstanding Grant's humble demeanor, the Tschetters had evidently viewed the President as a kind of American Tsar whose influence was substantial. Their very insistence on meeting with him showed a very "Russian" way of thinking and corresponded to Tschetter's own failed attempt to make a personal appeal to the Russian Tsar earlier that same year. Though 8,000 of the 18,000 Mennonite immigrants had put down roots in Manitoba in the 1870s—owing to the more favorable arrangements available to both groups—the Hutterians took their chances on the nation to the south.

Interaction with the—admittedly few in number—residents of the Dakotas had provided more positive experiences than those sustained from Manitoba encounters. The Manitoba landscape as well had appeared bleak, with flooded, swampy terrain and unbearable mosquito infestation. Paul Tschetter had been particularly favorably impressed with Dakota Territory's northeastern corner, which incorporated the rich soil of the Red River valley. Dakota Territory itself wanted more farmers and had advertised the benefits of settlement in the following way: "Dakota Territory, the richest grainery of the world; a land of sunshine, healthy climate, happy people. Its fertile fields, blooming cities and growing industries invite you and offer you golden opportunities for an existence."[68]

Dakota Territory sought Germans-from-Russia for their agricultural skills and desired "as many as possible." The Hutterians were impressed by the expression of such interest.

The Emigration

The Hutterian communities in Russia decided to relocate in North America "for the sake of faith," even though many village buildings and houses had only recently been constructed. The development of their fields and businesses had taken considerable time and labor, and economic prosperity had either arrived or was beckoning. Nevertheless, the Hutterians' commitment to the peace position and other Anabaptist principles made them turn their backs on the promise of hard-earned security. As the Hutterite chronicler instructed, "Persecution is the true sign of the disciples of Christ."[69]

Some Hutterians came to America with nothing, and all traveled on the cheapest class available. To secure reduced rates available to passengers under age one, many Hutterians had apparently given false information to shipping companies. Arnold M. Hofer found that ship records showed an overabundance of babies and significantly fewer two- and three-year-olds.[70] Communal and noncommunal Hutterians, who sailed together, listed more children under age one, for example, than in the entire one-to-three-year-old age group.

The Hutterians sold most of their land and untransportable possessions to Mennonites and other German-Russians. According to Hutterite Peter Janzen's diary account, *"Reise Nach Amerika,"* the whole village of Scheromet, for example, had been sold to Mennonite Peter Epp.[71] Because such a large group of Hutterians and Mennonites had decided to emigrate within a short period of time, most property had been sold for less than market prices, though a few people, who had originally purchased properties from Russian noblemen and military officials, realized some profit from land sales. Residents of Neu Hutterthal village were also said to have made "good deals."[72]

It is important to note that delegate Paul Tschetter had come to view the whole migration not simply as an escape from the Russification policies of Alexander II but as a divinely arranged means to take the Hutterian people away from the materialism and worldly ways of the Russian Mennonites, to wean them from, for example, smoking tobacco, for which many Mennonites had developed a taste. The Hutterian people had "departed far from the path of (the) forefathers."[73] Tschetter hoped migration would bring them back to God.

Yet, though he was a distinguished Hutterian minister committed to maintaining a conservative way of life for his people, neither in Russia nor

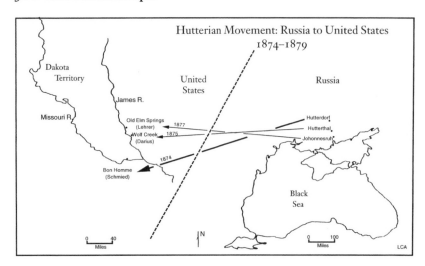

Map 2. Hutterian movement: Russia to the United States, 1874–1879.
Larry Anderson Collection, courtesy of Tony Waldner.

in the Dakotas did Tschetter express support for community of goods. He did not believe that Christian communism was the way to keep Hutterian traditions pure and unspoiled. In his "Report of Why We Had to Leave Russia," and in entries in Neu-Hutterthaler congregational records, Tschetter noted the increasing lack of spirituality among his people and their association with "war lords" (as he described the Russian government). Tschetter viewed the entire emigration as "an awakening."[74] But he did not associate such an awakening with communal life.

Hutterian settlement in the United States was assisted by North American Mennonites through the Mennonite Church (MC) Board of Guardians. The organization raised a small fund for initial start-up costs and helped make arrangements with steamship and railroad lines. Dakota Territory immigration commissioners, who had enthusiastically promoted their area, were also helpful, because they wanted the Hutterians to establish themselves in the territory in order to offset, as they described it, "the humiliating ratio between man and land in the territory." They did not, evidently, consider the native Lakota people to be truly "civilized men."[75]

"Swimming around on the stormy ocean," as Paul Tschetter characterized their journey, the Hutterian people came to what is now the state of South Dakota, across the delegate's "great world ocean." They had not enjoyed the journey across that large body of water. Being thrown together with all sorts of people on the ships was "the worst," according to a member of the communal Darius Walter group who seemed to be particularly upset with fellow travelers of Jewish ancestry. He noted in traditional xenophobic and anti-Semitic fashion that "Jews can't be without trickery."[76] Still, some hardships would be endured "for the sake of the gospel."

Only a few Hutterites remained in Russia. These included descendents of Andreas and Mathias Miller, as well as individual members of Stahl, Tschetter, Knels, and Wollman families.[77] David Knels, for example, remained with his spouse and five children. Andreas Wollman, known as "Millionaire Wollman," also stayed in Russia. This wealthy industrialist had made his fortune partially through an advantageous marriage to the daughter of affluent Mennonite factory owner Peter Lepp. The Lepp family later lost everything during the Russian Revolution, and the Lepp-Wollman factory in Zaporozhye was converted into an automobile production plant.[78]

Some Hutterians had difficulty leaving for other reasons. Anna Wurtz, for example, left behind a boyfriend whom she intended to marry. He had planned to come to North America later, on a different ship. During the first winter in the Dakotas, therefore, Anna spent considerable time sewing clothes for her anticipated wedding, until a devastating letter from a friend in Russia convinced her that her intended had been spending time with another girl. Anna married John Hofer instead. Later, when her first love arrived from Russia, she discovered—too late—that the rumor about him had been false.[79]

An unsolved mystery continues to surround the life of one Franz Wollman, who returned to Russia in 1884 in order to "get financial help" from his affluent relatives.[80] Franz never returned to Dakota Territory. A trunk containing a Russian fur coat and about $300 eventually arrived, but Franz himself never appeared. Investigations at the time determined that the young man had disembarked at New York City after his sojourn in Russia. What took place thereafter is an enigma; no discernible trail was ever discovered. Perhaps Franz was murdered; maybe he changed identities and slipped away into the swirling ethnic mix of New York City. A few months later Franz's exasperated spouse, Sarah, along with their three children, joined the Jamesville Hutterite Colony. Before joining the colony, she and her husband had not lived communally.

Joshua Wollman, a single man who owned a flour mill, also remained in Russia, as did a number of Hutterian women who had married Mennonites.[81] Barbara Tschetter Unger, for example, stayed in Russia and suffered through World War I, the Revolution, and the famine and persecution that followed. Some of her descendents had left Russia during World War II, making their way to Canada by way of Paraguay. A number of young Hutterian men, under obligation for five-year periods of alternative military service, left Russia later than other residents of their respective villages.[82]

Fig. 2.4. Sarah Wollman and her three children, circa 1884.
Photograph courtesy of Hutterian Centennial Committee.

Establishment of a Prairieleut Identity

In 1875, Bon Homme Colony ministers Michael Waldner and Joseph Waldner had returned to Russia for the express purpose of recruiting more members for their communal village. During that trip, while riding on a train, the visionary Waldner fell into a trance and performed a miracle. In his vision, he saw a large rock on the track ahead, which might have caused the train to derail had it not been brought to the attention of the conductor.[83] While visions continued to play a very powerful role in the early history of Waldner's communal assemblage, the two men were unsuccessful in convincing many additional Hutterians who left Russia to join them in Bon Homme Colony.

At the time of the Hutterian departure, only thirty-two of approximately one hundred Hutterian families in Russia had lived with community of goods. They included, as noted, members of two separate communal groups that had, at one time, lived in the same village of Hutterdorf. In the Dakotas, again, only one-third of the Hutterian brothers and sisters opted for a communal way of life. And those who opted for communal life were not necessarily the same ones who had lived communally in Russia. Nor did all of those who had lived communally in Russia choose colony life when they arrived in the Dakotas. In any case, the large majority of Hutterians had decided in favor of private property and did not join the Dakota colonies. They continued to preserve Hutterian traditions without community of goods, living on private farms with family-controlled finances.

It is significant that, in North America, those Hutterians who chose communal life came to monopolize the name Hutterite. Those who did not, though they, too, originally thought of themselves as Hutterites, came increasingly to accept the appellation Prairieleut, in order to distinguish themselves from their communal relatives. As noted, this work uses the alternate term, Hutterian, to describe all descendents—communal and noncommunal—of the European Hutterites, as well as the traditional beliefs and practices associated with that assemblage. In the North American context, the word Hutterite is used only to describe those persons who joined communal colonies, while the terms Prairieleut, Prairie People, and, on occasion, Hutter, are employed to designate Hutterian immigrants who did not opt for communal life.

The Prairie People, having left Russia and relocated in Dakota Territory, faced the awesome task of preserving Hutterian traditions without, Paul Tschetter hoped, the intrusive demands of a federal government or the dominating influence of the Mennonites. In Russia, the Mennonites had attempted to turn all Hutterians into ideological and behavioral replicas of themselves. Tschetter hoped to escape from those assimilative pressures in the United States.

In the Dakotas, however, the noncommunal Hutterians found themselves once again situated right next door to their "fallen" Anabaptist cousins. Some Prairieleut wondered whether it would be possible, in that situation, to create an ethno-religious society unaffected by the conceptual and functional influence of Mennonite as well as non-Mennonite citizens. Paul Tschetter thought it was possible, and he felt the best way to achieve success was to practice a noncommunal rendition of the Hutterian way of life. He felt God would bless such an endeavor but did not anticipate the powerful impact of unfamiliar social, economic, and ideological conditions.

3

. . . .

Life on the Plains

Welcome, thou fatherland, afar,
Where favored gates stand wide ajar
We now our land of birth disown,
We've chosen a home in lands unknown.
**From *"Ein Auswanderungs Lied,"* a song sung by Hutterians
before leaving Russia**

I attended school at seven different places. I sat 26 months
on a school bench, from ABC's to my 16th year. The rest of
my youth was spent on the farm.
David J. Mendel, recalling early settlement years

Dakota Territory

From 1874 to 1879, all of the Hutterian immigrants put
down roots in what became southeastern South Dakota. It was not the site
preferred by the Rev. Paul Tschetter, who had wanted to settle in the Red
River valley of northeastern Dakota Territory. A change of plans had come
about as a result of railroad company maneuvers; because Tschetter did not
accompany the first Hutterian settlers; and because a group of Mennonites,
who had earlier established themselves in the territory's southeastern corner, lobbied for the Hutterians to join them.[1] The emigrants were heavily
influenced by Daniel Unruh, who, together with fifteen Mennonite families from the Russian Crimea, had decided to homestead near what became
the town of Freeman.[2] It seems an odd choice if one considers Tschetter's
strong interest in living away from Mennonite influence.

Based on conversations with his grandfather, Paul G. Tschetter suggests
that, when the Rev. Tschetter arrived in Yankton, he grabbed the arm of the
Chicago, Milwaukee, and St. Paul Railway land agent and asked, "Where

36

are we? I've never been here before," implying that he had been misled and had expected to be deposited somewhere near the Red River (hundreds of miles north), not the Missouri river.[3]

Tschetter had been told, in response, that if he wanted to get to the Red River valley, he and his people would first have to return to Chicago and then start the last part of the trip all over again.[4] The railroad company, in association with Dakota Territory officials and representatives of the Mennonite Board of Guardians, had evidently preferred that the Hutterians settle elsewhere.

In the 1870s, Dakota Territory was still, in many ways, a Native American frontier. Chief Crazy Horse did not lead his successful charge against General George Custer (in what was then eastern Montana Territory) until April 1876, two years after many of the Hutterians had arrived. As late as the mid-1860s, only 2,400 European-Americans inhabited the entire Dakota Territory. Land in the Dakotas had been sold at going rates, irrespective of the natural rights of the Lakota population.

The Homestead Act, passed by Congress in 1862, priced a quarter section of land (160 acres) at $1.25 per acre. The Timber and Culture Act of 1873 allowed individuals to buy an additional quarter section at the same price if trees were planted on the property. Railroad companies owned strips of property, twenty miles wide, on each side of their laid track, with alternating sections, that is, 50 percent of the land, remaining in government hands. Railroad land was usually priced between $2.50 and $7.50 per acre.

In the 1870s, southeastern Dakota Territory was home to a diverse group of people. Yankton, located thirty-five to fifty miles south of most Hutterian settlements, was a frontier outpost with a predominately male population. The Missouri river, which no bridge traversed until 1907, was an avenue for bootleggers making their way toward backland districts and Native American settlements. Yankton's saloons consistently outnumbered its churches, and newspapers openly advertised opium cures.[5] Because of its location on the river, Yankton was a stopping place for transients of all kinds, from steamboat workers to army camp followers, from wandering traders, to gamblers, soldiers, and prostitutes. The territory had a notorious reputation for destroying marriages.

The Dakota Territory Bureau of Immigration, created in 1871, actively encouraged Hutterians, as well as other Germans-from-Russia, to move to the Dakotas due to their renowned success in agriculture and interest in bringing along entire extended families. "To acquire land and still more land was for them the joy of their lives, increased by the hope and satisfaction of leaving it to their children," noted historian George Rath.[6] Dakota Territory wanted hardworking farmers of European ancestry to bring "social stability" to the area.

Before embarking for the American midwest, the Hutterian immigrants first spent a few days in New York City. In his autobiography, David J.

Mendel recalled visiting the zoo when he was six years old and described the outing as "the greatest thrill" of the whole journey.[7] When they arrived in the Dakotas, Hutterians who wanted to live communally divided into three main branches: the Schmiedeleut, followers of blacksmith (*Schmied*) and visionary Michael Waldner; the Dariusleut, disciples of Darius Walter; and the Lehrerleut, adherents of teacher (*Lehrer*) Jacob Wipf, who had been licensed as such by a Mennonite secondary school in Russia. In at least one case, a single Hutterian family was represented in each of the three communal groups.[8] Decisions about which communal colony to join were based variously on family connections, specific leaders, and/or personal associations in Russia.

Those Hutterians who decided not to live communally, the Prairie People, organized their own independent churches. The first noncommunal assemblage to arrive in the Dakotas had accompanied the Darius Walter communal group and settled near the Wolf creek, west of present-day Freeman, on homestead land. David Waldner, Wilhelm Tschetter, and Johannes Hofer were ministers in that group. The second Prairieleut group to arrive was led from the Ukrainian village of Neu-Hutterthal by Paul Tschetter. They settled nine miles north of the Wolf creek group, near what became the town of Bridgewater.

Schmiedeleut Hutterite founder Michael Waldner employed a metaphor first used by sixteenth-century Hutterite leader Peter Walpot. He compared the separated, nonworldly life of the colonies with the "saved" lives of those spared by God in Noah's ark in Genesis.[9] The Prairie People decided to live outside the family shelter of the 'ark,' taking their chances on divine election without observing fully communal theological principles and social practices, because, as one Prairieleut recently put it, "The ark was so full of holes you could only drown in it." The ark of communal living proved, however, to provide a kind of security not found on the prairie.

Considering themselves true Hutterians, the Prairieleut, in their Russian villages, had observed a great many semi-communal practices. In contrast to Mennonites, for example, two Hutterian families had often lived in one basic house structure, much like the duplex found in some Schmiedeleut colonies.[10] But in North America, the Prairie People lived a separated and isolated existence on private farms. This was due, in part, to their inability and unwillingness to procure large contiguous sections of land, but opponents of the "Mennonite Bill" also helped to create the predicament.

Early Religious Life

Prairie People and communal Hutterites struggled with Mother Nature and with government policies as they established a new way of life in a foreign land. They also communed with God. While the Hut-

terites held daily church services on common colony grounds, the Prairieleut met together only on Sundays in private homes. The religious life of
neither group, however, had favorably impressed Samuel S. Haury, the first
missionary licensed by the General Conference Mennonite Church. Haury,
who visited churches throughout the Dakotas in the fall of 1877, gained a
very low opinion of local Prairieleut, Hutterite, and Mennonite spirituality, referring to the Dakota Anabaptists, in general, as "spiritually dead."
But he had been particularly shocked by the lack of religiosity found among
the Hutterische (Prairie People), who did not live in colonies.[11] Haury viewed
the whole area as one big "harvest field" for Mennonite missions, an even
larger mission field, he insisted, than the American Indian reservations.

Early years of settlement for any immigrant group are difficult times, and
so it is, perhaps, not surprising that the Rev. Haury reacted as he did. One
might anticipate spiritual matters taking second place in the lives of people
whose priority was to find a way to put food on the table. But Haury sin-
gled out the Prairieleut for particularly scathing mention. There was something about the way in which the noncommunal Hutterians expressed their
commitment to the Christian faith that had troubled the evangelist. But
possibly, the highly formal and ritualistic worship practices of the Prairieleut congregations, the great importance given to 200-year-old sermons,
were not fully or fairly understood by Haury. One wonders, additionally,
whether Haury ever encountered the very spiritually minded Paul Tschetter.

In addition, it was customary for missionaries, regardless of denominational affiliation, to find spiritually deficient the people they evangelized.
The primary function of missionaries is to convert people to a new way of
thinking and living. Existing religious life is inherently suspect, even though
a rich, indigenous ecclesiastical tradition may just as well support as detract
from a deep underlying spirituality. The Hutterian *Lehren*, for example, provided biblical exegesis filled with earthy agricultural references. The sermon content was therefore highly relevant for late nineteenth-century
Dakota farmers. Traditional hymns, as well, reminded Hutterian worshipers
of the religious commitment of historical predecessors who had themselves
dealt with economic hard times.

One older Prairieleut told John D. Unruh, however, that "his family probably went to church two or three times a year."[12] The writers of the Neu Hutterthaler Church history stated, furthermore, that in the early years "children
probably did not attend church until they were of school age."[13] Erstwhile
Prairieleut settlers David and Barbara Hofer said they joined Wolf Creek
Colony because they "saw how much better the church organization was
among the Hutterite people."[14] These comments show us why Haury might
have been concerned about the spiritual state of the Prairieleut he visited.

On the Dakota plains the Prairie People continued to think of themselves as Hutterians, and just as much representative of the Anabaptist tradition as the colony people. That is not, however, how they were perceived

by neighboring Hutterites and Mennonites. Though an occasional reference to "the other brothers" was found in colony documents, the Hutterites, in general, found the Prairieleut spiritually wanting and therefore initiated little contact with them, since the Prairie People were unwilling to pay the cost of communal discipleship.[15] Mennonites, conversely, tried to convert the Prairieleut to their own rendition of Anabaptist Christianity.

The Prairie People had developed distinctive ethno-religious traditions, however, which they had no intention of giving up. In the Prairieleut view, the community of goods practiced by their relatives in the colonies was not biblically mandated. Other Anabaptists did not preach community of goods as a central Christian principle; neither did the Prairieleut. The Prairie People still engaged, however, in many community-oriented practices. Neighbors, for example, often threshed, sheared and butchered together.[16]

The noncommunal Hutterians had developed a philosophical position for the very different path they proceeded to follow. While the communal Hutterites thought in terms of the community and collective responsibility and one's obligation both to God and to one's Christian brothers and sisters, the Prairieleut placed greater emphasis on the individual and on personal responsibility. Like other Anabaptists, the Prairie People believed in the notion of stewardship. According to this way of thinking, God had entrusted property to individual Christians as his trustees, who were then held accountable for the way it was used. It need not, however, be pooled together to establish a single, collectively owned entity.

Rolf Brednick, somewhat ironically, has attributed long-term Hutterite success in living communally to strong leaders, to "persons of authority, model individuals who [embodied] and [passed] on the value system of the brethren."[17] In North America, the communal Hutterites looked to the leadership of the various *Leut* elders. In the early years, the Prairieleut, as well relied on the authoritative influence of important personalities such as Paul Tschetter. Hutterian leaders in both assemblages, however, were subject to the collective direction of the church community. Theological understandings resident in the sermons provided an additional overarching check on individual influence in both communal and noncommunal societies.

In North America Prairieleut congregations continued to place major emphasis on adherence to decisions made authoritatively by the church as a collective spiritual agent. But because they did not live in separated communal villages, the Prairie People eventually found themselves much more influenced by the spirit of American individualism than did the Hutterites. The Prairie People did not have the ability that their communal relatives had to remove dissenters and their influence from the local community. Noncommunal Hutterians could excommunicate offenders from their churches, but this did not remove them from neighboring farms and businesses. There was no geographically defined borderline inside of which the church controlled all religious, social, and economic relationships.

Table 3.
North American Hutterians in 1880[a]

Hutterians	Location
Hutterites (443 colony residents)	
Schmiedeleut	Bon Homme Colony, Tabor, South Dakota
	Tripp Colony, Tripp, South Dakota
Lehrerleut	Elmspring Colony, Ethan, South Dakota
Dariusleut	Wolf Creek Colony, Olivet, South Dakota
Prairieleut (825 church attendees)	
	Hutterthal Church, Freeman, South Dakota
	Neu Hutterthaler Church, Bridgewater, South Dakota
	Associated House Churches, Olivet/Bridgewater Area, South Dakota
	Hutterdorf Church, Freeman, South Dakota

Note:
[a]This table shows Prairieleut and Hutterite demographic statistics based on the 1880 census.

Institutionally, a number of churches had been established in the Prairieleut community by the late 1870s. Ministerial visits to individual families were also extremely important, since a significant minority did not participate in worship services of any kind. Most of the Prairieleut churches operated in traditional Hutterian fashion without full communal emphasis. Though ministers were divided over whether to include or delete the parts of the seventeenth-century sermons that emphasized communal life, the Hutterian *Lehren* were the only sermons delivered in Prairieleut churches at that time.[18]

The only hymns sung in Prairieleut church services were those contained in the Hutterite *Gesangbuch*. That hymnal, through the lyrics of the songs, the *Lieder*, offered a running historical commentary on the spiritual struggle undertaken by Hutterian and Anabaptist saints in the face of violent oppression. Ursula Lieseberg's research showed that, compared to other Anabaptist groups, the Hutterites had written "the most and longest martyr hymns."[19] Each song or set of songs was dated, and the order of hymns chronological, beginning in the 1520s and continuing into the eighteenth century.[20] It is interesting to note that the Hutterite songbook was not formally published until 1914. For nearly four hundred years, Hutterians used a collection of handwritten volumes.

In Prairieleut churches, men and women sat on opposite sides of the center aisle as was customary. As late as the year 1930, when a Mr. Glanzer walked into an independent Hutterian church in the Huron, South Dakota, area with the intention of sitting together with his new wife, he was confronted by a minister who informed him, "This will never happen while I'm here."[21]

Fig. 3.1. Traditional Prairieleut attire. The Joe M. Hofer family, circa 1900.
Photograph courtesy of Hutterian Centennial Committee.

Prairieleut ministers were unsalaried and selected from within the membership by the casting of lots, with the traditional expectation that the Holy Spirit played a determinative role in deciding where the lot fell. Modern-day Hutterites still select ministers in that manner. "The fear is that were men to make the final decision, they might choose a hypocrite!" exclaimed one minister.

Prairieleut services were always conducted in the German language, though some Sunday school classes used the Hutterisch dialect. Noncommunal Hutterians also observed the traditional custom of rising for the reading of scripture and kneeling with hands folded for prayer. First names were almost always biblical. Musical instruments were not permitted.

The Rev. Paul Tschetter, who had evidently been tipped off, had once met a parishioner on the street and asked him point blank, "Do you have a piano in your house?" When Joe A. Hofer replied "yes," that he had purchased one, Tschetter responded by exclaiming, "You're out of the church."[22] Tschetter did not tolerate games associated with gambling either. In 1884, Tschetter's Neu Hutterthaler Church established that a third offense with regard to playing pool, referred to as "a great evil and black spot," would automatically lead to excommunication.[23]

There was also very little difference between the style of clothing worn by the Prairie People and that worn by Hutterites. In the 1870s, all Hutterian men, in contrast to their Mennonite neighbors, wore plain dark clothes, beards, and long hair.[24] Women wore simple wooden shoes and dark blue or black dresses. Homes were simply furnished, and women in both communal and noncommunal groups were not permitted to wear jewelry, hats, or colorful dresses. As one Prairieleut put it, "We would say they were dressed like peasants, but they more closely resembled the colony people of today."[25] Hutterian dress emphasized humility, preventing clothing from being used as a means of self-expression or self-assertion. It also provided a visible manifestation of a life separated from the world "outside."

Paul Tschetter had once refused to marry a couple because the groom wore a coat with a starched collar, donned a shirt with stiff cuffs, and sported a moustache, which Hutterites in Europe had traditionally associated with military officials.[26] Wedding gowns, too, were unacceptable for Prairieleut brides. Instead, church leaders insisted on the simplicity of a traditional dress with apron and shawl. Women braided their hair, which like men's hair was parted in the middle. Their dresses had common gathers instead of pleats.

In the late nineteenth century, the Hutterisch Austrian dialect was one of the primary mechanisms that both kept the Prairieleut community together and ensured that relationships with communal Hutterites would continue to exist. Terms of deference, as well, promoted the retention of customary sensibilities. One heard older members, for example, referred to with the appellation *Vetter*, for males, or *Basel*, for females, to indicate an attitude of respect. Also functioning as an effective social glue were distinctive ethnic foods, as well as methods of food preparation. And probably as strong a cement as anything else was the 450-year separation of all the Hutterian people, Prairieleut and Hutterites, from non-Hutterians, or "outsiders" as they were commonly called. A common history of persecution, adversity, and confrontation created a unique social bond.

That historic sense of collective separation, based on religious belief and practice, did not leave Hutterians when they settled on privately owned Dakota farmland. In this way, a history of cultural isolation helped set the Prairieleut apart from Swiss and Low-German Mennonites who had settled in the same geographical area. Later on, this phenomenon was noticeable, as well, in central South Dakota, North Dakota, Alberta, Saskatchewan, and on the West Coast, wherever Prairie People established communities.

Homesteading

In many ways, a visit to a modern Hutterite colony is a journey back to what European village life was like in the late nineteenth century—a good deal of closeness in personal relationships and very little privacy. The colony resembles one large extended family.

It is that familial form of life that pulled at the Prairieleut during their early settlement years. All Hutterians had lived at least semi-communally in eastern Europe, but in North America, the Prairie People were unable to duplicate the residential closeness of that social structure. Instead, an intense loneliness confronted many people, a sense of detachment experienced, as well, by other midwestern immigrants. Without complete community of goods, it was simply not feasible, economically or politically, to create the village community to which all Hutterians had grown accustomed in Russia. In the Russian villages, every family had lived on either side of one main road with "beautiful orchards and gardens" in between their homes.[27] In the Dakotas, noncommunal Hutterians often constructed primitive sod houses by themselves, while relatives in the colony worked together side-by-side.

Hutterian life, in general, had been very different in Russia. In the late nineteenth century, the Russian Empire was one of the most dictatorial states in Europe. Hutterians, however, had been authorized to administer the villages in which they lived as mini-democracies within that authoritarian national political structure. Hutterians, Mennonites, and other German-Russians thus represented geographical and cultural islands in a sea of foreign culture. While Russian peasants had virtually no social or political rights, Hutterians elected their own government officials, controlled schools, and worshiped as they pleased.

Anabaptists in Russia had developed a strong sense of uniqueness and separateness, representing a closed Germanic society in the midst of a majority Ukrainian population. Mennonites and Hutterians spoke a different language and held heretical religious beliefs, such as believers' baptism and pacifism. The Russian government did not want those traditions to have any influence on non-German citizens of the Empire, so they left the Anabaptist colonists alone and never asked them to recognize the spiritual authority of the Russian Orthodox Church.

Hutterians and Mennonites, like other German-Russians, had preserved to a considerable extent an eighteenth-century German peasant way of life, but they had lost touch with contemporary social, political, and intellectual trends in Germany itself.[28] That which was referred to as "Mennonite" furniture, for example, had in actuality perpetuated the Biedemeier style, popular among middle-class Germans in the early nineteenth century. Yet it had continued to be the most popular style in Mennonite homes into the following century.[29] Since Prairieleut immigrants had been conditioned by an isolated and insulated way of life in Russia, they were able to successfully retain old world customs and traditions in North America much longer than German-speaking immigrants from the homeland.

The Russian Empire had also prohibited intermarriage between "Germans" and Russians (without forfeiture of numerous government privileges) and had made proselytizing a criminal offense. The prohibitions ensured,

Table 4.
Hutterian Settlements in North America since 1874[a]

Hutterians	Location	Date
Prairieleut		
	South Dakota	1874
	North Dakota	1895
	Saskatchewan	1901
	California	1911
	Alberta	1922
Hutterites		
	South Dakota	1874
	Montana	1911
	Alberta	1918
	Manitoba	1918
	Saskatchewan	1949
	North Dakota	1950
	Minnesota	1958
	Washington	1960
	British Columbia	1977

Note:
[a]This table shows the eventual movement outward from South Dakota to new Hutterian settlements across the western United States and Canada.

in additional ways, that indigenous peoples and German settlers would be situated in different social and ideological camps. Both limitations—proscriptions on intermarriage and on evangelism—guaranteed a continuing ethnic, linguistic, and emotional separateness for German-speaking minorities, who had also developed a sense of ethnic superiority. In Dakota Territory, the Prairieleut continued to discourage marriage outside the ethnic group, a phenomenon representative of all Germans-from-Russia who had immigrated to the Dakotas.[30]

Even though most Prairieleut had not lived communally in Ukrainian Russia, they had established residence in close-knit villages, in which houses stood side-by-side, and seeding, harvesting, and cultivating were done together with neighbors, following traditional European strip-farming practices. But now in Dakota Territory, the limitations imposed by the Homestead Act and the liberal contributions of land given to the railroads by the federal government made it difficult for any one group of people to purchase large connected sections of land. Communities could not be easily re-created according to the eastern European model. Though Mennonite settlers in Canada had been successful in re-establishing a village social structure there, with one broad main street, strips of land extending back from the houses, and semi-communal farming structures, this was not possible in the Dakotas without a highly organized and concerted effort, which had not materialized.

The Homestead Act also forced settlers to live on their own quarter sections, creating an additional barrier to the establishment of village-style residential and economic structures. Some Prairieleut families got around this regulation by placing immigrant houses in corners of adjoining quarter sections, to form a kind of four-house mini-village. But long walks to places of work in the fields of distant properties eventually made the practice economically and physically difficult to justify. Railroad land did not have the same restrictions, but much of it had already been sold to non-Hutterians.

It is interesting to note, however, that in three early Prairieleut settlements there were places where families managed to secure homesteads in the shape of long rectangular strips as opposed to the common square pattern. This is shown on old county maps, and it duplicates an eastern European village design in which houses were built as close to one main road as possible.[31] The Prairieleut Hutterthal and Hutterdorf church buildings, for example, had eventually been built in what might be described as "main road" positions.

Some Prairieleut families had refused to purchase Homestead land for ideological reasons. Government forms required signatures after a statement declaring the signee's intention to become a United States citizen. Many Prairie People felt citizenship might lead to military service obligations. It is for this reason that the communal Hutterites, for example, had at first declined to purchase any government land.

Some Prairieleut, in addition to or instead of homesteading, had purchased farms from struggling settlers who wanted to go elsewhere. Others had staked their claims in questionable ways by putting up shacks on the land they "homesteaded," to satisfy residence requirements, but never actually living in them. Once federal residency requirements had been met, the land was sold to the highest bidder. As one individual noted:

> Instead of actually living on the homestead land a small house or shanty was moved or built on the land and the party who was to make his or her home on this land only spent some nights sleeping there occasionally and then after the required time claimed ownership before the authorities. This was easy to do if the available land was close to the home of the parents of a young person who was of age.[32]

The vast majority of Prairieleut Hutterians did not engage in such practices. It is true, however, that many Prairieleut families who had been considered rather poor in Russia had become at least "land wealthy" in Dakota Territory.

In any case, severe loneliness encircled many noncommunal Hutterians

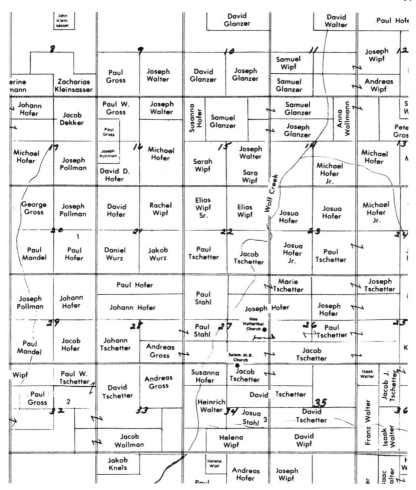

Map 3. Detail of Hutchinson County land map showing Neu Hutterthaler Church area, circa 1880. Map courtesy of Hutterite Mennonite Centennial Committee.

as they established homes on an unpopulated frontier that offered few neighbors to talk to without walking a long distance and no one, outside of the immediate family, with whom to share daily life experiences. In the European villages they had left behind, Hutterians could get quickly to any place or person they desired. In North America, great distances separated people, accentuating the semi-conscious state of shock already inundating anxiety-laden psyches. Some Prairieleut individuals became so disenchanted they had even talked about going back to Russia.

Elements of a semi-communal social and religious ethic had still existed, however. Much work was done collectively, and machinery and tools were

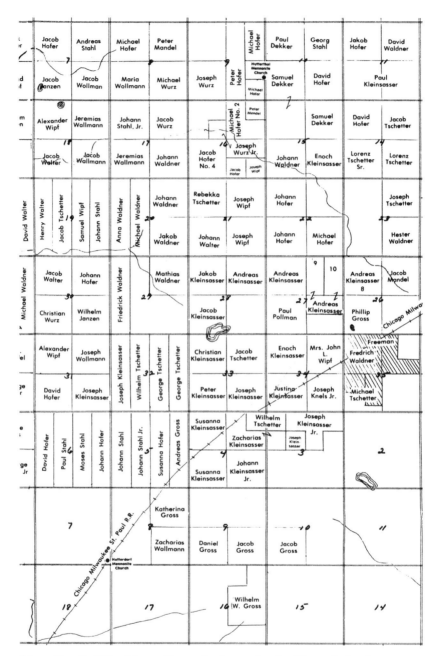

Map 4. Detail of Hutchinson County land map showing Hutterthal and Hutterdorf Church areas, circa 1880. Map courtesy of Hutterite Mennonite Centennial Committee.

Fig. 3.2. Prairieleut hog
butchering scene, circa
1920. Photograph courtesy of
Hutterian Centennial Committee.

often borrowed or loaned. Some neighbors, even when not related, co-purchased expensive machinery, and later, this included combines, windrowers, and bailers. Some neighbors also planted and harvested together. "We took a lot from each other," noted one Prairieleut. "People had to learn to get along with each other and never let the sun go down on their arguments." "We couldn't have made it on our own," stated another person. "I combined, my neighbor hauled the grain." There were also barn-raising bees, quilting sessions, and hog- and steer-butchering community events. And when someone was ill, neighbors would sit and talk with the afflicted individual as long as he or she desired company. In what became the Neu Hutterthaler Church area, Prairieleut settlers had creatively positioned eight homesteads along the banks of the Wolf creek—where four would typically have been placed—to equalize access to water sources.[33]

This was not, however, the life noncommunal Hutterians had known in Europe. One might interact with close neighbors, but everyone else, as the complaint went, "lived so far away." Life in the Hutterite colonies was in many ways less stressful because of the more intensely communal aspects of the cooperative socio-economic and religious venture. The colony way of life more closely replicated the world all Hutterians had known in Europe. Working together, breaking up the sod with a team of oxen, sharing

Fig. 3.3. Hay making on the Jacob L. Hofer farm, circa 1920. Photograph courtesy of Hutterian Centennial Committee.

all material possessions, the communal Hutterites had an advantage in terms of psychological and physical resources.

Prairieleut immigrants, like other Germans-from-Russia, built homes that resembled those in the "old world," even though, in the early years, prairie homes may have had dirt floors and chairs constructed from wooden crates. Other immigrant groups did the same. Finnish settlers in the Dakota counties of Brown and Hamlin, for example, constructed traditional saunas for bathing purposes.[34] "Siouxland" novelist Frederick Manfred—of Frisian ethnicity—had once noted: "We now have things so beautifully done in our toilets, you hardly know you're going to the bathroom."[35] During early settlement times, however, everyone had used outhouses with their un-inviting scents.

For cooking and heating, Prairieleut settlers installed centrally located Russian ovens, attempting to replicate the architectural design that had served them well in eastern Europe. Water from rainfall and individually dug wells was stored in cisterns and pumped by hand into pioneer kitchens. Even the American style of roof construction was not adhered to until the early 1900s, by which time most traditional forms of structural design had been discontinued.

The Russian-style kitchen consisted of a stove made of earthen bricks,

Fig. 3.4. Prairieleut hay-making crew, circa 1920. Photograph courtesy of Hutterian Centennial Committee.

which extended up to the second floor of the house into a central chimney at the roof. Meat was hung and cured in the chimney. The settlers then laid brick, attached to the oven, throughout the livingroom to produce a central heating system. The resulting heat was so intense that one had to be careful not to get too close to the fire.

In the late nineteenth century, twelve-year-old Katherina Hofer Kleinsasser got too near an oven and set her clothes on fire. Fortunately, her brother Peter noticed and quickly threw a heavy blanket over Katherina, extinguishing the flames.[36] Another girl, four-year-old Anna Glanzer, was not as lucky, dying as a result of "a neglected fire" in 1891.[37]

Prairieleut pioneers also constructed their homes as house-barn combinations, so that family members could walk from the living areas, through a walkway, straight into places that housed animals and farm equipment. According to Jacob J. Mendel (Prairieleut publisher of the Freeman *Courier* from 1916 to 1960), even those families who had moved into town, "had a cow for the milk supply."[38] Outdoor summer kitchens were constructed for use in warmer weather and also for butchering ducks, geese, chickens, and hogs in the winter.[39] Flower gardens were typically placed in front yards and included a mix of perennial and annual varieties planted from carefully preserved seed.

The immigrants had initially constructed their houses of sod, often dug halfway into the ground. Adobe bricks, consisting of an appropriate mixture of dirt, straw, and water were very efficient, holding warmth in the winter and keeping living quarters cool in the summer. Walls were whitewashed

Fig. 3.5. Prairieleut house-barn combination, a building style common in eastern Europe, circa 1900. Photograph courtesy of Hutterian Centennial Committee.

both inside and out. Floors, however, were made of good Dakota dirt, sometimes strewn with sand to provide a cleaner surface, and insects were a perennial problem. Candles provided the only form of light inside the houses and barns of the early settlers.

After a few years of mice tunneling in and out of the sod, and continual complaints about the vermin and bugs, and as they became able to afford building materials, Prairieleut settlers slowly replaced their sod residences with houses constructed of wood. Since the wind-swept plains of the Dakotas contained few forested sections, lumber had to be transported from great distances and was an expensive commodity. A primary source of lumber was the Missouri river, forty or fifty miles to the south, from whose banks oxen transported many loads of wood.

In the late nineteenth century, food was plentiful in southeastern Dakota Territory. There was a large supply of fish in the rivers and streams and prairie chickens in such abundance that, according to Jacob J. Mendel, they could be killed from one's doorstep.[40] During the first year of settlement Prairieleut pioneers cleared stones from the rocky soil and planted crops such as oats or flax. They had also raised livestock, leading to the development of a mixed economy. The second year saw the cultivation of corn and wheat. Vegetable garden produce, fish, crabs, eggs, and milk comprised the staple Prairieleut diet, though some individuals raised more exotic crops. In 1910, for example, one individual planted sugar cane, which produced thirty-six gallons of syrup.[41] A few Hutterians had also planted mulberry trees, seeking to duplicate the silk industry which had been successfully developed in Russia.

The Prairie People, in general, preached an ideology of frugality and

Fig. 3.6. Breaking the Dakota sod on the Paul P. Kleinsasser farm, 1915. Photograph courtesy of Hutterian Centennial Committee.

hard work and were considered "tight-fisted" because of their propensity for saving money and their aversion to "worldly" celebration. It later became a tradition, for example, for Prairieleut parents to attempt to leave a quarter section of land to each male heir. Not everyone achieved this, but it was an important motivational goal. Most of the immigrants refused to take financial risks.

Farming was an arduous and uncertain endeavor in the late nineteenth century. There was no modern machinery with which to till the soil, and grain had to be cut by hand with scythes. Plowing was done on foot with oxen and horses, and locusts as well as antelope threatened the settlers' crops. Though antelope could be shot, there was no effective way to reduce the level of insect infestation. A blue sky darkened suddenly by a cloud of grasshoppers, which could destroy the crops in minutes, was not a scene found on the Ukrainian steppes. Worms and gophers were also known to destroy the settlers' crops.

Fuel often consisted of buffalo chips or hay twisted into knots. Prairieleut children also spent considerable time gathering grass, cow chips, and dried sheep manure for fuel. The soil was rocky in the Dakotas, composed of glacial outwash from the last Ice Age. In order to prepare the soil for planting, "rock-picking" was an unavoidable and unending chore. Even in the 1990s, one finds piles of stones in the corner of virtually every southeastern South Dakota farm field. Though a few wagon trails crossed the Dakota landscape in the 1870s, the roads were primitive, extremely muddy during certain parts of the year, and few in number.

Prairieleut immigrants cleaned their clothes with a washboard, a task that

Fig. 3.7. Prairieleut house-barn residence, Margaret and John L. Hofer family, circa 1895. Photograph courtesy of Hutterian Centennial Committee.

demanded backbreaking physical labor and was performed almost exclusively by women. Prairieleut women were heavily involved in the entire farming operation, a common occurrence among German-Russian immigrants. As Betty Bergland put it, "Unlike other farm wives, German-speaking immigrant women did field work and sustained family gardens."[42] They also made most of the family clothing. Brooms were also handmade, usually by men, from corn, a tradition carried on by the Hutterites.

It is interesting that terminology used in connection with the Ukrainian environment took on a slightly different meaning in the American Midwest, even as it continued to be employed by the Prairie People. When one was not in one's own farmyard, for example, one was said to be "out on the steppe." When communal Hutterites used the phrase, however, they meant life outside the colony, and more specifically, that life which was lived by Hutterians who had not committed themselves to true Christian gelassenheit.

Frustration on the Plains

A major frustration for the early settlers was the extreme cold of North American prairie winters. In the Prairieleut Langham (Saskatchewan) settlement in the early 1900s, for example, most travel had to

Fig. 3.8. Pioneer Prairieleut stacking straw, circa 1890. Photograph courtesy of Hutterian Centennial Committee.

be undertaken by bobsled with occupants wrapped in "a horse blanket or a buffalo robe with heated stones at their feet."[43] Along the travelers' way frost "glued their eyelids shut."

Prairie fires were also potentially devastating because of the flat terrain, the marginal rainfall, the undeveloped nature of the land, and the dry, damaging winds. As early as October 1875, a "great prairie fire" had been noted in the Rev. Joseph "Yos" Hofer's diary account.[44] Natural prairie grasses had grown so tall that, according to one individual, "if a cow would lay down, or a horse, they could not be seen or found until they would get up."[45] Once started, fires took off quickly in such terrain. Settlers constructed prairie fire lines to inhibit the spread of conflagrations, but the burn lines were not always sufficient to stop flames from spreading. Early settlers also complained about the annual flooding of certain properties.

Frontier medical practices were extremely archaic; disease was often treated by bloodletting. There were no hospitals and few doctors. Prescription drugs, which were easy to obtain from traveling salesmen, were often dangerous, having undergone only minimal testing. Sara Wipf Janzen died from an overdose of a medicine taken to relieve a backache.[46]

Farm accidents, as well, were often fatal. In June 1876, for example, Paul Glanzer was killed in a windmill mishap. In the early 1900s, Paul Stahl went into a shed to brace the roof on which he had been shoveling ears of corn. While he was inside, the roof collapsed and crushed him.[47] In 1915, thirteen-year-old Joe Pullman hit a rock while on a mower "cutting grass" and was thrown to his death.[48] Seven years later, Susie Wipf, age three, was playing too close to a mower. Her foot had to be amputated at the ankle.

At the turn of the century, infant mortality rates were extremely high, and accounts of deaths were common in church records.[49] Noncommunal Hutterian Barbara Waldner, who later joined Wolf Creek Colony, described her many children who had died as infants as "nine little angels in heaven."[50] As a result of widespread poverty among immigrants, Prairieleut children were often asked to go barefoot during the summer. And for many, winter footwear consisted merely of burlap wrapped around their feet.

Sitting in insect-infested sod houses, or in homes laboriously constructed from limestone, gathered from James river hillsides, then fired in ovens, some Prairieleut settlers became discouraged. Later, though, daily routines were interrupted by welcome visits from hobos and gypsies who offered their labor or music in return for provisions.[51] Modern transportation made it possible to organize popular singing schools, where participants and observers could also socialize. Gypsies and singing schools were not part of the experience of the earliest years, however.

In the early years, some Prairie People purchased guns, and whether as a diversion or through suggested necessity, the practice quickly became a common one, much to the dismay of the Rev. Paul Tschetter. The guns were used to hunt prairie chickens and antelope, but they were also used for purely recreational purposes. The children, alternatively, used their imaginations to create inexpensive toys out of leftover building materials.

The unusually cold winters, the nearly unbreakable sod, the locusts, and the gophers made life as difficult for the Prairie People as that pictured in O. E. Rolvaag's *Giants in the Earth*.[52] The immigrants also faced blizzards and tornados, unknown in mother Russia, and the year 1884 was a particularly devastating one. In addition to the inscrutable disappearance of Franz Wollman, three Prairieleut were killed by the tornado that also led to the "mental derangement" of Jacob Knels, Jr., who died at Yankton State Hospital fifty-eight years later.

The three persons killed were twenty-one-year-old Maria Hofer Wipf, her father-in-law, Elias, and a seven-year-old son, Joseph. They had been in the fields leading a yoke of oxen hitched to a hay wagon when the tornado appeared. It tossed Maria and her father-in-law into a nearby ravine after first "stripping" Maria's scalp "almost entirely off her head" and tearing out Elias' eyes and nose. The head of one of the oxen had also been completely torn from its body.[53] Maria's husband, Elias, Jr., managed to get their three youngest children and his mother into a storm cellar before the twister hit.

Nearby, the same tornado lifted Andrew Dekker straight up into the sky, then gently placed him back on the ground, unharmed. The same twister ripped both arms from the body of Jacob Tschetter.[54] This was also said to be one of the first tornados ever to be photographed (by Prairieleut Jacob Janzen).[55]

In that same year, Paul Tschetter's six-year-old daughter, Barbara, was killed when her dress got caught in a threshing machine. And that year, also, four individuals had been struck dead by lightning.[56] Lightning also killed Susanna Glanzer Wipf on Pentecost Sunday, 1885, and, two years later, Peter Hofer.[57] The immigrants, unaccustomed to North American climatic conditions, sometimes wondered whether God had really wanted them to leave eastern Europe. In desperation, perhaps, twenty-four-year-old Prairieleut Rachel Wipf killed herself.

A number of additional tragedies struck the Prairieleut community in the early 1900s. Two suicides, for example, were mentioned in a single diary account covering the years 1900 to 1920.[58] Although one might find a similar or greater ratio of suicides to total population in other ethnic immigrant groups, these occurrences, nonetheless, show the stressful nature of life on the plains. There was also speculation that the accidental shooting of eleven-month-old Jacob Tschetter in 1897—in a moving buggy—had been precipitated by personal rivalry over a woman.

There were so many economic and psychological challenges in the new world that the Prairie People sometimes forgot how much worse off they could have been elsewhere. When a number of Prairieleut families resettled in Saskatchewan in the early 1900s, they had had to undergo the early settlement experience all over again. Twelve-by-sixteen-foot shacks were eventually constructed, but at first, the pioneer women had slept in tents and the men under the wagons.[59]

Geneticists have suggested that Hutterians are some of the most prolific people on earth. Notwithstanding the common occurrence of fatal illness, as well as tragedies related to inclement weather and farm machinery, Prairieleut families were still large, with ten to twelve children being not uncommon. Individual members did not, therefore, grow up with as much emphasis placed on their own personal identity as one finds in late twentieth-century North American families.[60]

One person interviewed, who had grown up in the early 1900s, could not even recall exactly where she had stood in the order of twelve brothers and sisters. "Some died," she said. That same individual remembered that one sister had "passed away" at age seven. Asked how this had come about, she had responded, "I guess she got hurt somehow." Virgil Kleinsasser noted that his grandfather, John Z. Kleinsasser, who had sixteen children, had not even known him by name.[61]

Prairieleut farmers often felt a special closeness to God because soil and crop conditions relied so heavily on weather conditions, which were outside the sphere of a farmer's will. One person noted that, by working in relative solitude for long hours each day, a farmer could become an open vessel for the inpouring voice of the supernatural. Women, too, did field work, and both male and female tillers of the soil had much time to reflect in silence and voice inner thoughts in song. God was said to speak to Prairieleut farmers through deliberation and intonation, as well as by imparting physical and emotional strength.

Nineteenth-century Prairie People placed much emphasis on the close connection between life on earth and the supernatural dimension of existence. Death was all around and was thus portrayed as a natural transition to a more blessed form of existence. It was for this reason that the immigrants did not fear death as much as people tend to in the late twentieth century. Grandparents were also heavily involved in raising their sons' and daughters' children. The extended family of the Prairieleut was at least as close-knit then as the North American nuclear family became later. The Prairieleut social scene, indeed, represented a tribal society in transition.

Schooling

In the early settlement years, the Prairieleut had so many physical and material obstacles to deal with, they did not spend much time educating their children, though some sent sons and daughters to Hutterite colony schools. During the first two decades of Lakota homeland colonization, the Prairie People guarded themselves against assimilative cultural pressures by isolating themselves as much as possible from non-Hutterians. This was purposefully done by adhering to traditional customs and theological principles. It was also achieved, somewhat unintentionally, by not participating in the public school system.

The fact that education was not a top priority for Prairie People is not surprising. Only two of the 1254 Hutterian immigrants had been educated at the secondary level in Russia—Lehrerleut Hutterite founder Jacob Wipf and a man named Peter Gross. Some Prairieleut immigrants were not even literate. Many had signed land abstracts, for example, with an "X."[62] These farmers had been most concerned with issues of survival, not with formal education, which they deemed a luxury. Though storytelling was a popular pastime, older Prairieleut noted that very few books had been read by family members and friends.

Paul L. Hofer, for example, recalled that in his own home "no one ever read anything," not even a newspaper. The only time he had read was at school.[63] Since schooling was not a priority, instructors were paid little more than room and board. John P. Kleinsasser, himself an educator, noted that teachers were "sometimes men who had nothing else to do or who couldn't do any other work."[64] Teaching was not a prestigious profession.

Regarding education in general, the Prairieleut had a saying, *"ye gelehnter, ye verkehrter"* (the more learned, the more confused), which succinctly summed up the community's view of academic learning. A number of additional common expressions, such as, "No educated person has fallen from heaven as yet," and "He who wants to know everything does not live long," symbolized a peasant culture's disdain for theoretical learning.

The pragmatic Hutters also enjoyed telling folk stories about the futility of higher education. John P. Kleinsasser in his "Memoranda" told the following representative tale:

> Another farmer sent his son to school. When he came home he started a chicken ranch. A few days after the chickens were hatched he came to one of the neighbors and said his chicks were dying. The neighbor asked him what he was feeding them. The young man said, "why feed them, don't they suck?"[65]

Yet, Kleinsasser himself read heavy works, such as Tolstoy's *Anna Karenina*, into mid-life.[66] One wonders whether the numerous comments deriding reading and educational pursuits reflected primarily the perspective of Prairieleut men. A very different viewpoint was expressed in the accounts of many women. In her memoirs, Barbara Entz, for example, noted, "We all liked to read and get books from the library."[67] Another Prairieleut woman, Edna Tschetter, said she had read Sinclair Lewis' *Main Street*.[68] Some Hutter women, furthermore, attended the Mennonite Brethren Tabor Academy in Hillsboro, Kansas.

Still, hard physical work was required to make a living on the prairies. There was little time for recreational or purely intellectual activities. Joseph Kleinsasser noted that the day after their marriage, he and his spouse had gone "into the wheat fields . . . and shocked wheat" for their self-described "honeymoon."[69] Though older Prairie People had attended school occasionally "for the fun of it," they still enjoyed telling anyone who would listen, that a "Ph.D." stood for "post-hole digger."[70]

State-mandated attendance policies in the early 1900s eventually forced the Prairieleut to become more involved in the educational process, and their children attended public schools at least some of the time. One Elizabeth Hofer, for example, went to school in the Olivet area until the seventh grade, after which her parents refused to let her continue. They had become concerned about non-Hutterian dating interests and exposure to modern clothing styles.

What little public schooling was provided for Prairieleut children emphasized the basic skills of reading, writing, and arithmetic. David P. Gross told the story of a singing festival *(Sangerfest)* held in the schoolhouse of District 68, west of Freeman, which had been broken up by a Hutter board member who was, perhaps, under the influence of alcohol. According to Gross, "He came with a buggy whip and chased out everybody saying this is a school for education not for a singerfest."[71] Later Prairieleut generations made formal musical training part of the curriculum in the schools that they helped establish. But in the early years, school attendance itself had not been considered terribly important. A noncommunal Hutterian in Saskatchewan told the author that he "never went to school very much" and had left as soon as he had "been able to get away with it."[72]

Stricter compulsory attendance laws imposed during the 1930s and 1940s changed matters radically, forcing young Prairieleut to spend significant periods of time in school alongside children of various cultural and religious backgrounds. The influence of non-Hutterian peers, at the time, caused concern for many Prairieleut parents, particularly at the secondary and college levels.

A few attempts to provide private education from a Christian perspective followed. John Z. Kleinsasser, for example, operated a school north of Huron, South Dakota, from 1909 to 1911. That institution, Bethel College, closed its doors when Kleinsasser moved to California. Despite its name, Bethel College was actually a combination grade school and Bible school, in which German language instruction and choral training received significant emphasis.

Many Prairie People were also supporters of Freeman College and Academy, schools associated with both the Prairieleut churches and the Mennonite congregations. The Rev. John L. Wipf, who had been ordained at the Hutterthal Church in 1878, was a member of the committee that organized the college (then South Dakota Mennonite College) in 1900. Wipf, at the time, served as secretary of the school's first Board of Directors. In those days of nonsalaried ministers with second occupations, Wipf had also been one of the first teachers employed by the Freeman public school system.

Other Hutters were also involved in the establishment of Freeman College. Joseph "Yos" Hofer, for example, had attended the school's organizational meeting. John Gross donated the three acres of land on which the college had been built. And David J. Mendel served as the governing board's first treasurer. Many noncommunal Hutterians served the institution in a variety of positions in subsequent years, though Freeman College, which closed in 1986, never had a Prairieleut president. Prairie People also dominated the first public school board in Freeman, holding all three positions.

In later years, a number of persons with Prairieleut background served as college professors in other communities as well. One of the first to do so was Jacob M. Hofer, who began his teaching career in 1925 at Tabor College in Hillsboro, Kansas. He did not stay there long, however, moving first to Bethel College, another Kansas Mennonite institution, then to the University of Chicago, and finally to Chicago Junior College. Hofer served these various institutions as a professor of history and education. In 1934, however, after nine academic years in four different colleges, Hofer returned to South Dakota to farm.[73]

Prairieleut Identity on the Frontier

Early Hutterian life on the prairies was certainly not easy. Midwestern plant, insect, and animal cultures required much crop experimentation, leading to as many failures as successes. Climatic differences were hard to get used to and often intimidating. The Prairieleut confronted this plethora of new experiences and conditions without the traditional village institutional structures that might have provided the kind of secure social grounding that sustained Hutterite relatives in the colonies.

The Prairieleut attempt to face this new-found existence with traditional Hutterian intellectual and social principles presented a major test of will. The Prairie People were successful in establishing a number of churches, which followed historic operational and theological patterns. Those spiritual centers provided comfort and support for persons recently uprooted from their European homes. Church discipline had been strictly enforced, and the ancient sermons read every Sunday, while Hutter ministers continually directed the attention of congregants to God's unending guidance and support.

Simultaneously, however, an assortment of unfamiliar environmental manifestations and basic survival requirements led many Prairieleut to consider changing not only the way they worked and interacted with each other but also the manner in which they worshiped and communed together. Ideological and social structures indigenous to an eastern European cultural and geographical milieu were re-evaluated in the context of life on the northern plains. The Prairie People looked to the past for help but often found their attention diverted instead to the dry, rocky ground lying in front of them.

4

· ·

Communal Life or Private Property

When a brother leaves community and returns to private
property, it is a sure sign that he has turned away from God
and left the first love.
Peter Rideman, Hutterite Servant of the Word, 1537

Nearly all of them have returned to private property, leaving
the house of the Lord to wrack and ruin.
Peter Rideman, 1538

Jesus Christ, as soon as he began his teaching, was in community with his disciples. And when the Holy Spirit descended
on them, they began community.
Hutterite sermon on Acts 2, circa 1650

The Big Decision

Upon arrival, the most serious and difficult determination
Hutterian immigrants had to make regarding the future of their lives in
North America was whether to choose communal life or private property.
Prairie People initially chose the noncommunal Hutterianism that most
were familiar with in Russia, but they were confronted continually, through
the *Lehren* and hymns and by Hutterite relatives and friends, with the very
different life they might be living if they gave up personal possessions and
joined one of the colonies. As Bon Homme Colony schoolteacher Peter
Janzen reminded, "For in Heaven is complete communion in all things and
Heaven is in you now."[1]

Close relationships between Hutterites and Prairie People were not uncommon, particularly during the first years of settlement. Many families

Fig. 4.1. Margaret Decker and John L. Hofer, an early Prairieleut immigrant couple, circa 1900. Photograph courtesy of Hutterian Centennial Committee.

had been divided, some members living in community, some not. Many persons changed their minds about their initial choice, leading to much movement in and out of colony life. Prairie People and Hutterites visited with one another often, with Hutterites usually hosting, and the resulting interaction led to many marriages across Hutterian boundaries, much to the chagrin of communal as well as noncommunal assemblages.

The Prairie People disliked intermarriage, because it meant the possibility of losing female children to the colony. And few Hutterite girls married Prairieleut boys. But Hutterites, too, hesitated to encourage intermarriage. Noncommunal spouses were often uncomfortable in colony households, creating potential problems that would influence the commitment of both husband and wife, as well as their friends and relatives, to a communitarian way of life. Both Hutterian groups, of course, worshiped and dressed similarly, so in this respect, there was no great cultural gap for young mixed couples to overcome.

The most extensive movement between the colonies and the private farms of the Hutters occurred during the pre–World War I era. Previous published works underestimated the magnitude of exchange. John Hostetler, for example, suggested in a footnote that "scarcely more than" ten Prairieleut families had joined the colonies before 1895, and that "parts of" seven families left the colonies before 1918.[2] But Prairieleut journalist Jacob J. Mendel, in a book based on Freeman *Courier* articles, identified nine Prairieleut families by name who had joined colonies and twelve Hutterite families who had moved to the prairie.[3]

In addition, Mendel mentioned a large number of "crossovers," people who had lived initially on the prairie, had later joined a colony, but eventually had returned to private property, as well as the reverse. Mendel had not equated crossovers, furthermore, with the many families who had entered colony life permanently nor with the twelve who had left. Since Mendel had only mentioned these situations in passing and had conducted no formal study of the matter, older Prairieleut, including farmer/historian, Arnold M. Hofer, always believed there could easily be three to four times as many crossovers as Mendel had specifically named.[4]

Hostetler based his figures on statistics provided in linguist A. J. F. Zieglschmid's addendum (1947) to the Hutterite *Kleingeschichtsbuch* (literally, the "little history book," the extension of the *Chronicle* that had originally covered the period 1665–1802).[5] Zieglschmid himself had relied on "Hutterite informants," who had evidently not included much of the continuous movement back and forth occurring during the first decade on the plains, when many families had had a difficult time deciding which direction to go.[6]

Even after the first ten years, the figures underrepresented communal and noncommunal intermovement, since they failed to include the many single men and women who went one way or another without their families. Stories confirming extensive movement back and forth are provided in the pages that follow. Before reviewing that evidence, it is important to note the reasons why many Hutterians were attracted to colony life in the first place and, conversely, why many communal Hutterites left the colonies for "the steppes."

In general, Hutterites thought the noncommunal Prairie People were less committed to the Christian faith than they, because the Prairieleut lifestyle was seen as less demanding and more individualistic. Colony life required daily cooperation, openness, group discipline, and an emphasis on simple living. Hutterites felt Hutters were selfish and materialistic.

The communal Hutterites believed in the philosophy of *gelassenheit*, a complete yielding of the individual to God's will as mediated through the church as a body of believers. This meant a willingness to give up all possessions to the colony as exemplified in the Book of Acts in Jesus' own "little colony of disciples" and in the early apostolic churches. The Hutterites believed that all New Testament groups had lived communally and they supported this view with numerous biblical references that at least implied that such had been the case.[7] The spiritual attraction of a communal way of life was deeply felt by many Prairieleut, who were not only aware of the communal past but recognized the communitarian focus of many Hutterian sermons. Many erstwhile Prairieleut thus became Hutterites.

However, noncommunal traditions, too, enticed many people, who had

Fig. 4.2. Breaking sod with oxen, 1880. Photograph courtesy of Hutterian Centennial Committee.

joined the colonies when they arrived, to return to private property ownership. Living communally meant focusing less attention on oneself and one's family than on the community at large; it also meant strict adherence to decisions made at colony meetings. Many Hutterians could not abide living in such a regimented atmosphere.

One Montana Hutterite told Samuel Hofer that an ancestor had once discovered her Hutterite father in tears, in a horse stall, disappointed that he had released all of his worldly goods to the colony. "We would have done better had we not joined," he had told his daughter.[8] He now wished very much that he had settled on the prairies instead. There were also a few instances in which communal Hutterians had applied, as individuals, for free homestead land, with the intention of eventually deeding it back to the colony after fulfilling five-year residency requirements. In a number of cases, colony members reneged on such promises. Early on, this had caused further bad feeling between Hutterites and Prairie People.[9]

In any case, by the turn of the century a number of important economic relationships had been established between communal and noncommunal groups, owing especially to extensive Prairieleut use of Hutterite flour mills and syrup presses. Hides, too, were taken to the colonies for stretching and tanning. Joseph "Yos" Hofer once visited a colony to purchase lamp oil.[10] Relationships were sustained, as well, by numerous informal visits. Since Hutterian families were often divided over the communal/noncommunal

Fig. 4.3. Kathryn Hofer on corn-picking rig, circa 1920. Photograph courtesy of
Hutterian Centennial Committee.

issue, Prairie People dropped in on colony relatives frequently. There were
references to such visits in virtually every published Prairieleut family history and diary account.[11]

In 1903, for example, Prairieleut minister, Jacob J. Hofer attended the
funeral of his uncle, Dariusleut Hutterite patriarch Darius Walter.[12] Once
described as a "common man with somewhat meager education," the Rev.
Hofer had, in fact, visited Walter "on the point of death," one day prior to
his decease.[13] Michael Stahl, who was originally a Prairieleut but eventually
became a minister at the Wolf Creek Colony, preached Walter's funeral sermon. One of Jacob Hofer's brothers had also been a member at Wolf Creek,
and he claimed a sister at Rockport Colony, where his mother-in-law had
also lived. The life of the Rev. Hofer's extended family was thus a socially
mixed communal/noncommunal conglomeration.

Jacob Hofer visited the colonies repeatedly, as was noted in diary entries.
Though he was a minister in a Prairieleut congregation, Hofer referred to
the communal Hutterites as his "brethren." When someone got sick, the
Rev. Hofer seemed to know about it and a visit was made. He noted, for example, that when Hutterite minister Paul Hofer died, there had been many
Prairieleut at the funeral.[14] In June 1912, Hofer volunteered to drive a number of Dariusleut Hutterites to Parkston, South Dakota, where they had
boarded a train that took them to north-central Montana, one of the locations where many Dariusleut eventually resettled.

Some Prairieleut families also sent their children to colony schools because of what was described as "superior education and spiritual training."[15]
Hutter Marie Waldner, a retired Freeman College professor, stated that her

grandfather had attended school at Wolf Creek Colony because there had simply been no public schools in the area where he lived.[16] In the process, the Waldner family had developed close relationships with the Wolf Creek people, and Marie remembered visiting there often as a child. She recalled that though her father and his family were allowed to eat in the communal dining hall, her grandfather had been asked to take meals in a separate room. In Russia, he had at one time been a member of the communal Dariusleut, and though the Hutterites treated him with kindness, he was also continually reminded of broken vows from the past. Other Prairie People remembered ancestors attending school at the Tschetter Colony located a few miles west of Wolf Creek.

Marie Waldner's Prairieleut family had many Hutterite relatives. A great-aunt, for example, who had been raised Prairieleut, had married into Rockport Colony. Marie's great-uncle Christian, also brought up on the prairies, had become a member of Wolf Creek Colony, as had one of her uncles. As a young married man, Christian, who had evidently been pulled by communal Hutterianism for some time, promised God that if He helped him survive a terrible illness, he would join the colony. Christian recovered, kept his promise, and was later chosen by lot as a Dariusleut minister.[17]

In the early settlement years, many Prairieleut felt guilty and spiritually uncomfortable about not living communally. Others developed the art of apologetics. Marie Waldner noted that visiting the colonies had been like being with family, and that they often stayed late. Her Uncle Christian used those opportunities, however, to preach the communal gospel unceasingly. He continually told her father, "I'm so sorry we didn't take you along," indicating his heartfelt wish that Marie's family too had been brought into the colony. Marie's father usually defended his decision to live "outside" by pointing to the alcohol abuse and lack of personal responsibility in the colonies. "You have your problems too," he would exclaim.[18]

Like Christian Waldner, Bon Homme Colony schoolteacher and shoemaker, Peter Janzen had also spent much time trying to convince skeptics that the New Testament established the foundation for communal life. He did this through letters written to, and published by, the *Mennonitische Rundschau*, a German-language Mennonite periodical.[19] Hutterite evangelism was indeed not dormant at the turn of the century, at least not with regard to noncommunal relations.

Blood lines ran thick between communal and noncommunal Hutterians. Christian Waldner's brother Martin, for example, a minister in a Prairieleut congregation, had ultimately been buried in the Wolf Creek Colony cemetery. That was a highly unusual practice and had happened only because Martin had maintained very close relationships with members of that colony. Many older Hutters living in the 1990s either recalled playing with cousins in the colonies or remembered parents and/or grandparents telling them of such occurrences from their own life stories.

Excursion to Pennsylvania

In 1880, a highly unusual event transpired, when four single Prairieleut men, Paul F. Gross, Jakob J. Wollman, George D. Hofer, and Samuel Wipf, journeyed to Tidioute, Pennsylvania, northeast of Pittsburgh, in order to join the communal Harmony Society. Whether they did so on an adolescent whim, from a spirit of adventure, or were attracted to communal life but did not want to join Dakota Hutterite colonies was difficult to determine based on available records and personal interviews. Paul Gross, for example, had been raised as an orphan at the Schmiedeleut Bon Homme Colony. He left in his teens, however, and eventually, after he returned from the east, became a Prairieleut minister.

In the 1880s the Harmony Society (also called Rappites), a communal Christian organization founded by George Rapp in 1804, had an aging and dwindling membership as a result of internal schisms, unfulfilled millennial hopes, and the Society's belief in celibacy. Still, the Rappites had significant financial resources and owned 12,000 acres of oil-rich land in Warren County. The Rappites (like the Inspirationists in communal Amana) had also loaned thousands of dollars to certain Hutterite colonies. Perhaps that is what attracted the Hutter soldiers of fortune. Their unmarried status certainly met one of the qualifications for membership. Whatever the case may be, the young Prairieleut men eventually returned to the Dakotas, and we know virtually nothing about the circumstances of their sojourn in Pennsylvania.

In 1884, however, in a more publicized case, the entire Tripp Hutterite Colony (a second Schmiedeleut assemblage), under the leadership of Michael Waldner and Peter Janzen, temporarily took over the Rappite Colony site near Tidioute. Harmonist leaders by that time had expressed interest in deeding the property in total to a trusted, like-minded, and German-speaking communal society. They embraced the Hutterites, even though the two groups differed on a number of theological issues.[20] How the experience of the four Prairieleut sojourners had influenced decisions on either side is not known.

In 1885 the Schmiedeleut Hutterites accepted a formal offer from the Harmonists, including the nonnegotiable condition that the "entire" Hutterite population of "380" would leave South Dakota and relocate to the east. That requirement caused numerous "troubles," since the Schmiedeleut did not have the authority to act on behalf of the other two Hutterite groups.[21]

The Hutterites who moved to Tidioute developed a small lumber industry but were unsuccessful in transforming the Warren County properties into farm land. The Hutterites had expressed disinterest in establishing nonagricultural industries in the oil-rich region, and according to Rappite leader Jonathan Lenz, they had simply not been successful economically.[22] In 1886, they were either "sent back," or they "returned" to Dakota Territory, depending on which Hutterite or Rappite account is consulted. It appears that at least one Hutterite remained in western Pennsylvania, however. Samuel Kleinsasser evidently defected from the Schmiedeleut after fleeing punishment for arriving late for a church service. He was photographed for a short news article in 1922 (republished in 1955), one which discussed the local history of the Tidioute area and implied, throughout, a strong abhorrence for communal life, associating it with Soviet communism.[23]

Crossing Over

One of the most interesting manifestations of the intense struggle for the hearts and minds of all ethnic Hutterians was the crossover phenomenon. Examples of the interconnected relationships of Prairieleut and Hutterites during the early years of settlement are too numerous to explore fully, but the following examples are a representative sampling.

In Russia the Rev. Michael Stahl had been a noncommunal Hutterian elder in the village of Hutterthal. When he first arrived in the Dakotas, Stahl continued a noncommunal existence on the prairie. His conscience bothered him continually, however, and within a year, on July 31, 1876, he left his farmstead and joined the Dariusleut Wolf Creek Colony.[24] Noncommunal Hutterians who decided to join colonies were usually accepted into membership by the "laying on of hands."[25] Previous baptisms were, in this way, fully validated. Michael Stahl's brother, Johann, had joined him at Wolf Creek, three days later. Stahl had, at that time, allied himself with a Wolf Creek faction that had successfully opposed the unification of the Dariusleut, Lehrerleut and Schmiedeleut Hutterite groups.[26]

When early Hutterian settlers joined or left colonies they were often accompanied by large families. The lives of hundreds of people, perhaps one-sixth of the entire Hutterian population, were irrevocably changed in transit, somewhere between the prairie and the colonies. This movement was not a minor phenomenon involving merely a few individuals.

The Johann Hofer family, for example, had settled in the Lehrerleut Elmspring Colony originally but left sometime in the 1880s.[27] Two of Johann's sisters had departed for the Prairieleut "steppes" even earlier.[28] George Hofer, one of the ministers at Wolf Creek Colony, had a son, another "Johann Hofer," who followed him in the ministry. But Johann did so at the Hutterdorf Church, which was a Prairieleut congregation located near the town of Freeman.[29]

Ship list records indicate that one Peter Entz joined Elmspring Colony when he arrived in the Dakotas.[30] Many of his children, however, did not join. Benjamin Stahl homesteaded on the prairie, but his two sons, John and Michael, joined Wolf Creek Colony. Many families were split in this manner as both individuals and families disagreed about whether or not they should join the colony river settlements. Joseph Wipf, for example, decided to live among the Prairieleut, but his children did not uniformly follow his lead. Three children joined him; three others entered the life of the colony.

It is important to note that families were sometimes divided not only on the issue of communal life versus private property, but also about which of the three Hutterite Leut groups to join, creating an even more complicated situation. Tremendous familial tension emerged at a time when the lives of all persons involved were undergoing tremendous stress as a result of geographic relocation.

There are numerous additional illustrations of the crossover phenomenon. One Paul Mendel, for example, opted for communal life when he arrived in Dakota Territory, and he remained there until his death thirty-eight years later. One of his children, however, joined the Prairie People. A daughter of Prairieleut Matthias Waldner, on the other hand, married a boy at Wolf Creek Colony and took up residence there. A son of Prairieleut Johann Wipf also joined the Wolf Creek assemblage.[31]

The Rev. John Kleinsasser, one of the first ministers at the Hutterthal Church, also sold his private farm and joined a colony, the Elmspring Colony. Another Hutterthal minister, John Waldner, made a similar decision but opted instead for the Jamesville Colony. This was a very strange story indeed, since two Prairieleut ministers joined colonies associated with different Hutterite Leute—the Lehrerleut and Dariusleut, respectively. Later in life, Waldner left Jamesville and re-established himself on private land near Freeman![32]

One of the most bizarre antecedents to a decision for communal life occurred in the late 1800s when a young Prairieleut male was hung from a tree by jealous brothers who, as the story goes, had hoped to benefit from a larger inheritance. The young man's sister, however, had seen what had transpired and had cut him down in time to save his life. Taking this as a sign from God that he needed to do something different with his life, the man sold his property and joined the Wolf Creek Colony.[33]

The Yos Hofer Story

Joseph "Yos" Hofer is another example of someone who moved back and forth between communal and noncommunal life. Hofer, a "private owner" in Russia, joined the Hutterites upon arrival in Dakota Territory and was well connected to influential colony leaders. His brother-in-law, Darius Walter, for example, was the senior minister at the Dariusleut Wolf Creek Colony, where Hofer and his family first established residence. Joseph was also the nephew of another Wolf Creek minister, George Hofer. In addition, Joseph, nicknamed "Yos," was a nephew of the Rev. Peter Hofer, who had helped found the Lehrerleut Hutterites. He also had relatives among the Prairieleut. Yos was, furthermore, quite wealthy and had managed to bring much of his capital with him from Russia.

Much of what is known about Yos Hofer is derived from diary accounts of the years 1873–1905. Hofer's journals, discovered in the early 1990s, and painstakingly translated by Arnold M. Hofer, included commentary about a heretofore unknown visit to St. Petersburg on behalf of communal Ukrainian Hutterians in 1873, showing that even in Russia Hofer had been attracted to community of goods. Hofer's journal also described his sojourn with the Wolf Creek Colony Hutterites, from 1874 to 1877, and his life as a Prairieleut leader thereafter.

At Wolf Creek Hofer served on the colony's governing council and as the community's schoolteacher. He was also a leading advocate of a plan to unite the various Hutterite Leut branches, supporting the efforts of Schmiedeleut leader, Michael Waldner, who had made that endeavor one of his primary goals during the 1870s.[34]

In February 1876, according to the Hofer account, the Dariusleut Wolf Creek membership had voted to accept Michael Waldner as common Elder of both Wolf Creek and the Schmiedeleut Bon Homme Colony. Six months later, in September 1877, all three Leut leaders—Michael Waldner, Jacob Wipf from the Lehreleut, and Darius Walter from the Dariusleut—met together at Wolf Creek to discuss formal merger arrangements.

Integration was doomed, however, because of continual disagreement on land title issues; the collective refusal of Darius Walter and Jacob Wipf to give up control of their respective Leut organizations; and the differences of opinion about who should hold title to colony property. There were also many heated discussions regarding allocation of both work responsibilities and clothing.[35] Much of the conflict appeared to represent an extension of the century-old feud between parts of the Walter and Waldner families. The Waldners traditionally blamed the Walters for the failure of the communal experiment at Raditchewa. Hofer's account clearly delineated the interpersonal and structural difficulties involved in establishing a communal organization from inception, with members often at each other's throats for visiting too much or not working hard enough.[36]

Hofer's greatest complaint was that, although the colony membership had, by majority vote, decided in favor of unification in September 1877, the Wolf Creek leadership had not recognized that plebiscite. According to Hofer's account, the Rev. George Hofer, an antimerger advocate, ultimately exclaimed: "Schmied Michael [Michael Waldner] should take his people, those whom he dragged together, and take them away."[37] Hofer also accused his nephew, Yos of "rudeness" for openly criticizing the leadership.

In response, a meeting of the entire Wolf Creek Colony membership voted not only to "discipline" Darius Walter for not honoring the expressed preference for unification but also decided to excommunicate George Hofer.

In defense, the charismatic Walter not only refused to be disciplined but threatened to excommunicate anyone who disagreed with him.

One has to bear in mind that, while the Yos Hofer journal opened new lines of thinking with regard to early inter-Leut relationships, it also reflected the personal bias and perspective of the diarist. It was clear, however, that Darius Walter had retained a strong hold on the Wolf Creek membership as no action was taken against him or George Hofer. Ironically Yos Hofer once spent 112 days in St. Petersburg with his present adversaries, one of whom was his uncle.

In 1877, greatly upset with the entire Dariusleut assemblage, Yos loaded up his family, and four others, and moved away. Retaining commitment to a communal way of life, the Hofer group established residence at the Schmiedeleut Bon Homme Colony, where Yos served for eleven months as farm manager. Hofer never actually became a member of Bon Homme, however, holding back money he had inexplicably managed to take with him from the Wolf Creek Colony.

The possession of the money was an extremely unusual occurrence, since all of Hofer's material and financial holdings should have gone permanently into the Wolf Creek treasury at the time of his joining. The Bon Homme Colony leadership evidently got wind of this, because they instructed Yos to lay all of his privately held assets "at the Apostle's feet," as the early Christians had done. Hofer decided to leave instead, since, as he later put it, "there was nothing there."

Hofer told Bon Homme members he intended to rejoin the Wolf Creek Colony. It is said, however, that enroute Hofer stopped to visit with one of his sisters, a Prairieleut living in the Olivet area. In the course of their conversation she exclaimed, "What do you want on the colony?" Whatever went on in that dialogue evidently convinced Yos not to go back "in." He proceeded to purchase private land on the prairie and was eventually selected as minister by the small Olivet Prairieleut fellowship. The fellowship met biweekly in private homes, where Hofer read Sunday sermons both morning and afternoon.

The Yos Hofer story raises the fascinating question of what might have happened if there had not been three dueling communal factions among the Hutterites at the time of settlement. One could legitimately speculate that unification would have made colony life much more attractive to non-communal Hutterians than had ultimately been the case. The prospect of finding oneself in the midst of interpersonal conflict based upon family factions, charismatic leaders, and minute differences in social organization, was not an inviting one for many Prairieleut who were already, at least minimally, averse to full community of goods.

Following Yos' defection, his diary had continued to document numerous visits to Hutterite colonies, though he rarely appeared at the Wolf Creek community. Hofer also engaged in regular correspondence with Hutterite friends and relatives. Hofer's journal showed many visits, as well, to the Salem Krimmer Mennonite Brethren Church (KMB), where his son Jacob, and many other Hutters, had established membership. Yos had remained a member of the independent Prairieleut church community, however, noting with regard to his initial attendance at the revivalistic Salem Church, "It had but little influence on me; for they had little spirit and were nothing less than *zundent* (inflammatory)."[38] Still Hofer continued not only to attend a number of KMB services, but he invited KMB ministers, including Paul Tschetter's two ordained sons, to preach the Sunday morning sermon in his home congregation. (The Krimmer Mennonite Brethren phenomenon is discussed in chapter six.)

Another surprising find in Hofer's diary was his notation that, in 1892, five people from Sabatisch, Slovakia—evidently Habaner—had visited the Freeman area. Two of the Habaner remained for half a year working, first for Yos' son, Jacob, and then for Hutter David Wollman. Nothing further was mentioned, but this entry suggests that the Slovakian Habaner retained some sense of where their distant relatives had settled.[39] John Hostetler, in his 1974 work, *Hutterite Society*, noted that Habaner Ignatius Pullman had visited the communal Hutterites in 1893, bringing some "old books" with him.[40] We now know that there were other Habaner visitors as well. The significance of locating a single diary is shown clearly by the information contained in the Yos Hofer account.

The communal Hutterites held on to one story about Yos Hofer, which was retold often during the next eighty-five years. It involved Yos' wife, Anna, and went as follows: According to this frequently told account, which had mysteriously appeared in written form as an addendum to the only extant copy of Yos' diary, Anna Hofer had never wanted to leave the colony and continued, throughout her life as a noncommunal Prairieleut, to insist that she be dressed in "colony clothes" when buried. "When I die," she requested, "dress me in the clothes that are in my closet."[41]

Anna's family did not follow her wishes. They placed her in a casket in Prairieleut garb, which had over the years become increasingly stylish. But for no apparent reason, the burial clothes kept getting wet, causing all kinds of problems. After changing Anna's attire a couple of times, the family finally gave in and put colony clothes on her instead. Those clothes stayed dry and Anna went to her reward in peace.

I first heard this story from Michael Waldner, a Hutterite minister and colony-recognized historian who died in 1991. Waldner, a grandson of the Schmiedeleut founder, told the story with enthusiasm and conviction. He also reeled off ten to fifteen more stories with the same theme. In Hutterite accounts the story was usually completed with the following statement referring to Yos: "This showed him that he did wrong in leaving the colony." The problem with such moralizing, as Arnold M. Hofer pointed out in his translation, was the fact that Yos actually died seven years before Anna. Also interesting was the fact that no one remembered Prairieleut Hutterians ever telling any part of the story.

Older Hutterites were adamant, however, that the incident had taken place as described, whether or not Yos had by that time gone to his grave. It had at least shown his descendents that they had "been wrong." Even if the story was apocryphal, it was significant with regard to what it said about relationships between Prairieleut and Hutterites. The two groups were constantly trying to convince one another that God had blessed their uniquely different endeavors.

Families Torn Apart

Individual Hutterians often had a difficult time deciding whether to take communal or noncommunal paths. Two blind orphaned sisters, Rebecca and Katherine Wollman, for example, went in opposite directions. Rebecca joined a colony; Katherine joined a Prairieleut Krimmer Mennonite Brethren congregation.[42] One-time Prairieleut Katherina Stahl also joined a colony.[43] KMB minister, John Z. Kleinsasser, went the other direction. Kleinsasser had lived in the colonies for many years before buying land on the prairie. Though John Z.'s father, Zacharias, accompanied his son when he left the colony, John Z's sister, Maria Waldner, never gave up community of goods.[44]

While at Wolf Creek, Yos Hofer had continually noted persons who "came to the congregation," including one "John Hofer with his old Susanna" and the entire Elias Kleinsasser family.[45] Three of John Hofer's brothers joined him at the Dariusleut Wolf Creek; three others became Lehrerleut Hutterites. John Hofer's father, Jacob, however, settled on the prairie, the only member of his family to resist the appeal of colony life.

Grandson George M. Hofer told the author that his mother always said, that if his father died at a young age, she too would take the children and join a colony. This was a commonly expressed intention of Prairieleut women in the early 1900s. If their husbands died, these women and their children knew they would have much greater economic and social security in the colony. Even in the late 1990s, it was still customary for colony women to retire from major work responsibilities when they reached their mid-forties. The communal assurance of colony life was undeniably attractive to someone forced to contemplate single motherhood. Much more help would be provided there. That was why Sarah Wollman joined the colony after her spouse, Franz, disappeared in New York City.[46]

Jacob Janzen, a Mennonite originally from the Ukrainian Chortitza Colony, also represented the historic Anabaptist tendency to drift. After receiving high recommendation from Mennonite leader Johann Cornies, Janzen had his first encounter with Hutterians in 1845 when he began teaching ninety-one students in the Hutterthal village school. Soon after his first wife died in 1848, Janzen went one step further and joined the Hutterian Church. He then married Maria Waldner, a sister of soon-to-be Schmiedeleut elder Michael Waldner. At the Hutterthal church, Janzen had also inexplicably been given authority to perform marriages, though he was not an ordained minister.[47]

Upon arrival in the Dakotas, Janzen and his family had originally joined Bon Homme Colony.[48] They left soon thereafter to homestead northwest of Freeman. Jacob, thereafter, made many attempts to get the one son who had remained at Bon Homme to join them. The son, Peter, became well known as a teacher and shoemaker and as a contributor to the continuation of the *Kleingeschichtsbuch* for the years 1874–1899. Jacob was unsuccessful in his attempts to convince Peter to leave community life. Once, his son even hid in the barn to avoid Jacob's entreaties.

In the years that followed, Peter Janzen sent many reports on colony affairs—sometimes via his father—to Hutter Jacob J. Mendel's Freeman *Courier*, as well as to the *Mennonitische Rundschau*. Peter remained committed to the communal Hutterites, however. In 1893, he even convinced his youngest sister, Maria, to join the colony, where she met a young man and was married.[49] Jacob himself, as noted, provided an historic eyewitness account of the infamous 1884 tornado, which was published in the *Rundschau*.[50]

In the twentieth century, one finds fewer and fewer incidents of communal/noncommunal crossover. In 1923, right before his death, Prairieleut farmer Sam S. Hofer joined Rockport Colony. He made that move at age seventy, after spending his entire life "on the prairie." Communal life had evidently retained a hold on him. But the Sam S. Hofer case was not a typical one. It was generally assumed that the pressures of American and Mennonite assimilation had convinced almost all Prairie People that Hutterite life was not a viable option for them. Thus Prairieleut girls quit marrying Hutterite boys and vice versa. Equally important, however, was the fact that few Hutterites remained in the state of South Dakota after World War I (see chapter 7). If they had, there might have been closer relations for a longer period of time.

The following are a few final examples of colony–prairie movement. Between 1874 and 1888, an extended family of Tschetters had been particularly active in moving back and forth between communal and noncommunal forms of existence. Most of the family eventually joined Bon Homme Colony.[51] In 1890, Prairieleut Mary Glanzer married Andrew Kleinsasser and joined Bon Homme Colony, exemplifying Jacob J. Mendel's contention that, "for many years girls on the farm were married to young men in the colony."[52]

In 1894, the Rev. Joseph Waldner and his family went in a different direction, leaving Milltown Colony for the prairie. Waldner had originally joined Bon Homme Colony and, in 1876, accompanied Michael Waldner on the missionary journey to Russia, to invite remaining immigrants to join the colony. But Joseph Waldner eventually grew tired of living communally and left for the "steppes." Peter Hofer, a noncommunal minister in Russia, joined the communal Lehrerleut when he got to America. His son Dave P. Hofer, however, left the colony at age nineteen, joining Hutterite-turned-Prairieleut John Z. Kleinsasser on his trek to the West Coast. This meant leaving behind many brothers and sisters.

Sarah Wurtz Tschetter and husband Isaac, as well as Sarah's sister, Katherina Wurtz Hofer, chose to live on the prairie. But Sarah's brother, Johannes Wurtz, and two half-brothers (Joseph and Andrew) joined Elmspring Colony. Sarah's mother, Katherina, was also a member at Elmspring, as was her grandmother, Sarah Kleinsasser.[53] One Jeremias Wollman grew up as a Hutterite but eventually left, settling among the Prairieleut.

Andreas A. Wipf, Freeman, South Dakota's first medical doctor, was born in Russia and lived on the prairie until his father died. After his father's death, his mother, Susanna Glanzer Wipf (later struck by lightning) married Hutterite Johannes Waldner of Wolf Creek and joined that colony. Andreas lived at Wolf Creek for three years, from 1876 until 1879, when his parents changed direction and left for the steppes.[54] Most of Andreas' brothers and sisters, however, chose to stay in the colony, and one sibling who left eventually rejoined.[55] There are numerous additional examples of these types of Prairieleut/Hutterite movements and crossovers, which made early life on the plains extremely stressful for many individuals and their families. Prairieleut E. J. Wipf's mother, for example, had lived at Rockport Colony. Dr. J. H. Wipf's sister married colony member Paul Stahl.[56]

Previous estimates of colony–prairie intermovement have been radically understated, particularly due to the crossover phenomenon and the fact that so many young persons married across the colony/"steppe" border. Examination of documented residential transitions from the earliest years found in diary accounts, ship lists, marriage documents, and nineteenth-century church records, confirm an unusually broad series of Prairieleut/Hutterite interrelationships.[57]

Previous assessments, furthermore, did not include the many persons who lived without community in Russia but had immediately moved into a colony on arrival in the Dakotas. Arnold M. Hofer, for example, had three great-uncles who joined Wolf Creek Colony when they arrived in Dakota Territory, even though they had not lived communally in Russia. A number of people from the noncommunal Russian village of Neu Hutterthal also joined the colonies.[58] Ship passage lists from the noncommunal Russian village of Johannesruh, too, showed a mix of colony and noncolony people in the group.[59] And what about those Hutterians who had lived communally in Russia but chose noncommunal prairie life in the Dakotas? There various transpositions demanded radical cognitive and experiential alterations. In his diary account Yos Hofer noted significant interpersonal conflict both at Wolf Creek Colony and in the Prairieleut community.

Fig. 4.4. Johann "Schwag-
ger" Wipf, Hutterite colony
beekeeper, circa 1910.
Photograph courtesy of Hutterian
Centennial Committee.

Two Kinds of Community

Since communal and noncommunal Hutterians journeyed
together across the Atlantic, they had much time to try to convince each
other of the spiritual correctness of their different plans for the future.
Though the majority of Hutterians did not feel community of goods was
biblically mandated, significant ambivalence about the value of the communal past caused great difficulty for families deciding whether or not to join
the Dakota colonies. Hutterians in Dakota Territory came to realize that,
if they did not choose communal life, they could not simply re-establish the
semi-communal village organization to which they had grown accustomed
in Russia. They would have to live in greater physical isolation and do more
things on their own.

As the Hutterian settlers came to terms with life in a strange land, they
were confronted with the reality of two visions of Christian community.
The Hutterite view demanded submission of the individual to the ultimate

authority of a group of people acting together as God's representatives and servants on earth. The Prairieleut view, which continued to support collective decision making on religious issues, allowed for significant individualization of judgment with regard to economic concerns. The Hutterites, on the other hand, put faith in a community that regulated the economic lives of its constituents. Even work assignments were based on the will of the group as a whole, not simply on the basis of individual interest. The Prairie People, conversely, believed in a community that called its members to be responsible for their own livelihoods.

The acceptance of either concept of community had important implications for the way one viewed social, psychological, and economic issues and obligations. Family life, for example, meant very different things, depending on whether one lived communally or noncommunally. Already, in the late nineteenth century, Prairie People began making more and more decisions as individuals and as families without consulting the church even on issues of moral import previously dealt with by ministers and other members of the congregations. Perceptions of what was meant by "community" were transformed in the process, the Prairieleut moving increasingly in the direction of privatization.

5

. . . .

Prairieleut Congregational Patterns

There was one thing I did not approve and that was the fact
that some of the women smoked and chewed tobacco.
Paul Tschetter, 1873

What will you do with the world? World is world and will
remain world until the Lord will come and end it all.
Paul Tschetter, 1873

The independent renegades . . . live on farms or in the cities
individually. Their forefathers left the communal life in Russia
or America, and very few of them returned.
Paul S. Gross, Spokane Hutterian Community, 1965

Hutterthal

One of the first items of business for the noncommunal
Hutterian immigrants was the establishment of churches. Though the Prairieleut congregations eventually affiliated with Mennonite conferences, they
remained independent for over sixty years, until the eve of the Second World
War. And when the congregations did integrate, it was because the Prairieleut
hoped that young males would fare better in their quest for an alternative to
military service if they belonged to a larger historic peace church conference.

Beginning in the 1880s, some Prairie People had chosen to join the small
Krimmer Mennonite Brethren assemblage, but the majority had affiliated
with the independently organized Prairieleut churches. These congregations attempted to maintain historical Hutterian teaching and tradition in
the face of continual invitations from Mennonite and evangelical Protestant
denominations to amalgamate.

Fig. 5.1. The Hutterthal Church, founded in 1879, circa 1920. Photograph courtesy of Hutterian Centennial Committee.

In the 1870s, three Prairieleut churches, Hutterthal, Neu Hutterthaler, and Hutterdorf were organized in the Freeman/Bridgewater area. Five additional Dakota Territory congregations were established in subsequent years. These included another congregation called Hutterthal (near Carpenter), Zion (in Bridgewater), Fairfield-Bethel (near Hitchcock), Emmanuel (near Doland), and Mt. Olivet (in Huron). The Bethany Mennonite Church (in Freeman) was established as a joint Prairieleut/Mennonite effort.

The Hutterthal Church, which became the largest Prairieleut congregation in Hutchinson County, took its name from the Ukrainian village where most of its members had previously resided, a village located on Mennonite entrepreneur Johann Cornies' model estate, "Tashchinak." The practice of using Russian village names for churches was not unique to the Prairieleut. Other Russian-German settlers christened their churches in a similar manner.[1]

The Hutterthal Church was formally established in 1879 by ministers John L. Wipf and John Waldner. Waldner, following the social pattern discussed in the previous chapter, eventually left Hutterthal and joined the Jamesville Colony. Hutterthal families met for worship in homes and in a schoolhouse until a church building was constructed in 1901. The practice of holding services in schoolhouses was nothing new and continued to be a common practice in Hutterite colonies.

The early Hutterthal Church employed a lay ministry composed of a group of preachers without seminary training. All ministers held additional occupations and relied on supplementary "love" offerings—voluntary gifts —for financial support. Hutterthal had no salaried minister until Peter P.

Table 5.
Independent Prairieleut Congregations in America[a]

Congregation	Location	Date Established
Neu Hutterthaler	Bridgewater, South Dakota	1875
Hutterdorf	Freeman, South Dakota	1875 (disbanded, 1961)
Hutterthal	Freeman, South Dakota	1879
Hope	Chaseley, North Dakota	1900 (disbanded, 1960)
Bethany[b]	Freeman, South Dakota	1905
Hutterthal	Carpenter, South Dakota	1906
Zion	Bridgewater, South Dakota	1920
Emmanuel	Doland, South Dakota	1922
Fairfield-Bethel	Hitchcock, South Dakota	1927 (disbanded, 1963)
Mt. Olivet	Huron, South Dakota	1945

Notes:

[a]This table shows the location and date of establishment of the various independent Prairieleut congregations. All the independent Prairieleut congregations had associated with the General Conference Mennonite Church by 1952.

[b]Bethany, which many Prairieleut families attended and helped found, was, from the outset, an interethnic Mennonite congregation.

Tschetter began receiving minimal compensation in 1921. And until 1937, the church selected ministers by the casting of lots and usually chose spiritual leaders from within the congregation. An ecclesiastical structure that included more than one ordained preacher had also been in place into the early 1940s.

The fact that Hutterthal continued for so long to select ministers from within the congregation and to select them by casting lots exemplified the ongoing vitality of two important Hutterian theological principles. The first principle was that one must know one's spiritual leaders well; one must know their families, their general character, and even their youthful indiscretions.

The second principle was that God must be given a direct role, even if through a seemingly chance event, in selecting appropriate individuals to serve as spokespersons in the church. The presence of the Holy Spirit in the casting of lots procedure was assumed. Following a time of prayerful reflection, persons recognized to have suitable spiritual and leadership qualities were first nominated by the membership. The names of those nominated were then written on pieces of paper, which were inserted into a Bible. Then the lot was cast as one slip of paper was removed, giving God final determination in the pastoral selection process. This practice was modeled after a procedure described in the New Testament Book of Acts.

Critics maintained that the nomination process operated more crudely than it was supposed to. According to Hutterthal member and former South Dakota state legislator John P. Kleinsasser: "The ministers were usually the

Fig. 5.2. Early Prairieleut immigrant couple, with daughter, circa 1900.

Photograph courtesy of Hutterian Centennial Committee.

most successful farmers. They did not get any pay so they had to be good farmers to make enough money and also to have the respect of the people. Most people measure the success by how much money you could make, and how much land you had."[2]

Kleinsasser (nicknamed "J. P. Morgan") wrote straightforwardly, not allowing political considerations to influence what he perceived to be the truth: the collective discernment process, which preceded the casting of lots, tended to nominate those with land and money.

Many Prairie People held opposing opinions, believing that God preselected ministers with a variety of gifts and abilities. Personal deficiencies in the economic realm, for example, might in fact be God's way of confirming a call to ministry. Many examples were given of persons being selected for ministerial positions who were not cut out for farming or who were not good with their hands. In the 1920s, for example, relatives told Californian Jacob D. Hofer, after spiritual ruminations had caused him continually to run his tractor into the ditch, that perhaps God was calling him to the ministry.[3]

Other Prairie People believed that the ministerial typologies described above represented only a small minority of those who had actually served as clergymen. In their view, the spiritually gifted, those most committed to God and the church, were the ones selected as pastors. Nevertheless, those chosen were often quite capable in nonecclesiastical assignments. Some contemporary Prairieleut even suggest that the less democratic ministerial selection procedures of the past, including the casting of lots to make final determinations, had brought forth stronger and more competent leaders than could be found in the present.

It was extremely important, especially during the first years of settlement, for the noncommunal Hutterians to have strong leaders who could creatively articulate a unified Prairieleut response to the communal Hutterites, as well as to the seductive challenge of numerous evangelical Protestant groups. Neither individual "calls" to ministry nor modern democratic selection processes carried the spiritual force of the casting of lots, which tapped into the power of divine intervention.

It is significant that there were, at times, as many as four active ordained ministers at Hutterthal. Hutterian tradition accepted the notion that a church needed many spiritual leaders so that no one person would monopolize theological interpretation and ecclesiastical decision making. All of the Prairieleut churches adhered to this philosophy and practice into the 1920s and 1930s. After that time, members usually elected one person, who was salaried, elected democratically, and who generally came from outside the community. And, seminary training was considered essential preparation for pastoral work.

Hutterthal was a church with a highly homogeneous population, which never selected a nonethnic Hutterian as pastor until 1955. According to the official church history, all the ministers were "of our own Hutterisch people," implying that ethnicity carried special weight in that congregation.[4] When Prairie People spoke of joining the church, they expressed it as "coming to the people," a manner of speaking employed, as well, by the Hutterites.

In all the Hutter congregations, into the 1920s, church services followed the colony pattern of a short sermon (Vorlehr) followed by a long sermon (Nachlehr). The already prepared hand-copied manuscripts of the forefathers that were used were always read in German. Marie Waldner noted that she and her childhood friends had referred to those sermons as the "short one" and the "long one."[5]

Since English was used in public schools, and the sacred tongue was heard only in church, most young persons grew up with only a marginal understanding of German. They did not always fully comprehend what the sermons and hymns were teaching although they participated worshipfully in an atmosphere of love and devotion. At home, first, second, and third generation immigrants communicated in the Hutterisch dialect. And Sunday School teachers, too, often spoke Hutterisch to help children understand the lesson. In church, however, the only language used was German.

To deal with the language problem, most Prairieleut churches, in the early 1900s, established "German schools," which met for a couple of months during the school year or on Sunday afternoons to instruct young people in the German language. This was accomplished by studying the Bible and

Fig. 5.3. Prairieleut settlers
John L. Hofer Sr. and
Michael Hofer, circa 1900.
Photograph courtesy of Hutterian
Centennial Committee.

memorizing Bible verses, as well as by discussing Sunday morning sermons
and learning catechism. A similar curriculum continued to be found in Hutterite colony "Sunday Schools" in the late 1990s. Prairieleut German schools
had not been very popular. Unlike those in the colonies, they met less and
less frequently over the years and disappeared by mid-century. At Hutterthal
English replaced Hutterisch in Sunday School classes in 1936, at which time
monthly English church services were also introduced.

It is ironic that there was little discernible interest in translating the sacred
Hutterian sermons and songs into English. Instead, older Prairie People
worked assiduously at maintaining German as the living language of the
church. Ultimately the rigid adherence of traditionalists to German-only
congregational life became so interconnected with loyalty to the *Lehren* and
songs that the sermons and hymns themselves were attacked as irrelevant,
archaic, and dry. Their special vibrant character had been lost for most
younger Prairie People.

The only persons who could have successfully supervised translation of
the sermons and hymns into English, thus preserving a unique noncommunal Hutterian interpretation of the Christian faith, were unfortunately
the same individuals holding out for German. These people had no interest in translation projects that might kill the ancient tongue.

Fig. 5.4. Paul Kleinsasser
and John L. Hofer Sr.,
with son and daughter,
respectively, circa 1900.
Photograph courtesy of Hutterian
Centennial Committee.

It was also true that the older generation did not generally have the academic training required to undertake major translations. Thus when the Prairieleut churches threw out the German language, they threw out the unique theological interpretations of the *Lehren* and *Gesangbuch* as well. In the 1990s, a seventy-year-old Hutter minister noted that he had never in his life seen or read one of the traditional Hutterian sermons.[6]

In the early years, Hutterthal members held very conservative positions on issues of lifestyle. As late as 1921, Hutterthal's pastor had stated from the pulpit that women should wear triangular-shaped shawls, not hats, as head coverings.[7] Women were expected to cover their heads even when praying in the privacy of their homes. Marie Waldner, who taught at Freeman College from 1935 to 1972, confirmed that when she prayed without a head-covering it had seemed "disrespectful" to God and had made her feel extremely "uncomfortable," even when she was not in a church building.[8]

In describing Prairieleut social standards of fifty to sixty years ago, a number of older Prairie People stated that "there was much sin then." In other words, much that had been considered sinful then is not considered iniquitous in the late twentieth century. The requirements of Prairieleut lifestyle during the first half-century in America had differed little from those ad-

Fig. 5.5. Prairieleut children, circa 1900. Photograph courtesy of Hutterian Centennial Committee.

hered to by Hutterite relatives. In earlier years Yos Hofer had met a group of well-dressed "Protestant" women whom, he insisted, had not even looked like "people." Yos described their general appearance instead as an unnatural "miscarriage."[9] He did not appreciate modern clothing styles and was very outspoken about it.

Marie Waldner noted that when her family had first started attending the more progressive Prairieleut/Mennonite Bethany Church in Freeman, she had once exclaimed to a friend who had worn a hat instead of a shawl, "Aren't you afraid you'll go to hell?" Marie had been raised to believe that there was a connection between the way one dressed and one's eternal spiritual state.[10]

Hutterthal women began to cut their hair and to wear rings and jewelry in the later 1920s. By the end of that decade, head coverings were disappearing among younger people. Until that time, however, high heels had been forbidden for women, and after church services men, starting from the back of the church, had walked out first, row by row. The women followed behind, just as they do in modern Hutterite colonies.[11]

Evangelicalism

The Hutterthal Church promoted and displayed histori-
cal Hutterian beliefs and practices until the 1920s and 1930s, when the
influence of evangelical Protestantism brought significant change to the
congregation. Evangelical religious literature, local revival meetings held
by Krimmer Mennonite Brethren preachers, and the leadership of the Rev.
Peter P. Tschetter conveyed new ideas that were then institutionalized. Since
a major evangelical emphasis was placed on mission work, Hutterthal, in
1926, began to train its young people in "public witnessing" at Sunday evening "Christian Endeavor" meetings.[12]

The very idea of teaching Christians to be active propagandists was a
significant departure from post-sixteenth-century Hutterian tradition. Tradition focused attention, instead, on the responsibility of Christians to serve
as ethical role models. With the exception of those times when one felt obligated to proselytize sister Hutterians, aggressive evangelism had not been
the norm. The controversial nature of public witness can be understood
when one considers that Hutterthal did not establish a missionary society,
as such, until 1943.[13]

Into the 1920s, the Prairieleut majority had turned their backs on the
evangelical revival preachers who frequently came through the Freeman area.
The exception was those Hutters attracted to the Krimmer Mennonite Brethren Church. Generally recognized as the leader of the Prairieleut churches,
Paul Tschetter attended an American revival service in 1873 and had noted
that "a comedy could hardly offer more entertainment." He referred to the
methodology employed by one revivalist as "a great indiscretion."[14]

Before Peter P. Tschetter's pastorate, Hutterthal had steadfastly remained
true to Hutterian ancestral traditions, both theological and cultural. The
Hutterian *Gesangbuch*, for example, was the only hymnal used at Hutterthal
until the year 1910. Singing had, therefore, been done by rote and most
strains memorized, since the *Gesangbuch* had no printed notes in early editions. Melodies in the traditional songbook indicate a German folk heritage;
many are the same tunes used in Lutheran hymns.[15] All lyrics were passed
on orally, and the same strain was used for many hymns.

Gesangbuch lyrics had been composed to a great extent by early Anabaptist
and Hutterite leaders. A few Mennonite and Amish pieces were also included.
Forty-five of the hymns had been written by sixteenth-century Hutterite
leader Peter Rideman.[16] During the service, ministers or other members of
the congregation named the tune to be followed, read the verse ahead of
the singing, and then led the congregation in song. In one case, the Prairieleut
songleader had been an older woman who had known the melodies well.[17]

Into the 1920s, the Hutterthal Church had forbidden stringed instruments of any kind. They were viewed as "instruments of Satan," as induce-

ments to vanity and self-glorification at the expense of worshiping God. All singing of hymns was done a cappella, as is still the tradition in Hutterite colonies. In the early years, only congregational singing had been allowed in church services. Any group or solo performance was thought to be self-serving and ostentatious. The Hutterthal Church had not, therefore, organized a choir until 1924. No piano was placed in the church until 1936; an organ was not purchased until 1955.

The first English hymnal authorized for occasional use at Hutterthal was the *Tabernacle Hymnal*, an evangelical songbook that was popular in many Prairieleut churches and adopted in 1930.[18] The *Tabernacle Hymnal* went through numerous editions and included light gospel songs, like "Sunlight," with its choral refrain:

> Sunlight, sunlight in my soul today,
> Sunlight, sunlight all along the way.
> Since the savior saved me
> Took away my sin
> I have had the sunlight of his love within.[19]

The hymnal had also introduced deeply pietistic hymns, such as "Open My Eyes That I May See," which included the following chorus:

> Silently now I wait for thee,
> Ready my God, Thy will to see
> Open my eyes, illumine me,
> Spirit, Divine.[20]

The adoption of an evangelical hymnal proceeded, despite opposition from older members of the church who preferred hymns that were Anabaptist and more theologically substantive. As one Prairieleut professor put it, "They [the old hymns] were deeper in content than later gospel songs."[21] Most traditionalists, however, simply preferred to sing the songs they had grown up with; songs imbued with powerful emotions and mental images. The views of both sides were taken into consideration in 1952, when Hutterthal purchased the *Mennonite Hymnal*, with its mix of traditional and gospel hymns.

The very fact that it took some time for traditional Hutterian beliefs and practices to lose their hold on Hutterthal congregants caused a significant number of Prairieleut to leave the church in the early 1900s, to join the Krimmer Mennonite Brethren who conducted less formal meetings, did not read the Hutterian sermons, and were very evangelistic. KMBs were always telling the Hutterthalers they needed to "get saved."[22]

Early Prairieleut church services were, indeed, long ones. Sermons were at least forty-five minutes in length, and the service format varied little from Sunday to Sunday. During the 1920s and 1930s, however, things changed;

ministers started writing their own sermons, people prayed aloud, and small group musical performances were introduced.

The Rev. Peter P. Tschetter, who served Hutterthal as pastor from 1921 to 1937, was the greatest influence on the development of evangelical and fundamentalist theological emphases. Tschetter, who later served as a "field representative" for the fundamentalist Grace Bible Institute, held many revival meetings emphasizing "spiritual renewal" and promoted the same "born-again" experiences Hutters had protested when Mennonite and other Protestant evangelicals had tried to "save" them.[23]

Tschetter, an evangelist recognized by the General Conference Mennonite Church, not only pushed evangelical positions at Hutterthal but at other South Dakota Prairieleut congregations as well. He was not always well received. Many Prairie People held great respect for the historic sermons and hymns and did not consider themselves in need of "salvation." This was especially true of members at the Neu Hutterthaler Church. And one person in attendance at Tschetter's services suggested that Hutterthal "throw him [Tschetter] out."

Within the Prairieleut churches, many accused Tschetter and his followers of superpiety, the same charge they directed at other evangelicals. Even at Hutterthal, not all members agreed with everything Tschetter was doing. They made sure that Hutterthal maintained its independence and did not join the General Conference Mennonite Church until 1941.

Individuals who remembered those times said that Tschetter had been somewhat cautious in introducing change, however, and was careful to affirm the salvation experiences of those who had not experienced "climactic" conversion. Tschetter was also recognized for steadfast adherence to the Hutterian position on peace and for being personally well liked by Hutterthal parishioners. His supporters agreed that some members felt he had pushed evangelical emphases too strongly, but they, themselves, were pleased that such changes had been made.

At Hutterthal, Tschetter had refused to read either the seventeenth-century Hutterite sermons or his own. Instead he spoke "from the heart." And from that time on, an interesting mix of Hutterian and evangelical Protestant emphases created a philosophical balance of interests in the Hutterthal congregation.

Neu Hutterthaler

The other large Prairieleut congregation established in southeastern Dakota Territory (in 1875) was Neu Hutterthaler, which took its name, as well, from the Russian village where most members had lived. Early records also referred to Neu Hutterthaler as "the Wolf Creek *Gemeinde* (community)" due to its physical location.[24]

The Neu Hutterthaler Church was founded by Paul Tschetter, who with his infamous uncle had once met with President Ulysses S. Grant. The first Neu Hutterthaler church building was constructed in 1888, though members who lived at a distance continued to meet in schoolhouses with their own associate ministers.

Neu Hutterthaler introduced Sunday school classes in 1908. Sessions were initially conducted in the afternoon but were moved to Sunday morning, in 1912, when it was determined that members were absent because they preferred to spend the afternoon fishing.[25] As at Hutterthal, Sunday school sessions were conducted in Hutterisch, so that younger persons could better comprehend what was being discussed.[26]

Known affectionately as "Paul Vetter," Paul Tschetter, with a full beard, his black hair parted in the middle, and commonly attired in a vest buttoned up to his neck, was a towering figure at Neu Hutterthaler and in the entire Prairieleut community.[27] He served as minister at Neu Hutterthaler for forty-five years, from 1874, until he suffered a fatal stroke in 1919.[28]

Tschetter had initially been selected for the ministry in Russia, at age twenty-one, and had been ordained by the "honor worthy" Mennonite minister Peter Wedel.[29] In 1883, Tschetter, now in Dakota Territory, was ordained to the higher position of elder, or senior minister, by another Mennonite, the Rev. Friedrich Schartner. Ironically, in that same year, Schartner left the congregation he pastored and started his own splinter "Schartner Church."[30] It is noteworthy that both of Paul Tschetter's ordinations had come at the hands of non-Hutterian ministers.

Tschetter himself was a traditionalist, and Neu Hutterthaler was known to be more conservative than Hutterthal. One member continued to drive a horse and buggy into the 1930s, long after most Prairie People had purchased vehicles. Tschetter's son Joseph—who along with sibling David left Neu Hutterthaler for the Krimmer Mennonite Brethren—noted that his father had been "very slow to accept . . . new teaching even though the Bible did not oppose it."[31] Paul's son had evidently defined "new teaching" as including the evangelical emphases and general informality of worship in his own congregation, a religious ambience similar, perhaps, to what Paul Tschetter had once described as ecclesiastical "entertainment."

Tschetter was an unusually adept leader, however, who did not cut himself off from the Prairie People who had joined the KMBs or from the communal Hutterites. In 1952, when Neu Hutterthaler remodeled and moved its church building, Paul's son David—a KMB minister—in turn made sure that land his father had set aside for the future use of that congregation was properly exchanged—even though he had no legal obligation to do so.[32]

Throughout his life, Paul Tschetter continued to read the Hutterian sermons, though he sometimes made relevant side comments on contemporary issues. On occasion, Tschetter also composed sermons of his own, some of which had been requested by friends in the colonies. The Rev. Tschetter was often asked to join the communal Hutterites and once asked congregants to take an offering for a colony that had experienced a destructive fire.[33] Tschetter, married to his wife, Maria, for fifty-five years, was known to be fair though strict in his relationship with parishioners.[34]

Paul Tschetter fought an ongoing battle against the worldly practices he considered unfit for Hutterian Christians. Strongly opposed to smoking in the Mennonite community, Tschetter saw that habit become an increasingly popular pastime of Neu-Hutterthalers in the 1880s. Tschetter once even threatened to withdraw from preaching responsibilities until members refrained from tobacco use. From 1888 to 1892, in particular, the Neu Hutterthaler smoking controversy was often mentioned in Yos Hofer's diary.[35]

Near the end of his life Tschetter found it increasingly difficult to hold the fort against ecclesiastical and social innovations. He "could not forget the flock [he] had served for fifty-three years," and through the "frustrations of illness," he had once done a very "foolish" thing, as he described it to a grandson. Distressed by the placement of a picture behind the Neu Hutterthaler pulpit, he had gone to the church one Saturday evening and nailed small pieces of wood over the representation. His son David, noticing what had happened, later removed everything—wood, nails, and picture—so that on Sunday morning only a few small holes remained in the wall.[36]

The Neu Hutterthaler Church began to pay its ministers in the 1920s—after Tschetter died. However, no services were conducted in English until 1947, after the arrival of the non-Hutterian Rev. Albert Ewert. More significantly, the seventeenth-century Hutterian sermons were read at Neu Hutterthaler worship services into the early 1940s. Neu Hutterthaler, like the Hutterthal Church, did not join the General Conference Mennonite assemblage until the onset of World War II, and like Hutterthal, it only did so then because of the potential benefit of collective peace church negotiation in support of alternative nonmilitary service.

Like Paul Tschetter, other Neu Hutterthaler ministers, too, occasionally made instructive comments during the course of their sermon reading, offering practical advice relevant to contemporary issues. The Rev. David J. Wipf, for example, was remembered to have removed his glasses whenever he spoke of "women's problems." He would then upbraid women in the audience for their "worldliness."[37] Prairieleut men received similar admonishment. But the seventeenth-century sermons were still considered specially blessed by God, and reading them consumed a considerable part of Sunday morning services.

Neu Hutterthaler took a strong congregational stand against bowling, gun ownership, and musical instruments into the 1920s. The use of guns, particularly, and hunting for any reason, was considered militaristic and un-Christian. In his 1873 diary account, Tschetter forcefully criticized American Mennonites of Swiss heritage for their use of firearms. When he heard about an individual who enjoyed hunting, Tschetter had declared, "What a fine example of a nonresistant Mennonite."[38] Eventually "the spirit of gun ownership" entered the Neu Hutterthaler congregation as well.[39] Tschetter battled the spirit successfully in some cases, unsuccessfully in others.

The impact of Tschetter's forthright position against guns was in evidence as late as 1918, when Hutter draft evaders Paul L. Hofer and his brother Jacob, both of whom had fled to Canada, had "shivered" at the sight of "guns standing all around" in the Prairieleut home of a Mr. Wollman, near Langham, Saskatchewan.[40] At its sister congregation, Hutterthal, pastor John Waldner had taken a more favorable position on gun ownership, prohibiting only hunting for sport.[41] But Neu Hutterthaler held fast to a universal antigun position.

Until 1946, when a piano was purchased, singing at Neu Hutterthaler was without instrumental accompaniment; only a tuning fork directed pitch.[42] It is said that, on the first Sunday musical instruments were introduced, one gentleman seated himself in the front of the church and cried openly, lamenting the fact that an important Hutterian tradition had been lost. The first English hymnal, the *Tabernacle Hymnal*, replaced the German Hutterian songbook in 1945, fifteen years after a similar transition had taken place at Hutterthal.[43] Neu Hutterthaler, like its sister congregation, also eventually accepted evangelical Protestant theological positions, though it was not until the 1940s that a majority of congregants were willing to accept those viewpoints.

Hutterdorf

The Hutterdorf Church, a third, smaller, Prairieleut congregation, again, named for a Ukrainian Hutterian village, had been organized in 1875 by ministers William Tschetter and David Waldner, a few miles northwest of what became the town of Freeman.[44] Hutterdorf constructed its first church building a quarter-century later, in 1901, after meeting for many years, as was customary, in a local schoolhouse.

The Hutterdorf Church, following Hutterian traditions, never in its entire history selected a minister from outside the congregation nor paid established salaries to its pastors. A piano was not installed in the church building until 1944, about the same time that an English hymnal was also adopted.[45] When introduced, the innovations caused older members great distress, as had also been the case at Hutterthal and Neu Hutterthaler. Until 1946, the Hutterdorf congregation sang a cappella, and Hutterdorf never united with the national General Conference of Mennonite Churches, though it did join that conference's regional Northern District organization.

Hutterdorf record-keeping was extremely limited, making it difficult to get a good sense of congregational positions on theological and ecclesiastical issues. The most influential figure in Hutterdorf's history, however, was the Rev. Peter J. Stahl. He served as minister for forty-five years, from 1916 to 1961, at which time he announced that on a certain date he was going to preach his last sermon.

Stahl had "done his duty" and felt it was time to retire, after nearly a half-century in the ministry. "You will have to find yourselves another church," he had announced. And the congregation did not survive his resignation, being by that time composed substantially of older persons.[46] Stahl's ministry exemplified how the ordained-for-life ministry had functioned in times past, before the general acceptance of salaried pastors who came from outside the community and who generally did not stay for more than five to ten years. Stahl himself received only minimal compensation for fulfilling the church's ministerial reponsibilities.

In 1961, a majority of Hutterdorf members followed the Rev. Stahl to the Bethany Mennonite Church in Freeman while others joined Hutterthal. Stahl himself was well liked and respected in spite of his traditionalist inclinations, and former members recalled a warm family atmosphere at Hutterdorf church services. The church was not successful at local evangelism, however, and its membership dwindled over the course of the century.

Hutterdorf became the most conservative of all the Hutter congregations. The Hutterdorf Church held on to the German language longer than any other Prairieleut group and did not even install electricity in the church building until the late 1940s. By the early 1950s, however, Hutterdorf, like other Prairieleut congregations, had accepted a strongly evangelical interpretation of Christianity and had turned its back on many distinctive Hutterian theological positions and ecclesiastical practices.

Other Prairieleut Congregations

A fourth church, which many Prairieleut had joined in southeastern South Dakota, was the Bethany Mennonite Church, originally established as a joint venture by Prairie People and Swiss Mennonites who lived in the town of Freeman. In the 1930s and 1940s, people of diverse Protestant backgrounds, many of whom had moved to Freeman to teach in local public schools, also joined the Bethany Church. Historian John D. Unruh described Bethany as "a somewhat conglomerate" group.[47]

Bethany began as a Sunday school fellowship in the mid-1890s and was formally organized as a congregation in 1905, under the leadership of Henry A. Bachman, a teacher at Freeman College. At that time, Bethany also became a member congregation of the General Conference Mennonite Church.[48]

The first Bethany minister of Prairieleut background was Peter P. Kleinsasser, who accepted that position in 1923. Three of the five members of the initial Bethany committee of trustees, however, had been Hutters. Still, as an older individual from a country church put it, "We never called Bethany our church (i.e., a Prairieleut church)." At the time of this writing, only one additional person of Prairieleut background had served as a minister at Bethany. That fact, plus a mixed ethnicity and early association with Mennonites, made it difficult to define Bethany as a "Hutterian congregation." Nevertheless, over the years, many Prairie People who were members at country churches attended Bethany when the weather was bad. Hutterians within the congregation, furthermore, held on to numerous ethnic sensibilities, as well as to some theological traditions.

Early on there had also been a small Prairieleut church fellowship in Olivet, eighteen miles southwest of Freeman. It was one of a number of small congregations that were supervised by the Neu Hutterthaler Church. Joseph "Yos" Hofer, as noted, led this group in home and schoolhouse meetings from 1900 until his death in 1905.[49] Hofer's diary indicated that the fellowship had not always operated in complete unity with the mother congregation. On Easter Sunday in 1899, for example, there had been "no preaching because of dissension."[50] Hofer attributed that discord to Paul Tschetter's "reoccurring new narrowness."

Hofer's account revealed more controversy with regard to Paul Tschetter's leadership than is found in official records. One conflict, for example, was related to the Olivet Fellowship's interest in selecting a minister from within the congregation. Olivet members had not wanted that decision to be made by the Neu Hutterthaler Church, which had customarily supplied the congregation with self-selected traveling preachers. At one point Paul Tschetter had, in fact, "invalidat[ed]" Yos Hofer's own selection as minister at Olivet.[51] It seemed that Yos often found himself in controversial situations.

After Hofer's death, the Neu Hutterthaler Church once again supplied preachers for the fellowship, but regular services were discontinued in 1920. In 1939, John S. Mendel revived what remained of the Olivet group under the Krimmer Mennonite Brethren Church banner.[52] That group died a second death in 1941, however, when the Rev. Mendel moved west due to an asthmatic condition.

Another small Hutter fellowship in the Bridgewater area established itself independently as the Zion Mennonite Church in 1920. That assembly, too, had been an affiliated branch of the Neu Hutterthaler Church. In 1900, a now-extinct independent Hutterian church called Hope was established in Chaseley, North Dakota, after a number of Prairieleut families moved to that area seeking better economic opportunities. Other noncommunal Hutterians had moved to Montana, where they joined Mennonite or Protestant congregations rather than establishing their own churches.

In all of the Prairieleut churches there was a tendency for social relationships, and even spiritual ones, to involve other Hutterians. "All our friends were Hutters," noted one individual.[53] Even during the great revival meetings of the 1920s and 1930s, very few "English" (i.e., non-German-speakers) came to the services. Because the horse and buggy mode of trans-

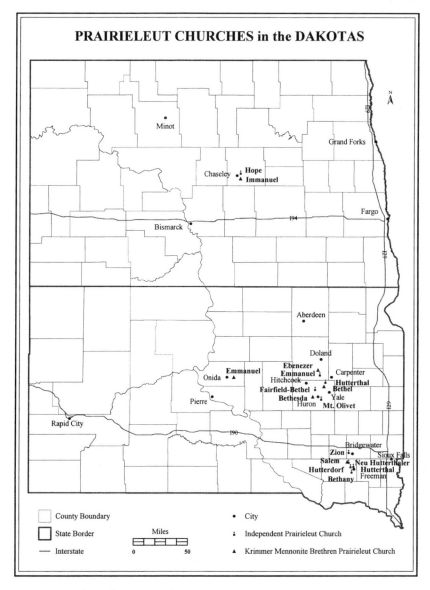

Map 5. Prairieleut churches in the Dakotas. Map by Bill Slusser.

portation limited travel, and since most Prairieleut families had settled in similar geographical areas, a natural ethnic separation was the norm.

For the "town Hutters" who attended Bethany, life was a bit different. These Hutterians associated with a variety of Swiss and Low German Mennonites, as well as people from other denominational backgrounds. Everyone lived and worked side by side, and eventually a large number of Bethany Prairie People married into Lutheran, Reformed, Catholic, and Methodist families, breaking out of traditional ecclesiastical and ethnic boundaries and providing the town of Freeman with the unique character it retained at century's end.

Preserving the Hutterian Identity

Within the boundaries of the various Prairieleut church communities, a number of traditional customs continued to be observed. Some of these were tightly connected to theological traditions, others were not. Many social and cultural practices were indeed identical to those observed in Hutterite colonies. Weddings and courtship procedures, for example, were essentially the same. Hutter parents asked for the hands of the young women their sons wanted to marry. Prospective grooms then sealed those arrangements with a glass of wine or whiskey.[54]

Wedding ceremonies were lengthy and in German. No ring was given; no photographs allowed. Kissing games, designed to bring single persons together, were played after a large meal, which followed the wedding ceremony. Free-flowing consumption of liquor (not found during or after Prohibition) helped reduce anxieties associated with such serious occasions. As one Prairieleut noted, "They served beer from five- or ten-gallon kegs." Wedding celebrations continued for three days, as in the colonies, with bride and groom eventually moving in with the groom's family. There was no honeymoon, but there had been quite a celebration.

In the early 1900s a number of noncommunal Hutterians also served in significant leadership positions in the Freeman and Bridgewater communities. Andreas A. Wipf, as noted, was Freeman's first medical doctor, while Jacob H. Wipf served as the community's first dentist. In 1902, John Gross and Jacob M. Wollman were named President and Vice-President, respectively, of Freeman's Merchant State Bank, which, according to local tradition, was "where all the Hutters bank." Another Prairieleut entrepreneur, Jake T. Gross, started Freeman's first telephone company.

Jacob J. Mendel was, perhaps, the person most responsible for preserving the cultural heritage of the Prairie People. Born in Russia, he began publishing the Freeman *Courier*, a podium for stories, recollections, local news, and editorials in 1902. He continued to run the business, as well as to farm, until his death in 1960.

Mendel represented well those Prairieleut individuals who had developed a sense of multicultural, interdenominational, civic responsibility, yet were simultaneously concerned that historic Hutterian mores and cultural traditions be recognized and passed on to future generations. Mendel actively promoted progressive economic development in the town of Freeman, while concurrently telling all who would listen about "the way things had been."

Of significance to the later work of historians was Mendel's extensive interest in the Hutterian legacy, which had manifested itself in a large collection of manuscripts, articles, records, and photographs. Exemplifying the traditional custom of marrying within the ethnic group, all three of Mendel's spouses (he was twice widowed) were Hutterians.

Another early Prairieleut notable was Michael R. Hofer, commonly known as *"Rutschield,"* the ultimate survivor. Hofer's personal story began in the Hutterian community at Raditchewa, where he was born in 1829. At age thirteen, Hofer moved with his parents to the newly established villages near the Mennonite colonies and then made not only the transatlantic voyage to North America in middle age but lived for another forty-eight years as a member of the Prairieleut community. Hofer lived to be 103 years of age.

Recognized as a wealthy man in Russia, Hofer transported gold bars with him to North America in the bottom of a large trunk. The last half-century of Hofer's life took him from the rough early settlement years to times of financial security and into the beginning of the Great Depression. He saw the unfolding of three major periods in Hutterian history (from Raditchewa, to the Russian Mennonite village areas, to the Dakotas). It is also striking that, in 1855 at age twenty-six, Hofer's family had nearly buried him, thinking Michael dead after watching him endure a lengthy illness. Michael was about to be placed in a coffin when his eyes miraculously opened. He lived seventy-seven years longer.[55]

Prairie People in the independent churches continued to observe numerous Hutterian traditions of a markedly ecclesiastical nature. As in the colonies, men and women continued to sit on opposite sides of the church. This practice did not end until as late as 1966 at one Prairieleut congregation. It continued in the late 1990s at the Stirling Mennonite Church in Alberta (see chapter 8).

All Prairieleut churches celebrated Pentecost as the birthdate of the Christian faith. Hutterites had always placed major emphasis on Pentecost Sunday, believing God had empowered the church on that day to move in a communal direction by the power of the Holy Spirit. The Prairie People retained that celebration, but they did so with noncommunal interpretation.

Prairieleut congregations also recognized Ascension Day with special services and commemorated Epiphany, Easter Monday and Tuesday, Pentecost Monday and Tuesday, and the two days following Christmas, as holy days. New Year's Eve, too, was treated as a sacred occasion.[56]

Prairieleut churches also took a strong stand against taking photographs, a practice that continued to be officially taboo (though increasingly accepted) for their communal relatives. In the 1980s, South Dakota Hutterites told the story of an attempt by Prairieleut visitors to photograph them that had gone awry through what was described as divine intervention. What fol-

lows is an eye-witness Hutterite rendition and interpretation of that incident, which showed Prairieleut/Hutterite difference of opinion concerning
the making of graven images.

In the summer of 1982 Prairieleut descendent Frances Janzen Voth, in
the process of writing a family history, visited Pearl Creek Colony (near Iroquois, South Dakota) accompanied by a local Prairieleut farmer. While
there, Voth discovered that the Rev. Michael Waldner possessed a copy of
the *Hutterite Chronicle* that had been hand-copied by her ancestor Peter
Janzen.

Because she had other appointments, Voth had to leave the following
day, but the Prairieleut farmer returned and attempted to take a photograph
of Michael Waldner's wife holding the copy of the *Chronicle* in her lap. Mrs.
Waldner (also a direct descendent of Peter Janzen) disliked the idea of being photographed but remained silent. She prayed as hard as she could, however, that God would not allow the photograph to be taken. As we listened
to the unfolding of this story in the Waldner's home at Pearl Creek Colony,
my wife and I could see a knowing sparkle appear in Mrs. Waldner's eyes.

Rev. Waldner told us the tripod holding the camera had repeatedly fallen
over during the photo session and the camera malfunctioned again and again.
The camera took a picture of Mrs. Waldner, but the film came back blank
from the developer. According to the Hutterites, God had given a final response.[57] When asked for a personal reaction to what happened, Mrs. Waldner just looked at the author and smiled.

The contemporary narrative sounds very similar to stories told by early
Prairieleut leader Paul Tschetter. In his continuing battle with "the world,"
Tschetter had once exclaimed, "What will you do with the world? World is
world and will remain world until the Lord will come and end it all."[58]

It is said that Tschetter had once, himself, backslid, allowing photographs
to be taken during his well-known visit to North America on behalf of the
Russian Hutterians. Tschetter's uncle, Lohrentz, evidently convinced him
to have the photographs taken while the two were in New York City. Perhaps one of these was the obviously posed and only extant photograph of
the Rev. Tschetter.

During the course of their voyage home, however, Tschetter's ship encountered a bad storm in the Atlantic and, like Jonah in the Old Testament
account, "Paul Vetter" decided that God was speaking to them. Tschetter
exclaimed to his uncle, "We are the Jonahs on this ship." In response, the
Tschetters tossed the photographs overboard and the seas had calmed. Paul
Tschetter's mischievous uncle, however, had then pulled one remaining photograph out of his pocket and laughed at his pious nephew.[59]

Sunday School Conventions and the
General Conference

The Prairieleut congregations in South Dakota made numerous attempts to maintain close relationships with one another in the climactic times that followed the early settlement years. In the early 1900s, for example, a number of Hutters moved to Beadle, Spink, and Sully counties in east-central South Dakota, in pursuit of more favorable economic conditions. Prairieleut churches organized in those areas were also composed almost entirely of ethnic Hutterians and functioned much like the congregations in the Freeman/Bridgewater area.

Together the Prairieleut churches began to hold annual Sunday School conventions in 1924. The conventions had a strong evangelistic emphasis and focused on how to properly train young persons to be disciples of Jesus. But an additional reason to establish the conventions was to share ideas on how to create programs vital enough to halt the exodus of Prairie People to the Krimmer Mennonite Brethren.

The Prairieleut conventions included reports from the various participating members and much singing and worshiping.[60] These events facilitated the establishment and maintenance of close relationships between noncommunal Hutterians, even after the congregations they attended had joined Mennonite organizations. The conventions were conducted in German until 1938.

Though five of the once independent Prairieleut churches continued to hold the assemblies into the 1990s, the Hutterthal Church (Freeman) discontinued participation in 1978 due to scheduling problems and the existence of alternative Sunday School workshops conducted by General Conference Mennonite Church personnel. Many Hutterthal members had become concerned by the extensive involvement of non-Anabaptist presenters at conventions during the 1970s. Others criticized the conventions for lack of support for Mennonite *Adult Quarterly* Sunday School materials.

Workshops conducted by General Conference Mennonite representatives were, in turn, criticized by the more fundamentalist of the Prairieleut churches, which were, as one Mennonite representative put it, "not too enthusiastic about them."[61] The pastor of one Prairieleut congregation reprimanded the service-oriented Mennonite Central Committee—the international relief and development agency—for being too ecumenical (specifically for accepting Catholics as associates). Ties between Hutterthal and other Prairieleut assemblages had thus been loosened dramatically.

In 1996, the Prairieleut Mt. Olivet Church (Huron, South Dakota) voted itself out of the General Conference Mennonite Church; a majority of members felt the conference had gotten "too liberal." Conflict with regard to Sunday School conventions and difference of opinion on conference affiliation indicated a rift between conservatives and progressives within the Hutter church community (see Chapter 10). Throughout most of the twentieth century, however, Prairieleut solidarity was intensified by means of annual conferences. In a 1991 publication, the Mount Olivet Church still described itself, for example, as "the most Hutterisch" in ethnic composition of all the Mennonite churches.[62]

By mid-century all of the independent Prairieleut churches had joined the Northern District Conference of the General Conference Mennonite Church (GC). The General Conference, established in 1860 by progressive defectors from the North American Mennonite Church (MC), had also been the denomination of choice for the majority of Russian Mennonite immigrants.

The once independent Prairieleut congregations joined the General Conference rather than the more evangelical Krimmer Mennonite Brethren as a result of longstanding interpersonal conflict, nonimmersionist baptismal practices, and the General Conference's more open stance on how individuals might enter the Christian community. Some Prairie People had never accepted an evangelical Protestant focus on climactic salvation experiences and, like many General Conference Mennonites, had viewed the pathway to Christian faith as a long process of Christian nurture that might or might not occur on a specific date.

Association with General Conference Mennonites was not an uncomplicated transition, however. Significant numbers of Prairie People had accepted the more dramatic conversion theology of American evangelicalism. It was difficult, furthermore, for Hutters to join a conference that held more liberal views on lifestyle issues and practiced a latitudinarian church discipline. The latter positions had been forcefully attacked earlier. Prairie People with more evangelical leanings had been comforted, however, by the establishment of Grace Bible Institute (Omaha, Nebraska) by GC conservatives in 1943. Grace provided a fundamentalist/evangelical alternative to mainstream General Conference Mennonite schools and colleges.[63]

General Conference Mennonite historian John D. Unruh ascribed the Prairieleut hesitancy to join other conferences to "extreme conservatism" and "aloofness."[64] This was essentially true; the Prairie People had tried "conservatively," and with an "aloof" nonworldly perspective, to follow as closely as possible biblical teachings as they understood them. What they did not like hearing was the word "extreme," though one older Prairieleut noted that Jesus had been an "extremist" as well.

Sounding like Paul Tschetter, many older Prairie People accused Mennonite leaders of being condescending and patronizing. They also criticized Mennonites for holding what they described as "ultraliberal" theological, as well as social lifestyle positions. Some Prairieleut churches began to employ pastors who had received their theological training at non-Mennonite fundamentalist seminaries, which quickly pushed those congregations down non-Anabaptist pathways.

In general, the independent Prairieleut churches—even as they were transformed into "Hutter-Mennonite" congregations—remained extremely conservative with regard to social and ecclesiastical practice. Church regulations were strictly enforced into the 1960s. Church discipline and excommunication, though redemptive in purpose, was fervently put into practice.

The Prairie People considered themselves more conservative than the similarly privatized Mennonites nearby, even as they found their churches joining together institutionally. Norman Hofer, a lay leader in the General Conference Mennonite Northern District, noted that when he was a teenager card-playing, movie attendance, participation in sports, and the wearing of makeup and fashionable dress had all been frowned on and even "preached against from the pulpit."[65] Hofer said that such practices had been more commonly accepted in Freeman-area "Mennonite" congregations.

In the Prairieleut view, Christianity was not to be taken lightly. Life on earth was serious business and important preparation for a future heavenly existence with God. Mid-twentieth-century Hutters did not use the hooks and eyes on their clothing as their immigrant descendents had done. And they went swimming in public places and visited beauty parlors. Still, in contrast to many mainstream American social values, they held very conservative opinions.

Will this Style Work?

A Prairieleut minister once asked the deacons in his congregation whether the tendency of church members to follow the "style" of life of their neighbors was "working." He wanted to know whether it was possible to modernize without compromising religious principles.

Up until the 1930s and 1940s the tradition of a noncommunal Hutterianism, as practiced in the independent Prairieleut churches, had been preserved with love and devotion. The Prairie People established a number of congregations, worshiped in traditional Hutterian ways, preached a simple, hardworking lifestyle, and maintained the use of the German language.

Hutterite relatives in the colonies viewed the noncommunal ethos of the Prairie People as unbiblical, representative only of historical periods of spiritual decline. They felt the Hutters were selfish, materialistic, and worldly. Prairieleut evangelicals who had left the mother churches concurred. They believed the noncommunal Hutterian congregations they had been raised in were in need of radical revitalization, though they suggested more individualistic avenues to the truth than did the Hutterites.

Prairieleut families that remained in the traditional churches, however, thought pejorative analyses were unfair and exaggerated. They had been successful for many decades in maintaining the traditions of the Hutterian ancestors, without adopting the markedly individualistic, and often culturally Anglo-Saxon, emphases of midwestern Protestant evangelicalism. The Prairieleut had been more successful than many other ethno-religious enclaves on the North American steppes. They had done so, furthermore, without establishing communal economic structures to keep the "world" out.

The Prairie People in the independently functioning congregations had preserved Hutterian conventions without communalism by adhering to a number of powerful cultural forms, which in addition to the Hutterisch dialect and historic sermons, had included the singing of traditional hymns that provided theological interpretations of important historical events. The Prairieleut had also established strict behavioral guidelines for church members and had practiced their faith fervently, though perhaps not without a glass of wine in hand.

Increasingly, as the mid-twentieth century approached, Prairieleut Hutterians began to engage in practices not traditionally accepted by their forefathers. These included smoking, the use of guns, more liberal dress styles and the like. One also saw significant movement toward more individualistic and evangelical positions with regard to theology and ecclesiology.

As long as the Rev. Paul Tschetter lived, his very presence and powerful personality had seemed to ensure that major changes in Prairieleut beliefs and practices (in the independent Hutterian churches) would not materialize. But, following almost a half-century of service to the Neu Hutterthaler congregation, Tschetter suffered a paralyzing stroke and died in 1919, at age seventy-seven. Not many years after his death, Prairieleut ministers stopped using German, quit reading the sermons, introduced Protestant gospel hymns and began to question numerous Hutterian religious traditions.

The impact of nationalistic American patriotism also changed the Prairieleut community. The onset of World War II in particular proved a critical juncture for the entrance of many non-Hutterian beliefs and practices as large numbers of Prairie People joined the armed forces for the first time. This was also the time period when most of the Prairieleut congregations joined the General Conference Mennonite Church. Though most of the once independent Hutter congregations continued to meet annually for Sunday School conventions, they did not control the agenda at district or national denominational conferences.

These combined occurrences sparked a major ideological reanalysis, raising the question of whether it was possible for the Prairieleut community to successfully dress the ancient Hutterian faith in modern theological clothing. Before discussing that particular issue and others, it is important to look at the Krimmer Mennonite Brethren, a small group of conservative Mennonites, who convinced large numbers of Prairie People to join them as an alternative to the independently organized congregations.

6

· ·

The Attraction of the Krimmer Mennonite Brethren

One day when I thoughtfully meditated and prayed about
my lost condition in the field I experienced a strange feeling;
my heart became soft and I had to weep a long time. This
I considered a witness of the Holy Spirit upon which . . .
a true new birth follows.
Jacob A. Wiebe, 1867

A wedding in Margenau without brandy was really
unthinkable.
C. F. Plett, 1985

Sermons From the Heart

This chapter focuses on that substantial Prairieleut minority
who were attracted early on to the vibrant evangelical conservatism of a
small Mennonite sect called the Krimmer Mennonite Brethren (KMB).[1] In
this book members of KMB churches are often referred to as "KMBs,"
reflecting most accurately the way in which Krimmer Mennonite Brethren
were commonly described, by themselves and others.

Already in the 1880s, some Prairie People had begun to feel that there
was something spiritually lacking not only in the Hutterite colonies but also
in the independent Hutterian churches. Concerns included a lack of church
discipline, sporadic church attendance, and a too rigid attachment to Hutterian rituals. Particular consideration was given to the seventeenth-century
Lehren, to what critics felt was an excessively limited interpretation of the
Bible by those who wrote the sermons.

The Hutterites believed that the Lehren, written in the sixteenth and seventeenth centuries by at least six different persons, provided divinely inspired interpretation of the most significant teachings found in the Bible. The sermons contained annotated interpretation of Bible passages from the Old and New Testaments, often amounting to a verse-by-verse exegesis, which ensured standardization of biblical interpretation. The Lehren followed an established liturgical calendar and were written in an antiquated seventeenth-century German *(Shrifschsprache)* recognized by Hutterians as the language of the Bible.

One of the more important sermon writers was Servant of the Word Hans Friedrich Kuentsche who led the Hutterite community at Kesseldorf, Slovakia, until his death in 1659. Kuentsche was the author of the "Pentecost *Lehren*," some of the most revered of the sacred works. Hutterites believed that the sermons provided guidance to Christians in every historical period, if they were properly understood and if contextual transmediations had been made by the ministers doing the reading.

Although the Hutterites were often attacked for not allowing fresh interpretations of the Bible to emerge, thereby providing more relevant commentary and spiritual enlightenment, Prairieleut and Hutterite ministers alike made connecting comments when appropriate. This often occurred outside of the church service and provided modern extrapolations of the sermon writers' instructive examples. The Lehren themselves—of which there are about four hundred—introduced numerous examples relevant to the general human condition. A sermon on Matthew 6, for example, included the following description of some attending church: "They sit during a sermon from the Word of God, their hearts and minds wander after some other temporal things which they love."[2] And another section of the same sermon continued that thought: "In the same way that a woman who besides her husband, looks at young boys, hangs her mind on them and wants to love them, is not true, honest and right."[3]

Prairie People and Hutterites also recognized a number of epistles written by early Hutterian leaders as spiritually inspired. Most of these letters came from the sixteenth century, and, as Robert Friedmann noted, provided the Hutterites with, "a higher education in the discipleship of Christ."[4] Some of the most famous were Jacob Hutter's own lengthy treatises. Hymns from the *Gesangbuch*, consisting of songs written by a variety of Hutterite lyricists in the sixteenth, seventeenth, and eighteenth centuries, also provided a rich source for theological instruction. The hundreds of pages of hymns continually emphasized thankfulness to God and the willingness to suffer for his cause.

The sermons themselves, as they interpreted and expanded on verses from the Bible, were certainly not dry, a fact that surprises modern Prairie People who scan them, anticipating that the sermons will be quite boring. Since they had always been read in German, the gist of what was presented was often missed.

The *Lehren* always included a selection from the Bible, which was followed by interpretation of a polemical character that was graphic and filled with earthy references to agriculture. Some of the metaphorical content was striking. Note the following description of the selfishness of non-Christians:

> As soon as the pigs are brought home from the field and driven to the trough, one hears and sees how they grunt, whine and scuffle, step into the trough, slobber and squeal so that others dare not approach. Therefore it is impossible for godless men to live together.[5]

And, another section of the same sermon notes:

> One cannot see any more evidence of rebirth in them than in a pig or a dog. They sit like the cowbird in their nests of human excrement, with their natural crown, their proud feathers.[6]

The sermons could be particularly critical of those Christians who did not live communally—those with "wide as barngates consciences" as described in the following entry:

> And in their gathering there is great love during exhortation but as soon as they depart the teaching they say again, "I am now with my people; what have others to do with me."[7]

At the time of their arrival in the Dakotas, all Hutterians believed the Bible should be interpreted according to the inspiration of the *Lehren*. They were persuaded that the writers of the sermons had been specially touched by the Holy Spirit. Thus it was only on rare occasions that ministers composed sermons of their own.

But this was not the practice of most Christian assemblages, nor even of most Mennonites. Though sermons might be written down beforehand, few Christian ministers read ancient sermons on Sunday morning. Those Prairie People who desired more spontaneity and contemporary relevance in their church services thus began to form separate churches associated with the Krimmer Mennonite Brethren Conference. This conference emphasized the importance of ministers composing and delivering their own sermons under the immediate guidance of the Holy Spirit.

KMB evangelists from Kansas first brought their message to Dakota Territory via revival services held in 1881. The Krimmer Mennonite Brethren Conference, a conservative Mennonite sect founded by Jacob A. Wiebe in the Russian Crimea in 1869, promoted a more evangelical type of Christianity than was found in the Russian Mennonite churches or in the various Prairieleut congregations. KMBs also placed major emphasis on strict holy living and adherence to church rules and regulations.

Prairie People attracted to the Krimmer Mennonite Brethren complained a great deal about the "materialism" and increasing acceptance of tobacco use among Hutters in the independent churches. KMBs were also opposed to the consumption of alcohol and insisted that drunkenness was "commonly evident" in the Prairieleut community. The accuracy of their characterization depended on how one defined "drunkenness." Prairie People did drink wine and beer and at public establishments, but they did so in moderation. Alcoholic beverages were also consumed at weddings, a tradition observed then and now by communal Hutterites. As KMB church leader and historian C. F. Plett noted regarding nineteenth-century Russian Mennonites, "A wedding in Margenau without brandy was really unthinkable."[8] KMBs, on the other hand, were teetotalers.

The Krimmer Mennonite Brethren also emphasized conservative lifestyle and dress much more than other Mennonite groups. Instrumental music, for example, was considered sinful, as were personal photographs and shiny shoes and buggies. One sinner was asked to repaint his buggy a "dull gray."[9] As C. F. Plett put it, "The KMBs were strict disciplinarians and were very much on the lookout for anything that was worldly."[10] According to an 1891 church regulation, bicycles, for example, were not to be used "for the purpose of pleasure riding."[11] Members of the church were also not supposed to play cards.

The historical Hutterian emphasis on a conservative, though not alcohol-free, way of life caused all ethnic Hutterians to be hesitant about "becoming Mennonite." But the Krimmer Mennonite Brethren Conference was different. Its rigid lifestyle requirements were easier to understand and accept than those practiced by the more progressive General Conference Mennonites. They were in fact quite similar to the regulations adhered to in the colonies. KMBs had even practiced shunning with regard to unrepentant sinners.

Anfechtung and Assurance

Hutterians, in general, experienced high rates of an emotionally destabilizing form of depression referred to as anfechtung—literally, "temptation." The condition is still recognized by colony members. The Krimmer Mennonite Brethren had a solution for this confusing problem: the doctrine of the "assurance of salvation." But before discussing that teaching, let us follow a Hutterian woman through an intense anfechtung experience.

In the year 1872, in the Russian Hutterian village of Johannesruh, Katherina Wipf was "visited with a serious illness from God," which had manifested itself in a "feverish sickness in the head."[12] The anfechtung experience was usually understood as a time of testing of personal faith by God through Satan's efforts to tempt the tormented one, or as a struggle between God and Satan for an individual's soul. In Katherina's case, her suffering and testing was compared to that experienced by Jesus himself.

Katherina had been so distraught at one point that she had cried out, "The devils are eating my flesh from my body." At another juncture she became blasphemous, exclaiming: "I have no God at all," and wanted nothing to do with ministers. Her tongue had turned blue and was "completely thick because of biting and tearing."

A person experiencing anfechtung characteristically acknowledged his or her sinful nature and asked for forgiveness. "Satanic" forces would then leave the stricken individual and he or she would go on with life. That was partially what happened to Katherina. She had ended the "great temptation of suffering," the demonic possession, by yelling, "Out with you, you evil spirits, you liars." Soon thereafter, however, Katherina had a vision of heaven and died, though she had left her material existence at peace with God.

Katherina's death did not represent a usual outcome of the anfechtung experience, but one can see the psychological devastation such an encounter had brought forth. In South Dakota, congregational records from the Neu Hutterthaler Church registered the "many anfechtungen" that one Susanna Gross had experienced before her death in 1892.[13]

Several modern Hutterites told Peter Stephenson that anfechtung was the result of being cursed or *schreied*, something akin to being the victim of the evil eye.[14] Contemporary Hutterite ministers interviewed by the author focused attention instead on God's use of anfechtung "to bring people back to him," noting that persons who had undergone such testing were "more worthy than previous."[15] Communal Hutterites were not in agreement, however, about whether or not God initiated the testing, though they often compared anfechtung sufferers with Job in the Old Testament.

One contemporary Hutterite leader, who believed Satan himself selected those whom he wanted "to play around with," noted that if the battle against Satan was lost, mental illness usually resulted. A Hutterite defector confirmed that the anfechtung experience had caused her to end up in a psychiatrist's office.[16]

As early as the 1950s, researchers Bert Kaplan and Thomas Plaut had described Hutterian anfechtung as a psychosis resulting from a heavy sense of guilt, leading to "a weakening of the ego's ability to deal with the moral struggle between ideology and impulse."[17] Karl Peter and Ian Whitaker, in 1984, suggested that anfechtung was particularly prevalent in Hutterite women who felt socially or spiritually inadequate and thus found themselves feigning "artificial" busyness in order to disguise their discomfort.[18]

However, contemporary Hutterites, and the Prairieleut traditionally, felt the anfechtung experience was simply part of the life struggle certain persons had been destined to endure. As one Hutterite minister put it, if one "got right with God" the temptation would end. No other psychological explanation was warranted or helpful. As one of the *Lehren* put it, "The great art is to obey the Lord Jesus Christ and to never oppose him, so long as one lives, and to endure everything in patience, whatever anfechtung or suffering may come."[19]

One finds, therefore, a variety of explanations for the anfechtung event. The Krimmer Mennonite Brethren position, however, suggested that anfechtung was the result of an overly negative or pessimistic attitude toward life, resulting from an individual lack of assurance that one was a true Christian. KMB founder Jacob A. Wiebe had believed strongly in the assurance teaching, which promoted the view that God had guaranteed an eternal resting place in heaven for those who committed their lives to the Christian faith. Wiebe supported that position with numerous New Testament references and made it a central focus for the denomination.[20] He believed that "deep experiences," that is, anfechtungen, could be avoided if one experienced "joy in Christ" and accepted the certainty of one's faith.

Hutterian KMBs on the West Coast noted that the anfechtung condition continued to affect church members until a number of young people were exposed to the "assurance" teaching at the fundamentalist Bible Institute of Los Angeles (Biola) in the 1920s. Evidently Jacob Wiebe's teaching on salvation assurance had not been emphasized enough by California KMBs. Biola students brought the "assurance" focus back to the San Joaquin Valley, creating an ambience of security in faith, which one could personally "claim" from God.[21] As is often the case, younger Prairie People were the ones most open to the new "assurance of salvation" teaching.

Similar events took place in the Midwest as Prairieleut KMBs were exposed to "assurance" teaching at Chicago's Moody Bible Institute and at Northwestern College in Minneapolis. "New ideas" associated with the fundamentalist movement had ironically confirmed a KMB teaching, promoted by the denomination's founder.

Though most KMB Prairie People did not believe that salvation was universally guaranteed (one could, after all, forsake one's commitment to God), as long as one was in communion with God and with the church, one's eternal state was never in question. This was essential to many Prairieleut. One individual who went forward at a KMB revival meeting felt such a surge of joy and comfort "come over him" that, in front of the congregation, he "jumped up and shouted," while the revivalist's arms were still around him. His salvation now assured, he no longer had to be anxious about life after death. A minority within the KMBs went even further, accepting the "once-saved, always-saved" position of "eternal security," the belief that those whom God had "saved" could never lose that spiritual status.

In any case the "assured" never had to live through the suffering endured by Justina Wiebe, spouse of KMB founder Jacob A. Wiebe, who had herself gone into a trance-like state that sounded very much like the Hutterian anfechtung. Justina experienced great "torture" which made it seem as though "lightning had struck [her]." She contended that she was "outside of her self" and had "screamed for some time: Hell! Hell! Hell!" Finally, after seeing an image of a man smoking tobacco, she developed a new commitment to God and left her depression behind.[22] This sounds very much like something the Rev. Paul Tschetter might have dreamt.

The Krimmer Mennonite Brethren thus placed much emphasis not only on the importance of a personal salvation experience with Jesus but also on having an eternal assurance of one's saved state of existence. The doctrine of "assurance of salvation" had emerged from the KMB reading of Romans 8:15, 16, wherein the writer had noted: "When we cry, 'Abba! Father!,' it is the Spirit himself bearing witness with our spirit that we are children of God." KMBs also emphasized John 3:36, with its injunction, "Anyone who believes in the Son has eternal life."

Notwithstanding the existence of the anfechtung experience, it is ironic that the communal Hutterites were thought to have created a way of life that provided a greater sense of security than that delivered by other religious groups. The Hutterite sense of "assurance" was ascribed to the "routinization of the certainty of salvation" in their communal way of life.[23] That was the very reason many first generation Hutterian immigrants had joined colonies. Jacob Hutter himself had once stated, "By his [Christ's] filial spirit we have been assured that we are the children of God, true heirs."[24] The ark of the colony preserved the faithful, protecting them from doubts and concerns about their eternal status.

Karl Peter noted that this sense of assurance had been lost, however, whenever Hutterians, at different points in their history, had given up communal life.[25] Perhaps, in certain ways, this explained the attraction of many Prairie People to the Krimmer Mennonite Brethren. KMBs promised eternal security—as long as one followed the teachings of the church—and members could still hold private possessions. As a KMB, you did not have to give everything to the colony but could still claim a secure eternal home. No longer did Prairieleut converts have to wonder whether God wanted them to join their communal brothers and sisters in the protected ark.

Yet, assurance of future blessedness did not always encourage spiritual arrogance. KMBs sang the lyrics, "Oh to be nothing for my Lord" and continued to emphasize a life of humility and self-abnegation. Expressions of ambition had, in themselves, been considered sinful. Not all members of one KMB church, for example, had blessed one congregant's high-profile excursions into youth, radio, bookstore, and Bible distribution ministries, even though these had all been church-related activities.[26]

The communal Hutterites, and most Prairie People in the independent churches, however, thought "assurance" speculation was unbiblical. They believed it was blasphemous for human beings to claim to know, absolutely, whether or not God had accepted them. The communal way of life might be a great aid in one's search to please God, as was the fellowship of the gathered Prairieleut congregation, but God's ultimate will could never be fully known. Though a recent Hutterite defector told Caroline Hartse that it was through a "born again" experience that she had been able to expiate her own personal sense of depression, Hutterians, in general, have always considered the whole "assurance" emphasis to be "full of pride."[27]

Krimmer Mennonite Brethren also pointed to the spiritual danger of waiting until one's early twenties, directly preceding marriage, before joining the church, as was the traditional Hutterian practice. KMBs emphasized experiential faith via a definitive conversion experience, personal witnessing, and discipleship. They were attracted to the American fundamentalist movement by its emphasis on an inerrant Bible. KMBs also proclaimed that Christians should be "separated" from the world as citizens of God's holy kingdom on earth. That injunction fit the Hutterian mindset well. KMBs in Kansas had even constructed a European-style village at Gnadenau.

KMBs believed that the world was "Satan's kingdom." The Christian's duty in this sphere of existence was to follow the teachings of Jesus literally, in a separated spiritual reality, allowing no compromise with trends and styles of the secular society outside. One therefore looked in vain for wedding rings on KMB brides and grooms. Funerals were conducted in the home of the deceased.[28] As late as the 1960s, the Zion KMB Church in Dinuba, California, heard public confessions from members who had done things unacceptable to the congregation.[29]

For Hutterian converts, the practices of KMB worship took some getting used to. KMBs expected, for example, that sermons not only "come from the heart" but be delivered without notes. In the mid-1990s, ethnic Hutterian Phil Glanzer was unable to provide copies of any of the hundreds of sermons he had delivered during the course of his eighteen-year pastorate at the Salem Church in Bridgewater, South Dakota, because none had ever been written down word for word.[30] Reacting to the traditional Hutterian practice of reading prepared sermons, Prairieleut KMBs felt the Holy Spirit spoke more clearly and directly when annointed ministers had not thought out everything ahead of time.

Revival Meetings

News of Hutterian openness to the KMB conference had reached the leadership in central Kansas in the mid-1880s. In the winter of 1886, the Rev. Heinrich Wiebe was sent northward to hold revival meetings and help organize a church. Baptisms had then been conducted in Wolf Creek on November 25, "after the ice was chipped."[31] What then became the Salem congregation met in the sod houses of parishioners for eight years, moved to a schoolhouse in 1894, and constructed its first church building near Bridgewater in 1900.

The Salem Church was the first Prairieleut KMB congregation. Other Hutter KMB churches were established in subsequent years. In South Dakota, these included Bethel (organized in 1902 near Yale); Ebenezer (established in 1920 near Doland); Emmanuel (founded in the same year near Onida); and Bethesda (started in 1943 in Huron).[32] Congregations were also established in Dinuba, California (Zion, in 1911); Langham, Saskatchewan (Emmanuel, in 1917); and Chaseley, North Dakota (Immanuel, in 1920).

In the early organizational years, KMB congregations, like the independent Prairieleut churches, were scattered over a wide geographical area with gatherings often referred to by the name of whoever had emerged as a spiritual leader of the particular small group. Thus one reads of a "Tschetter Assembly" and a "Tschetter Brethren," referring to the Rev. John Tschetter; and of the "Brother Joseph Walter gathering" and the "congregation by Brother John Kleinsasser."[33]

John Tschetter, a brother of delegate Paul Tschetter, had been a particularly energetic promoter of the KMB alliance and was the first Prairieleut minister at Freeman's Salem Church. Tschetter was described by one KMB church history as "the first of the Hutterisch people who publicly confessed to personal salvation through a spiritual experience with Christ."[34] Tschetter had found "real peace with God" after an extended spiritual struggle, precipitated initially by relationships established with local Pentecostals.[35] The Pentecostals emphasized two themes which had interested Tschetter—spiritual healing and "endtime" preparedness—but he became disenchanted with the group's "emotional exuberance" and joined the KMBs instead.

According to Tschetter, God had revealed himself in such a way that a dark cellar he was praying in had been "lit up by the love of God." Tschetter desired to be baptized so fervently that a hole was cut in the winter ice, and he was immersed in freezing water.

Born-again Prairie People attended KMB revival meetings and after experiencing a great release from their sins and securing "salvation," they established their own KMB churches. They continued to call themselves "Prairieleut," "Hutterisch," or "Hutters" to identify themselves ethnically but were divided about how much teaching from their Hutterian past should become part of their new Christian experience.

They appreciated, for example, the traditional emphasis on holy lifestyle but had no interest in retaining the sermons, nor did they any longer recognize the Hutterian interpretation of the more gradual process of attaining salvation through Christian faith. Since many KMB churches were predominately Hutterian in ethnic composition, however, it was common to see young ethnics joined together in marriage, a manifestation which helped preserve a Prairieleut identity.

Some early twentieth-century revival meetings continued for weeks at a time, until that point when the leaders of the congregation discerned that God had completed his work in the lives of those in attendance. Services

Fig. 6.1. Salem Krimmer Mennonite Brethren Church, circa 1920. Photograph courtesy of Hutterian Centennial Committee.

relied on the preaching gifts of a number of ministers. In 1921, a revival at the Bethel KMB Church (Yale) continued for seven weeks with Samuel J. R. Hofer, Jacob P. Glanzer, and John Tschetter preaching. That revival resulted in fifty-eight baptisms.[36]

Some Prairie People attending KMB revival meetings "walked up and went out" when called to the altar, causing a revivalist of the 1940s to note a great amount of antagonism from the independent Hutterian church community. But a significant Prairieleut minority were impressed and transformed by the KMB connection.

KMB evangelists did at times provide ambivalent instruction at revival services. One individual said she had been "saved" at a revival meeting but really "knew little about it," that is, what it meant for her life in the future. That person thus spoke of being saved twice. She had not been "instructed" fully the first time, so she asked for salvation a second time at a later revival service, conducted by a different preacher.[37]

The Krimmer Mennonite Brethren also emphasized evangelism, an activity that was not without its risks. According to one account, KMB evangelist and well-known entrepreneur John Z. Kleinsasser had once gotten into trouble because he decided to stay overnight at the home of a potential convert. Evidently John Z. and an associate named Hofer went witnessing one evening and decided to stay at the home of a woman whose husband had not returned home, and who was known to be a jealous man with a drinking problem. In those horse and buggy days it was customary to keep guests overnight since it was dangerous to travel unmarked roads in the dark. John Z. and his fellow evangelist had thus been offered a bed in the guest room. But when their hostess' husband came home and found two men sleeping in his house, he immediately went into the guest room and started "whipping" Mr. Hofer, who was sleeping on the side of the bed nearest the door.

Hofer took the punishment without protest or fighting back, but when he heard the man coming back a few minutes later, Hofer insisted that he and John Z. change places so he would not get hit twice. The husband then proceeded to whip Hofer a second time—in his new position on the bed. The angry man's accompanying comment had been: "Now I'll give it to the other guy." The man had evidently been more in control of his wits than they realized. In any case, it was common in the early 1900s to find KMB laypersons and/or ministers going out in pairs, from one home to another, Bibles and songbooks bound in handkerchiefs in tow, to "bring the gospel."[38]

Prairieleut detractors of emotion-laden revivalist techniques insisted that KMB preachers scared their audiences into submission rather than relying on the guidance of the Holy Spirit. David M. Hofer, a KMB pastor and evangelist who visited the former Ukrainian Hutterian homelands on behalf of the Mennonite Central Committee in 1923 and 1924, had been accused of "terrif[ying] his hearers with hell . . . instead of emphasizing the saving love of Jesus . . ." Still, during one of his meetings, it was reported that 167 people had "repented of their sins" and that, eventually, 300 had been "saved."[39] Human lives were transformed in radical ways. Hofer later served, for many years, as editor of *Der Wahrheitsfreund*, the official organ of the Krimmer Mennonite Brethren Conference.

Two Anabaptist Traditions Mix

As in independent Prairieleut and Hutterite colony services, singing in parts was not allowed in late nineteenth-century KMB congregations. Songbooks were handwritten and contained only lyrics.[40] Church services were conducted primarily in German into the 1930s, while German hymns were sung regularly into the 1950s.[41] KMBs, like Prairie People and Hutterites, recognized the Apocrypha as part of holy scripture. All of this made the Hutterian converts feel right at home.

The Salem KMB Church did not purchase a piano until 1932, and no organ was placed in the sanctuary until 1954, though musical instruments had by that time found acceptance in KMB homes.[42] At Salem, church services continued to be conducted once a month in German until 1956, the year after the traditionalist minister David W. Tschetter was killed in an automobile accident. Thereafter, those interested could still attend German Sunday School classes (into the 1960s).[43]

The Krimmer Mennonite Brethren did observe a few traditions that were uniquely non-Hutterian, such as the "holy kiss." After communion at KMB churches, a "love chain" was formed with one person kissing another, although the sexes were separated.[44] This practice was observed at California's Zion Church until 1943 (the same year the congregation purchased a Steinway grand piano).[45] When observing the Lord's Supper, Prairieleut KMBs used a large common cup symbolizing congregational unity.

Following the example of Jesus, the KMBs also practiced footwashing, which had accompanied every communion service and symbolized humility, service, and unity. As late as 1955, pastoral candidate Laverne Hofer had stated emphatically: "Feetwashing was ordained in connection with the Lord's Supper."[46] It did not matter what the tenor of one's relationship had been to another person during the week. One might still be called upon to wash that man's feet the next Sunday morning, and vice versa. A spirit of forgiveness and reconciliation had been institutionalized in this historic Mennonite and Amish—though not Hutterian—ritual.

In many other ways, however, KMB and Hutterian practice converged. Mennonite historian Peter M. Friesen once described KMB theology and practice as a "narrow partisan Mennonite tendency," but many Prairie People were attracted to it.[47] Even the "love meals" that opened KMB conferences made the Prairieleut feel at home, hearkening back to Hutterian traditions. In the colonies every meal had, in a sense, been a "love meal." Colony suppers, in particular, were imbued with special spiritual meaning, since they traditionally followed late-afternoon church services.

Krimmer Mennonite Brethren services were often day-long affairs, with Sunday School, Bible study, and testimony time in the afternoon. Morning gatherings were often followed by a "fellowship" meal: women took turns preparing the food; men were responsible for scripture reading and prayer.[48] *Zwiebach* (soft, two-sided rolls), jam, and coffee fueled and lubricated the spiritual fellowship that ensued. KMB Sunday morning services included two sermons of thirty to forty minutes, each by different preachers, duplicating the pattern of worship in the independent Hutterian churches.

These practices continued into the late 1920s, when the automobile and other technological innovations made the meals and afternoon events less popular. In 1948, the Ebenezer KMB Church (Doland) reinstituted Sunday afternoon young people's meetings under the ironic appellation "The Christian Soldiers," but they were only held once a month.[49]

The KMB emphasis on Bible verse memorization combined with German language instruction in Sunday School classes was also reminiscent of Hutterian practice. The Hutterites too had required their children to memorize scripture in German, giving even greater emphasis to that ability by establishing "German schools," which met daily before and after public school sessions.[50]

Early KMB Sunday school classes focused equally on German instruction and on Bible teaching; the two were creatively joined together. Children in the Huron area were also taught the rudiments of music by persons like Jacob A. Tschetter, a well-known instructor.[51] On the more progressive West Coast, Californians Joseph and David Kleinsasser helped form the popular Harmony Male Quartet, which once performed for President Calvin Coolidge.[52]

Since Krimmer Mennonite Brethren were extremely strict with regard to the "do's" and "don't's" required of church members, congregations had also established mediation committees (*Vermittungs*) to deal with moral infractions. Committee meetings at the Bethel KMB Church (Yale, South Dakota) were dominated by discussions of smoking incidents, inheritance squabbles, members working on Sunday, the wearing of moustaches, and participation in athletics.[53]

At the turn of the century non-KMB Prairieleut, as well, had opposed participation in sports and the playing of certain games. In 1884, as noted, special meetings were held at the Neu Hutterthaler Church because too many members were playing billiards. This resulted in the adoption of a church ordinance, stating that upon a third offence transgressors would be sent "out of church."[54] Neu Hutterthaler also forbade participation in basketball games. Prairieleut KMBs thought much the same way. They were strongly opposed to competitive athletics and attendance at sporting events.

KMBs held a negative position as well on business involvement. It was suggested, for example, that professional buying and selling made participants "vulnerable as to their own salvation and spiritual well-being."[55] Members were expected to consult with the church before assuming significant debt, and they were enjoined not to deal in horses, a profession associated with dishonest practices. They were also instructed not to raise mules, because of that animal's "unnatural" infertility.

As late as the 1920s, KMB men and women were not allowed to swim together, and women could not cut their hair. Dating was carefully supervised and chaperoned by adults. Mary J. Glanzer remembered sitting on the front porch swing with a date until ten o'clock at night. She also recalled, however, that she and her friend had sat on opposite sides of the swing, and that her parents had occasionally peeked out at them through the window.[56]

KMB families were expected to be involved in all activities of the church, regardless of time and financial constraints. There was no staying home on Sunday morning. The spiritual dimension of human existence was to be ingrained in one's children with regard to all aspects of their lives. One older KMB Hutter noted that when he was young he and his friends still occasionally "lived it up" by "playing marbles and flying kites." But his primary emphasis was on the seriousness with which KMBs viewed the human experience.

One can see that in organization and in many theological emphases KMB and non-KMB Prairieleut congregations were similar. Abundant resemblances to communal Hutterite beliefs and practices were also in evidence. Both KMBs and independent-church Hutterians had established and carried on very similar socio-religious traditions. And they did so simultaneously. In many ways, the KMB world was very much like the one these people had left behind.

By adding a strong revivalist emphasis, the born-again experience, to an ultraconservative set of ethical regulations, many Prairie People found the perfect mix of traditionalism and evangelicalism for which they had been searching. KMB Hutters could now feel a certain spiritual superiority to their communal relatives and those who lived on private property, for they believed they had experienced God and the assurance of his salvation in a way that members of neither of the other groups could possibly understand or replicate. The emergence of Prairieleut KMB congregations also meant that Hutterians now had three possible churchly avenues they might choose: Hutterite, independent Prairieleut, or Krimmer Mennonite Brethren.

Independent Prairieleut/KMB Conflict

The evangelical emphasis at Prairieleut KMB churches had major impact on the Hutterian community in general. Families often split apart over theological issues, and unfortunate things, difficult to forgive, were said and done on both sides. In 1920, for example, the Neu Hutterthaler Church lost one of its ordained ministers when the Rev. Jacob I. Walter transferred his membership to the Salem KMB Church. Walter had been rebaptized, by immersion, into what he had come to recognize as the truer faith of the Krimmer Mennonite Brethren. This was extremely upsetting to Neu Hutterthalers, who had just experienced the death of the Rev. Paul Tschetter. Friends of KMB minister Paul F. Gross, as well, had been greatly upset when Gross left the independent Prairieleut community.

It was significant that in the independent Prairieleut churches, even those parishioners who eventually accepted evangelical theological emphases, had often attacked and/or felt uncomfortable with KMB neighbors. The KMB refusal to accept nonimmersion forms of baptism was a critical point of contention. Residual bad feeling between Prairie People in the two groups had been propelled, as well, by a "we were there first" KMB mentality. As late as 1986, for example, the Salem Church published a congregational history, in association with its centennial celebration, which stated, one hundred years after the fact, that John Tschetter had been the "first one among the Hutterite people to have a personal conversion experience with the Lord and to openly confess Christ as his personal savior."[57]

That statement cut many non-KMB Prairie People to the heart. They felt the commitment of their forefathers to Jesus had not necessarily been weaker simply because they had not expressed their conversion and witness in the same public and pietistic way. "What about his [John Tschetter's] brother?" asked one individual, referring to the Rev. Paul Tschetter, "Will he have a lower place than the KMB's in heaven?"

The Salem Church history also noted that the Rev. David S. Wipf had "made several decisions for Christ as a youngster." He still, however, had not known Jesus "as his personal savior." One prominent non-KMB Hutter responded to that situation straightforwardly: "Imagine all the pain that guy went through trying to figure out what kind of feeling he was supposed to get. What was the difference anyway?" That was a significant, though caustic response, for it revealed the very different way in which many KMBs who believed there was a major difference, and some non-KMB Prairieleut who did not, viewed an individual's relationship with God.

Many Prairie People had felt that something important was missing in the independent churches. David J. Mendel, in his "Autobiography," noted that, although he had been actively involved at Neu Hutterthaler and Hutterdorf and had "tried to live an honest and righteous life," he had still not been "assured" of his "salvation."[58] After being nominated as minister at Hutterdorf in 1908, he had thus "refused acceptance" and instead run successfully for the South Dakota House of Representatives, where he served from 1909 to 1912. Mendel had simultaneously organized Hutterdorf's first Sunday School program and served as its first superintendent. He continued to be dissatisfied with his spiritual condition, however, and was eventually rebaptized at the Salem KMB Church.

Even after the institutional division, marriages across KMB and non-KMB Prairieleut boundaries continued nonstop. The young people could not be kept apart. And eventually theological changes moved the independent churches in more evangelical directions as well. "Freeman was glowing for the Lord in those years," as Mary J. Glanzer put it. "The ministers were full of fire."[59]

Evangelism

Another issue that Krimmer Mennonite Brethren felt strongly about was missions. This was an endeavor the Hutterian people, communal and noncommunal, had not much emphasized since the early 1800s. Mission endeavors, even at that time, had focused primarily on backslidden brothers and sisters in Slovakia.

At the turn of the century two diverse philosophies of mission were in evidence. One, the modern Hutterite position, which was adhered to by the Prairieleut in the independent congregations, focused on the preparatory activity of the Holy Spirit rather than on individual missionary activity. As Hutterite novice Eberhard Arnold once noted, "Mission has to be a challenge addressed only to people who are in some measure already drawn by God. No one can come to him unless the father draws him (John 6:44)."[60] Christians modeled the love of Jesus, and through that example, attracted those whom God brought to their churches.

The second philosophy, that of the Krimmer Mennonite Brethren, was one that said that God called his followers to actively recruit new members through preaching, writing, or individual witness, allowing God to work through the evangelist as well as in the heart of the listener. That had also, ironically, been the perspective of the sixteenth-century Hutterites, who had sent members on missionary journeys across the European continent. The KMB paradigm suggested that God brought the unsaved to the Christian faith in only such measure as Christians themselves worked actively to spread the message of Jesus. God might play a foundational role behind the scenes, but Christians were made responsible for those not reached.

The Hutterite and independent church Prairieleut point of view, alternatively, placed major focus on the work of God. One perspective emphasized lifestyle, the other vocal witnessing. The KMB position eventually became the predominant viewpoint among all noncommunal Hutterians, but this took a couple of decades to materialize. In the interim, non-KMB Prairie People unexpectedly found themselves targeted by their "assured" relatives.

Early KMB commitment to evangelism was in fact inhibited by the German language, which created a wall between members and many potential neophytes. Most South Dakota converts had thus come from the Hutterian population, "one church stealing from another," as one Prairieleut described it. The KMBs eventually extended their mission, however, sending evangelists beyond South Dakota state lines.

The first two Prairieleut missionaries commissioned by the KMB Conference were the Rev. Jacob M. Tschetter and his wife, Kathryn Decker Tschetter, who were sent to western North Carolina in 1903 to work with the African-American community as ministers, teachers, and social workers. The Tschetters developed a deep love for that community during their nine-year tenure and had at one time prophesied that "the United States would pay dearly for the way it treated the negro."[61] It was upsetting to the Tschetters that during their entire sojourn in North Carolina their children had not been allowed to attend school with the sons and daughters of parishioners due to segregationist sentiment.

In 1915, Joseph W. Tschetter, another North Carolina mission project veteran, and David M. Hofer, who later visited and evangelized Russian Mennonites, started the Lincoln Avenue Gospel Mission in downtown Chicago. That evangelistic effort, like the Carolina work, in which an orphanage was established, had attempted to feed "both body and soul" by providing supplies of food and coal accompanied by the Christian message. Unfortunately, conflicts between Tschetter and Hofer caused the KMB conference, at one point, to relieve both men of their preaching licences.[62] In 1933,

Joseph Tschetter began publishing a separate newspaper, *The Friend of Truth*, and the Lincoln Mission properties were ultimately divided between the Hofer and Tschetter factions.

As late as 1941, new pastor Jacob S. Mendel discovered that Sunday morning services on the Hofer side of the Chicago mission were conducted in German, though Sunday School and other meetings used English.[63] Mendel himself had dropped German altogether, and in 1957, when Joseph Tschetter died, the two chapels were reunified. In 1963, the mission was renamed the Lakeview Mennonite Brethren Church but was never successful in attracting a solid core of members. Mission personnel observed tremendous demographic mobility in the low income neighborhood, which had suffered from drug traffic and high unemployment. According to later minister George Classen, it was "like trying to evangelize a parade."[64]

Over the years, however, KMB Prairie People provided extensive financial and material support for the Chicago mission, which served as a beacon of hope for many people. As late as 1976, South Dakotans Joe G. and Emma Hofer came to Lakeview for two weeks to help repair buildings.[65] And Delbert and Ardella Hofer were actively involved in the church into the early 1980s.

Later KMB evangelistic efforts included successful overseas assignments as well (see chapter 11). With regard to domestic efforts, however, the longtime commitment to the German language, combined with a clannish Hutterian membership, made it extremely difficult to gain large numbers of converts. It was said, for example, that one reason the Rev. Samuel J. R. Hofer was never as effective as he had hoped to be was his "deficiency in English."[66]

Like the independently organized Prairieleut churches, South Dakota KMBs also held annual Sunday School/Christian Endeavor conferences for many years. They were joined by the Huron (South Dakota) Mission Church, a nondenominational group that many Prairieleut had joined. In the 1960s, however, the various congregations joined the interdenominational National Sunday School Association and attended its conventions instead.

One of the larger KMB congregations in east central South Dakota was the Bethel Church, initially organized by the Rev. John Z. Kleinsasser in 1902. Kleinsasser had paid for the original church building out of his own pocket from land sale profits. Kleinsasser had set aside a preselected percentage of his brokerage fees for that specific purpose and had invited members to meet in his own large home until construction on the building was completed.[67]

When Kleinsasser later moved to California in 1910, however, he sold the church building, along with the rest of his holdings, to the Lake Byron Hutterite Colony, forcing the Bethel congregation to construct a new meetinghouse in a different location. That caused many to question John Z.'s commitment to that assemblage, though he reimbursed those who contributed to the construction of the Bethel College building nearby.

Oddly enough, after members of the colony moved to Canada in 1922, the church building was resold by new Prairieleut owner, Joe Waldner, to the Ebenezer KMB Church, which had moved the sanctuary to Spink County. Into the mid-1990s, therefore, worship services were still held in John Z. Kleinsasser's building.

The Bethel congregation itself was served by ethnic Hutterian pastors until the 1940s and continued to sing one song in German every Sunday morning until 1952. Carolina missionary Jacob M. Tschetter pastored the Bethel congregation for almost thirty years.

John Z. Kleinsasser

Bethel KMB founder, John Z. Kleinsasser, exhibited a number of representative characteristics of early twentieth-century Prairieleut life. Born in 1864, on the Ukrainian steppes of the Russian Empire, John Z. Kleinsasser ("John Z.") crossed the Atlantic Ocean on the Pomerania at age twelve, and grew up at the Lehrerleut Elmspring Colony.

While a member of the colony, Kleinsasser—at age seventeen!—had married his widowed sister-in-law, Anna (nee Hofer), seven years his senior, who had two sons (one of whom was her own, the other a child of her deceased husband's first wife).[68] John Z. and Anna loved each other, but they did not love communal existence. They were attracted instead to the capitalist opportunities beyond the colony gates. And so, six years after marrying, they left colony life and soon thereafter converted to the evangelical Krimmer Mennonite Brethren Church.

Before leaving South Dakota, Kleinsasser served as a minister at the Salem Church in Bridgewater, South Dakota, as well as at Bethel, where he founded the short-lived Bethel College that the Hutterites later converted into colony residences.[69] Kleinsasser was also interested in music and had personally instructed sundry "brothers and sisters" in the art of singing. John Z. was occasionally also an evangelist (recall his overnight adventure with a jealous husband) who went from house to house looking for potential converts to tell about his new-found salvation.

But John Z. had a hard time focusing attention on any one interest. As an investor, he engaged in numerous land speculation endeavors, which made him a wealthy man but also raised the eyebrows of some church members. Those successful economic ventures and strong personal opinions caused the Salem Church (where he had been ordained) to at one time prohibit him from preaching there.

In 1910, John Z., along with many American contemporaries, caught the "California fever" and took his family and eight others, including nineteen-year-old Hutterite runaway Dave P. Hofer, from South Dakota to the fertile farmland of California's San Joaquin Valley. All forty-eight persons accompanying John Z. were interrelated; all hoped to find the good life in a warmer climate.[70]

John Z. packed his family into a seven-passenger Chrysler Imperial, and when they arrived in the Dinuba area, purchased 3200 acres of farm land, setting aside a small, hilly parcel of it for a church building. Today, as one walks through the grassless dirt cemetery of what became the Zion Church, one encounters gravestone after gravestone inscribed with the names "Kleinsasser" and "Hofer."

John Z. pastored the Zion Church from 1911 to 1919 while simultaneously caring for a large family. In addition to raising two of Anna's sons, John Z. had ten children of his own with Anna, five sons and five daughters. When Anna was killed in 1910 in the town of Reedley in an unfortunate collision between car and train, John Z. married twenty-eight-year-old Helena Fast. They had six more children, three sons and three daughters. In all, John Z. took on the responsibility of raising eighteen children.

John Z.'s eleven-year-old daughter, Anne, died with her mother in the train collision as John Z. was returning from a trip to South Dakota where he had assisted extended family members preparing to move west. Anna and Anne Kleinsasser were the first two persons buried in what later became the Zion KMB Church cemetery.

John Z. Kleinsasser was a crusader, described by son Zack as "restless" and "impulsive."[71] It seemed that he was never satisfied with any venture, spiritual or secular in nature. Before coming west John Z. had first explored land purchase possibilities in Canada and the American northwest. He arrived in California with substantial financial resources, as much as $100,000, but could not resist financial investments, locally and in southern California, which eventually caused him to lose much of what he owned. He then had to rely on the resources of his children, until the time of his death in 1944.[72]

Some say the financial acumen of Anna Kleinsasser had ensured more cautious investments earlier. Others simply confirmed that John Z. was never the same person after her death. A few blamed real estate developers for his misfortune, believing John Z. had been mistreated and taken advantage of.

John Z.'s younger grandchildren remembered only an old man with a fading memory who was served meals in a separate room. Older grandchildren like Lydia Hofer retained memories of a friendly and outgoing person with tremendous devotion to the church.[73] In any case, John Z. started a movement that brought numerous friends and relatives to California's Central Valley. As Mary J. Glanzer put it, "That whole outfit went to California leaving a whole corner [of farm land] empty."[74]

As a teenaged groom, John Z. had crossed over from traditional village-based and communal Hutterianism to a KMB-defined American evangelicalism. He gained salvation and a lot of money in the process. Eventually, however, he lost almost everything but his faith.

Fig. 6.2. Young Prairieleut men (Mike Wurtz, Paul Wipf, Jakob Wipf), Langham, Saskatchewan, 1903. Photograph courtesy of Edna Wurtz.

Other New Churches

Prairieleut KMB congregations were also established further north. In 1920, for example, David J. S. Mendel organized the Immanuel Church for KMB Prairieleut who had settled near Chaseley, North Dakota. The congregation did not survive, however, owing to the mobility of members and internal conflict related to an accusation of drunkenness against deacon Wilhelm Kleinsasser.[75] The church was dissolved in 1932. Many members then joined the independent Hutterian church (Hope) that met in a schoolhouse across the road. That congregation purchased the Immanuel church building in 1947.

In 1917 a KMB congregation was also established in the Saskatchewan community of Langham (northwest of Saskatoon) by a number of Prairieleut families who had moved to that area in the early 1900s seeking better economic opportunities.[76] The Langham immigrants had claimed homesteads in a contiguous, rectangular, fifty-square-mile block, establishing a completely separate settlement, which helped them retain a singular iden-

Table 6.
Prairieleut Congregations of the Krimmer Mennonite Brethren Conference[a]

Congregation	Location	Date Established
Salem	Bridgewater, South Dakota	1886
Bethel	Yale, South Dakota	1902
Zion	Dinuba, California	1911 (disbanded, 1990)
Emmanuel	Langham, Saskatchewan	1917 (does not hold regular services)
Emmanuel	Onida, South Dakota	1919
Immanuel	Chaseley, North Dakota	1920 (disbanded, 1932)
Ebenezer	Doland, South Dakota	1920 (disbanded, 1995)
Bethesda	Huron, South Dakota	1943

Note:
    [a]This table shows the location and date of establishment of the various Prairieleut KMB congregations. In 1960, the Krimmer Mennonite Brethren Conference merged with the Mennonite Brethren Conference.

tity for a long period of time.[77] Also helping preserve social specificity was the absence of Hutterite colonies in that area until the 1950s.

The Emmanuel congregation was led initially by Andreas Stahl who had started his ministry many years earlier by conducting services in members' homes. Stahl knew "from past experience," as he put it, "that without a church and apart from its teachings lies only chaos and disaster."[78] Stahl, who was never ordained and who died in 1920, had been blunt in pointing out exactly how church members should act.[79]

It was significant, however, that a large number of Langham-area Prairie People never joined Emmanuel or any other congregation. Although, a few of the unchurched attended Mennonite services during World War I so that young conscientious objectors might associate with an historic peace church.[80] Some Langham-area Prairie People also met privately, in family groups for Bible study and prayer. A few joined local Mennonite or Protestant churches.

A particular concern of the small KMB minority had been the common Hutterian practice of keeping children at home during church services. "Most of the young people went astray as a result," insisted one individual. Langham-area Prairie People maintained a strong Hutterian ethnic identity, nonetheless, with high moral standards. According to Catherine Masuk: "They were the salt-of-the-earth types—hard working, honest and pious."[81] The children of some nonattenders did later participate in Emmanuel KMB's "Young People's Meetings."

In the late 1990s the Emmanuel church building and graveyard continued to serve as a social/religious center and historic site for Prairieleut descendents (KMB and non-KMB) in or from the area. The premises themselves were carefully maintained by one Jake Waldner, who also preached funeral sermons when called upon. An active Ladies Aid Society pieced quilts for mission projects, and the church building continued to be used for marriages, an annual Thanksgiving service, and a summer barbecue. The Emmanuel congregation itself, however, did not function on a regular basis.

In the 1930s, many Langham Prairieleut moved further north to the Napawin area, clearing the forests and "breaking up the bush."[82] Many Hutterian families were still listed in a mid-1990s edition of the Napawin telephone directory. Other Prairie People settled near Calvington. But no churches were established in either of those areas.

Over the years Langham-area Prairieleut retained some Hutterian cultural practices as well as a clannish ethnic identity, which helped seal a localized social personality, as had Canada's promotion of diverse ethnic traditions. Hutterisch phrases and traditional foods continued to be known, even by some members of the Generation X age group.

In general, however, Saskatchewan Prairieleut became a more secularized people than their brothers and sisters in South Dakota, showing an interesting mixture of cultural insularity and societal assimilation. According to Prairieleut linguist Walter Hoover (born Hofer), "Perhaps no immigrants to Canada wanted so desperately to fit into the English society as the Hutterian prairie people."[83]

This, perhaps, represented a negative reaction to a KMB-only Prairieleut church option early on. The loosely organized, independent Hutterian churches in South Dakota had made no concerted effort to establish an ecclesiastical outpost in Saskatchewan. There had not been an Andreas Stahl among the non-KMBs to promote the establishment of an independent Hutterian congregation. The KMB pathway, in turn, had not been the choice of the Prairieleut majority.

On the American west coast, near Dinuba, the Zion KMB Church was established in 1911 by John Z. Kleinsasser and many of the same families who had accompanied him earlier from Hutchinson County to Beadle County, in South Dakota. Mennonites and people of diverse ethnic backgrounds who settled in the Dinuba community discovered quickly that the Kleinsasser colony people, as they were described, though they called themselves Mennonites, did not hold Low-German or Swiss names, nor did they speak the Plattdeutsch dialect.[84] Instead, the Zion folks spoke the difficult-to-understand Hutterisch and held surnames like "Hofer" and "Decker."

Not all Prairieleut Californians joined the Zion Church. A few, who had been members of independent Prairieleut congregations in South Dakota, joined a local General Conference (GC) Mennonite congregation instead. Others affiliated with Mennonite Brethren congregations.

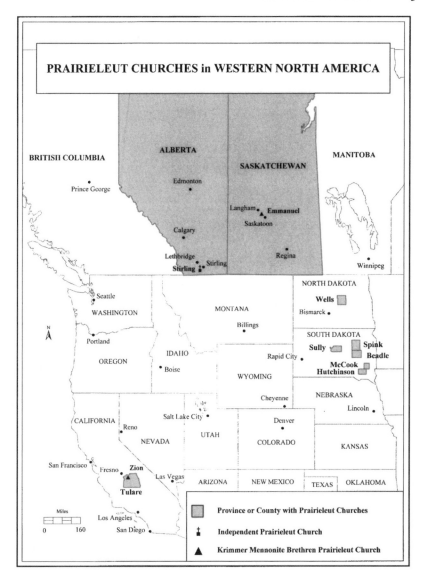

Map 6. Prairieleut churches in western North America. Map by Bill Slusser.

Jacob D. Hofer

The Rev. Jacob D. ("J. D.") Hofer presented a classic example of movement between the ethnic Hutterian community and Low German Mennonite congregations. Raised in an independent Prairieleut church in the Freeman area, J. D. accompanied his parents to California in

Fig. 6.3. Jacob D. and Agnes Fast Hofer, wedding photograph, 1911. Photograph courtesy of Center for Mennonite Brethren Studies and *California Mennonite Historical Society Newsletter,* Fresno, California.

1910. His stepfather, John L. Hofer, who was a first cousin of John Z. Kleinsasser, had not taken his family to the Zion Church because he disagreed with KMB theological positions.

J. D. Hofer himself, however, had been unhappy at Reedley's First Mennonite Church and had started looking elsewhere. After attending a nondenominational revival service in Fresno, he had asked himself the question, "What have those people got that I haven't got?"[85] Hofer had then attended services at the Zion Church, found "assurance," and was eventually baptized into that fellowship.

Soon thereafter Hofer made a more radical shift to the Reedley Mennonite Brethren Church after marrying one Agnes Fast. The Mennonite Brethren Conference (MB), like the KMB group, had been organized in Russia in 1860 as a pietistic and evangelical rendition of Anabaptism. The MB Conference was ten times the size of the KMB assembly, however. At the time he joined the Reedley MB Church, J. D. had also been the only ethnic Hutterian in attendance.[86]

After discerning a call to the ministry following unsuccessful attempts at farming, Hofer pastored a number of MB churches and was also a "conference evangelist." In that role Hofer not only provided a link between the Pacific District Conference organization and local congregations but had convinced many people to make decisions for Jesus. Hofer also held the position of Conference Chair for three terms, helped found the educational institution that in later years became Fresno Pacific University, and was generally influential in Mennonite Brethren circles until his ouster from the pastorate of the Fresno MB Church in 1947, due to accusations of "Pentecostalism."[87]

It was said, that at one "Young People's" meeting, the youth had "gone wild" and had "danced it up," which had greatly upset influential members of the congregation. Though Hofer insisted he was not a Pentecostal himself, he refused to discipline church members who had chosen to express their faith in nontraditional ways. After his ouster from Fresno, Hofer had still been called on to minister at South Dakota's Salem KMB Church. He and California Prairieleut Clarence Hofer, described by one person in attendance as "alive on the stage," had held what were portrayed as "very successful" revival meetings in the mid-1950s.[88]

Contemporary Prairie People tended to defend J. D. Hofer and to believe that what he had introduced at Fresno was simply "gospel from the heart" with accompanying "Amens" and "Hallelujahs," which, in their view, had been appropriate. They felt Hofer had been mistreated, as did the members of the Mennonite Brethren Board of Reference and Counsel, who had at the time unsuccessfully attempted mediation.[89] In the end, however, Hofer left the MB Conference completely, establishing the interdenominational Chapel of the Open Bible.

Among other things, J. D. Hofer's career showed the continuing importance of second occupations for Anabaptist ministers into the 1930s and 1940s. Hofer spent a considerable amount of time, for example, doing carpentry work to help supplement the small size of the "love offerings" he had often complained about. In 1935, for example, Hofer had received an annual salary of $660. In a letter to his congregation, Hofer insisted that there was no way he could support his family on that amount of income.

Back in Huron, South Dakota, the Bethesda KMB Church became the most innovative of the Prairieleut churches in later years, introducing services with a more informal character, encouraging attendance from nonethnic Hutterians, and seeking alliances with a variety of local evangelical organizations. In 1975, the congregation added an "Activity Center" of 8150 square feet, which included a basketball court to encourage alternative recreational activities for youth, which were often combined with evangelistic endeavors.

Families Split Apart Again

Perhaps the most difficult thing for the Prairieleut community to deal with was the family strife caused by the KMB conversions. Prairieleut families not yet recovered from the communal/noncommunal fissure now had to face another rending schism. All but one of Paul Tschetter's children, for example, became Krimmer Mennonite Brethren. Elder Tschetter's son, David, furthermore, began preaching at the Salem Church while he was still living in his father's house![90] Ministers representing churches whose members were at odds ate and slept in the same residence. Another son, Joseph W., had initially been selected for the ministry at the Neu Hutterthaler Church but had declined to serve.

It is said that Paul Tschetter once told his family, "Children, you are right to become KMBs but what will I do with my sheep here [at the Neu Hutterthaler Church]?"[91] Joseph W. Tschetter told people, additionally, that his father had had a "personal salvation experience."[92]

The preceding accounts and quotations, reiterated by many Prairieleut KMBs, require clarification in terms of what Paul Tschetter had actually meant. What, for example, was the context in which such comments had been made? Tschetter had also noted, for example, how "hurt" he was that his children had left Neu Hutterthaler but that he had decided "to [leave] it to God."[93] Intrafamily division could also be seen in Californian J. D. Hofer (a KMB who turned MB), who was the grandson of the Rev. Paul Hofer, a minister at the Hutterthal congregation.

Even after they left the independent Hutterian churches, Prairieleut KMBs continued to have a great deal of respect for Paul Tschetter. Some even attended services at the Neu Hutterthaler congregation and shared the communion cup, something they had not allowed Neu Hutterthalers to do at Salem.[94] KMB pastor Jacob M. Tschetter had even been asked to preach at Neu Hutterthaler. At the time, no non-KMB Prairieleut minister was known to have been extended a reverse invitation.

Movement between the Neu Hutterthaler and Salem KMB churches, two congregations located almost within sight of each other, continued for the next half-century, however, generally following a trajectory that pointed toward Salem. Prairieleut KMBs took an activist approach toward missions, focusing special attention on Hutterians in the independent churches whom they knew so well. Neither did they forget their friends and relatives in the colonies. They were aggressive and often successful in those endeavors.

Samuel J. R. Hofer, for example, joined the KMBs in 1908 after undergoing a "spiritual struggle" and securing "assurance of salvation," a theological position he insisted had been "problematic" at Neu Hutterthaler.[95] Jacob I. Walter, as noted, began his ministry at Neu Hutterthaler in 1916. Four years later, however, he was rebaptized and reordained at the Salem Church, a congregation he then served for the next thirty years. Walter insisted that the evangelical message had not been "appreciated" at Neu Hutterthaler.

In 1930, Jacob A. Hofer, another Neu Hutterthaler member, had also refused to accept a call to the ministry. He left instead and was rebaptized at the Salem KMB Church. Prairieleut historian Arnold M. Hofer left Neu Hutterthaler, as well, in 1938, at age twenty-two, after being "convicted" at a KMB revival service. The congregation Paul Tschetter led for so many years thus experienced a continuous stream of defections to the church up the road. As one individual put it, "Neu Hutterthaler was always on the short end of the stick in those situations."

KMB Prairie People also criticized Neu Hutterthaler for refusing to ordain a member who had very much wanted to be their pastor. David S. Wipf had claimed a special "call" from God to preach during a time when he was also teaching Bible courses at Freeman College. For unexplained reasons his "call" had not been recognized by the Neu Hutterthaler congregation. At Neu Hutterthaler one's "call" required extensive and collective congregational discernment, which in Wipf's case had not resulted in positive confirmation. A similar evaluation process at the Salem Church had led to a different decision.

The primary criticism directed at KMBs was that they were too quick to identify all independent church Prairieleut as "lost souls." Marie Waldner, for example, had been told by a KMB friend, "Your parents are not baptized." This upset Marie a great deal, but her parents assured her that they had indeed been baptized. Later, the KMB girl corrected herself and said, "Yes, that's true, but they aren't converted, so their baptism isn't worth anything."

Were the Krimmer Mennonite Brethren overly idealistic and intolerant? New revival movements always had those tendencies. One could make the same criticism with regard to the sixteenth-century Anabaptist ancestors of the various Hutterian groups. Prophetic movements caused people to focus attention on the supernatural realm of existence, encouraging in their adherents a tendency to condemn those who refused to follow the new way of thinking.

Some independent church Prairie People admitted that the KMBs were "ahead of [their] churches," in the sense that the KMBs had moved in evangelical directions more quickly than they had. Relationships had changed radically by the end of the twentieth century. In the early 1990s, for example, the Ebenezer Mennonite Brethren Church (originally KMB) and the Emmanuel Mennonite congregation (once independent Hutterian) were holding joint meetings whenever the pastor of either group was out of town.[96] In 1995, when Ebenezer closed its doors, a majority of its members had joined the Emmanuel Church.[97]

Earlier relationships between the two groups had not been as cordial. They were negatively affected by idiosyncratic interpretations of ecclesiastical rituals, particularly the form of baptism. Mary J. Glanzer, for example, said that her first baptism had been by sprinkling at the Bethany Mennonite Church in Freeman, a congregation that many Prairieleut had helped establish. She had been pushed in a "spiritual" direction at Bethany by the Rev. Henry A. Bachman. Later on, however, she felt the need to be rebaptized after recommitting her life to Jesus at revival services held at the Salem KMB Church.

Glanzer had thus been baptized again, this time by immersion, the required KMB form. Mary had later wondered, however, how to view her first baptism. One wise older member at Salem had told her this: "If I run the drag over this piece of field, the second time I do it, I do not condemn the first."[98]

The KMBs did not simply baptize by immersion but, more specifically, they dunked baptizands on their knees, face-forward under the water. In 1945, a pastoral applicant was rejected because he refused to support that specific form of immersion baptism as the most theologically correct.[99]

The independent Prairieleut churches, instead, followed Paul Tschetter; they baptized prospective members by pouring water on their heads. And baptized Prairieleut had difficulty accepting that their adult baptisms by poured water were not good enough to allow them to become members of KMB churches if they wanted to. This was a particular problem for spouses who happened to belong to the wrong congregation. They may have been baptized in what they considered meaningful adult experiences, but since water had not completely covered their bodies, they could not be members of KMB churches, again implying a sense of spiritual superiority.

The KMBs held firm, however, believing that baptism by immersion was the way Jesus himself had been baptized in the Jordan River. In the mid-1990s, the Salem Church still baptized new members in the James River and no nonimmersed Christians were allowed to join the congregation.[100]

One of the reasons Californian John L. Hofer had never become a member of his cousin John Z. Kleinsasser's church was related to his refusal to be rebaptized. Hofer had been baptized by pouring in South Dakota and had insisted that "one baptism is enough for me." Nonimmersed Hutterians had also not been allowed to participate in KMB communion services because of the denomination's "closed communion" position (altered in later years). At the same time KMBs could and did participate in Lord's Supper observances at the independent Prairieleut churches.

Annual KMB revival services with their Billy Graham–style calls to "come forward to be saved" created spiritual anxiety as well as hope for many people. Edna Tschetter described her experience as follows: "I really wanted to be saved so I went forward when the invitation was given. Rev. J. M. Tschetter would kneel by us and tell us to repeat the sinners prayer . . . I went forward every year until at age 14 I finally realized I was saved."[101]

Some Prairieleut KMBs looked for spiritual experiences at the revival services of other Protestant denominations as well. During the 1920s and 1930s, the Salem and Bethel KMB churches had major confrontations with members attracted to the Protestant Holiness and Pentecostal movements. Holiness preachers called for a "second work of grace" or "sanctification" as essential to the Christian faith. In the Protestant Holiness view, God did not grant his Spirit to believers at their initial conversion, but only after a second "work," which some preachers thought should lead toward sinless perfection.

Pentecostal preachers, similarly, emphasized a "baptism of the Holy Spirit," which both confirmed one's salvation and empowered Christians for holy living. The influence of Pentecostalism on Californian J. D. Hofer was evidenced by the fact that he always carried a bottle of oil in his suit coat, which was used to annoint the sick.[102] Pentecostals placed much emphasis on the supernatural healing of the afflicted.

Spiritual-minded Prairieleut were constantly seeking more profound ways to experience God. In her continual search for perfect spiritual enlightenment, Hutter Katherina Kleinsasser, for example, had gone forward "to be sanctified" at a Church of the Nazarene revival service. But, according to Katherina, "nothing had happened."[103] Katherina's son, Willis, remembered thinking, "Fellows, if my mother isn't sanctified, no one is."[104] As one of the Hutterite sermons put it: "And so it is with the children of man; they want to hear something new and strange. They prize highly what comes from afar."[105]

Revival services, "which came from afar," led many persons, however, to focus more seriously on the meaning and purpose of life. The services caused discomfort, but the resulting uneasiness often brought forth positive change in personal behavior. KMBs felt revivals provided a significant way in which God himself confronted the inherently secular nature of day-to-day existence. In any case, Prairieleut KMB converts were eager to share their new beliefs and practices with others. They were filled with love and joy and were determined to give all Hutterians the opportunity to experience something similar.

Alcohol and the Gospel

With regard to lifestyle issues, alcohol use was perhaps the Prairieleut pastime most strongly attacked by the Krimmer Mennonite Brethren. The issue caused many differences of opinion, since, historically, drinking was quite common among all Hutterians. As John P. Kleinsasser noted (with perhaps a bit of exaggeration), "When someone went to town he would usually go with a wagon load of wheat, and come home with just a load on."[106]

Kleinsasser was a farmer and teacher actively involved in Freeman's Hutterthal Church, where he often taught Sunday School. Kleinsasser also served in the South Dakota State Legislature and had been employed by the State Government's Agricultural Division. In his diary, Kleinsasser included an account of a meeting of the Hutchinson County Federal Land Loan Association where he consumed his "first glass of whiskey since the repeal of Prohibition."[107]

Kleinsasser indicated that it was common for Prairie People to frequent local saloons. According to Kleinsasser, some "got drunk in town and only their team of horses found and took them safely home to the farm."[108] Klein-sasser also published a true story about a Hutter farmer who, after buying some dynamite in Freeman, took "a few more refreshments" before leaving town and fell asleep on the way home. His wagon hit a hole in the road enroute, and the box of dynamite landed on top of him. Fortunately, it did not explode. In 1907, at the organizational meeting of the South Dakota Mennonite Aid Plan—a nonprofit insurance program—one Isaac Walter crawled into a photo session drunk. Since it was too late to push him out he had appeared in the official photograph of that meeting.[109]

The preceding stories were not representative of commonplace Prairie-leut practice, as drunkenness was not acceptable behavior. Social drinking in moderation, however, was generally approved, particularly before Prohibition. *"Trinch e bisl vain fir mottoch"* ("Drink a little wine for dinner") was a common admonition.

The pious Paul Tschetter, for example, was known to drink a jigger of schnapps each day before lunch.[110] Hutterians traditionally believed that drinking temperately was biblical. As a writer pointed out in the Hutterite *Chronicle*, Jesus in Matthew 26:29 implied that one day he would share a glass of wine with his followers in heaven in a transformed communion experience. Did this mean that true believers needed to develop a taste for the fruit of the vine while still living on earth?

Most Prairieleut at the turn of the century thought so. The Rev. Yos Hofer, however, had gone a different direction. Yos noted in his journal that he, too, customarily enjoyed having a glass of beer when he was uptown. In his account book, he used the symbol "x" to denote one drink. If he had two drinks, it was registered as "xx" and so forth. Hofer, however, eventually gave up drinking, feeling it had become a habit that was too distracting. One day, Yos told his family he was going "into the trees" until his alcohol problem had been "settled." He had returned later that day, and it was said that he never took another drink.[111]

In Russia, where one found drinking establishments in the various Anabaptist villages, most Hutterians and Mennonites consumed alcohol in moderation. Both groups became well known for brewing and distilling in their homes throughout Europe. In 1806, for example, German Mennonite, Cremer ten Doornkaats established a schnapps distillery, which now markets its product internationally. In Russia, the Anabaptists requested and were given special authorization by the Tsar to distill spirits and brew beer, privileges normally granted only to the Russian nobility.

As Reuben Goertz put it, "Now the Mennonites pushed into Russia. They wouldn't be worthy of their name if they didn't take advantage of a golden opportunity when it presented itself."[112] Proceeds from the Russian Mennonite liquor industry, in addition to ferryboat fees, were in fact a major source of income for the establishment of daughter colonies. It should also be noted that the oldest operating whiskey distillery in the United States

—Michters—was started by Pennsylvania Mennonite, John Schenk, who began converting his excess grain into whiskey in 1753.[113]

So the fact that Hutters in the Freeman area visited local bars for refreshment and conversation was not surprising. Even Prairieleut women occasionally frequented area saloons. Bar ledgers, which listed guests and the number and cost of drinks, showed that "abstinence was not considered important to the spiritual welfare of these people."[114] That was not the view of the KMBs; they had come to recognize alcohol as a tool of the devil.

As a result of Prohibition and the influence of evangelicalism, a teetotaling spirit eventually pervaded the independent Prairieleut congregations as well, though not all members were teetotalers. Prairieleut alcohol abuse, on occasion, led to sad results. One man, for example, who often imbibed whiskey from bottles hidden in the barn from his wife, fell head first onto the barn floor and "broke his neck."[115] One suspicious prairie fire, as well, was said to have been inadvertently started by an inebriated Hutterian. A number of such examples were given by temperance-minded Hutters as they pointed out the dangers of drink.

This was not to suggest that Prairieleut KMBs did not also occasionally consume a glass of wine, even if it was done secretively in one of the outbuildings (as a former KMB leader told me). Grain company sales representative, Paul Kleinsasser, for example, wrote that he always packed "liquor and cigars" in his automobile to give to potential customers. Kleinsasser did this even after he was "saved" and had joined the church.[116] Another KMB Hutter said, that as a child, he remembered vividly making wine from muscat grapes alongside his fervently religious grandmother. As that individual put it, "The Lord gave it to us. If correctly used, it's o.k." Furthermore, wine —not grape juice—was often used in nineteenth-century KMB communion services.[117]

Another difference of opinion converged around the issue of tobacco use. While, historically, all Hutterians had been opposed to smoking, the independent Prairieleut churches gradually adopted a position of unofficial tolerance; but the KMBs had held firm. This led to an ongoing KMB battle against nicotine.

Members of the Emmanuel Church in Langham, Saskatchewan, for example, discovered in the 1920s that a group of boys had "acquired the habit" of slipping out of church shortly before closing prayers. The boys had then "smoked frantically" for a few minutes (until services were completed) and reappeared "wholly innocent" when members filed out of the sanctuary.[118] In general, however, the KMBs were successful in eliminating smoking in their congregations.

A Third Way

The Krimmer Mennonite Brethren gained converts, as John D. Unruh put it, "largely through proselytizing from other Mennonite churches," playing on members' dissatisfaction with the level of spiritual vitality in their home congregations.[119] KMBs were committed to saving people. They wanted all the Prairie People to experience the inner spiritual warmth in which one became immersed through establishing a close personal relationship with Jesus. They exhibited the "extraordinary" characteristics of many new religious movements, discussed in detail by American religious historian Catherine Albanese. These characteristics included the emphasis on transcending "everyday" culture via a direct relationship with "some form of otherness."[120]

Non-KMB Prairieleut were more "church-oriented." Rather than a climactic salvation experience, the Prairieleut stressed the importance of a gradual nurturing experience in the faith and of catechetical instruction and parental nurture as part of the process whereby one became a follower of Jesus. It was sometimes difficult, therefore, for the two groups, especially early on, to find much favor with each other.

The Krimmer Mennonite Brethren Conference provided another Anabaptist option, a third way for Hutterians as they sought to most correctly practice the Christian faith. In addition to joining communal colonies or becoming members of the various noncommunal Hutterian churches, Prairie People might undergo a different type of conversion experience and become KMBs.

In the Krimmer Mennonite Brethren Conference, the Prairieleut found a group that imposed strict behavioral guidelines and rigid disciplinary regulations, many of which were similar to those adhered to by communal Hutterite relatives. This provided a corrective to what was perceived, by many, as an increasingly liberal lifestyle among noncommunal Hutterians in the independent churches. Even ministers like Yos Hofer maintained close relationships with KMBs and appeared to be attracted to many KMB social and theological emphases. As early as 1905, noncommunal Prairieleut ecumenicity had shown itself, when at Yos Hofer's funeral the audience had listened to the collective preaching of KMB John Tschetter, Neu-Hutterthaler minister Paul Tschetter, and Hutterthal Church pastor John Wipf.[121]

Prairie People in the KMB churches combined commitment to an assortment of elements of traditional Hutterian lifestyle—though communal life was not one of them—with an evangelical Protestant approach to theology and ecclesiology. Since most of the churches they joined were predominately Hutterian in ethnic composition, KMB Prairieleut also preserved the *Hutterisch* language and many social customs. This gave them immense comfort and helped indirectly to sustain a distinctive Hutterian identity inside the KMB Conference for a long period of time. Since Prairieleut Hutterians eventually comprised nearly 50 percent of the conference's membership, they were quite successful in retaining a unique ethnic personality within that Mennonite assembly.

KMB theology, with its focus on "assurance of salvation," provided an alternative form of security for the Prairie People, which they had in some manner relinquished by not joining one of the colonies. Hutterians now had a third way by which they might find spiritual security, and they could do so as individuals while still holding on to their private residences.

An unfortunate corollary to the Prairieleut-KMB connection was added family division within an ethno-religious group that was already extremely small. That development, in an ironic way, created a novel kind of social insecurity for the very persons who had just experienced spiritual security in "assurance of salvation."

Eventually, the assimilationist influences of twentieth-century North America entered the Prairieleut KMB world as well, altering social, ecclesiastical, and theological patterns. It was difficult to forestall the invasion of modernist ideals and practices without communal institutional structures firmly in place. But for a time, many Prairieleut found a place for themselves in a small and relatively unknown Mennonite sect.

7

· ·

Citizenship and the Political Order

> It is clear . . . that a Christian may neither go to war nor seek
> revenge. Anyone who does has abandoned Christ and His way
> . . . The sword of this world removes the person from earthly
> life, depriving him for evermore of the chance to repent.
> **Peter Walpot, Hutterite Servant of the Word, 1547**

> The teacher threw a book down and lunged at me like a man
> suddenly gone insane. And with all the strength in his hands
> . . . he started hitting my head, first on one side and then the
> other . . . I thought surely he would kill me.
> **Tillie Stern, 1976, concerning an incident that took place during
> World War I**

World War I

During the first forty years of frontier life, government institutions at federal, state, and local levels had essentially left the Prairie
People alone. This was exactly what they wanted. Things changed with the
onset of World War I, as the United States Government called upon young
Prairieleut men to fight and expected them to do so in gratitude for the
country's provision of political, social, and economic opportunity.

Until that time, KMB and non-KMB Prairieleut alike had managed quite
successfully to retain a cultural and religious identity that refused participation in war. There were occasional exceptions. One Alex Wipf enlisted in
the United States Army in 1898 and was sent to the Philippines.[1] More representative, however, were those Prairieleut who fled to Canada during that
same time period to avoid military service. World War I was, therefore, a
major test for the Prairie People, because they were harassed for the first time
by North American government officials, schoolteachers, and local citizens.

136

Some Prairie People had divided national loyalties, finding it difficult to understand how the cause of the Triple Alliance (Great Britain, France, Russia) was more just than that of the Central Powers (Germany, Austria-Hungary). In 1914, a Mennonite Brethren German-language periodical published a picture of nineteenth-century German Emperor Bismarck on the front cover. Yet most Prairie People were pacifists who wanted no part in a military struggle between two sets of superpowers. From 1914 to 1917, Jacob J. Mendel's Freeman *Courier*, for example, advocated a strong position of American neutrality.[2]

Beginning in 1917, however, Hutterians discovered that their cultural traditions, their customs, food, language, their entire way of life identified them as enemies. Three years earlier, the Salem KMB Church held a special congregational "festival" on the Fourth of July as an alternative to the patriotic celebrations that were of "the world."[3] Now participation in that sort of festival was considered treasonous.

During World War I, anti-German sentiment was especially intense in the state of South Dakota. The traditional pacifism of Hutters, Hutterites, and Mennonites outraged patriotic citizens of all ethnic and religious stripes, including sister German-Americans desperately trying to prove their loyalty to the United States. Harassment and discrimination resulted. Government officials, as well, treated pacifists of all persuasions with contempt.

Hutterites Joseph and Michael Hofer suffered the ultimate fate; they died as a result of mistreatment by military superiors at Fort Leavenworth. Many Prairieleut were related to the two men, and a number attended their funerals, including KMB minister, Jacob J. Hofer.[4] A January 1919 report tabulated by the House of Representatives Committee on Military Affairs noted that the deceased Hofer brothers from the Rockport Colony, sibling David, and a man named Jacob Wipf had been imprisoned for refusing to sign an oath of obedience to military commanders and refusing to drill or wear uniforms.[5]

The young pacifists were court-martialed and sentenced to thirty-seven years imprisonment. They were sent to federal prison on Alcatraz Island, where they were "stripped to their underwear," starved for five days, and then forced to sleep "on a cold, damp floor in the stench of their own excrement."[6]

The Hutterite prisoners were also beaten with sticks—Michael so badly that he passed out—and forced to stand for a day and a half with their "hands tied together above their heads and fastened to the iron rods above."[7] The four men were eventually transported to Fort Leavenworth, Kansas, "guarded by six armed sergeants and chained," where they were "driven through the street like pigs" with much fanfare and "the use of bayonets," all the time holding on to their Bibles.[8]

The pacifists were then ordered to remove their clothes and forced to stand outside in the cold, late November air for many hours. That final indignity caused Joseph and Michael to die from exposure. Adding insult to injury, military personnel then dressed the dead Joseph Hofer in the very military uniform he had refused to wear when living. Other Hutterites experienced similar mistreatment. One individual told Peter Stephenson (himself a 1960s-era draft resister) that "the guards used to like to dunk my head in a bucket of water 'til I couldn't hold my breath . . ."[9]

The Hutterites' experiences were made public by an army officer who listened to the stories of the Hofer brothers right before they died. But the Hutters, Hutterites, and Mennonites who knew about it did not talk about the incident, evidently out of fear that they would not be believed. Or perhaps they thought that such talk would unjustly—through the transmediatory interpretation of a wartime society—brand them as ungrateful "slackers."

The story was circulated instead by socialist political organizations opposed to government treatment of wartime dissenters. Socialist Party leader, Eugene Debs, for example, was imprisoned for advocating draft resistance.[10] A. J. F. Zieglschmid's 1947 report, based on interviews with David Hofer (brother to the deceased) and fellow prisoner, Jacob Wipf, was originally published only in German.[11] The first English translation did not appear until 1974. Jacob J. Mendel's Freeman *Courier*, furthermore, published only a brief reference to the two men's deaths.[12]

In South Dakota, the Prairie People, along with their Anabaptist cousins, the Mennonites, were harassed for speaking German in public places, for adhering to German culinary and cultural traditions, and for hesitating to buy war bonds. Even the "frankfurter" was renamed the "hot dog" during the war. This was indeed a difficult time for those who wished to hold true to German traditions. South Dakota's Council of Defense even prohibited telephone conversations in the language of the enemy.

Some Hutters remained intransigent. The Rev. John Tschetter, for example, responded to language restrictions by stating, "if the authorities wished to arrest [him] that would be acceptable to him," but he would go on speaking German nonetheless.[13]

The Jamesville Hutterite Colony suffered the most violent response from South Dakota citizens. It was raided by a group of patriotic Yankton-area residents, including a prominent local physician. The modern-day sons of liberty stole 100 head of cattle and 1000 sheep from the unresisting Hutterites and then sold them at auction for funds that they subsequently donated to the war effort.[14] Patriotic citizens also stole eighty-two gallons of colony wine, freely distributing the looted fruit of the vine to celebrants on Armistice Day.[15]

During the war, conscientious objectors in South Dakota were commonly referred to as "yellow bastards." After returning from a sojourn in Canada, one Hutter who had evaded the draft found his new buggy appropriately painted yellow.[16] Government reports showed that South Dakota's large population of Mennonites and Hutterians had struck fear in the hearts of many misguided federal employees. According to one report, the Mennonites represented a possible "cover front for a pro-German underground."[17]

In that same report, the Hutterites were referred to as "a rabidly radical pacifistic body . . . considered dangerous and under investigation."[18] Planned government surveillance included monitoring phones, recording private conversations, and intercepting mail. There was tremendous pressure, therefore, for young Prairieleut men simply to "give it up" for Uncle Sam and leave their unpopular religious scruples behind.

As conscientious objectors to war, most Prairieleut, Hutterites, and Mennonites refused to serve in the armed forces during World War I. At least thirty young Prairieleut men ran away to Canada in order to escape the physical and psychological "hell"—as one Hutter called it—of the military training camps.[19] American Mennonite historian James Juhnke suggested that the total number of "Mennonites" fleeing to Canada in 1918 might, in fact, have exceeded the more publicized "draft dodging" of the 1960s.[20]

Prairieleut Jacob S. Glanzer was one such draft evader. Jacob and his brother had been arrested at the beginning of World War I and were thrown in jail for refusing to buy the government Liberty Bonds that helped finance the war. It was said that in their cell the Glanzers had sung hymns like their imprisoned Hutterian ancestors in Europe, causing jailers untold discomfort. Upon release from jail, Glanzer and his family left immediately for the Langham, Saskatchewan, community, not even bothering to remove food from the kitchen table.

There were numerous cases of entire Prairieleut families giving up comfortable lives on the American plains to start all over again in Canada. They did this in order to protect their young sons from the draft and/or to avoid having to purchase Liberty Bonds, which they felt too directly benefited the war effort. The William J. Walter family, for example, joined the Glanzers in Saskatchewan. Henry C. Gross and family moved to Alberta, where some family members found employment at the Standoff Hutterite Colony.[21] Joseph E. Wipf settled in Alberta, as did the Andrew Gross family and Andrew's cousin, George. Unfortunately, toward the end of the war the Gross family were struck hard by the swine flu epidemic. The flu first killed George, and then both Andrew and his wife, Rebecca. A son and daughter, left behind, were temporarily taken in by the communal Hutterites. Prairieleut relatives eventually brought the children back to South Dakota.

Neu Hutterthaler Church records noted that many young men from that congregation fled to Saskatchewan during the war.[22] Paul L. Hofer and his brother Jacob were two such draft dodgers. In a 1991 interview, Hofer noted that, in early August 1918 he and his brother were told by their father, "with no warning," that they would be taking a train to Canada the next morning. "Fill up your trunks with clothes you think you might need," they had been instructed.[23]

With their mother in tears, and accompanied by their father, Paul and Jacob left the next day, first picking up appropriate legal papers from Prairieleut banker Jacob Stahl in Huron. Paul noted that, on board the train, "he never ate so many candy bars in his life." But he was anxious about what might lie ahead.

Paul and Jacob were taken to Saskatchewan, where their father enrolled them in Rosthern Academy, a Mennonite secondary school. There, they were to study and board the following school year. Since this was early August, Paul and Jacob "hooked up" with a threshing crew in the Langham area, which, to their surprise, was composed entirely of Prairieleut draft resisters from South Dakota, making them feel very much at home.

While a student at Rosthern Academy, pacifist Paul Hofer engaged in one rather violent encounter. Apparently, for the first time in his life, Paul was given the opportunity to box with gloves. Unfortunately, he proceeded to "knock out" his opponent, a fellow conscientious objector. He felt so remorseful he never boxed again.

After the war, Paul and Jacob had encountered some difficulty getting back into the United States. One immigration officer told them point blank to "go back where you came from."[24] On his return to South Dakota Paul also ran into trouble while shopping in the town of Dolton (near Freeman). Two local boys had grabbed Paul, pulled him into a barbershop, and proceeded to run a hairclipper "right up the center" of his scalp. The barber watched the whole incident without intervening. Paul's father refused to do business in Dolton from that time on.

During World War I, paranoid state officials even called the FBI into the Freeman area to investigate a number of conscientious objectors. Agents showed up, for example, at the home of Peter J. S. Hofer, another Hutter who later escaped to Canada. Peter was escorted in his flight northward by the Rev. John Hofer of the Neu Hutterthaler Church, who was showing official ecclesiastical support for the illegal endeavor. Peter Hofer remembered the Jacob S. Glanzer family meeting him when he arrived in the Langham area. And he recalled that he had "shocked bundles" for one Jacob Wurtz, along with South Dakotans Jacob Decker, Andrew R. Wollman, and others.[25] In Langham, Peter and most of the other Prairieleut young men attended the Emmanuel KMB Church.

Other young Hutters, however, strayed from the conscientious objector pathway, an easy thing to do during a time when there were no alternative service opportunities. One Jacob Hofer, for example, was one of the first 10,000 South Dakota volunteers in World War I and was killed in action in 1918 at Verdun.[26] Before he left the Freeman area, Hofer told Peter J. S. Hofer that he "[would not] come back unless I get the Kaiser's head." It is important to note, furthermore, that 48 percent of KMB Prairieleut draftees performed 1-A status military service, a striking phenomenon since the KMB Conference was strongly opposed to military service and had seriously considered immigrating en masse to Canada.[27]

The 48 percent refers only to those who were drafted, however. Many Prairie People secured family, medical, and farm deferments. It is quite probable that a greater percentage of those deferred, as compared to those drafted, held pacifist beliefs. Mennonite leader Harold S. Bender insisted on that proposition, though it could not be definitively confirmed. Californian David L. Hofer, for example, received a farm deferment during World War II but insisted that if he had been drafted he would have served as a noncombatant.[28]

Many Prairieleut civic leaders presented themselves as solid patriots, while simultaneously declaring continued commitment to Hutterian traditions. After war was declared on April 6, 1917, Jacob J. Mendel's *Courier*, for example, changed ideological course in a nationalistic direction. "We may not serve in the ranks," Mendel wrote to a largely Anabaptist audience, "but we can demonstrate our loyalty and devotion to our country by heeding the plea of the president in an increased production of food supplies."[29]

Even more surprising was Mendel's service on the Hutchinson County Council of Defense, an organization that had, among other things, discriminated specifically against communal Hutterites by refusing to provide military exemptions for colony men with dependent families. The reasoning of the Council had been that a communal society—unlike the extended or nuclear family—was perfectly capable of taking care of the wives and children of draftees. Mendel had also visited one of the military training camps and reported favorable conditions. Merle Funk thus concluded that Mendel and others "chose to believe the publicity campaigns rather than their own people."[30]

In any case, KMB leaders could see which direction the wind was blowing with regard to their stance on peaceful nonparticipation in war. After the war, a concerted effort was made, therefore, to protect that principle from the nationalistic influence of America's public schools and media. As late as 1924, David J. Mendel, writing as secretary of the Krimmer Mennonite Brethren Conference, drafted a letter to President Coolidge protesting the observance of Defense Day, since, as he put it, such was "not conducive to the promotion of world peace."[31] Yet the light of pacifism had grown increasingly dim among the membership at large.

The vast majority of young Hutterian men of the World War I era did not volunteer for 1-A status military service, nor did they escape to Canada. Instead, they reported as required to military training camps. And at the camps, conflicts with commanders sometimes materialized because the pacifists refused to carry weapons, to drill, and, in the case of the Hutterites, to wear army uniforms. Some Mennonites even refused to do KP duty.[32] Refusal caused the Hutters, Hutterites, and Mennonites to be the object of much disdainful harassment, though conscientious objectors were segregated from other draftees as much as possible in order to support what Merle Funk described as "a policy of subtle persuasion aimed at getting the C.O.'s to forget their convictions and fight like everybody else."[33]

In total, 136 Mennonites and Hutterians were court-martialed during the war years, primarily because of their refusal to follow orders.[34] Two Prairieleut men, Joseph H. Wurz and Joseph S. Walter, were court-martialed twice. They had evidently agreed at some point to perform noncombatant medical corps service, not realizing this meant they would be serving in the United States Army. On the basis of religious belief, Wurz and Walter later changed their minds and refused to serve.

Because of that change of heart, which was based on a misunderstanding, Wurz and Walter were court-martialed in September 1918 and sentenced to twenty-five years at Fort Leavenworth, where they remained until January 1919. At that time, they were told they would be released and were sent to Fort Dodge (for that purpose). On arrival, however, military officials reassigned them, once again, to the Army Medical Corps. Wurz and Walter promptly refused to serve and so were retried, court-martialed a second time, and sentenced to three months in prison.[35]

Even those South Dakota Prairieleut and Mennonites who complied with camp commander demands suffered personal insults and physical attacks from fellow draftees due to their belief in Christian pacifism. Though officers were continually instructed to go easy on the young pacifists, and Prairieleut draftees were not treated as badly as communal relatives (who often had their beards removed by patriotic conscripts during bus rides to military centers), they were still treated like "the scum of the earth," as one Hutter put it. It is significant and not surprising, then, to note that many descendents of those same pacifists decided to avoid personal attacks in World War II by dropping their pacifist stance altogether. The persecution endured by ancestral relatives was not to be experienced again. The same phenomenon was noticeable in Canada, where all of the young men in the Langham, Saskatchewan, Emmanuel KMB Church, for example, accepted straight military service during World War II.[36]

One Hutterite draftee, Jacob Waldner, kept a diary account of his experience in the military camps. In it he noted that there were *Eigenthumer*—"private owners," or Prairieleut—with them in the camp.[37] Hutterites and Prairieleut evidently felt a certain solidarity, as Waldner referred to one Prairieleut draftee as "one of our brethren." Other Prairie People, however, felt a keen embarrassment in being associated with bearded, archaically dressed distant relatives who had refused to wear army uniforms as ordered. Because Prairieleut men were more cooperative, none were sent as criminals to Alcatraz, as was the case with the Hofer brothers.

Another issue of great significance was related to the restrictions on using the German language. The German tongue and the Hutterisch dialect were indeed central components of the Prairieleut identity. Since sermons and hymns were written and presented only in German, and since Prairie People typically conversed in Hutterisch, many Prairie People did not feel comfortable communicating with God or with each other in any other language. Many believed it was not possible to express certain beliefs and feelings outside the boundaries of a specific linguistic tradition, following the findings of the Sapir-Whorf theory.[38]

On July 18, 1917, the South Dakota Council of Defense extended its prohibition on the use of German to church services. Until that time the restriction had extended only to public institutions. The new provision created a difficult situation for Prairieleut ministers who had never before preached in English. Ministers in the independent churches, furthermore, were accustomed to reading sermons that had never been translated. Many churches simply disobeyed state law and continued to use the outlawed tongue throughout the war. Peter P. Tschetter's response was typical. He insisted he would "rather go to jail than give up German."[39]

During World War I, even non-Hutterian citizens of German descent suffered harassment as a result of the super-patriotic temperament of the times. Freeman resident Tillie Stern noted that a teacher of Irish ancestry had roughed her up one day after school, because Tillie had called out to a friend, "Come here," in German. Tillie relates that, when he heard this, the teacher reacted as follows:

> [He] threw . . . a book down and lunged at me like a man suddenly gone insane. And with all the strength in his hands, I don't think he used his fists, he started hitting my head, first on one side then the other, continuously till I fell down. He jerked me up very roughly and kept on and on till all his anger was spent. I thought surely he would kill me. The other kids just stood and stared in fright.[40]

Pacifism as Embarrassment

The World War I experience brought much pain to the Prairieleut community. Some people endured with strengthened commitment to Hutterian Christian principles. Others, however, particularly those of the younger generation, felt shamed and embarrassed. Veterans' organizations actively attacked all varieties of pacifism, attempting to associate those who adhered to such positions with Judas, the betrayer of Jesus. In Canada, which had opened its doors to draft resisters, veterans groups issued press releases specifically designed to generate negative publicity against the communal Hutterites.[41] As John P. Kleinsasser put it twenty years later, after attending an Armistice Day rally, "It is just twenty years since the end of the World War, a totally useless war . . . our people have suffered enough from the anti-German hysteria . . ."[42]

Three hundred and fifty years previously, the Hutterite chronicler had cautioned, "Even in the church, especially among the young, many are bent on evil ways and delight in wickedness."[43] "Wickedness" and "evil" were characterizations that Hutterites historically associated with military service. Yet, desiring acceptance as patriotic American or Canadian citizens, a majority of young Prairieleut had begun to accept the for-God-and-Country ideology of North American civil religion, throwing off the embarrassing chains of their traditional pacifism (and the German language as well).

Many young Prairie People believed their willingness to defend the United States or Canada was biblically mandated and an expression of deep appreciation for the democratic freedoms bestowed upon them. America's distinctive worship of youth and historic denigration of the values and customs of non-Anglo-Saxon first- and second-generation immigrants was reflected in the refusal of third- and fourth-generation Prairieleut to place much stock in the wisdom of older persons in their communities. Most of the older generation stayed true to their position on peace.

The Prairie People had come to North America having never identified ethnically or nationalistically with their Russian homeland. In eastern Europe, Hutterians had actively protested military service obligations, even the alternative of service in government forestry or sanitation divisions. Yet in only two congregations, the Hutterthal Church (Freeman) and the Salem KMB Church (Bridgewater), was the pacifist position consistently adhered to in later years. In all of the Prairieleut churches, furthermore, pacifism eventually become an optional position with regard to church membership. Nonpacifists were even given teaching and leadership positions in most assemblages. And many congregations employed ministers who did not personally adhere to a position of conscientious objection to war.

As early as 1938, California's Zion KMB Church ordained the Rev. John J. Kleinsasser, who had served in the military as a noncombatant medic during World War I. The minutes of a Zion congregational meeting held on December 10, 1941, three days after the Japanese attack on Pearl Harbor, note that one Paul Hofer donated an American flag to the congregation and that it had been placed inside the church.[44] The congregation also moved to have all official records henceforth written "in the American language." This church was not going to be accused of consorting with the enemy.

A significant minority of Prairieleut draftees continued to request alternative service assignments during World War II, registering as conscientious objectors and joining the Mennonite-directed Civilian Public Service (CPS) program, which operated independently of American military structures. Most Prairieleut congregations had, by that time, joined Mennonite conferences. Though KMB Prairie People had been part of the Mennonite institutional world since the late 1800s, the more recent joining together of most independent Hutterian congregations with the General Conference Mennonite Church was done for the specific purpose of providing a pacifist alternative to military service. It was hoped that young men could avoid military training camp experiences altogether. As it turned out, however, a majority of young Prairieleut had no interest in conscientious objector alternatives. A strong sense of duty to country, at whatever cost, prevailed and was documented in diary accounts.

One Prairieleut who had remained loyal to Anabaptist traditions was Paul

G. Tschetter, a grandson of the Rev. Paul Tschetter, and a CPS camp director in the Black Hills. Correspondence showed Tschetter indicating that alternative service had stirred the "depth" of his own soul. He described the dam that CPS workers had constructed as a "Monument of Peace." According to Tschetter:

> Social, cultural and religious differences and backgrounds: All these and more have been carried into this Monument of Peace. There may be no public marker announcing to the world what you did here but when you stand on the crest of Deerfield Dam you too will feel that stirring of the soul and that swords have been changed into pruning hooks.[45]

Mennonite church leaders had envisioned CPS as a model for positive democratic action via the creation of numerous, as Paul Toews called them, "colonies of heaven."[46] CPS had been established in May, 1941 and began operations before any American declaration of war.[47] It was indeed a model of inter-Mennonite cooperation, the various denominations raising four million dollars to cover administrative and operational costs.

On the West Coast, Prairieleut Jacob D. Hofer served as the MB Pacific District Conference "liaison" with young men in the CPS camps.[48] All of the Prairieleut KMB churches, and even Joseph E. Wipf's interdenominational Huron Mission Church, gave financial assistance to the CPS program.[49] Many Hutter women, as well, worked in the camps, taking on a variety of responsibilities.[50]

In some South Dakota counties, conscientious objector status was still difficult to obtain. Hutchinson County, for example, was notorious for creating difficulties for pacifist applicants. Arnold M. Hofer remembered accompanying "numerous" young men to hearings in Sioux Falls as a result of critical evaluations by the local draft board.[51] At times it was even necessary to appeal above the state level, to the federal courts. Difficulties with Hutchinson County draft boards continued into the 1950s and 1960s as board members gave "a rough time," as it was described, to certain conscientious objectors. One could imagine, in that context, the powerful impact nonpacifist Christian peers must have had on young Prairieleut males who wanted to be viewed positively.

While a majority of young Prairieleut were turning their backs on pacifism, it is important to remember that even the most evangelical of Prairieleut had not felt uneasy with the peace position earlier. Exemplifying that commitment were Joseph W. and Katherina Hofer Tschetter, who, in the early 1900s, had served as KMB missionaries in North Carolina. One finds strong pacifist viewpoints throughout Katherina Tschetter's 1945 autobiography.[52] The Tschetters gave an uncompromising nonresistant response when confronted with hostile acts from local white citizens and vigorously refused to be guarded by armed men, even when warned they were in great danger.

According to Katherina, they had looked to God for protection instead. Even fundamentalist KMB ministers such as Samuel J. R. Hofer held strong pacifist beliefs.[53]

By the 1940s, however, much of the traditional Hutterian pacifism was gone. One section of Freeman's American Legion was, in fact, called the "Weber-Hofer Unit."[54] Many with Hutterian names were part of that unit, including Hofers, Walters, Kleinsassers, Stahls, Wollmans, and Wipfs. Dentist Michael J. Wollman was an American Legion commander and served simultaneously as a deacon in a local Mennonite congregation. Hutterians Joseph Walter and Arnold Kleinsasser were killed in action, and other Hutterians served as officers. One California Hutterian served as a personal chauffeur for General Douglas MacArthur and loved to tell stories about it.[55] This was mainstream American thought and action. These men gave their lives for a moral cause. To criticize their willingness to die for the new Hutterian homeland seemed thankless as well as treasonous. Most were commended instead by members of the Prairieleut churches.

Many Hutterians simply took positions of neutrality and/or silence on the peace position. In his diary account, John P. Kleinsasser, for example, included notations about Prairieleut killed in action, as well as those being "trained as bombardiers." Military personnel on leave often visited Kleinsasser's home. Yet Kleinsasser also made appearances at CPS camps and attended CPS choir concerts. His daughter, Marian Towne, recalled preparing food that was sent to the Hill City CPS camp in the Black Hills.

In his wartime journal, however, Kleinsasser expressed no opinion—either way—on the moral necessity of any particular course of action.[56] Ideologically, he was a pacifist; in practice, he remained nonjudgmental. Kleinsasser's daughter once asked her brother, "How come some boys in our church go to the Army and some go to the C.O. camps?" He responded, "It's a difference of belief. The Mennonite people dictate non-resistance . . . but some Mennonites don't go along with that anymore . . . we follow our own conscience."[57] That statement pretty much typified the majority opinion among younger Prairieleut.

By the early 1940s, sentiment in the various churches had become so nationalistic that conference leaders in the KMB and GC were forced to reflect seriously on what had gone wrong. Church leaders often noted that peace had not been a major concern during the 1920s and 1930s. Younger members, therefore, were not prepared to deal with the heady and seductive patriotism of the 1940s. There were few trained theologians available during those years to forcefully articulate traditional peace theology in the face of ideological attacks from evangelicals. The same could be said with regard to the pre–World War I era, but forces of assimilation had not been as potent then, in a pre-radio age, as they had become by the 1940s. Kaiser Wilhelm, furthermore, had not seemed as dangerous as Chancellor Hitler.

After World War II, KMB Conference leaders belatedly attempted to resurrect support for the peace position by conducting a number of seminars and publishing special literature dealing specifically with nonresistance. But even when such attempts were made, few Hutters listened. Too many Prairieleut families had children, parents, or relatives who had served in the military. Churches themselves were attended by conscientious objectors and soldiers alike. Most Prairieleut churches—KMB and GC—had thus taken a middle position, supporting whatever point of view individual members had decided to take. In December 1943, for example, California's Zion KMB Church decided to send presents both to its boys in CPS camps and to those who were serving in the armed forces.[58]

Prairieleut congregations, for the first time in their history, began to perform intricate balancing acts with regard to their position on peace, eventually relegating it, by silence and/or accommodating actions, to a belief considered to be of only secondary importance. Even though applications for the KMB ministry, for example, continued to confirm personal belief in pacifism, pastors in that conference increasingly took a public position of silence on this very divisive issue. In 1944, KMB ministerial candidate Paul H. Glanzer had suggested, "Let everyone decide for himself according to his conscience."[59] Nine years later, missionary Joe Walter responded to a question on the peace position by stating, "All who participate in war are responsible to God for all that they do."[60] He did not elaborate further, believing that the church should not demand that individuals accept nonresistance unless they "claimed it for themselves." Anything else would be hypocritical.[61]

By mid-century many Prairieleut Christians had also introduced a new theological angle in the debate on the peace position. Many now insisted that the peace position made their churches unattractive to potential converts. They had come to view pacifism as a potential stumbling block, a hindrance to successful evangelism. As the Rev. Virgil Kleinsasser put it, "I really believe that during the war [and] after the war . . . Mennonitism was over-emphasized at the expense of evangelization." He believed "this wrong emphasis" had even "grieved" God.[62]

In total, only 46 percent of the Mennonite men who were drafted served in Civilian Public Service camps during the period 1941–1947. The remaining 54 percent had done either straight military service (39 percent) or noncombatant duty (15 percent).[63] In the Prairieleut churches, one finds an even greater percentage of persons who became just-war advocates. In Prairieleut KMB congregations, for example, 71 percent of those drafted served in the military with either noncombatant (26 percent) or straight military (51 percent) assignments.[64] In the GC Hutter churches 67 percent registered for noncombatant (14 percent) or straight military (53 percent) service.

It is noteworthy that the Salem KMB Church had the strongest pacifist response of all the Prairieleut congregations. At David W. Tschetter's Bridgewater congregation, six men who were drafted chose the alternative service option, another became a noncombatant, and only one—who was not a member of the church—went "straight into the military."[65] This was in contrast to one Huron-area congregation, which had seen all fourteen of its young men accept 1-A status military assignments. The most striking balance is found at the Hutterthal Church (Freeman), where six men requested 1-A status, two were noncombatants, and eight registered as conscientious objectors.

Ministers, perhaps, had significant influence on the route taken by the young men in their congregations. For example, during the war, Peter P. Tschetter, a committed pacifist, found himself pastoring a non-Prairieleut Mennonite church in Pretty Prairie, Kansas. At that church, thirty-three young men served in CPS camps, while only fifteen accepted military service assignments.[66]

The changing nature of Prairieleut teaching on peace was exemplified in the experience of California KMB John Kleinsasser who in the late 1930s had applied for United States citizenship but was denied due to the fact that he had answered "no" when asked if he would be willing to take up arms to defend the nation. After "spending a lengthy time reviewing his understanding of scripture," Kleinsasser had gone back five years later and answered "yes" to that same question.[67]

At the same time, the Zion KMB Church—Kleinsasser's congregation—was engaged in heated debate about a suggestion that the congregation "pray" for young men in the military. At a Wednesday evening service, the Rev. John J. Kleinsasser (whose son, Virgil, was a noncombatant) supported the suggestion and was successful in getting it passed. He was aided by the fact that he was a well-loved and influential minister who had encouraged many young people to become missionaries.

Virgil Kleinsasser later became Zion's pastor and served for many years as a missionary in Nigeria and Ghana. In 1946, when Clarence Hofer returned to California—after completing studies at Biola and at Bob Jones College—he noticed significant "friction" between church members owing to differences of opinion on the peace position. Hofer told the author that the "non-pacifists" had won out in the end.[68]

At Zion, positions changed rapidly during the 1950s. Laverne University professor Phil Hofer—who grew up in the congregation during the 1950s and 1960s—said that he could not recall any teaching with regard to peace and nonresistance, either in sermons or in Sunday School classes. With regard to the peace position, the post–World War II era had evidently been a time of retrenchment at Zion. In order to preserve internal unity, ministers and lay leaders had not taken a vocal position on the issue, leaving it up to individual families to decide what to tell their children. When Hofer and his friends were drafted in the 1960s, only Phil registered as a 1-O status conscientious objector. He noted that some church leaders had even criticized him for taking that historically Hutterian position.

Similar stories were part of the history of other Prairieleut congregations as well. The Bethel MB Church historian, for example, noted that during the late 1940s and early 1950s, "the peace position was not heavily stressed in either preaching or teaching . . ."[69] Willis Kleinsasser wrote that the ideological scene at the Mennonite Brethren Tabor College—which many Prairieleut KMBs had attended—also gave one a negative impression of pacifism, which was, as he put it, "not a popular position in pre-Vietnam days."[70]

The United States itself represented a positive image for most Prairieleut Hutterians. It was difficult to say "no" when the government asked for help in the international post–World War II battle against communism, even if that assistance meant engaging in violence. It is true, however, that many Prairieleut had continued to request noncombatant military assignments. Walter Kleinsasser, for example, served as a chaplain's assistant in the army.[71] Clifford Walters served in the United States Army Finance Corps.[72]

In the 1960s and 1970s, the peace position became even more controversial. Even the pacifist Prairieleut minority, for example, had difficulty supporting a stance associated with individuals who were experimenting with drugs and sex, engaging in public demonstrations against government policies, and questioning the morality of America's capitalist economic system. Prairie People preferred public identification with evangelical Christians, most of whom thought pacifism was unbiblical, heretical, cowardly, and naive. This presented a complicated theological maze for Prairie People; few knew how to walk through it without feeling dazed and confused.

Most evangelical Christians viewed pacifism as misinterpretation of scripture, and many Prairie People, four hundred years after the death of Jacob Hutter, concurred. Though Hutterian ancestors had often turned the other cheek to the point of death, most North American Prairieleut did not want to be identified with secular antiwar protestors or pacifist church groups such as the Jehovah's Witnesses, Quakers, and Seventh-Day Adventists. Evangelical Christianity was, in many ways, a great lifesaver for the Prairie People. It not only gave Hutterian Christians theoretically purer "born again" moral and devotional qualities, but provided theological support for tossing out an embarrassing historical belief.

This was also the era when prayers and sermons were shortened and kneeling for prayer began to disappear in the various Prairieleut churches. Prairie People—like other ethnic assemblages—had become more sophisticated and up-to-date. In Jacob D. Hofer's California congregation, the church council began to add disinfectant to water basins used for footwashing services.[73] (In many congregations footwashing itself was no longer observed.) The gospel of Jesus was to be made palatable for a cleaner, more cultivated people. That was the logic used, as well, to support assignation of the peace position to secondary theological status. One did not want to place a stumbling block—such as the unpopular peace emphasis—in front of those who might otherwise be interested in the Christian faith. Too much was at stake in the effort to bring people to Jesus.

Politics

During the Depression years, most Prairie People suffered alongside their neighbors as a result of national and international economic policies and conditions that were exacerbated by climatic instability. This period followed a time of tremendous economic prosperity, particularly for Prairieleut farmers in South Dakota's Hutchinson County. Things changed in the late 1920s and 1930s. Drought, crop failures, low prices, inability to make loan payments, all of these characterized Hutter life during that era.

In addition, during the summer of 1936, a tornado had picked up the Emmanuel KMB Church in Onida "and spun it around an exact quarter-turn."[74] Many stories were told of Prairieleut families struggling to survive, getting by with limited food, entertainment, and clothing. John P. Kleinsasser's journal notes the many winter days when school was canceled due to lack of coal supplies for heating.[75]

Adverse economic conditions caused many Prairie People to take an interest in political issues, as well, as they discovered the close relationship between global market prices and their own financial well-being. The emergence of a spirit of communal goodwill had indeed accompanied economic struggle, but conditions were not good. They were particularly bad for Prairieleut living in South Dakota's Beadle, Spink, and Sully counties, where the drought had hit hardest and crop losses were heaviest.

Seventy-five percent of Mennonites in that area—predominately ethnic Hutterians—lost their land during the Depression years.[76] Government assistance via Works Progress Administration jobs—often related to road construction—eventually helped revitalize the area's economy, but a lot of suffering was endured before such New Deal programs became fully operative.

Some Prairie People had even gone on relief, accepting government-provided food and clothing, including dried canned beef and plain denim overalls. Walter Kleinsasser wrote that his family moved to California in 1934 specifically because of poor economic conditions in South Dakota. During his high school years, Kleinsasser worked in a print shop as an employee of Franklin D. Roosevelt's National Youth Association.[77]

These various Depression-era experiences caused many Prairieleut to follow state and national political movements more closely. Though strongly separatist in the organization of their churches, South Dakota Hutterians evolved a feature conspicuously absent in the American Mennonite world until recently: support for political activity among the membership.

Though many Prairie People had been actively involved in local politics from the 1880s on, post-1920s activity increasingly focused attention on

Fig. 7.1. Turkeys on the Paul M. Waldner farm, circa 1940. Photograph courtesy of Hutterian Centennial Committee.

higher levels of government. Political involvement of that nature was particularly prevalent among Prairieleut who had joined Krimmer Mennonite Brethren churches. This is a phenomenon that has been overlooked by Mennonite political scientists and historians, who have often suggested, alternatively, that there has been little, if any, such involvement among Mennonite groups in the United States.[78]

The small size of the KMB denomination, in particular, provided an opportunity for many people to develop leadership capabilities, as the services of virtually every member were required to make the conference function effectively. Some persons ultimately utilized those skills in the political arena.[79] Many non-KMB Prairie People, too, sought political office, feeling that in a state as small as South Dakota there was a great opportunity to "make a difference."

One might, in fact, go back to the traditional organization of European Hutterian settlements—both communal and noncommunal—to find a preparatory foundation for civic leadership. John Bennett has written, for example, that "the social management system of the [Hutterite] communal colony at a population level of around 100, is more complex than the government of a typical town of 5000."[80] Hutterian management skills are thus highly developed. In North American colonies in the 1990s there were generally two ministers, one farm manager, and one business manager for every 120–130 people. In the 1980s, Terry Miller, a former Hutterite novice, was elected to the South Dakota State Legislature.[81]

Hutterians also experienced many forms of self-government in the past, administering local affairs in virtually every place in Europe where they had

Fig. 7.2. Three Prairieleut children, circa 1930. Photograph courtesy of Hutterian
Centennial Committee.

established colonies and villages. In their last place of residence in Russia
some Hutterians had even held the position of magistrate. But political
power exerted in the past had been designated for sister and fellow Hutterians, not for a mass citizenry.

Such was not the case in the United States, and, from the earliest years,
Prairieleut Hutterians served as local civic leaders. In 1884, Jacob Tschetter,
for example, was elected to the office of Marshall in the town of Bridgewater. The following year he was appointed United States Deputy Marshall
by Democratic president Grover Cleveland. Tschetter also served the town
of Bridgewater as an alderman, justice of the peace, and, for sixteen years,
as mayor. He gained local notoriety for arriving late for the hanging of out-
law Jack McCall after McCall had murdered Wild Bill Hickok in a Black
Hills bar. According to one Prairieleut authority, Tschetter "had been raised
in a Christian Mennonite home and so did not feel he wanted this honor."
Another source noted: "I knew this Tschetter well and I can easily imagine
him coming on the scene late with a big cigar in his mouth. He made cigars
from tobacco he raised himself. No doubt he shook hands with all the digni-
taries there and apologized for coming too late."

By the early 1900s, many South Dakota Prairieleut had also joined the
Farmers Union and were active in Lions Clubs and Chambers of Com-
merce. David D. Wipf served as South Dakota's Secretary of State from
1905 to 1909. Many other Hutterians held state legislative positions (see

Fig. 7.3. Prairieleut businessmen in Freeman, South Dakota, circa 1900. Photograph courtesy of Hutterian Centennial Committee.

Appendix B), including membership in the South Dakota State Legislature and the State Senate.

John P. Kleinsasser's diaries were particularly helpful in documenting late 1930s campaign strategies as the candidate traversed his legislative district in search of votes. When Kleinsasser ultimately lost a re-election bid in 1938 —by a single vote—he intimated that heavier voting among the "Hutterische" might have made a difference.[82] (In the 1990s, Kleinsasser's daughter Marian Towne ran unsuccessfully for a seat in the Indiana State Legislature.)

A cursory look at the Freeman community showed extensive Prairieleut political involvement at the local level, beginning in the 1890s. As early as 1893, Michael Wollman had been elected to the town's Board of Trustees. Andreas Kleinsasser became City Assessor that same year. In 1896, S. A. Kleinsasser assumed the position of City Marshall and was succeeded by Emmanuel Hofer in 1899, and by A. C. Wollman in 1901.[83]

There were numerous additional examples. In the Huron area, KMB physician John S. Tschetter served as chair of the Beadle County Democratic Party and as mayor of the city of Huron. In Freeman, the list of Prairieleut mayors included Sam Walter, John J. Wipf (who later served in the South Dakota House and State Senate and was a charter member of the South Dakota Historical Society), J. M. Wollmann, John A. Wipf, and Jacob L. Hofer. Of twenty-five ethnic Hutterians and Mennonites who served in the South Dakota State Legislature from 1903 to 1988, 52 percent had Prairieleut roots.[84]

It is significant that Prairie People who went into politics often did not hold pacifist positions. There were exceptions. John P. Kleinsasser, for ex-

Fig. 7.4. Prairieleut-owned grain elevators, Bridgewater, South Dakota, circa 1900. Photograph courtesy of Hutterian Centennial Committee.

ample, spoke out forcefully against the death penalty during his term in office in the 1930s and advised some young people at the Hutterthal Church to become conscientious objectors. Most Prairieleut politicians in the past half-century, however, were not pacifists. This reflected theological changes in the Prairieleut churches and may also have influenced the direction of such changes.

During the period between World War I and World War II, an increasing number of Prairieleut individuals entered the political arena, following Mennonite political scientist John H. Redekop's belief that "a thoroughgoing political abstention in our society is both impossible and undesirable . . . "[85] Political involvement continued in the years that followed. In the decade of the 1970s, for example, one found Democrat Menno Tschetter serving ten years in South Dakota's House of Representatives and Democrat Paul S. Tschetter, two years in the State Senate. Some Prairie People had developed close relationships with important national figures such as Senate minority leader, Tom Daschle.

In the 1980s, Democrat Harvey Wollman served as a South Dakota State Senator, as Lieutenant Governor, and as Governor, while continuing to sing in the choir at a Prairieleut congregation. Wollman once noted, "To be a Christian is also to be a model; to be politically responsible." He also told the author—with a mixture of honesty and humor—"I think if you read the Scriptures carefully, you'll become a Democrat."[86] Wollman's brother Roger served as Chief Justice of the South Dakota State Supreme Court and as a justice on the United States Eighth Circuit Court of Appeals. Also in the

Fig. 7.5. Main Street, Freeman, South Dakota, circa 1920. Photograph courtesy of Hutterian Centennial Committee.

1980s, Harris Wollman held the position of Secretary of Education and Cultural Affairs, and Republicans Leland Kleinsasser and Benny Gross represented their districts in the State Legislature. Gross, a World War II veteran, lost an arm at the battle of Iwo Jima.

Most of these individuals were members of or were raised in Krimmer Mennonite Brethren congregations. Everywhere, Prairie People were encouraged to be actively involved in the political process. In 1984, California's Zion Church, for example, encouraged members to vote in a particular way by inserting a flyer in the Sunday morning bulletin published by the conservative American Coalition for Traditional Values.[87]

Civic Obligation and Peace

Beginning in the 1920s, the Prairie People in South Dakota developed an increasing interest in fulfilling civic obligations through active political involvement at the state level. The increase in political involvement was influenced by a combination of factors, including the citizenship ideology promoted by public schools, evangelical Protestant theological positions, and a generally positive feeling about life in North America. Hutters also began to see the economic benefits associated with certain political positions. Most Prairie People who went into politics felt that in a state as small as South Dakota they had been given a great opportunity—perhaps a moral imperative—to make a difference.

Fig. 7.6. Main Street, Freeman, South Dakota, circa 1920. Photograph courtesy of Hutterian Centennial Committee.

This burgeoning interest in public service represented a novel development for Hutterians, who had, in the past, been interested only in issues that affected their own people. To force one's opinion on others had not been considered consistent with a nonresistant pacifist belief system. Experience in self-government in eastern Europe had prepared Hutterians for public service in North America, however, and from the earliest settlement years, a number of Prairie People had held local government positions.

Along with a growing concern for the political order, Prairieleut Christians now had to deal with the question of how much an individual could legitimately compromise in the political arena without undermining Christian principles. The Prairie People were thus confronted with a citizenship dilemma with which communal Hutterites had never had to engage. Isolated in communal agricultural villages, the communal Hutterites had generally refused to vote or in any way impose their viewpoints on other people. Their radically different lifestyle had also made it easier for them to resist nationalistic social pressures. The Prairieleut, conversely, had to deal with issues of civic obligation head-on.

A sense of social responsibility very naturally pulled Prairieleut individuals away from traditional ideological principles that had emphasized separation from the world, nonresistance, and conservative lifestyle. Engagement in the general affairs of American society demanded a willingness to accommodate ideological and behavioral difference, leading Prairie People to accept an ethic of toleration not adhered to historically.

During the World War I period, the Prairieleut found themselves hated simply because they belonged to a particular ethno-religious group with unique beliefs and practices. From that time forward, younger Hutterian generations in the United States moved quickly away from traditional ideals such as pacifism, feeling an increasing attachment to "America" as a way of life. They questioned ecclesiastical traditions and folk customs, as well, and they identified themselves more and more as mainstream Protestant evangelicals. When asked what "Mennonites" believed, they simply responded, "We're like the Baptists."

The development of a sense of civic obligation had thus evolved simultaneously with a growing embarrassment about historic Hutterian ideals and customs. And tradition was submerged in midwestern America's distinctive rendition of the "melting pot."

8

. . . .

Embarrassment, Respect, and Rivalry: Prairie People, Hutterites, and Mennonites

A small number of these former Mennonites joined the church [Hutterian] at different communities, but they were more of a burden than a help to the church. All they wanted was to argue and eat and drink and there was much impurity among them.
The Chronicle of the Hutterian Brethren, 1604

Previously we did not know you [Mennonites] but now we [Hutterites] have come especially close to you and have experienced the Christian compassion that characterizes you, the warm affection, the unity of love . . . the divine influence that inspires you to help us.
The Chronicle of the Hutterian Brethren, 1665

Each ethnic group had its contributions to make. The effortless friendliness and hospitality of the Swiss, the unswerving persistence of the Low Germans, and the straight-forwardness of the Hutterites together produced an enrichment greater than would have been possible had there been ethnic solidarity.
Marie Waldner, 1951

The Prairieleut/Hutterite Relationship

This chapter looks at the relationship between Prairieleut, Hutterites, and Mennonites. The Prairieleut/Hutterite association is reviewed first, in some detail, followed by a discussion of the rather complicated connection between the Prairie People and different Mennonite groups.

The relationship between noncommunal and communal Hutterians in North America has been a stressed one. An ambivalence characterized personal contacts and collective opinions, both sides freely criticizing the other. Over the years the tense and somewhat paradoxical relationship underwent a variety of transformations but never resulted in heartfelt mutual understanding.

Modern-day Prairie People are quick to point to negative aspects of Hutterite life, often noting alcohol abuse, theft, and a legalistic form of Christianity.[1] The Hutterites do make chokecherry, dandelion, and grape wine and drink it in moderation. This occasionally has led to alcohol abuse, as is readily admitted. In former Hutterite Samuel Hofer's "fictional" work, *Born Hutterite*, the main character noted that, at the end of a particular wedding, "a few of us were walking wobbly already."[2] Another Hutterite who drank a great deal had once stated, "Everyone knows about my drinking but only I know about my thirst," pointing to an underlying spiritual/psychological problem. Still, immoderate drinking is not condoned or practiced by most Hutterites.

Hutterite children, who have a more generalized perception of what is "mine" and "yours" than people on the "outside," have sometimes been accused of, or caught, stealing by Prairieleut and non-Hutterian shopkeepers and neighboring farmers. Similar examples can, of course, be found in any cultural group. A personal survey of county sheriffs, policemen, shopkeepers, and farmers in South Dakota communities, where large numbers of Hutterites resided and/or shopped, found that individuals on the "outside" believed communal Hutterites engaged in a lot less theft than other ethnic groups.[3] Local officials often laughed when I brought up this issue.

One got the sense, however, that more was expected of the Hutterites because their way of life was so different. They were common targets of unsubstantiated gossip, which at times had become part of the prejudicial folklore of the northern Plains. Many prominent persons, for example, had suggested to the author, in all seriousness, that they "were sure" the Hutterites hired male outsiders to impregnate young Hutterite women. The ethnic slur was a ridiculous idea given specious credibility as a result of the general public's knowledge of how inbred Hutterite culture had become and what seemed, to some, a logical way to deal with what was perceived to be a negative phenomenon.

Many contemporary Prairieleut, as well, do not recognize the value of communal Hutterite theology, considering it unbiblical and overly legalistic. It would appear from discussions with some that few beneficial ideas or practices could be attributed to the Hutterian past. Prairieleut critics appreciated the fact that their communal ancestors had given their lives and possessions for the Christian faith, but they did not agree with the way that faith had been interpreted. Hutterites, in response, accused the Prairieleut of selfishness, egotism, and a lack of gelassenheit, the full surrender of self to God manifested in communal living.

According to Karl Peter, the Hutterites had strengthened their ideological commitment historically during those times "when only committed members were left in the group."[4] In making that observation he had pointed conversely to the cultural and religious "assimilation of the Prairieleut to the larger society." That was indeed the contemporary Hutterite viewpoint. Modern Hutterites did not insist the Prairie People were eternally damned simply because they did not live communally, but they did emphasize that Christians were enjoined to be in community with God on a personal basis. They felt material possessions seriously detracted from that connection and assumed that the Prairie People were therefore not as "committed" to God as they were.

Compared to the average Hutterite, noncommunal Hutterians, like most Americans, had accumulated abundant material possessions. Though the Prairie People had perhaps adopted mainstream American cultural values and practices at a slower pace than certain other ethnic groups, contemporary distinctions were hard to make. As Miriam Warner noted with regard to California's Mennonite Brethren, "While the religious value system emphasizes equality, the ethnic value system looks with favor on business and material success."[5] Hutterites placed greater emphasis than the Prairieleut on the "next world" by not placing too much faith in the present "vale of tears." They too, however, had increasingly entered into competitive marketing relationships with noncommunal enterprises and had continually upgraded the standard of living in colony homes.[6]

South Dakota Prairie People also accused the Hutterites of allowing too much wild behavior from teenage boys and girls.[7] As one noncommunal Hutterian put it, "They are not always successful in keeping their young people away from the world." The Hutterites did tolerate a certain amount of reckless behavior, particularly among young men prior to joining the church (which usually occurred in their twenties). This got the rebellion "out of their systems" but was not tolerated once those same individuals became full-fledged members. One young Manitoba minister told me that the most difficult thing for him to give up—after joining the church—were those times of frivolity and "running around" which had been a central feature of his "growing up" years. Hutterite pastor and schoolteacher John S. Hofer once described the teenage years as that period of time when individuals "go up fools hill."[8] Shortly after making that statement a group of this writer's students, engaged in a three-day study experience, had been found dancing with young Hutterites in the colony dining hall.

Prairie People tolerated less adolescent experimentation, expressing a stronger concern for strict discipline in this area. Prairieleut descendent Delbert Wiens put it more bluntly and caustically: "Unlike my mother, who was expected to grow up, we were expected to begin to do the work of a Christian when still young. And that was logical for a Christianity that had been reduced to a level that could be understood by adolescents."[9]

Fig. 8.1. Hutterite broommaker Chris Tschetter, circa 1975.
Larry Anderson Collection, courtesy of Tony Waldner.

Prairieleut memoirs, too, suggested more wildness than might have been anticipated. Paul Kleinsasser, for example, wrote that before he married and settled down (at age twenty-one), he and his Hutter friends had rolled their own smokes and consumed a lot of beer at local pool halls.[10] Phil Hofer noted that a number of young people at California's Zion Church had also "gone up fools hill." The expectation was that eventually most would come back to the faith.[11] For a short time one had to tolerate the pack of cigarettes sticking up out of the offender's shirt pocket.

It was perhaps most ironic that the Prairieleut had become such loyal supporters of United States military endeavors. That manifestation, too, had, at times, led to ideological conflict between Prairieleut and Hutterites, since members of the communal group did not serve in the military nor generally exercise the right to vote.

As early as World War I, Prairieleut physician Andreas A. Wipf had served as a member of the South Dakota Council for the Defense, an organization that pushed an antipacifist and anti-German philosophy, which was diametrically opposed to KMB and non-KMB Hutterian theological and cultural positions. Since the 1940s, continued Hutterite commitment to pacifism and refusal to defend the United States militarily had become an embarrassment to many Prairie People as they pursued acceptance by the dominant culture.

Some of the strongest opponents of government privileges for Hutterites were also distinguished Prairieleut. That opposition had developed due to high-stakes competition for available farm land throughout the past half-century. Prairieleut farmers often felt the Hutterites had a big advantage over them at land auctions, much as the Montana-area residents accused of "hate crimes" against the Hutterites felt in the late 1990s.[12] Hutterite settlement decisions also had an impact on school district territorial designations. Because of these matters, some of the most negative statements about Hutterites have come from Prairie People.

In the mid-1950s, for example, during a time when South Dakota's legislative bodies were debating a bill proposing restrictions on the incorporation of Hutterite colony operations, a prominent Prairieleut farmer spoke out publicly against the colonies at the state capitol. Anticolony feeling had run particularly strong among Prairieleut farmers in Beadle, Spink, and Sully counties, where families had been most adversely affected by the agricultural depression of the 1920s and 1930s.[13]

Embarrassed By the Relatives

The Prairieleut Hutterians' "in-tune-with-the-times" way of life certainly differed from the sixteenth-century peasant ambience and the dated social customs of communal Hutterites. Since they desired association with mainstream American culture, their embarrassment about their past had become an obsession for some. This residual shame was related to common public association with Hutterites. "They don't have to live that way!" one person exclaimed in consternation. "I wish people wouldn't confuse us with them."

This manifestation was common among second and third generation Americans who experienced immigrant embarrassment as a kind of identity crisis, propelled by the essential cultural differentness of parents and grandparents. Sons and daughters desired acceptance as "good Americans," to be like the people they went to school with, worked with, and, from the 1950s on, the people they saw on television. Their need was accentuated by ridicule they received from those American citizens who were further along the road to assimilation.[14]

Derision of their cultural traditions is particularly difficult to take for young people, who spend years in age-segregated public institutions and are thus highly susceptible to attacks on personal and social characteristics, particularly during their adolescent years. Disparaging assaults thus influenced the destruction of ethnic uniqueness not only in language, cultural practices, clothing styles, and religious rituals but also in basic value interpretations and foundational ways of knowing. It was difficult, then, to "get it back."

Most ethnic groups in America were eventually assimilated, and the past

Fig. 8.2. Communal residence at Bon Homme Hutterite Colony, Tabor, South Dakota, 1998. Photograph courtesy of Samuel Hofer.

was lost, only to be rediscovered as a quaint historical interest or hobby, a source of pride in one's ancestors, long after the ancestors were dead (which made it easier to appreciate them).[15] Herbert Gans referred to that phenomenon as "symbolic ethnicity."[16] In his book, *Multicultural America*, historian Ronald Takaki discussed the tremendous impact of that social and psychological process on virtually every immigrant assemblage in the United States.[17]

The Prairie People had a difficult time following that historical pattern, however, owing to the continuous and increasing presence of a large number of Hutterites all around them. The communalists nearby represented an older immigrant tradition, now fossilized in the sense that Hutterites held fast to customary ways of doing things. The Prairie People found it difficult to escape from their communal cousins. They were constantly associated with them even if it was only through identical surnames. One found little embarrassment only in California and Saskatchewan.[18] In California, communal Hutterites were virtually unknown. In Saskatchewan, no colonies had been established in Prairieleut areas until the 1950s.

Some South Dakota Prairie People believed that a confusion of identities with Hutterites had even affected church growth. At a late 1960s meeting of one congregation, the secretary had noted, "Emmanuel feels a bad image of Mennonites, confusion with Hutterites, makes witness difficult."[19] Now the relatives could be blamed for lack of church growth as well.

Fig. 8.3. Old flour mill at Bon Homme Hutterite Colony, Tabor, South Dakota, 1998. Photograph courtesy of Samuel Hofer.

Prairie People often joked about the uncouth—as they described it—lifestyle of distant relations in the colonies and reiterated their appreciation that their families, sometime in the past, had left that way of life. Prairieleut women, in particular, frequently held that view, seeing the manner in which Hutterite women dressed, worked, and were treated. "You think I was dressed like a colony?" one woman responded, after being queried about early Prairieleut dress styles.

Former Hutterite Ruth Baer Lambach has emphasized that Hutterite women, in reality, have tremendous inner integrity, exert forceful influence in colony affairs, and in no way should be characterized as "put down."[20] Caroline Hartse, in a recent study, discerned increased personal freedom and influence, which manifested itself not only in women securing drivers licences but in the increased merchandising of such items as homemade dolls and down pillows.[21] Many Prairieleut women focused instead on the proscription of female attendance at colony business meetings and the fact that they had often seen Hutterite men "ordering the women around." (see chapter 10.)

It was, perhaps, in the Huron, South Dakota, area that Prairie People sought disassociation from the Hutterian past most fervently.[22] But other areas of South Dakota and the northern plains had been affected as well. In the 1980s, one Prairieleut minister used to get very upset when anyone called him a "Hutter." Other Prairie People remembered being referred to, jokingly, as "communists." They got tired of being identified with their communal brothers and sisters (whom they often did not consider "brothers and sisters").

Ethnic ideals and varying lifestyles create cultural mosaics invigorating society with myriad solutions to social problems, as well as providing aesthetic enrichment through a variety of definitions of beauty, different types of food, and dissimilar styles of architecture. Multicultural manifestations also cause separateness, however, with an accompanying inclination to fear the other.[23] These different results of ethnic identification can work at cross-purposes. While peculiar customs and beliefs provide innovative examples for society at large, the only way to preserve cultural distinctiveness is, often, to keep mainstream culture at a distance.

Hutterians and Mennonites in the former Soviet Union, for example, were very successful in holding on to linguistic and cultural traditions.[24] The Soviet government, to the very end, sponsored German broadcasts and published a German journal. Maintaining ethnic traditions had been extremely helpful in offsetting the impact of ideological rigidity in Soviet public schools. It had not, however, created positive relationships between Soviet Germans and other cultural groups, nor had ethnic distinctiveness encouraged Anabaptists to exert much influence on Soviet society as a whole.[25]

In North America, the communal Hutterites had preserved their ethno-religious islands from wholesale assimilation through commitment to geographically isolated and communal socio-economic structures. The Prairieleut had not created a similar kind of insular institutional edifice. They had opened themselves wide to American society, in the process losing touch with many ethno-religious traditions that they now find embarrassing.

Coming Together

It is significant that, just when much Prairieleut ethnic and cultural separateness had disappeared, and in the very midst of a community still strongly affected by different forms of ethnic embarrassment, a new interest arose in preserving written materials, photographs, and artifacts telling the noncommunal Hutterian story.

In 1973, a century after Paul and Lohrentz Tschetter's fateful journey to North America, a group of interested South Dakota Prairieleut decided that something needed to be done to preserve the Prairieleut part of the Hutterian story. They established the Hutterian Centennial Committee to coordinate publication of a book commemorating the one hundredth anniversary of the immigration of all ethnic Hutterians to North America.

The Centennial Committee, under the leadership of Arnold M. Hofer, continued, after original projects were completed, to pursue the goal of preserving communal and noncommunal Hutterian history. They honored Prairieleut and Hutterite ancestors and their founding traditions and focused particular attention on making history come alive for younger generations of Prairie People. As a result, many developed a strong appreciation for and understanding of the Hutterian heritage.

The Hutterian Centennial Committee published various Prairieleut and Hutterite documents, letters, diary accounts, short histories, genealogical records, ship lists, and other manuscripts, and they assembled a not inconsiderable archival collection. Members of the Committee also interviewed older Prairie People on audio and videotape. In addition, the Committee sponsored historical tours, not only to Dakota Hutterian sites, but also to the eastern European homelands. The Committee encouraged positive relationships with the communal Hutterites, as well, and a number of Hutterites, including Dariusleut minister Paul S. Gross and South Dakota Schmiedeleut senior elder Joseph Wipf, participated in celebratory meetings held in Freeman in 1974.

The work of the Centennial Committee had, at minimum, helped Prairieleut descendents develop a greater appreciation for early immigrant leaders. For example, a few years ago, Ben Hofer, a Mennonite Brethren lay leader and farmer, brought out an old framed portrait of delegate Paul Tschetter, a direct ancestor, and hung it up in the living room. Until that time—according to spouse, Elsie—Ben had expressed little interest in his ancestral past.[26]

Notwithstanding negative comments about Hutterites, some Prairieleut had always maintained close relationships with colony members. As one person put it, "They are mostly a good people." Older Prairie People used the word *gmanschofter*, a form of the German word gemeinschaft, to indicate "those who lived communally," and particularly to denote relatives in the colonies. In recent years a Prairieleut widower who had colony friends had briefly courted a Hutterite woman. Although increasing numbers of Prairie People have developed friendships with Hutterites and are proud of their Hutterian ancestry, they invariably look the other way when confronted with invitations to join colonies, understanding that professional and material interests cannot be realized within the parameters of colony life.

With regard to the general context of Hutterian social relationships in the late 1990s, Saskatchewan Prairieleut Lesley Masuk made the following comment: "Hutterites have a tendency to treat Prairieleut as long-lost kin, which we usually are."[27] In the spring of 1984, a number of Prairieleut Hutterians, and one Hutterite defector—all enrolled in a "Hutterite Studies" course at Freeman College—spent an afternoon at the Bon Homme Colony trying to make sense of the ambience of colony life with the Rev. Jacob Waldner and his community. After a brief tour, the students were invited into the homes of colony residents, and the rest of the afternoon was spent conversing in both Hutterisch and English. The talk was candid and respectful. Prairie People and Hutterites seemed pleased with the opportunity to talk to each other. One saw no expression of bitterness or displeasure.

One Hutterite told the author that the Prairieleut "don't know much about our history," but that situation was slowly changing. One Hutter, a nineteen-year-old, who had been part of the Bon Homme visit, wrote that when the Rev. Waldner spoke about sixteenth-century Anabaptist history it had "seemed like he was talking about something that took place about fifty years ago." "I've never met a more friendly group of people," he added.[28] That comment resonated with one made by another student a few years later. In a presentation to his peers, the sixteen-year-old had exclaimed, "These were the most accepting people I have ever met!" denoting a non-judgmental straightforwardness not heretofore encountered.

Chuck Stahl, another student with Prairieleut ethnic background, wrote, "Being Stahl is a fairly common name among them, I've thought that it could be me living there, or that it was half-way possible that I could have ended up in a colony." Other students found that colony visits brought back memories from the past. Fifty-five year-old Amos Kleinsasser, a member of a 1985 student group, noted that a colony noon meal had reminded him of his "mother's cooking" when he was a child. Others expressed appreciation for the communal rationale. Twenty-year-old Jon Wollman noted, "I had a deep down good feeling, sort of like I was walking with 'real friends.' With everyone working together, they are able to get all their work done, while on our farms, we just don't have the time to do everything at once and so we get behind. I can see how they have an advantage in this way by living all together."[29]

Many Prairie People visited the colonies in the evening or on weekends for fellowship, exchange of stories, discussion of farming practices, a glass of homemade wine, or to sample the Hutterite cuisine. Those Prairie People who did not visit colonies often suggested that those who did were primarily interested in the wine. Doland area teacher and former track star "Smokey Joe" Mendel noted, however, that relationships with colony neighbors had usually been formed for other, what he called "good," reasons, and that there had been numerous visits "back and forth." He also admitted that the first request of many colony guests had been to turn on the television.

Mendel recalled that whenever his family had needed extra help on the farm the colony had always "sent boys" to assist them.[30] John P. Kleinsasser's diary account, as well, mentioned both the hiring of young Hutterite men to help with farm work and occasional visits to the colonies. Visiting back and forth continued in the late 1990s, but not as frequently as ninety years ago, when it had been a major Sunday afternoon pastime.

Another Prairieleut complaint about Hutterites was the latter group's lack of emphasis on evangelism. This contrasted sharply with the general Prairieleut interest—by mid-century—in active proselytizing. One Hutterite minister had agreed, noting: "I am uneasy because we have no missions."[31] As the Hutterites in the 1980s and 1990s experimented with evangelism for the first time since the wide-ranging efforts of the sixteenth century, Prairie People were pressed to tell a somewhat different story.

The Rev. Jacob Kleinsasser, for example, had helped establish a colony in Nigeria in the 1980s and had even visited potential converts in New Zealand. Manitoban Joshua Hofer had initiated contact with what became a small Hutterite colony in Japan. Many Prairieleut did not agree, however, with the communal message that Hutterites asked potential converts to embrace.

Evangelistic emphases within traditional ethno-religious groups often led, in an ironic form of piggy-backing, to more rapid assimilation with the dominant culture. As ethno-religious groups sought to properly contextualize the Christian message, they often, in that very process, compromised unique interpretive forms that were expressed in cultural practice.[32]

Ethno-religious groups that practiced separation and isolation were much more successful in retaining cultural identity than those that placed emphasis on outreach and openness. In the Prairieleut community, an emphasis on evangelism often played an important role in increasing the swiftness with which assimilation had proceeded.

It was ironic that the cultural isolation of the Hutterites had also—through the manifestation of "bedroom evangelism" and the retention of high percentages of members—led to much greater numerical growth than was found in the culturally assimilated Prairieleut churches. That phenomenon was confirmed in the burgeoning membership of both the Hutterites and the Old Order Amish in comparison to the more progressive Anabaptist assemblages.[33]

Some conservative groups insisted that a traditional approach to Christianity was in itself highly attractive to non-Christians. As Beachy Amish minister Philip Yoder told John Roth, "Conservatism is of course supposedly a detriment to our outreach. Yet we feel it is actually a great advantage. People looking in from the outside see us as clearly different from the world."[34] A more inclusive Prairieleut mission emphasis had in fact brought fewer people into church membership—in terms of total noncommunal Hutterian church numbers—than had the cultural isolation of the Hutterites.

New members have often been influential in pushing tradition-bound religious groups toward theological and ecclesiastical change. The Bruderhof, a group of 2,500 communitarians centered in upstate New York, provided the impetus, for example, for renewed Hutterite interest in evangelism, education, and worship style innovations after affiliating with them in 1974.[35] Less than twenty years later, however, differences of opinion with regard to theological and social emphases split the Schmiedeleut into two competing factions.

In the past two decades, there has been an increasing amount of defection from Hutterite colonies, particularly from the divided Schmiedeleut.[36] This has included the exodus of entire families, a phenomenon not commonly seen until recently.[37] Informal observation showed increased openness to family ownership of private property in colony apartments, as well as less ascetic consumption patterns.[38] Barbara Mathieu suggested correlation between increased emphasis on private prayer and lessened commitment to the communal ethos.[39] Still, the colonies continued to experience exponential growth.

Some individuals who left the colonies were still deeply affected by the communal experience. Ex-Hutterite Edna Hofer, who was born and raised at Riverdale Colony (Gladstone, Manitoba), and who later worked for the Mennonite Central Committee, returned to visit a Hutterite colony in the early 1980s. She wrote, "When I first learned that we were going to visit the colony, I was reluctant to go because of my Hutterite background . . . But when I saw their warm smiles of welcome as we were led into the house and introduced, I was able to relax."[40]

At the end of her visit Edna noted, "I have never been so homesick for a community way of life, ever, since I left the colony, as I was that one day." Other defectors, however, followed the more typical practice of heaping criticism on what had formerly been presented as a sacred way of life.[41]

One distinctive case involving Prairieleut/Hutterite contact occurred during the 1950s, when David Decker, from the Tschetter Colony (Olivet, South Dakota), enrolled at Freeman Academy. David was married and had children at the time so he did not attend high school classes as such. Instead he periodically picked up assignments and worked on a directed studies basis. After graduation, Decker proceeded to attend classes at Freeman College to prepare for teacher certification. His peers enjoyed having him on campus. At times they had even convinced him to stay for basketball games.

Decker had especially enjoyed getting to know Prairie People with whom he could converse in the Hutterisch dialect, though younger high school students had occasionally "snickered" at his "strange" dress and lack of cultural sophistication.[42] As Decker described the situation, he had "stood out." Decker found chapel services and many classes "helpful" but characterized some of the coursework as "impractical." He eventually became the first Hutterite to be granted teaching certification by the state of South Dakota and was later ordained as a minister.

The Hofer/Stirling Colony

Third and fourth generation Prairieleut descendents almost never joined Hutterite colonies or lived communally, but there were occasional exceptions. Barbara Glanzer Suess, for example, grew up in the Freeman-Bridgewater area and had attended the Neu Hutterthaler and Salem KMB churches at different times. She eventually, however, joined the Hutterites. Barbara had an aunt, also named Barbara, who had made the transition from Prairieleut to Hutterite earlier, marrying into the *Dariusleut* Wolf Creek Colony (Olivet, South Dakota) in 1912.

Before looking at the Barbara Glanzer Suess case, it is important to tell the story of Barbara Hofer, the aunt, and the unusual Hutterian community at Stirling that she helped establish.[43] Prairieleut "Aunt" Barbara, sometime after her first husband died, took an injured son to a colony bonesetter, where she had been introduced to Hutterite John B. Hofer, whom she later married. In 1918, Barbara and John had accompanied their colony to Raley, Alberta (near Cardston), to escape World War I–era persecution. Personal and ideological conflicts there led John, his brother David, and their families to move to Grassrange, Montana, in 1919, however, in an effort to establish a new colony. Unsuccessful, they had moved back to the Raley area in 1922.

John and David Hofer then formed their own independent "Hofer Colony," which functioned much like traditional colonies but had never been officially recognized by the Hutterites. The "Hofer Colony" initially comprised primarily the large extended families of the two brothers but had eventually attracted a diverse group of Prairieleut and Hutterite families, particularly through intermarriage. The Prairieleut/Hutterite ethno-religious mix is what made this group unique.

Hutterite Jacob D. Hofer, John B. Hofer's son, for example, had married Prairieleut Elizabeth Hofer. Hofer Colony member Katherina Hofer married Peter P. Hofer, a Prairieleut Hutterian from Saskatchewan.[44] Hutterite Anna Hofer had married Prairieleut Sam Wipf. There were many examples of this phenomenon, all of which have been researched by present member Jerald Hiebert.

A number of Hofer Colony members had also rejoined Hutterite colonies. One of "Aunt" Barbara's stepsons, another "David Hofer," for example, married Hutterite Barbara Hofer and had joined the Granum Colony.[45] The parents of leader John B. Hofer had, on arrival in the Dakotas, themselves lived as Prairie People.

In 1944, the Hofer Colony relocated to the Stirling area because of the construction of a dam near the Raley property. They began to call themselves "Stirling Colony." A few families stayed behind in Raley, however. Under the leadership of George Hofer and Eli Walter, they moved north four years later (in 1948) and established the "Brocket Colony," in the Pincher Creek area.[46] Eli Walter's two sons, George and Eli, had then continued to read the Hutterite sermons and to sing from the *Gesangbuch* into the 1990s, even though Brocket, too, had not been recognized by the Hutterites. (George Hofer, the father, had even composed his own "Hutterian" sermons.[47]) The Walters served, simultaneously, as pastors for the excommunicated Monarch Colony nearby.

Stirling itself represented a unique attempt by Prairieleut and Hutterites to establish a new communal assembly. Membership figures for 1994 showed that 61 percent of those in the church had some Prairieleut ethnic background.[48] Stirling was indeed the only example of successful communal/noncommunal unification in contemporary Hutterian history.

In the 1990s, in many ways, Stirling also exemplified what turn-of-the-century Prairieleut life, beliefs, and practices must have looked like. The only other significant ecclesiastical association of Prairieleut and Hutterites was found in the scattered house churches of the charismatic Global Mis-

Fig. 8.4. Stirling Mennonite Church, 1993. This congregation was founded by persons of Prairieleut and Hutterite background. Photograph by the author.

sions organization, which in 1993 had 150 former Hutterites and twenty persons of Prairieleut background in its membership.[49]

Stirling, like its predecessor, the Hofer Colony, was never recognized by the Hutterites, even though numerous attempts were made to establish some form of affiliation. The communal structure itself became optional in 1947. Members ate in the community kitchen and dining hall until 1962, however, and farmed collectively until 1990.[50]

In the mid-1990s the Stirling community buildings were still being used, and a sense of communalism was still vibrant. Many members lived in former colony living quarters and appeared to operate as one large extended family. As the Stirling Church *Standards* put it, "Our possessions are not our own to be used in self-interest and accumulation."[51] Throughout its history Hofer Colony members maintained close connections with the Hutterites, and a number of intermarriages had materialized, bringing to Stirling a continual influx of persons intimately familiar with communal life.

In 1964, the Stirling congregation affiliated with the Western Conservative Mennonite Fellowship, which was predominately Swiss ethnically and had close connections with various Amish groups. Six years later, in 1970, Stirling established the first private Christian elementary and secondary school in the province of Alberta. That action precipitated legal charges of truancy from local school officials, but the charges were thrown out by the courts the following year.

In the mid-1990s, John J. Hofer, son of the aforementioned (Aunt) Barbara, served the church as Bishop; Jerald Hiebert, who held a degree from the Associated Mennonite Biblical Seminaries (in Elkhart, Indiana), held the position of deacon. Hiebert and spouse, Barbara Walter (herself the daughter of long-time Stirling residents), also operated a bookstore and tract distribution center.

The Stirling church building itself was nondescript, a spare, clean, white building located on the east side of the former colony quadrant. As in Prairieleut churches a few decades ago, males and females sat on opposite sides on light maple benches, though one young girl insisted on running over to sit on her father's lap. The church service followed a Hutterian structure with hymns sung before, between, and after two sermons. The major sermon, delivered and prepared by the Rev. Hofer, focused on First Corinthians 9 and stressed that, without a willingness to suffer, the church would die. Emphasis was also placed on the lifestyle of the Anabaptist forefathers. The singing reminded one of Hutterite services, with a deep, heartfelt, almost chilling depth of commitment, expressed in loud voices, with no sense of reservation.

Services at a South Dakota Prairieleut congregation a week later created the sense that one had embarked on a journey outside the boundaries of the human time-frame. The modern Prairieleut congregation, in its more ornate sanctuary, sang in four-part harmony, with instrumental accompaniment, from non-Anabaptist hymnals. Men and women sat together and were dressed like businessmen and businesswomen. Many women wore makeup and jewelry; men, suits and ties. Most striking, however, was a large American flag propped up in the right front corner, and three smaller flags placed on a shelf underneath the cross, next to a vase of flowers.

At Stirling, alternatively, members of the congregation had knelt for prayer. Women wore headcoverings and did not cut their hair.[52] Members were not allowed to own televisions or radios, and, though photographs were tolerated, no family pictures had lined hallways proclaiming the significance of individuals. Stirling emphasized church discipline very strongly. Genealogical records revealed no hesitancy with regard to the administration of disciplinary action, including excommunication, when necessary.[53] The church also stressed pacifism and the Anabaptist heritage.

One difference between Stirling and the communal Hutterites was Stirling's opposition to alcohol use. Stirling also emphasized active evangelism and climactic salvation experiences. Stirling thus exhibited a unique mix of Hutterian and evangelical Protestant positions, which had occasionally attracted people of non-Anabaptist backgrounds. But, in general, because the fusion was, in many ways, prescriptively Hutterian, the membership had remained small. Still, Stirling offered a fourth model for Hutterians seeking to retain ethno-religious identity, a model somewhat different than that presented by Hutterites and by those Prairieleut who had joined General Conference Mennonite or Mennonite Brethren congregations.

Other Hutterian Encounters

A few Prairieleut relatives of Hofer Colony charter members had also embraced the communal gospel at different points in their lives. Barbara Glanzer Suess, for example, a niece of Stirling's Barbara Hofer, joined the Hutterites in 1946.[54] Previously she had taught school for nine years at the Rockport Colony (near Alexandria, South Dakota).

It was at the Huron Colony (near Elie, Manitoba) that Barbara first met and later—in 1949—married John Suess, a member of a small and rare group of nonethnic Hutterites.[55] The Suess family had at one time belonged to the Julius Kubassek communal group, which was associated with the Hutterites from 1936 to 1950. In February 1967, Barbara and John left the Hutterites and rejoined the Kubassek-led Community Farm of the Brethren, near Bright, Ontario. In the late 1990s, Barbara, now widowed, was still a member of that group, which had established close connections with Messianic Christian organizations. David S. W. Glanzer, Barbara's father, was known to have had great affection for many Hutterian traditions.[56] Colony members recalled that David S. W. had visited them often and had even attended Hutterite baptismal services.

Prairieleut/Hutterite relationships suggested that minimal residual interest in communal life as God's preferred way of existence continued to exist in the Prairieleut community. In contrast, with the exception of the Stirling assemblage, it was nearly impossible to find a Hutterite defector who had joined a Prairieleut church after the 1920s. One exception was a man named Dave Hofer (nicknamed "Colony Dave"), who had joined the Salem MB Church in 1971 after spending many years worshiping in a variety of Pentecostal fellowships.[57] Another exception was Hutterite Jake Waldner, who, in 1955, left the Clark Colony and joined the Emmanuel Mennonite Church (Doland, South Dakota). In 1960, Jake, a mechanic, had married Mary Gross, also a member at Emmanuel. They later moved to Huron and were, in the mid-1990s, members at the Mt. Olivet Mennonite Church.[58]

There were a couple of additional, albeit rare, examples of Prairie People who married communal Hutterites. In the mid-1960s, for example, Prairieleut Oscar Hofer married a Hutterite woman and joined the Spring Creek Colony (Lewistown, Montana).[59] In 1996, alternatively, Prairieleut descendent Lesley Masuk married Schmiedeleut defector Edward Waldner.[60]

In recent times, however, very few Prairieleut/Hutterite marital relationships had ensued. Most Hutterite defectors, furthermore, had not joined Prairieleut, or even Anabaptist, churches. Because of that fact and the absence of ongoing Hutter/Hutterite residential movement, the Hutterites no longer used the term "Prairieleut" to indicate persons who had turned their backs on community of goods. Hutterites used the term only to distinguish those Hutterians (and their descendents) who left colony life, or who had never chosen it during the first forty years of Hutterian settlement in North America.

The word "Prairieleut" itself was increasingly problematic for younger noncommunal Hutterians who did not understand German and thus did not fully comprehend what the word had once signified (though the term was recognized). Since an increasing number of Prairie People lived in towns and cities, not on farms established on the prairies, the term's literal meaning had also often become irrelevant.

Hutterites who left colony life from 1874 to 1914 had tended to settle in Prairieleut communities and join Hutterian churches. But, in the 1990s, most Hutterite defectors associated with charismatic and/or fundamentalist Protestant churches or attended no church at all.[61] Hutterite defector Samuel Hofer, a Saskatchewan publisher, for example, noted personal disinterest in organized churches at this point in his life.[62]

Former Hutterites who joined evangelical or Pentecostal congregations often had harsh words for the religious perspective they had left behind, generally associating it with an emphasis on doing good works. As one ex-Hutterite Pentecostal minister had put it (in a public sermon): "Now in the Hutterite colony, we were always taught you got to work your way into heaven. Work. You can't be . . . you can't do good enough."[63]

One family of ex-Hutterites had attended the Bethesda Mennonite Brethren Church in Huron for almost a year in the early 1980s but had eventually joined an Assemblies of God congregation instead. Bethesda pastor Eldon Busenitz suggested that the attraction of former Hutterites to Pentecostalism represented a reaction to the Hutterian formality they had consciously left behind.[64] Caroline Hartse proposed something similar in her 1993 study of Hutterite defector acculturation, noting that charismatic Protestant churches had often de-emphasized hierarchy, promoted missions, and conducted highly emotional and participatory services.[65] The latter characteristics were welcomed by ex-Hutterites who, in some parts of Canada, had created what Hartse described as a "network of evangelical Hutterites." The evangelical group actively proselytized in the colonies, even smuggling in tapes of sermons and church services.

That same kind of occurrence was evident in Sioux Falls (South Dakota), Grand Forks (North Dakota), Lethbridge (Alberta), Winnipeg (Manitoba), and in other places where significant numbers of ex-Hutterites had settled. The many Anabaptist churches located in those areas were not able to attract many Hutterite defectors. One colony member had informed a Prairieleut farmer that his "spiritual birth" had taken place at a Hutterthal Church (Freeman, South Dakota) worship service. That individual's commitment to communal life, however, had kept him in the colonies.[66]

Colony Schoolteachers

It is noteworthy that a great many Prairie People served as public schoolteachers in Hutterite colony schools. A 1992 study noted, remarkably, that 22 percent of non-Hutterite colony teachers had understood the Hutterisch dialect.[67]

Most Hutterite children studied in colony schoolhouses, where they were provided with certified teachers by local school districts. Prairieleut educators had often requested or were assigned to those positions. Paul Glanzer, for example, a descendent of one-time Hutterite schoolteacher, Jacob Janzen, had taught at the Millerdale Colony (Miller, South Dakota) for many years. Since Prairieleut teachers traditionally spoke Hutterisch and had maintained common cultural memories, if not practices, Hutterite schoolchildren had warmed up to them quickly. This made it easier for the children to adjust to the "outside" educational system they were forced to be part of.

Prairieleut schoolteachers noted that Hutterite children were less competitive than "outside" students and had a markedly limited awareness of world events.[68] Students at one Hutterite colony asked the author and his spouse, for example, if they were "Hofers" or "Deckers." They were the only two family names found at that colony.

Life aspirations, too, often conflicted with teacher expectations. One Prairieleut teacher noted, "If I encourage them to study hard so they can become a boss or minister, they reply, 'who wants to be a boss or minister?'" That response was not hard to understand, since Hutterites did not encourage active pursuance of leadership positions. In the Hutterite view God looked favorably only on the humble and self-effacing. An academically gifted young man, who was part of an experimental class established by the author and a Hutterite minister at the Wolf Creek Colony (Olivet, South Dakota) in the mid-1980s, had not been allowed to complete teacher certification requirements for a number of years, because it was thought that he might develop a proud disposition.[69] Hutterite children were very willing, however, to share materials and cooperate in classroom activities.

A controversial yet common practice was the utilization of Prairieleut schoolteachers as contacts between Hutterite individuals and the outside. Prairieleut teachers had occasionally served as conduits, for example, for the sale of black market Hutterite goods, such as beautifully decorated rolling pins and embroidered dish cloths. Markets had thus been expanded, and proceeds diverted from the colony treasury.

Some Prairieleut schoolteachers got involved in other questionable dealings as well. Some, for example, had arranged to have photographs developed for students and their families (who had indeed encouraged this). These operations were not acceptable to Hutterite leaders, even though almost every Hutterite had photographs in his or her possession; some even had wedding albums.

Subversive practices facilitated by Prairie People and other public school-teachers did undermine fundamental principles of communal existence. Many Hutterites, however, viewed those activities as "minor" divergences, believing they provided a necessary outlet for individualistic inclinations, which if not given catharsis might lead to large-scale defection and/or movement in noncommunal directions. One Hutterite put it another way: "Just go look in the minister's desk. You'll find all the pictures you're not supposed to have."

Prairieleut collaborators often felt sorry for their Hutterite students. Desiring to make life more pleasant for pupils and their families, they had felt there was nothing unethical about helping them, on occasion, subvert the communal system. Hutterite leaders were well aware that members sought out such collaboration but still labeled those activities as "sin."

Another "sinful" practice engaged in by Hutters, in association with Hutterites, related to unusual financial arrangements between employers and laborers. Prairieleut farmers who hired Hutterite boys had sometimes paid the workers twice, first with a check for the colony treasury, and second with cash to be pocketed by the workers. This practice was engaged in by many non-Prairieleut employers, as well, throughout the northern plains.

A Recent Visit

Contemporary noncommunal Hutterians engaged in a variety of relationships with the Hutterites. In the summer of 1992, Phil Hofer, for example, had visited Lehrerleut cousins in Montana along with his father, Egon, and two brothers. Phil got the sense that he was still accepted as a member of the Hutterite extended family.[70] A two-hour videotape of that Hofer-inspired Prairieleut/Hutterite interaction showed representatives of the two groups working and singing together, visiting, exchanging gifts and stories, and generally kidding around.[71] Watching the Hofer family engage the communal past and present while fishing, listening to a group of Hutterite girls playing harmonicas, and throwing horseshoes, one saw the display of a deep sense of mutual love and respect. This was confirmed by the large group of Hutterite people of all ages who had gathered on one colony yard at the time of the Hofers' departure.

Thirteen-year-old Emily Hofer, Phil's daughter, noted that her grandfather had promised to take her along on a return visit.[72] Though Emily did not appear to know a great deal about the reasons why her distant Hutterite cousins had lived communally, she was genuinely curious about their way of life and noted that by attending middle school at a Mennonite Brethren junior high school (in Reedley, California), she had been able to study alongside other girls with the "Hofer" surname.

A rare example of a Hutterite couple who had become Mennonites is provided by former Forest River Colony (Fordville, North Dakota) members Dave and Anne Waldner. They visited the colonies many times with their son, Ernie, during his growing up years, just as families had done at the turn of the century.[73]

In general, however, North American Prairieleut and Hutterites had become as different in the way they lived as two groups could become. In Ukrainian Russia, communal and noncommunal Hutterian groups had been virtually indistinguishable except for differences in economic arrangements. In America, a vibrant spirit of assimilation had caused the two groups to become radically different from one another; as different as the Old Order Amish are from members of the Mennonite Church.

The Prairieleut/Mennonite Relationship

The historical relationship between Hutterians and Mennonites is a complicated one. Relationships have ebbed and flowed in both positive and negative directions, depending on the era and place analyzed. This ambiguity is shown in the two quotations from the Hutterite *Chronicle* which precede this chapter. Each group criticized the other, yet they also exchanged money, personnel, and ideas. Both had Anabaptist theological roots but neither had accepted the other's interpretation of what the Bible demanded with regard to social and economic structures.

Personal relationships between the two groups increased after the Hutterites moved to Ukrainian Mennonite village areas in the 1840s. Two Hutterites had attended Mennonite secondary institutions, and some Mennonite schoolteachers held positions in Hutterite village schools. In addition, there were a number of marriages across ethno-religious lines.

Still the dominant Mennonite culture did not encourage the communal lifestyle of historic Hutterianism, nor did it look favorably on Hutterian social traditions. Since Russian Mennonites considered themselves culturally and educationally more sophisticated than the Hutterians, and since they had greater wealth and political influence, many Hutterites had indeed been attracted to the Mennonite way of life. Similar Anabaptist religious traditions helped further that relationship, so that Mennonite leaders had often referred to the Hutterians as "Hutterite-Mennonites." Before Russian law changed the political structure in 1870, the villages of Hutterthal and Johannesruh had, in fact, been under the administrative jurisdiction of the Molotschna Mennonite Colony.

Some Hutterian ministers even received ordination from Mennonites. Paul Tschetter, as noted, was ordained in 1866 by Mennonite minister, Peter Wedel. Jacob Wipf, Michael Stahl, and Peter Hofer were also ordained by Wedel, who had thus ordained men who became ministers in both communal and noncommunal Hutterian groups in North America.

Many Hutterians were also baptized by Mennonites. The busy Peter Wedel, for example, baptized forty-one Hutterians during his lifetime.[74] Marriage services, as well, had occasionally been conducted by Mennonites. In 1848, for example, Mennonite schoolteacher Daniel Janzen performed the marriage ceremony of Johann Hofer and Rachel Kleinsasser.[75] (Why a Mennonite schoolteacher had been authorized to oversee that ceremony has yet to be explained.) In any case, the eventual integration of the Prairie-leut churches with different Mennonite conferences made a certain amount of sense, whereas the merger of the communal Hutterites with a Roman Catholic monastic order—as was once suggested by an idealistic priest— would be difficult to fathom.[76]

Historic relationships were evidenced, as well, by the existence of Low-German Mennonite names among the Hutterian people. That occurrence was the result of a number of visits, marriages, and subsequent conversions, all of which had taken place in eastern Europe in the eighteenth and nineteenth centuries. In 1783, for example, three Low German Mennonite widows, Elsie Decker, accompanied by five children, her sister Maria, with one daughter, and Liset Knels, with two children, had joined the Hutterians while they were living at Wischenka, in Ukrainian Russia. Two years later, one Maria Isaak had been baptized into membership after marrying Lohrentz Tschetter. Maria was Tschetter's fourth wife and outlived him by thirty-one years.

In 1796, three Swiss Mennonite Schrag sisters from Volhynia had also joined the Hutterians. Since their offspring did not carry the "Schrag" name it had disappeared among the Hutterians (as had the name "Isaak"). In 1810, Low German Mennonite Peter Ratzlaff and spouse, Freni, joined the Hutterians at their new colony, Raditchewa.[77] The Ratzlaff children later married into Hutterian families.

In the end, male heirs of the Decker and Knels families had introduced two Mennonite surnames into Hutterian society. The Ratzlaffs, however, had no male heirs. But Prairieleut leader John Z. Kleinsasser's first wife, Anna, was a granddaughter of Peter Ratzlaff.[78]

It was hard to keep the Mennonites and Hutterians apart. After the Hutterites had relocated near Ukrainian Mennonite villages, a number of additional marriages had taken place. A Mennonite Janzen family from the Chortitza Colony had been involved in many of these marriages.[79] Jacob Janzen, a schoolteacher in the village of Hutterthal, for example, had married Maria Waldner, a sister of Schmiedeleut Elder Michael Waldner, sometime after the death of his first wife.[80] Jacob Janzen was probably a son of the aforementioned Daniel Janzen.[81] In 1870, one Helena Janzen had joined the Hutterian Church by marrying another Michael Waldner. Six years later, one Paul Glanzer married Katherina Janzen, a daughter of schoolteacher Jacob.

Mennonite A. W. Fast also married a Hutterite girl, though that marriage, like many others, did not appear in official Hutterian records since it had evidently taken place in a Mennonite church. Strangely, when his spouse died a few years later, Fast gave up their three children for adoption. They were taken in by different Hutterite families and the name Fast entered Hutterian society. In the Dakotas, most members of the Fast family had joined the Prairieleut Hutterthal Church.[82]

Others had participated in similar interethnic marriages. The Mennonite surname Entz entered the Hutterian world in 1846, for example, when one Peter Entz was married to Maria Wipf. Twenty years later, Peter's son, also named Peter, had been married to Hutterite Sarah Dekker by the Rev. Michael Stahl. Another son, Johann, married one Susanna Hofer in 1871 (Stahl conducted that ceremony, as well), and Johann's uncle, Jacob Entz, was married to Hutterite Rebecca Glanzer. The Entz men had obviously been greatly attracted to Hutterite women. As noted earlier, Hutterites Andreas and Mathias Miller had joined the Chortitza Mennonite Colony as early as 1819.[83]

Recent research by Fresno (California) genealogist Alan Peters has suggested the need for a radical reanalysis of commonly held Anabaptist ethnic interpretations. Peters believed that many names that were commonly accepted as Dutch/Low German were in fact Hutterian, or at least Austrian/South German, in origin. This came about, according to Peters, as the result of a numerically significant migration of Anabaptists from Moravia and southern Germany to Prussia—where many Dutch Mennonites had relocated—in the seventeenth century.[84]

This was a fascinating hypothesis based on Peters' study of surname spellings but did not explain why the Prussian Mennonites had continuously defined themselves as Dutch/Low German and had continued to use the Dutch language in church services until the mid-eighteenth century.[85] If the ethnic infusion happened as Peters suggested, the Austrian/South German enclave must have been, in some way, unilaterally assimilated by the dominant Low German Mennonite culture. That same phenomenon had indeed occurred when Mennonites "became" Hutterians and vice-versa.

In another interesting historical twist, many persons in the East Freeman (South Dakota) Mennonite community were in fact the direct descendents of Swiss Mennonite Katherina Schrag and Hutterian Andreas Waldner. Katherina, one of the Schrag sisters who had joined the Hutterians while they were living at Wischenka, had eventually married one Andreas Waldner, with whom she had six children. After Andreas died, however, Katherina had taken her sons and daughters back to the Mennonite villages in Volhynia. Her three male children had then continued the Waldner name, now spelled "Waltner."[86] Andreas Waldner himself had been a son of Johannes Waldner, the well-known Hutterite minister who had written the *Kleingeshichtsbuch* and had actively promoted a communal Hutterianism.

Mennonitization and Assimilation

The fact that Low German Mennonites had influenced the character of Hutterian life in Russia did not please many Hutterian leaders. In South Dakota, Hutterian leaders convinced most Hutterians to stay in the ethnic churches, and they continued to conduct services in a traditional manner. But it was difficult to keep the young people apart. In at least one case, a Low German Mennonite, Peter Becker, and a Hutterian, Christina Wollman, had had a child out of wedlock.[87]

In South Dakota, the initial refusal of the independent Prairieleut churches to join North American Mennonite conferences was thus not surprising. It was foreshadowed in Paul Tschetter's essay, "Report of Why We Had to Leave Russia," wherein Tschetter insisted that the Hutterian people in Russia had departed from the "path of our forefathers."[88] Tschetter had not referred to a departure from communal Christianity. He was alluding instead to Mennonite disinterest in Hutterian traditions.

Tschetter described the Russian Mennonites as "proud" and "presumptuous" people who would, as he put it, "crowd themselves into any office they possibly could." Tschetter spoke out against "business deals and quarrels" and a "spirit of the world," which, he felt, had negatively influenced Hutterians of that era. In Tschetter's view, the Tsarist ukase, announcing elimination of many Hutterian privileges, had provided divinely directed impetus for a Hutterian spiritual "awakening" in North America.[89]

Eventually all of the independent Prairieleut churches, however, had merged with Mennonite conferences. Hutterdorf, the last holdout, had joined in 1952. All of the churches had united with the General Conference Mennonite Church, the same group, ironically, that the majority of Russian Mennonites had joined earlier. Similarly, in 1960, all but one Prairieleut KMB congregation had affiliated with the Mennonite Brethren Church, another large group comprising primarily Russian Mennonite descendents.

These were not easy decisions for the Prairie People to make. It was particularly difficult for those who had continued to attend the independent Hutterian congregations. The federation of those churches with the General Conference Mennonites diminished the possibility of preserving a unique noncommunal Hutterianism. It indirectly, but powerfully, sealed ongoing Prairieleut disassociation from the traditions of the Hutterites. Even for KMB Prairie People, merger with the predominantly Low German Mennonite Brethren had meant a dimunition of ethnic Hutterian influence.

Other forces of assimilation, such as the public school system and patriotic wars, had significant influence on the concurrent Americanization of Prairie People in the United States. Prairieleut Hutterians had jumped somewhat hesitantly into the steamy waters of the melting pot, desiring acceptance as legitimate American denominationalists. Mennonitization provided assistance by

Table 7.
Prairieleut Denominational Affiliations in North America[a]

Prairieleut Churches	North American Mennonite Conferences
Independent Prairieleut congregations (1874–1952)[b]	
	General Conference Mennonites (1952–)
KMB Prairieleut Congregations (1886–1960)	
	Mennonite Brethren (1960–)

Notes:
[a]This table shows the joining together of all of the Prairieleut churches with two of the largest North American Mennonite conferences.
[b]The independent Prairieleut congregations joined the General Conference Mennonites individually, at different times, during the years, 1941–1952.

allowing the Prairie People to retain some traditional customs and religious practices while simultaneously modernizing at a rapid pace. It had also, however, caused Prairie People to think less of their original ethno-religious identity.

It was ironic that for many centuries Hutterians had prided themselves on following biblical teachings that called Christians to be "in the world but not of the world" with regard to dress, culture, language, and political philosophy. Now a desire to become "of the world," and as quickly as possible, had enveloped Prairieleut communities. That desire was then rationalized by emphasizing that the world was not such a bad place after all, at least not in rural North America. Mennonitization made that process palatable and less stressful. It provided theological rationalization and identificational redirection. It did for the Prairie People exactly what it has done historically for disaffected Amish families who turned Mennonite.[90]

Relationships between Prairieleut and Mennonites were not always as positive as they have become in recent times. Notwithstanding a number of marriages across ethnic lines, intermarriage, in general, had been actively discouraged both in Russia and in North America, and a selective Hutterian genetic pool maintained for decades. In the United States, a tradition of marrying within the group prevailed into the pre–World War II era, with Swiss and Low German Mennonites, as well, advising against such "intermarriages." One Prairieleut said he recalled the purchase of land in South Dakota "Mennonite areas" described as "moving across the Iron Curtain."

In the 1990s "Hutter jokes" were still told in Dakota Swiss Mennonite circles and were much akin to traditional "Polish" or "Irish" jokes.[91] In retaliation, Prairie People created their own repertoire of "*Schweizer*"—Swiss—jokes or was it the other way around? In actual fact, as Norman Hofer noted, most of the jokes were typical ethnic jokes, with each group telling the same stories and then "filling in the blanks."[92] Prairie People also told jokes about Hutterites. Most contemporary ribbing was good-natured, although it, perhaps, spoke to underlying prejudice.

The question, "How many (select an ethnic group) does it take to replace a lightbulb?" for example, incorporates the name of whatever assemblage is being made fun of, with the answer reflecting idiosyncratic social traditions within the group under assault. If the group attacked were the Hutterites, the answer might sound something like this, "You need four people. Two preachers to give you permission, one boss to get the light bulb, and one man to screw it in."

At mid-century, relationships between Prairie People and Low German Mennonites also occasionally showed some strain. One Prairieleut writer noted that, "Contrary to modern practice [at church conferences] lodging and food were provided free of charge as were full meals during the sessions at the church. This was in contrast to our Low German Brethren when often it was announced for their meetings, *"fur heises Wasser wird gesorgt"* [hot water will be furnished]."[93] This statement—which I assume was written with no prejudice intended, and perhaps humorously—was read to a seventy-year-old farmer of Prairieleut ethnicity in the summer of 1993, after he had suggested that relationships between Low Germans and Hutters had always been excellent and without friction. Upon hearing the quotation he had immediately laughed and said, "There are certain things you shouldn't read." Cultural insularity did breed difference.

Californian David L. Hofer recalled that during his first visit to South Dakota after marrying Low German Mennonite Sylvia Kliewer, he had often been asked: "Is she one of ours?"[94] In the early years of South Dakota's Salem KMB Church, Prairieleut and Low German groups had even met separately for worship, so there was a "Hutter Salem" as well as a "Low German Salem."[95] The two groups had joined together on the first Sunday of each month. According to David W. Tschetter, the two groups had met separately because "they lived far apart," not for reasons of ethnic difference. But, as Alan Peters put it, "The Hutterites soon took over."[96]

In Onida, the Emmanuel KMB Church did not employ a non-Prairieleut minister until 1959. The Salem Church maintained an even stronger record. From 1886 to 1960, when Kenneth Ontjes (who was married to a Hutterian) served as interim pastor, the congregation always had Prairie People in ministerial positions. From 1975 to 1993, the Rev. Phil Glanzer resurrected that tradition.

Ethnic Relations in Zion

Members at the Zion Church, in Dinuba, California (which closed its doors in 1990), also noted the occasionally strained relationship between Prairieleut and Low German members. Patriarchs of the congregation noted the "discomfort" many older Prairie People felt with regard to relationships with any non-Hutterians. One person said there had been difference of opinion even with regard to the kind of food prepared for church social events. Another emphasized that Prairieleut conservatism had manifested itself in a rigid adherence to traditional music—in reality to evangelical gospel hymns introduced in the early 1900s. Others attributed difficulties in local evangelism to Hutterian ethnic exclusivity.[97]

Though there were a few Low German Mennonites on Zion's list of charter members, the majority had been part of the Kleinsasser extended family assemblage. Particularly during the first few decades, church leadership positions had been dominated by Hutters. As Alan Peters described it, "When the church council met it was a family reunion."[98]

The Zion Church relied heavily on gifted Prairieleut spiritual leaders into the early 1970s, ordaining a striking succession of John Z. Kleinsasser descendents, including son, John J., and grandson, Virgil. California Hutters noted that local non-KMB Mennonites had sometimes told jokes about them, but that such comments had focused, primarily, on the KMB practice of baptizing forward and were not directed at ethnic distinctives.

Over the years, and particularly before the 1960 merger with the Mennonite Brethren, the Zion Church had sent out a remarkable number of international missionaries, as had KMB congregations in general. This was particularly notable owing to the small size of the conference, which never had a membership that exceeded 2000. In 1953, for example, the Krimmer Mennonite Brethren had thirty-six missionaries positioned on five continents.[99]

Zion, in its heyday, also operated two temporarily successful mission chapels in white migrant towns in the Reedley/Dinuba area, settlements that had originally been developed by eccentric Mennonite philanthropist Henry Bartsch. These were places in which the larger Mennonite Brethren churches in the region had often feared to tread.[100] Letters from those leaving Zion in the 1980s, however, revealed dissatisfaction with the congregation's "closed-in family" character.[101] According to one Low German member, "love of the family has usurped the love of the scripture."

A concerned member with Prairieleut background noted unrest, dissension, and the existence and influence of "parking lot committees."[102] In August 1988, the Young Adult Sunday School class drafted a letter to the congregation that stated, "We can no longer fellowship in a worthy manner at Zion Church."[103] The attraction of a number of members to Los Angeles-based charismatic organizations caused additional tension. One individual who left in the early 1970s wrote exuberantly, "There is no need to transfer my membership to any place other than Heaven. Praise the Lord!"[104] It was extremely difficult, however, for older members to "end it all." Even those no longer in attendance had been saddened by what transpired at Zion. Former member and pastor, Clarence Hofer, told the author that Zion's closing had in fact been "the tragedy of [his] life."[105]

Prairieleut KMB Influence

Perhaps the Prairieleut "invasion" of the Krimmer Mennonite Brethren Conference in the late nineteenth century had been comparable, in terms of ethnic and ideological influence, to the infusion of the Carinthian ancestors of Hutter KMBs into the Transylvanian Hutterian villages a century earlier. The KMB Conference, while it existed, had been the only Mennonite denomination in which the Prairie People had consequential numerical influence.

Of the twelve KMB congregations in existence at the time of the merger with the Mennonite Brethren in 1960, half had been heavily Hutterian in ethnic composition. Fourteen of the twenty-four KMB national committee members, furthermore, were noncommunal Hutterians.[106] Since this was a small conference with high membership expectations, active involvement in ecclesiastical affairs was demanded and people had come to know each other very well. Theologian Marlin Jeschke, who grew up in a Low German KMB congregation in Waldheim, Saskatchewan, described a tremendous sense of "informality," "family warmth," and "goodwill" between Low Germans and Prairie People, who, at annual conferences, had "worked things out together."[107] Low German KMB churches in Kansas, however, had actively promoted the MB alliance, isolating and upsetting South Dakota congregations.

Since the 1960 merger, many Mennonite Brethren leaders had sensed a diminished sense of conference-wide commitment from the Prairieleut congregations. One Hutter leader responded to that concern with the following statement: "What do they expect from us? We no longer have any say as to what goes on at the higher church levels." Others noted a downward spiral with regard to Prairieleut congregational membership.

The Rev. John J. Kleinsasser, who pastored the Zion KMB Church and two South Dakota Prairieleut churches from 1938 to 1959, had continually opposed the integration of KMBs and Mennonite Brethren. KMB missionaries polled in the 1950s had also strongly opposed the merger.[108] A particular fear of the missionaries was that they would no longer be recognized, as Joe Walter described it, as "the missionaries of every KMB church" and would be assigned instead to single congregations within the large MB denominational superstructure.[109] In 1953, the KMB Board of Foreign Missions put it this way: "We have an ever-increasing missionary zeal and if we join [merge] we are afraid this missionary zeal will be dampened. The value of a small conference which affords a personal acquaintance . . . would be lost."[110]

Some California Prairie People blamed the KMB/MB merger for the death of the once-vibrant Zion church community. In 1993 Clarence Hofer told the author that though he had supported integration in the late 1950s he now regretted it had ever happened. An almost identical sentiment was expressed by Mennonite Brethren leader J. B. Toews, who had supported the movement toward unification from the other side.[111] Others, however, reminded critics that the MB Conference had been true to its word in offering ongoing support to former KMB mission activities, and that the KMB Conference was too small to have ultimately "made it" on its own.

In any case, before 1960, Zion's outspokenly committed membership had held an outpost status in a small geographically diverse denomination. Much of the *raison d'être* for Zion's existence had emerged from a sense of denominational ownership—interconnected for many with Hutterian ethnicity—which in no way could be duplicated within the arms of the larger 36,000 member, and predominantly Low-German constituency, of the Mennonite Brethren Conference.

The Schools and Interethnic Relationships

In southeastern South Dakota, Freeman College and Academy played a major role over the years in bridging the gap between the various Prairie People and Mennonite assemblages. An interesting mix of Prairieleut, Swiss, and Low German Anabaptists, representing three different Mennonite conferences, plus the independent Hutterian group, had helped found the institution and had served together on the school's Board of Directors. Daily personal contact and similar religious training encouraged positive relationships and, ultimately, numerous marriages between the various Anabaptist student groups.

This does not mean everything ran smoothly. Prairieleut publisher and Board member Jacob J. Mendel contended that the initial fund drive for the college had not attracted many Prairieleut donors.[112] Hutters, in turn, pointed to the numerical dominance of Swiss Mennonites on the faculty. Interpersonal relationships established by generations of young people, however, had helped to break down many ethnic and religious barriers.

Although KMB students were definitely in the minority, the Salem Church had been a strong supporter of the schools, providing many students and significant financial assistance. The Rev. David S. Wipf, as noted, served as head of the Bible Department in the 1930s. Salem's 1986 history stated, furthermore, that ministers from outside the community had been struck by the "quality of services," which they "credited mostly to the effect of the local college on the church."[113]

There were times in the 1980s, however, when there were more Salem members on the faculty than students attending the schools. There were a number of reasons for Salem's defection, including the sense that East Freeman Mennonites dominated decision making processes through a larger corporate voting bloc. Others complained about limited athletic possibilities and academic electives and/or viewed support for public schools as a civic responsibility. Theological differences between Mennonite Brethren and General Conference Mennonites also influenced some Prairieleut dissatisfaction with the College and Academy.

Two hundred and sixty-eight students with Hutterian family names had been graduated from Freeman College and/or Freeman Academy at the time of the fifty-year celebration in 1950.[114] Fourteen Prairie People had served on the Board of Directors, one as President (Sam Walter), seven as secretary, and four as treasurer. Yet of one hundred and thirty-two instructors listed during that period, only eight names could be identified as Hutterian. Perhaps there was a correlation between numbers of teachers of Prairieleut ethnicity and traditional Hutterian skepticism with regard to academics.

In any case Freeman College and Academy had played a major role in helping alleviate tensions between Hutter, Swiss, and Low German Mennonites. The location of three different Anabaptist ethnic groups in one geographic area made Freeman a community with particularly unique problems and opportunities. To get the three ethnic groups to understand and accept each other had been a slow but successful process.

On the West Coast, KMB Hutters and Low German Mennonite Brethren had joined together in 1943, to establish the Immanuel Academy secondary school in Reedley.[115] That was an easier marriage to hold together, since there were no major theological differences with which to complicate matters. Clarence Hofer, a principal advocate of the school and a member of the school's first faculty, had encountered significant opposition, however, from public school supporters.

During the years 1943–1993 only six persons with Hutterian names served on the Immanuel faculty, yet numerous Prairie People sat on its Board of Directors.[116] The most prominent Prairieleut supporter of the institution was Ferd Hofer, who served two terms as Board Chair, five as Treasurer, and one as Secretary. Since one found much greater Hutterian representation on the Board of Directors, and in the student body, than on the faculty itself—as had also been the case in Freeman—one inferred a lingering hesitancy with reference to academic and/or pedagogical pursuits.

One noted, alternatively, the conspicuous presence of the Rev. Jącob D. Hofer, in the founding, organization, and operation of the early Pacific Bible Institute (later Fresno Pacific University). Not only had he served on that school's Board of Directors (1942–1947) but, as David L. Hofer noted, "That idea [for a Bible college] was in his mind years before anything was ever started."[117] In the view of many Prairieleut, Fresno Pacific's official history, published in 1993, had not given enough credit to the Rev. Hofer.[118] (Others felt Clarence Hofer had not been appropriately recognized for his role in the establishment of Immanuel Academy.)

In 1956, KMB and non-KMB Prairie People, along with Low German General Conference Mennonites and Mennonite Brethren, founded yet another school, James Valley Christian, near Huron, South Dakota. That school was another place where various Anabaptist ethnic groups worked together on a common project.

In conjunction with a mutual interest in Freeman College and Academy Low German, Swiss, and Prairieleut Mennonites had worked together, as well, in the annual *Schmeckfest* (festival of tasting) activities. Schmeckfest, which has become a major tourist attraction, was started in 1959 by the Freeman College Women's Auxiliary for the purpose of raising money for the enlargement and remodeling of college kitchen facilities. In the late 1990s, the festival was a three-day event that attracted visitors from across the United States. Schmeckfest included a bill of fare that featured a variety of Hutter, Swiss, and Low German ethnic specialities, and a country kitchen that sold an assortment of cheeses, sausages, poppyseed pastries, and homemade noodles. Also included in the festival were musical productions; historical presentations; tours of the Freeman Academy Museum, Archives, and Historical Village; and crafts demonstrations.

Prairie People, Hutterites and Mennonites

Near the end of the twentieth century, relationships between Prairie People and their communal kinfolk show improvement. This is ironic, since there is, perhaps, less to agree on (with regard to mutual interpretations of Christianity) than ever before. Still, many Prairie People are engaged in a search for their Hutterian roots. Though the late twentieth-century interest in ethnicity has often degenerated into a fad that moves people to seek out only the quaintest of historical customs, those who engage in such explorations often find themselves simultaneously exposed to traditional ideological positions. Cultural artifacts sometimes serve as conduits for deeper, transformative understandings.

What made the South Dakota Prairieleut situation unique was the fact that the historical beliefs of progenitors were still adhered to by a dynamic socio-religious communal organization situated close at hand. Possibilities of mutual impact increase substantially in that kind of circumstance.

In many ways KMB, MB, and GC Mennonites have made the Prairieleut transition from traditional Hutterianism—to a more mainstream evangelical Protestantism—a less stressful one, though acceptance of characteristic beliefs and practices has not been achieved without conflict. In the General Conference, for example, a strong Anabaptist stream continually pushed Prairieleut Christians in that group to resurrect historical beliefs and practices. Simultaneously, however, association with GC Mennonites had meant the quickened expiation of Hutterian cultural distinctives—and even many ecclesiastical and theological emphases—which had given the Prairieleut a unique identity within the Anabaptist family.

Prairie People, Hutterites, and Mennonites all had Anabaptist social and theological roots. Because they agreed historically on a variety of religious issues—and particularly because of their joint adherence to pacifism—it had been easy for people to lump them together. In this century, however, the Hutterites, like the Old Order Amish, established a definitive and separate identity via distinctive dress, lifestyle, language, and belief traditions, successfully withstanding the forces of American assimilation. Prairie People and Mennonites, alternatively, were acculturated at a very rapid pace.[119]

Contemporary Prairieleut often expressed embarrassment with regard to their communal Anabaptist cousins. Because of a similar history and kindred traditions, they had also, ironically, felt the need to compete with the Hutterites, even on issues of spirituality. One thus heard comments about one group being better at evangelism than another.

Since the early 1970s, however, many Prairieleut Hutterians have developed a new sense of respect for the integrity of historic Hutterian—or at least Anabaptist—principles. One finds a similar stance taken by many non-Hutterian Mennonites attracted to a more community-oriented interpretation of the Christian faith. The Hutterites, in response, have simply continued to follow religious guidelines contained in the *Lehren* they have been reading for 300 years.

9

Folk Beliefs, Dreams, and Visions

For such persons today, visions and apparitions still come, the Lord revealing to him what he intends and what shall happen. But not to those who occupy themselves with fool's follies, and lay themselves open to sleep like an ass or a pig.
Hans Friedrich Kuentsche, 1659

Whatever the true fact, a minister was eventually called out to the house to pray 'against the bad spirits.' This ruined all their fun.
Mary J. Glanzer, 1981

Folk Beliefs

This chapter documents a number of cultural folkways that provided a common bond for persons of Hutterian ethno-religious background. North American Prairie People continued into the twentieth century to accept a number of southern and eastern European folk superstitions. They, too, illuminated the general character of the Prairieleut and, for a long time, helped define Hutterian uniqueness.

In eighteenth- and nineteenth-century Hutterite *Kirchenbuch* (church book) birth records, for example, the sign of the zodiac had at times accompanied the birth date.[1] This continued to be the practice of a few North American Prairieleut. Stirling minister John J. Hofer's father, for example, placed an astrological sign next to his birthdate in the family Bible.[2] More recently a Hutterite woman ascribed a plethora of underweight colony children to the power of an "evil planet," believing that the heavens above had some influence on such happenings.

More significantly, the Prairie People believed that one should never say anything nice about a child, such as, for example, "what a beautiful baby girl." That would lead, it was thought, to "something terrible" happening to the infant. Neither should one say to a neighbor, "That's a beautiful team of horses." Something bad might then happen to the horses. A better thing to do, in fact, was to spit on the animals.[3]

To comment favorably on anything that belonged to someone else was considered covetous and idolatrous. This was particularly relevant for communal Hutterites, who had worked hard to eliminate manifestations of individualism. Prairie People, as well, placed a good deal of emphasis on giving up self-will and being obedient to God and the church. "Careful you don't schreien" a child, older Hutters would say, referring to a curse often delivered unintentionally.

If a baby was good-looking, therefore, it was said to be "pretty enough to be schreied."[4] Older Prairieleut remembered parents and grandparents using that expression in the belief that negative power lay dormant, ready to explode, whenever one person praised another. The curse might manifest itself, for example, in dangerous fevers and illnesses. Lesley Masuk noted that a Lehrerleut woman in the mid-1990s had commented with regard to Masuk's previous visit: "You looked so beautiful that day that I thought I cursed you."[5]

The word "schreien" itself was derived from the German "*Schrei,*" meaning "scream." The schreien curse was thought to predominately affect infants and young farm animals. Thus it was sometimes referred to as *kinderschreien,* though it could, as a satanic force, strike anyone.

Some Hutterites continued to tie red ribbons around the wrists of infants to protect them from the schreien malediction, the color "red" being associated with the protective "blood of the lamb" in the Old Testament. To effect a cure for stricken victims, one simply wiped "the eyes and face with a red cloth" or had the infant's mother lick out the eyes.[6] The first time anyone saw a new baby it was best, once again, to spit on it.[7]

It was also believed that being schreied might cause the person cursed to be greatly desired or admired. This in turn could lead the individual, for social and/or theological reasons, to withdraw from others, constituting the onset of the anfechtung experience (see chapter 6).[8] In that rendition the schreien curse reminded one of the eastern European evil eye imprecation. A Hutterite minister had thus described (to Peter Stephenson) a feeling of physical debilitation after a congregant praised him for a sermon he had delivered.[9]

Schreien belief had certainly represented an effective way to deal with the problem of "natural" gifts, whether intellectual, artistic, or physical, which might lead one person to be given more attention than another. It provided strong support for a system of communal self-abnegation. An academically gifted Hutterite boy in the 1990s might thus be held back from achieving all that he could, for fear that he might become proud and self-centered. South Dakotan Levi Tschetter, the only Hutterite with a masters degree, had achieved that honor "on the sly," without colony permission.[10] Schmiedeleut young men, who were securing college diplomas in increasing numbers in the late 1990s, had still been cautioned against making statements indicative of individual pride.[11]

Older Prairie People noted that Hutterians in general did not compliment each other very much fearing the development of self-centeredness.[12] Evelyn Hofer noted that her parents had never praised her "for anything" while she was growing up.[13] There had been no fear of schreien in all of this —it had also not indicated a lack of love or concern in any way. Evelyn's parents had approached childrearing in that manner because they wanted their children raised with humble spirits, in the "fear" of God.

A number of Prairie People used the term *"obschreien,"* to describe the form of schreien indicated when individuals had been "praised up" for significant accomplishments. Deserved compliments might again lead to something disastrous for the individual praised.[14] Hutterites, however, suggested that opschreien really meant to discontinue the schreien spell. The latter made more sense, considering the way in which the prefix *"ob"* was defined in Hutterisch. Perhaps the former interpretation had emerged from an anglicized rendition of the prefix *"ob"* which sounded like the English "up." That miscommunication showed the way in which Hutterisch phrases had changed and differed even between and within the various Hutterian groups.[15]

Folklorist Alan Dundes noted that in all cultures believing in the evil eye, "to praise" was to "invite disaster," and that it was commonly thought that the use of saliva, or even urine, was helpful in treating those who had been cursed.[16] This all fit Hutterian belief and practice. It is significant, though, that the Hutterian religious injunction against individualism had become associated through the years with something akin to the southern and eastern European evil-eye superstition. A paranormal belief had been reconstructed to ward off iniquitous self-glorification.

Peter Stephenson—who has studied this issue more than anyone—also noted the close relationship between schreien belief and the traditional Hutterite opinion that "seven evil spirits" were engaged in constant battle with the Holy Spirit.[17] Based upon his understanding of certain Hutterian sermons, Stephenson suggested theological foundation for schreien belief. Though modern Hutterites appeared perplexed by such associations, many agreed that Stephenson's analysis "made a little sense." Schreien belief was closely related to the constant sense of struggle between "flesh" and "spirit" Hutterites readily acknowledged.

The Prairie People had also thought that one could cure a sick horse by pulling off one's sweatshirt or undershirt, then wiping the animal with it.[18] This was also an effective way to cure human illness. If a dog howled at night, furthermore, that meant someone was soon going to die. Saskatchewan Prairieleut Edna Wurtz said she was taught that if one hit the ceiling with a whip this also meant somebody was near death.[19] Some Prairie People thought that throwing a small egg over a barn would bring bad luck, and that calves should only be castrated when the moon was full.[20]

Prairieleut folk sayings often had as their focus an encouragement to work hard from sun-up to sun-down. "Just only thinking about it does not tie up the cow," expressed that sentiment, as did the saying, "Hunters and fishermen often sit by empty tables." These sayings all had their contradictory renditions, as well, creating a sense of paradoxical humor, as was found in the following examples: "Work makes life a pleasure but laziness strengthens the body," and "The early riser eats himself into the poorhouse but the long sleeper keeps warm."[21]

One found analogues to Prairieleut folk beliefs among other ethnic groups in the upper Midwest, as well, and particularly among Germans-from-Russia. The Rev. Eric Kaempchen, who served numerous German-Russian churches in South Dakota, including a Protestant congregation in the Freeman area from 1939 to 1963, found his parishioners to be a very superstitious people, even into the 1960s. They had treated his own presence, for example, as a kind of "holy protection."[22]

Laverne Rippley noted that, according to Germans-from-Russia tradition, if one baked an extra loaf of bread for the cat and dog at Christmas it would help ward off hunger for the rest of the year.[23] Some Hutters remembered hearing parents and grandparents say the same thing. According to Reuben Goertz a few East Freeman Swiss Mennonites who lived nearby had even practiced the "black arts" from the so-called sixth and seventh books of Moses.[24]

The Prairie People had also developed folk remedies for illness and nagging ailments. One of the most widespread practices was the production of salves to bring health to "man or beast." One Prairieleut remembered being asked by his grandmother to gather "sheep pebbles" in a half-gallon pail. He thought it was ridiculous at the time and had been teased by friends who found out about it. But his grandmother made a salve out of the manure, purportedly quite effective in healing boils. Medical salve had also been made from cow udders.[25] Goose fat, too, had been used to promote the healing of wounds, as had soft cow dung.[26]

Walter Kleinsasser noted that, whenever he cut himself as a young boy "or had anything that caused bleeding," his mother had told him to "urinate on the sore." According to Kleinsasser—who wrote about this in 1990 —"that saved a lot of money on medicine."[27] Much earlier, Prairieleut Jacob Janzen suggested that the tips of poplar leaves, mixed with lime blossoms, provided the base for an excellent medicinal "tea" that was an effective cure for gout, arthritis, and asthma.[28] A number of Prairieleut had also practiced bonesetting, which has been continued as a medical tradition in some Hutterite colonies.

Publisher Jacob J. Mendel and his wife once laid a sick child on the floor of their living room and had a rat terrier jump across the baby, to effect healing. It was evidently a common practice to have dogs jump over colicky babies to make them feel better.[29] It was considered unwise, on the other hand, to let babies eat apples. The thinking here was that infant digestive systems were not developed enough to deal with such an Eve-tainted fruit. "Don't give them apples until they're grown," was a common saying, and some modern holistic health practitioners agreed.[30]

It was also conventionally believed that bloodletting would cure disease. Blood was sucked out of the body by leeches or with flexible cups with a lot of suction. It was also popular in Prairieleut communities to use German herbal tonics such as *Alpenkrauter* (for stomach aches) and *Heiloel* (for sore muscles).[31] Alpenkrauter, with its high alcohol content, was sometimes asked for by those who only "acted like [they] needed it," according to one individual, "and," he added, "boy was it good."

Some contemporary Prairie People, and many Hutterites, used "ZMO Oil," a mixture of camphor, oil of eucalyptus, and other ingredients, which was similar in nature to Heiloel. Older Prairieleut preferred Heiloel, however, which was still available.[32] "Genuine Green Essence"—called "green drops" by Hutterites—had also been taken for stomach aches and head colds. It was similar in character to Alpenkrauter, having a high alcohol content, intermixed with oils of aniseed, fennel, rosemary, bay leaves, and other natural elements. Katherina Hofer Tschetter, who grew up in the Neu Hutterthaler Church, wrote in her autobiography about a bad eye infection she had contracted at age ten. Her parents had taken her "to the Colony People" since one of the men there "claimed to know something about the treatment of eyes."[33] Her eye trouble had disappeared after "several weeks" of treatment.

Ghost stories had also been prevalent among the Prairieleut, though, along with folk remedies and superstitions, they were not much in vogue in the late 1990s. Some ghost stories had been told to entertain and frighten listeners and were not thought to be true. But others had been believed. Certain narratives caused a lifelong fear of cemeteries and dark places for some listeners.[34]

One story concerned the ghost or ghosts said to have resided at Mary J. Glanzer's home near Huron, South Dakota.[35] The house itself had originally been constructed by a Hutter who had moved to California with the John Z. Kleinsasser clan in 1910. According to Glanzer, "It [the apparition] always came in the morning, about four o'clock." Evidently, its first appearance to Glanzer had occurred one night, after she had told her sister Annie (who lived with her) that she needed to get up early the next morning to prepare for a wedding.

At 4:00 the following morning, a tall man and a woman wearing a shawl had entered her room, lifted up the covers, and pulled her out of bed. Mary, after the initial shock, thought that she had perhaps been confused and that Annie had woken her. But Annie insisted that she had been asleep.

Mary Glanzer saw the ghosts three times subsequently. On one occasion, a guest who had been given the haunted room had appeared running down the stairs late one evening, screaming that he was "fleeing from a ghost." Others who were interviewed said bones had been found in the wall of the haunted room and that a murder had once been committed there. Whatever the true facts, a minister had eventually been called to the house to pray "against the bad spirits." According to Glanzer, this had "ruined all their fun."

It was popular in some families to tell ghost stories often. The children had not always believed them, yet it still scared some so much they had a hard time sleeping. One woman was known to tell stories—she insisted were true—about "chairs moving."[36] Ghost stories were still used by some Hutterites in the 1990s to scare children into staying away from places where they were not wanted, such as tool sheds.

Another folk superstition suggested that if a door opened and no one was there that "something bad had happened" to someone. After listening to four different people tell this story one day, it was difficult not to become concerned when the front door of a Prairieleut residence opened and no one came in. But it was just the wind. Still, spirits of the dead had often been sighted by Prairie People in the past. Women, especially, were thought to be susceptible to the workings of ghosts and more superstitious than men.

Family Stereotypes

The communal Hutterites have traditionally considered certain individuals and families to be *Sabot;* that is, they were thought to have inherited physical or psychological characteristics that caused them to exhibit singular leadership abilities, stubbornness, laziness, stinginess, obesity, wisdom, or whatever. Characteristics were defined negatively only by nonmembers of a particular Sabot group. These portrayals then aided social identification and were, perhaps, related to generations of inbreeding.[37]

Older Prairie People continued to recognize many familial characterizations though they were unfamiliar with the word "Sabot." Studies conducted by Karl Peter and Ian Whitaker suggested that the Hutterites themselves used the word only (as they put it), "in relatively private circumstances when speaking among themselves, and usually not in direct conversation with persons who are being differentiated by the ascription of characteristics . . ."[38] The word *"Sabot"* itself was probably derived from the archaic German word *"Schabab,"* used to indicate persons with whom one wanted "nothing to do."[39]

It was more typical, however, for Prairie People and communal Hutterites simply to associate certain psychological and social characteristics with particular surnames. Persons with the family name Mendel, for example, were described by many Hutterians (communal and noncommunal) as "quick learners and big talkers." One Hutterite minister added: "You know the Mendels, you can't deal with those people." Another person noted that the Mendels "start a lot of projects and are impatient." Mendels also had the reputation of being people you could "count on to get things done quickly" and were excellent bonesetters, a gift that older Prairieleut and Hutterites said was rapidly being lost. Still, as one Hutterite put it: "There are a few good ones left." That same individual noted that the Mendels had the ability to heal "in their blood."[40]

With regard to another surname, one Hutterite had remarked: "No Decker ever suffered from lack of material resources and travel allowances." Peter Gordon Clark demonstrated that there were, in fact, significant correlations between some family names and the persons who had served in colony leadership positions.[41] A study of positions held by persons named Decker, for example, showed that the Deckers were more highly placed than any other Schmiedeleut family assemblage.[42] Deckers were also said to be people who "go to extremes."

No similar determinations of accomplishments and/or liabilities have been made with regard to Prairieleut community surnames. Hutterites and older Prairie People hold definite opinions, however, about the characteristics associated with all eighteen existing Hutterian names, even though continual marriage across family lines has, perhaps, rendered the descriptions somewhat meaningless.

In the colonies, family loyalties continue to influence decision making. Social typologies are thus extremely important. As Hutterite minister Paul S. Gross once put it, with regard to Pincher Creek Colony in Alberta, "The Hofers had the advantage, and could outvote the other three."[43] In other words they were able to outvote the Wollmans, Grosses, and Stahls.

Since so few family lineages had interconnected over the course of centuries, many commonly held perceptions were connected to specific surnames among both Prairie People and Hutterites. One could thus go into a room with virtually any group of ten to fifteen older noncommunal Hutterians or Hutterites and get an immediate response with regard to name characterizations, though unanimous agreement with regard to representations was not always possible to obtain. I tried this—many times. What follows is what I discovered.

The Hofers, for example, were often described as "stubborn" and "ambitious"; Glanzers as "sensitive," "good organizers," and "proud." Stahls were known to be "easy-going"; the Tschetters, "quick learners." Wurzes were portrayed as "poor businessmen" but "tolerant" and "open-minded"; Wipfs as "shrewd" but "unsophisticated."

Kleinsassers were known to be "good leaders" and "innovators." One person, recognizing individual differences, noted, however, that this was only the case if they were the "real Kleinsassers." This statement took me aback. One could evidently distinguish between those Kleinsassers who exhibited stereotypical Kleinsasser characteristics and those who did not. To continue, the Entzes were "progressive" and the Wollmans "quiet and reserved." The characterizations were neverending and not entirely consistent. Hutterians had pointed to individual Wollmans, for example, who were not "quiet and reserved." "Hofers," furthermore, though they were generally described as stubborn, had also been characterized by some as "open to changing their opinions."

Some portrayals were based on rather speculative historical/genetic foundations. Grosses, for example, were described by many Hutterites as "not deeply spiritual." Sources then ascribed that tendency to the fact that in 1782 Andreas Gross (the father) had refused to join his family when they became members at Wishenka. Since all contemporary Hutterian Grosses were descended from Andreas, genetic influence on family disposition was assumed.

Among Hutterites and older Prairie People the traditional names were often associated with idiosyncratic traits. In general, though, it was more compelling to think in terms of general Hutterian characteristics than about the peculiarities of specific families. That which distinguished one family assemblage from another in colony life, or from among an older generation of genetically unified Prairie People, was not nearly as great as that which differentiated Hutterians generically from the North American population as a whole.

Characteristic designations were much less applicable for contemporary Prairie People, in any case, than for Hutterites, owing to the increasing number of outside marriages. At one time, however, those distinctions had helped clarify what made one's "brothers and sisters" tick. The Prairie People also used nicknames extensively to denote family relationships and/or personal characteristics. Prairieleut birth records and church membership lists, as well as conversations with older Prairieleut, thus abounded with references to "Silver Fox," "Dafatal," "King David," "Blind Anna Basel," "Tatala Jacob," and even "Loose" (Hofer), to give a few examples.[44] Hutterthal Church Records referred to "Pickle Bill," "Baer Yop," "Diamond Dick," and "Peach," among others.[45]

Dreams and Visions

Many Prairieleut in the past also believed in the significance of dreams and visions, some individuals even consulting books on dream interpretation. Some Prairieleut described a condition they called a *"Frass,"* in which stricken individuals—usually older people—had been so scared they could not stop from shaking.[46] In recent times such phenomena have not been as evident, though they have occasionally resurfaced. One Prairieleut farmer in the Olivet, South Dakota, area was known, for example, for a vision in which he had been physically lifted up into the air by angelic beings.

The Hutterites have placed a significant emphasis on dreams and visions since at least the year 1859, when Michael Waldner reinstituted communal life in the Ukraine. It was a vision from God, as noted, which had caused Waldner to give up private property. Even though some Lehrerleut and Dariusleut Hutterites believed Waldner's various visions to be semi-delusional, the Hutterite *Chronicle*, the Hutterian epistles, and the *Lehren* also affirmed the reliability of dreams and visions, when given under the right conditions and with God's specific direction. Jacob Hutter himself had had an important vision that moved him toward communitarian Christianity.

Michael Waldner's own seminal vision proceeded in the following manner: In a "trance," a "spiritual guide" had appeared to Waldner and directed him to journey to two different places. First, the guide showed him the indescribable beauty of heaven and a collection of many thousands of angels. He had then directed Michael's attention to hell with its terrible pain and suffering.

After observing both locations, Michael asked the spirit, "Where will my place be?" The spirit responded with a question: "Can you tell me, whether at the time of the flood, anyone was saved from the judgment who was not in the ark?"

Michael answered in the negative, that "No one outside of the ark had been spared." The spirit continued: "Then you know where your place will be. The ark is the communion of the Holy Ghost, which you do not observe."

This pronouncement caused Michael to weep bitterly as he realized the "lost" state of his own soul and the hell-bound future of the Hutterian people. The spirit then instructed Waldner to give up his private property and to live in community. Waldner had obliged and become the founder of the Schmiedeleut Hutterites.[47] The image of the colony as "ark" was of course an old one, originally suggested by Hutterite leader Peter Walpot in the sixteenth century.

In the years that followed, Waldner continued to have other meaningful dreams and visions. One of them dealt specifically with the Prairie People. In a "spiritual dream," as it was characterized, Waldner said he had seen "many of our people [Prairieleut] among the damned."[48]

Waldner also reported the dream of an unmarried Hutterite woman who had foreseen the unification of the three communal Leut groups, something that Waldner had tried very hard to bring about. According to Waldner, the woman had seen three fountains, one leading toward the Schmiedeleut, another toward the Dariusleut, and a third in the direction of the Lehrerleut. She noted that, "when they took water out, one from the other," the water from "all three" fountains had run "together."[49] That prophecy was never fulfilled, however, owing to the interpersonal conflicts discussed in Yos Hofer's diary account and in *Das Klein-Geschichtsbuch*.

There were also numerous stories of dreams and visions leading noncommunal Prairie People to leave the steppes and join the communal brother-hood. Below are a few examples of that phenomenon.

According to most sources, sometime in the late 1880s, Prairieleut settler Fred Waldner had a dream while napping on a *Schlafbank*, a traditional German sleeping bench.[50] In that dream, Waldner had seen Jesus lying dead in a corner of his living room, an apparition that was terribly upsetting to Fred. He had no interest in seeing Jesus dead and especially not in his own house.

At this point in the dream, Jesus had slowly come to life but appeared to have been resurrected not in Waldner's house but in what Fred recognized as Michael Waldner's home at Bon Homme Colony, where Fred had occasionally visited friends and relatives. As is common in dreams, Fred Waldner awoke before the scene was completed, just as Jesus was being resurrected from the dead.

Three days later the meaning of the dream became clear to him: Fred Waldner's house was not really "his own." In fact, while Fred lived in it, Jesus was, in a spiritual sense, dead. Jesus would give life to Fred's house, via his spirit, only if Fred chose to live in community. In essence, Jesus would empower him with supernatural direction only if he sold his farm and joined a colony. Amazingly enough, Fred had proceeded to do just that.[51]

Another version of the Fred Waldner dream, told less often, had the corpse of Jesus flying from one Prairieleut church to another, trying to find true believers. In that version, Schmiedeleut elder Michael Waldner played a major role, clarifying for Fred that Jesus was "alive" only in the colony. After listening to the dream, Fred Waldner's wife was said to have announced to him, "Your place is amongst the Hutterites."[52]

Hutterite Fred Waldner was later recognized for raising an amazingly pure group of communal offspring. Thirty-six of thirty-seven grandchildren, for example, stayed in the colony. Fewer than ten of his great-grandchildren defected, providing an abundance of Waldners for the Schmiedeleut.[53]

Another Prairieleut settler, the Rev. Michael Stahl, who in Russia held the position of Senior Hutterite Elder, had an equally striking vision.[54] According to most sources, in an initial dream—which Stahl experienced while still in Russia—an angel had taken him by the hair, like the Old Testament prophet Habakkuk, and carried him across the Atlantic Ocean. The heavenly spirit had then set him down in "nice, flat country" on a stone, somewhere in Dakota Territory, and showed Michael some people living in small shacks out on the prairie. "They call themselves Hutterites," the angel had said, "but they are all corrupt—even the ministers—and will not last." Michael dreamt this sequence twice in one night but had not been sure what to make of it. When he arrived in the Dakotas, Stahl decided to farm his own privately owned land and had not joined the colonies.

One day Stahl had hitched up his oxen and headed down a river trail north of present-day Freeman, toward a farm where he intended to purchase some cows. On the way he sighted a peculiar stone that seemed so familiar to him he stopped and reflected on when he had seen it before. "Suddenly it seemed," he later noted, that it was "exactly the rock which I had seen in my dreams in Russia." This was a great shock for Stahl, as the angel in those dreams had said that the Hutterian people living in that area were headed toward a damned state of eternal existence. Stahl was particularly concerned because he was a Prairieleut spiritual leader.

Deciding to deliberate further on what he had just seen, Stahl sat down on top of the rock that had precipitated his deja vu experience and looked first to the left, noting that all the Prairie People lived in that direction. To his right, then, Stahl could envision the colony people, the Hutterites. He noted that this was exactly how the new world scene had been pictured in his original dream in Russia.

So stricken was the Rev. Stahl by that whole experience, that he had gone home and told his wife they were joining the colonies immediately. They loaded up all of their personal belongings, even taking wet clothes from the line outside, and had moved into the Wolf Creek Colony. Stahl was then placed "on trial" for a short period of time but had been allowed to retain his ministerial status.[55] Parts of the Stahl revelation were very reminiscent of Michael Waldner's vision of a fire-burning future for noncommunal Hutterians.

The pre-twentieth century experience of various Anabaptist groups showed at least occasional confidence placed in God-given dreams and visions. Noncommunal Hutterian Wilhelm Janzen, for example, a "heavy drinker," who was at times brought home from bars by his children, had a dream in which he was told that the devil was going to "get" him. This scared him so much that he quit drinking completely and become a "zealous" Christian.[56] Wilhelm, who had settled in Yorkton, Saskatchewan, in the early 1900s, was a brother to Hutterite schoolteacher Peter Janzen. Contemporary Hutterite ministers too placed a certain trust in messages given via supernatural suggestion as did some Prairie People.[57]

Anabaptist recognition of supernaturally infused reverie was essentially confined in the late twentieth century, however, to members of charismatic Mennonite congregations. Perhaps this was one reason many Schmiedeleut defectors were attracted to Pentecostalism. In the past, however, dreams and visions had been given much greater credibility. Noted KMB leader Jacob A. Wiebe's wife, Justina, had a number of visions while in a trance-like state, which took her "outside of" herself and included revelations of heaven. God revealed himself to early KMB Hutter convert John Tschetter by lighting up a dark cellar where Tschetter had been praying. Nineteenth-century Amish-Mennonite "sleeping preacher," Noah Troyer, had delivered sermons of one to three-and-a-half hours in a trance-like state.[58]

Mary J. Glanzer—of ghost story fame—had also had a vision of her sister Annie's upcoming funeral.[59] Some of the details in her vision, such as Annie's casket being taken out of the house through a window, and the eventual marriage of Mary to her widowed brother-in-law, corresponded to what ac-

tually happened later. At the end of her life Mary had also expressed an unusual desire to have one of her grandchildren die with her. Evidently she
feared going to the grave alone. That desire may also have been related to
the traditional Hutterian view that the deaths of children were a kind of
"blessing," since the children were thus spared earthly temptations, and
everyone knew exactly where they would spend eternity. One Hutterite had
thus told John Hostetler: "I sure wish I would have died when I was a kid."[60]

In the 1950s, apparitional beings had returned to earth once again to
spread the communalist message. In 1956, a man named "Alfred" wrote a
letter to a Hutterite acquaintance in which he described an encounter with
"two men" who had been suspended in air, "several inches from the ground."
The meeting had taken place near the town of Freeman and the ghosts had
been "dressed as Hutterites."

They had introduced themselves, furthermore, as the two Hofer martyrs
from the World War I era and told "Alfred" they were "waiting for the resurrection of the dead." In the interim, they felt compelled to preach the
communal gospel—along with the horrors of alternative Christian models
—just like the spiritual beings who had presented themselves to Michael
Waldner in the 1850s.[61]

In the late 1980s, Paul G. Tschetter (a grandson of the Rev. Paul Tschetter)
recorded an "imagined" dream sequence based on early recollections of his
grandfather's character, as well as what he described as a "personal incident."
In that speculative re-enactment, the Rev. Paul Tschetter had a dream—in
the course of undergoing a second and fatal stroke—which found him standing by a river beckoned by someone on the other side. Jesus had then appeared, taken Paul's hand, and escorted him across the water, where, on the
other side, the two met Paul's wife, Maria, who had died four years earlier.
At that point Jesus disappeared, and Paul and Maria had "walked hand-in-
hand to that New Jerusalem."[62]

Myths and Memories

Folk beliefs and practices, ethnic myths, and supernatural
visions, provided a central cultural focus for the Prairie People, perhaps, as
important as the various social and religious customs noted earlier. In many
ways, folk traditions were as consequential to the continued existence of a
sense of peoplehood as language or ecclesiastical structure.

The various folk customs were not, however, valued by most modern
Prairie People whether or not such persons had interest in other Hutterian
traditions. Beginning in the 1930s, many "old wives tales"—as they were
called—had been attacked forcefully by the better-educated individuals who
began to assume leadership in the Prairieleut churches. These individuals
viewed many of the folk traditions as unbiblical and downright dangerous

to the development of a newly vitalized evangelical faith. Even the belief that God might show his discerning presence through the process of casting lots sounded too magical and unscientific for a sophisticated modern audience.

Although that (third) generation was not successful in completely eliminating the various folk conventions, the age group that followed, beginning to accede to positions of influence in the 1960s and 1970s, had even less tolerance for ancient superstitions. Older Prairieleut were thus often laughed at, or at least laughed with, when they attempted to introduce Hutterian folklore to their grandchildren and others. Most folk traditions gathered dust and were eventually lost.

Contemporary noncommunal Hutterians also associated some manifestations described in this chapter with various "New Age" beliefs and practices. Hutterian folk traditions were thus not allowed to continue to provide the kind of central experiential denominator that might have assisted in the reconstruction of a modern Prairieleut identity. The traditions of the folk continued to be observed, however, in the Hutterite colonies.

IO

. . . .

Contemporary Religious Beliefs

Do not let the way be lost completely and the old boundary
stones moved!
Andreas Ehrenpreis, 1662

Membership in a religious ethnic group affords a sense of
personal security which is unattainable in the same way in a
wider society. This membership gives continuity with the past,
rationale for the present and hope for the future.
Miriam E. Warner, 1985

Conservatives, Neoconservatives, and Evangelicals

During the winter of 1987, a car driven by a man from the
Freeman area hit a section of ice on state Highway 1 and ended up skidding
off the road and into the frozen-over Silver Lake. The car broke through
the ice, and the man found himself standing in freezing water "up to his
neck, calling and waving" for help. Many cars drove past on the highway
nearby, but no one stopped until a Prairieleut man noticed him. The individual was pulled out, "near death," and was then taken to a hospital where
he recovered.

This story was told by a retired farmer in an attempt to show that in terms
of general character Hutters today were the same "Good Samaritans" they
had always been, having consistently stressed that word and deed be interconnected. That may be true. Prairieleut ways of thinking and acting have
undergone major change, however, in the past fifty years.

After World War II, the Prairieleut community discovered peace and
prosperity. Economic conditions improved significantly until the national
agricultural crisis of the 1980s, which created financial hardship for farmers
and accelerated the process whereby large majorities of young Prairie People

entered nonagricultural professions. Within the Prairieleut-Mennonite churches a number of different subgroups emerged, each holding a different vision for the future.

Into the 1940s, an older generation of Prairie People had held on tenaciously to traditional religious customs, such as the use of head coverings for women, the German language, the common communion cup, kneeling for prayer, a multiple ministry, and the separation of sexes in church meetings. Traditionalists had not been successful, however, in maintaining any of those observances. As they moved in the direction of the graveyard, so did those rituals and practices.

Other historic Hutterian beliefs had greater longevity. A remnant of older "conservatives" and a number of younger "neoconservatives," for example, continued to believe in conscientious objection to killing for any reason, a less materialistic way of life, and an ethic of mutual aid and semi-communal accountability.

Discussion of contemporary Prairieleut church life, in both the General Conference Mennonite and Mennonite Brethren conferences, is perhaps most appropriately undertaken via a tripartite definitional categorization of general viewpoints. Contemporary Prairieleut had, essentially, taken three positions with regard to theological and ecclesiastical issues.

The "conservative" position was held primarily by an older group of church members, generally born before 1930, who wanted to preserve many Hutterian social rituals and customs. Some conservatives were at least minimally interested in maintaining historic theological viewpoints, as well. Many were not.

A second position, "neoconservativism," was held by a younger group of Prairie People who were not particularly interested in resurrecting ancient Hutterian social customs, but who had developed a significant interest in Anabaptist theological emphases. Though neoconservatives had little interest in living communally, they were curious about other theological aspects of the Hutterian past. Some were also interested in Hutterian folk traditions.

A third position, referred to in this work as "evangelicalism," was more specifically concerned with constructing a social and theological pathway that connected the Prairieleut churches to mainstream evangelical Protestantism. That was the position held by the Prairieleut majority, incorporating all age groups.

It is important to note that the term "evangelical" has multiple definitions in modern North America. It was thus at times employed by all three Prairieleut groups to describe their respective positions. All three, for example, differentiated their beliefs from historic Hutterianism by emphasizing the importance of a personal relationship with God, through Jesus. The collective Prairieleut perception was that the Hutterites had focused too much attention on holy living and the observance of historic rituals.

For purposes of analysis, however, the term "evangelical" receives a more limited definition in this chapter. Prairieleut "evangelicals," as defined here, are those persons who had little interest in Hutterian cultural or theological roots.

The second position, neoconservatism, was the frame of mind most open to making connection with the Hutterian ideological past. Neoconservatives accepted the traditional pacifism of the sixteenth-century Hutterians and placed major emphasis on the social dimension of the Christian faith. Neoconservatism was a minority emphasis, however, which was at times assisted, sometimes hindered, by the fact that Prairieleut congregations (KMB and non-KMB) had decided, in the last half-century, to align themselves with large Mennonite denominations with tens of thousands of largely non-Hutterian members.

In the move from secthood to denominational status, religious groups in North America have tended to move from smallness, exclusivity, and strict ethical precepts toward more liberal interpretations of what it means to be a church member.[1] This was exactly what transpired as the independent Hutterian congregations joined the General Conference Mennonites and the Prairieleut KMBs merged with the Mennonite Brethren.

Both groups, who had previously worked only with other Prairie People (in the independent Hutterian churches) or at least much of the time (in the KMB Conference) now found their unique ethno-religious traditions overwhelmed by large non-Hutterian church organizations. Prairieleut congregations were then pushed to either accommodate to mainstream Mennonitism, join non-Mennonite denominations, or die like the Zion Church in the west and the Ebenezer Church in the midwest.

Simultaneously, communal relatives of the Prairie People had been discussed in a Calvinist denomination's Sunday School series under a subsection entitled, "Sects and Cults with Christian Roots," the appellation implying that Hutterites were Christian only with regard to a foundational belief in the Bible. According to that 1980s-era study guide, the Hutterite "view of the Christian and the world may be seriously warped."[2]

Though Prairieleut neoconservatives found the suggestion amusing, and though they had attempted to retain many Hutterian theological traditions, they did not usually hold positions acceptable to the majority of their Prairieleut brothers and sisters. Some neoconservatives criticized United States military involvement in Vietnam. Others attacked the materialism of American society and, more specifically, the materialism of the Prairie People themselves. Other neoconservatives became interested in environmental issues and the threat of nuclear proliferation. These positions created much new controversy in the various Prairieleut churches. The resulting tension was felt in a particularly dynamic way in congregations where there was significant, balanced disagreement between neoconservatives, evangelicals, and conservatives.

Fig. 10. Hutterdorf Church, circa 1930. Photograph courtesy of Hutterian Centennial Committee.

Dispensationalism

In order to attempt analysis of Prairieleut thinking and practice in the past half-century, one is forced to engage in some generalization, noting exceptions when necessary, and recognizing throughout that there is no one all-inclusive Prairieleut perspective. Each decade brought new interpretive analysis with regard to all of the positions described. But, in general, Prairieleut religious belief and practice in the late twentieth century, whether depicting Mennonite Brethren or General Conference Mennonites, looked something like that described below.

Prairieleut theology had been heavily influenced by dispensationalism, a method of biblical analysis developed by Plymouth Brethren founder John Nelson Darby and popularized through the *Scofield Reference Bible*.[3] This system broke history into a number of "eras" and suggested that many of Jesus' teachings were not normative for twentieth-century Christians. Jesus' Sermon on the Mount sayings, for example, were deemed idealistic statements meant for a future "Kingdom of God" era. In the dispensationalist view, beliefs such as pacifism, refusal to take an oath, and unwillingness to enter into lawsuits—all historically supported by Hutterians—were not tenets Christians were expected to follow.

As William Trollinger noted with regard to the theological emphasis at the fundamentalist Grace Bible Institute, "Nonresistance was optional at

Grace. Dispensationalism, on the other hand, was not."[4] Trollinger also found that despite many courses in Old Testament studies, Grace had offered few classes dealing with the four Gospels.[5] Many Prairie People had attended Grace, as well as the Moody Bible Institute in Chicago, and Biola, in the Los Angeles basin.

Dispensationalists also engaged in considerable speculation concerning the End Times, embracing a doctrine called premillennialism.[6] The traditional Hutterian position—amillennialism—suggested that no one could know definitively when Jesus would return to earth. That stance was rejected by dispensationalists. Whether or not Jesus would return to earth before or after establishment of a "millennial" Kingdom of God on earth, whether one could know this definitively, was a major concern for premillennialists, who believed Christians would be swept from the face of the earth sometime before that event, as depicted in the Book of Revelation.

It is important to note that premillennialism had not been the traditional position, even of the Krimmer Mennonite Brethren. Founder Jacob A. Wiebe, for example, had believed that in a sense Jesus was "already here," and had been since the Christian community had been founded. Still, as early as 1890, the KMB Conference, responding to difference of opinion, had decided to be "open to scriptural teaching" with regard to Wiebe's stance, since many premillennialist church members disagreed with him.[7]

End Times speculation became an important avocation for some Prairie People. Bethel KMB Church members, Elizabeth F. and Samuel J. R. Hofer, for example, published a 167-page treatise, entitled, *God's Way of Salvation in the Seven Dispensations*, wherein they speculated on futuristic topics and noted that "the new earth's blessing" would follow "Jesus Christ's second coming."[8] Pastor and evangelist Samuel Hofer, a perennial Sunday School teacher and missions worker, assisted his second wife, Elizabeth F., in a number of additional writing projects, always under the appellations "E. F. and S. J. R.," though Elizabeth was the "real theologian," according to many. Samuel Hofer himself was once described by a KMB leader as "on fire for the Lord."[9]

The evangelistic fervor and, apparently, high moral standards of dispensationalist leaders had, ironically, convinced many Prairie People to accept their unique and fairly rigid theological interpretations, which in turn caused many Prairie People to move away from traditional Hutterian and Anabaptist positions. The Bible itself continued to be recognized as an ultimate authority by all Prairieleut groups. All Hutterian church constitutions recognized the Old and New Testaments to be "inspired and infallible."[10] Differences of opinion related to the way in which holy writ was to be interpreted.

The dispensationalist approach called into question virtually the entire Sermon on the Mount canon, the central focus of historic Anabaptism. One Prairieleut neoconservative noted that when dispensationalists thus called themselves biblical literalists it was similar to hearing communists describe themselves as democrats. In any case, dispensationalists exerted major impact on the theological views of many noncommunal Hutterians, whether or not the average man and woman in the pew recognized the exegetical term "dispensationalism," which ministers on stage were promoting.

The Peace Position Under Attack

Most modern Prairie People also believed that Christians should be willing to kill other human beings in certain circumstances. In addition to employing dispensationalist arguments, contemporary Prairieleut supported that position by directing attention to the existence of violence among God's "chosen people" in the Old Testament and the way in which God himself had caused those who had worked against him to die.

Hutterians had traditionally viewed the Old Testament differently, as only a partial revelation of the truth, a truth not fully given until Jesus came to earth. Jesus' life and teaching had been recognized, correspondingly, as the full revelation of God's plan. Hutterians viewed the New Testament as foundational and the central focus around which other sections of the Bible were to be interpreted.

With regard to the peace position and the Old Testament, Hutterians had thus historically agreed with founder Jacob Hutter who had written, "David and others did fight. It was customary in their time . . . for at that time servanthood had not yet been distinguished from sonship and the road to glory had not yet been revealed."[11] That position helped provide rationale for the often violent displays by ancient Hebrews and by God himself, as pictured in the Old Testament.

In the Hutterian view, Jesus' Sermon on the Mount proclamation, "You have heard it said, 'An eye for an eye and a tooth for a tooth,' but I say to you, 'Do not resist one who is evil,'" overrode the Old Testament injunction as a kind of progressive enlightenment. In other words, the Jewish people had indeed "heard" something that was not a correct understanding of God's ultimate will for the future.

A majority of Christians, since at least the fourth century, however, had not accepted this Anabaptist/Hutterian belief in significant disjuncture between the Testaments—at least not on the peace issue. Throughout the centuries, Hutterians and other Anabaptists had been heavily persecuted for holding that perspective. In the late 1990s, however, Prairieleut nonpacifists were at times the most outspoken opponents of the nonresistant. "They are often more hostile than 'outsiders,'" noted one individual. This made young Prairieleut hesitant to accept the historic exegetical approach even though church leaders continued to teach Sunday School classes with titles like "Theology of the Anabaptists."[12]

It was noteworthy that, at the 1987 Triennial Convention of the North

American Mennonite Brethren Conference, delegates had never reached consensus on whether a minister in the conference should be asked to support the peace position. A motion to that effect, submitted by the Board of Reference and Counsel, had received 60 percent support when voted upon. There was so much vocal dissension, however, that no final decision had been reached. Simultaneously, the conference had no difficulty, however, gaining support for a resolution insisting that Mennonite Brethren pastors "both teach and preach" baptism by immersion.[13]

The traditional Hutterian method of biblical interpretation that had supported pacifism was not even known by many Prairieleut in the 1990s. Though most assemblages belonged to Mennonite conferences, whose confessions of faith supported and encouraged conscientious objection to war, and most Prairieleut church constitutions—both MB and GC—still gave creedal support to nonresistance, in practice, most Prairieleut congregations gave at least equal time to alternative interpretations, or simply avoided the issue.[14]

Elizabeth F. and Samuel R. Hofer's pamphlet, *Most Popular Bible Questions and Answers Everybody Ought to Know*, for example, included no discussion of the peace issue, nor were social issues, or even traditional Hutterian or Anabaptist practices, mentioned. The treatise had focused almost entirely on the issue of "assurance of salvation" and on End Times speculation, making the assumption that questions about other social and theological issues were not either "popular" or important. We know that Samuel Hofer was a pacifist from other sources, not from his books.

The great irony was that the very reason the Prairie People came to North America in the first place, giving up homes and growing economic strength in Russia, was to safeguard young Hutterians from military service obligations. As KMB leader C. F. Plett noted, "They risked coming to America to escape the draft. Their faith in the New Testament and the teachings of Jesus was strong."[15]

In 1947, the Rev. David W. Tschetter reiterated that the ancestors had "wanted to be free from compulsory military service."[16] Most modern Prairieleut, however, did not hesitate taking up arms if the situation demanded. Similarly, as noted, many persons who had moved to Canada to help their sons avoid the draft during World War I, found grandchildren actively supporting military service.[17] The Emmanuel MB Church (Onida, South Dakota) had not even included nonresistance as an essential belief in its *Constitution*, though it did state that the church was "in sympathy" with those who took a nonresistant approach.[18]

Middle-aged Prairie People noted that pacifism "just wasn't stressed," either by their ministers or at home. This was reflected by the fact that prominent Prairieleut leaders like former South Dakota Governor Harvey Wollman, State Senator Leland Kleinsasser, and Representative Benny Gross, two of whom (Wollman and Kleinsasser) had also served in influential positions in the Mennonite Brethren Conference, had all done 1-A status military service.[19] During times of war most young Hutterians naturally wanted to perform patriotic responsibilities, never having been introduced to the pacifist alternative.

Out west, as noted, Prairieleut Phil Hofer stated that he had "not once" received instruction with regard to the peace position, though his church's constitution had encouraged members not to participate in "carnal warfare."[20] Phil's models, early in life, were his Sunday School teachers, many of whom had served as a noncombatants in the military. Phil had tremendous respect for these persons; he appreciated very much their moral integrity and their commitment to missions and youth work. As indicated, however, Hofer eventually became one of the only persons growing up at Zion in the 1960s to register as a 1-O status conscientious objector.

It was noteworthy that the Prairie People themselves had not published many books or pamphlets on Hutterian or Mennonite history, or with regard to Anabaptist thought in general. Perhaps disinterest in their own history until recently had made it easier to accept mainstream Christian viewpoints on war and peace issues. Politician Harvey Wollman explained that non-resistance was not emphasized in the church where he grew up and that he had promoted it in his own family only as a "high ideal."[21] In recent times the Prairieleut political response has come almost entirely from a nonpacifist perspective.[22]

In the early 1950s nonpacifist sentiment was so strong in the South Dakota Prairieleut churches that the Krimmer Mennonite Brethren Conference, through its Peace and Welfare Committee, had commissioned Arnold M. Hofer to give presentations at the Ebenezer Church, near Doland.[23] At those meetings Hofer had discovered that many Prairie People feared that if they took a pacifist position they would be labeled "yellow" by their neighbors. They were embarrassed by Anabaptist pacifism; many had indeed been mistreated because of it.

Hofer had responded to the concerns of the discomfited by asking, "Who really are the slackers? Are they those people who bow to pressure and join the military or church members who stand by our beliefs?" Hofer noted that many people in attendance had not reponded favorably to his comments but that there had been "some positive results."

Members of the Peace and Welfare Committee of the KMB Conference, including South Dakotan David P. Gross and California pastor Clarence Hofer, had continually recommended that KMB ministers emphasize the peace position "in counseling, sermons, discussion and youth programs" in order to, as a committee resolution put it, "make this principle the personal conviction of our young people."[24] Some pastors, however, were not pacifists themselves.

The 1940s and early 1950s were periods of particularly strong patriotic sentiment, but nationalistic attitudes have not diminished in subsequent years. In some South Dakota congregations it was difficult to find male members who had taken the 1-O status conscientious objector position even during the unpopular and consciousness-raising Vietnam War. Concerning Prairieleut Mennonite Brethren in general, Arnold M. Hofer has written, "There is merely a remnant who consider some of these privileges [for example, nonmilitary alternative service] important enough to take advantage of them."[25] In 1980, the Zion MB Church *Constitution* still advised members —as had previous editions—not to participate "in carnal warfare."[26] Former members who were interviewed stressed that "carnal" had not, however, referred to "just" conflicts nor was it associated with noncombatant military assignments.

Still the tradition of biblical nonresistance had not completely died. George M. Hofer, a retired farmer and active member at Hutterthal Church, was a pacifist even though he had grown up in a church where many friends and acquaintances were not, including a brother who had served in the military. George noted that as a young man he had sensed, through the practical example of parents and church leaders, "that soldiering was wrong" and that he personally "couldn't go to war."[27]

General Conference Mennonite lay leader Aaron Glanzer underwent a more complicated pilgrimage, which took him from a "just war" philosophical position back to traditional Hutterian pacifism. His story follows.[28]

Glanzer was born in 1927 to parents actively involved in Freeman's Hutterthal Church. Glanzer did not recall hearing "anything" about the peace stance until his teen years, when Hutterthal joined the General Conference Mennonites; then he recalled "an occasional sermon or two."

When Glanzer was drafted in the late 1940s, his father—on his behalf —had requested conscientious objector status. Aaron, however, had refused to accept such interference. According to Glanzer, "I could not with a clear conscience go as a C-O because I really did not claim this for myself." Instead Glanzer joined the United States Army for a two-year tour of duty, a decision that, although it caused great concern for his parents, did not negatively impact his status in the church.

Upon his return to Freeman, Glanzer was well received by members of the ideologically divided Hutterthal, who had in fact invited him to teach the high school Sunday School class. Ironically, one topic for discussion had been "Peace Makers in a Broken World," which forced Glanzer to study New Testament sections dealing with issues of war and peace.

In the course of teaching that class, Glanzer had, quite unexpectedly, become a committed pacifist. As he described the process, "I accepted the truths of the Bible [with regard to pacifism] and applied them to my daily life." He also noted, instructively and ironically, that if the Hutterthal Church had condemned him earlier for joining the military he might never have become a pacifist.

The Conversion Experience

Greatly influenced by evangelical Protestantism, modern Prairie People also adopted a different view of how one becomes a Christian than that held by immigrant ancestors. In this regard, many Prairieleut in the independent churches admitted that the KMBs had been "ahead" of them.

A focal point was the radical conversion experience required for membership in Krimmer Mennonite Brethren congregations. As one older Prairieleut put it, "Now we have all been born again. We are now taught the importance of personal salvation." The latter statement implied straightforwardly that traditional Hutterian views had been deficient.

Contemporary Hutterites, and Prairie People traditionally, had viewed Christian salvation as a long process of enlightenment experienced by individuals as they received spiritual nurture within the Christian community. Many modern Prairieleut viewed salvation, alternatively, as a climactic personal revolution experienced as a result of face-to-face interaction between an individual and God.

Though not all Prairieleut General Conference Mennonites viewed the salvation experience in that way, many GC Hutterian churches did, and it caused many of them to openly criticize the summer camping program at Swan Lake Camp (near Viborg, South Dakota). One Prairieleut pastor had exclaimed, "Swan Lake seems to be a place for midnight swims." Another minister declined an invitation to speak at the camp, because he had not been given the right to give altar calls.[29]

The evangelical view of salvation was more individualistic than that held by Hutterites, who felt that relationship to God could not be separated from bonds to other members of the church. Most contemporary Prairie People viewed the more communal interpretation as lacking a personalized God-to-human being interaction, which they felt was at the heart of Christianity. They viewed the heavily structured character of Hutterite life as an open invitation to pharisaical legalism.

Emphasis on a personal relationship with God and on individual responsibility had thus replaced the Hutterian focus on collective accountability. As was commonly found in western Protestant denominations and Catholic parishes, personal freedom had replaced community-oriented rules and regulations. Prairieleut neoconservatives were more open to the traditional Hutterian position, a perspective adhered to by some in the General Conference Mennonite Church. They represented, however, a minority opinion.

The Prairie People had also been influenced by the "childhood evangelism" movement, which focused on "saving" children at as young an age as possible, giving particular attention to summer camp experiences. In the 1990s, South Dakota Prairieleut Myron Tschetter served as Leadership Development Coordinator at the Office of Child Evangelism's national headquarters.[30]

In this regard, Californian Phil Hofer remembered a "first conversion" at age five and a "second" when he was nine. The latter occurred at a revival service, where Phil said he had "fought the battle between good and evil" and had finally "given in." Phil was baptized two years later, at age eleven.[31] Hutterites and neoconservative Prairieleut questioned the level of understanding achieved by "born-again" children and wondered whether that was what Jesus had in mind. Many Hutterian evangelicals, on the other hand, felt the latter position represented that of Jesus' disciples when they had attempted to keep children out of Jesus' way, something for which they had been forcefully criticized. One Hutter conceded that it was "better to be safe than sorry."

In the midst of conflict on a number of theological issues, most contemporary Prairieleut had adopted more liberal positions on separation and divorce than were held earlier in the century. The most tolerant stances were held by General Conference Mennonite congregations. In 1954, the Bethany Church (Freeman) became the first congregation with a significant Prairieleut membership to receive divorced persons into membership.[32] Some GC Prairieleut churches also recognized the confirmation experiences of new members as the equivalent of believers' baptism.[33]

Fundamentalism and Mutual Aid

The Prairie People were also influenced by Protestant fundamentalists who in addition to emphasizing personalized salvation, believed in a wholly infallible Bible and the importance of evangelism.[34] Fundamentalists, like dispensationalists—who were in agreement on many issues—did not agree with persons who accepted the Bible's inerrancy, yet interpreted it differently, as did Prairieleut pacifists.

In 1963, Rollo Entz from the Bethel MB Church composed a master's thesis specifically intended "to establish the fact that the scriptures [were] verbally inspired," that, as he put it, "men of God wrote the scriptures exempt from all error, great or small, positive or negative."[35] Entz wrote this paper while studying at the Mennonite Brethren Biblical Seminary (in Fresno, California), which later employed faculty who accepted interpretations of the Bible that were much more contextualized, particularly with regard to the role of women in the church. That seminary, as well as the Associated Mennonite Biblical Seminaries in Elkhart, Indiana, was attacked forcefully by Prairieleut fundamentalists who often suggested that prospective ministerial candidates attend elsewhere.

Though Prairieleut fundamentalists placed major emphasis on the importance of individual relationships with God and an inerrant scripture, exemplary lifestyle and social action had not been neglected. The Zion KMB Church, in its Delft and New London missions endeavors of the 1940s,

1950s, and 1960s, for example, had provided significant financial as well as spiritual support to the poor white migrant workers it evangelized. This was laudable, particularly in the Reedley/Dinuba area, where residents had often stereotyped the people they called "okies," as socially backward. Poor whites had been used as a foil for comparison by central California Mennonites into the 1970s.

The social dimension of the faith was not forgotten in later years. In 1978, for example, the soon-to-be Rev. Jules Glanzer, a nephew of communal-life convert Barbara Glanzer Suess, wrote that love found its expression in "visible and measurable deeds," noting that love needed to manifest itself economically, socially, and spiritually.[36] It was notable too that, according to a 1985 questionnaire, 68 percent of Zion MB Church members had had some "involvement" with the social service–oriented Mennonite Central Committee.[37]

In comparison, the communal relatives of the Prairie People had engaged in almost no major social service endeavors, with the exception of emergency relief projects. In terms of participation in economic assistance activities, which focused on the needs of "outsiders," the Prairieleut had transformed belief into action much more effectively than had the isolationist Hutterites. Still, Prairieleut congregational records included much criticism with regard to the social service—as opposed to evangelistic—focus of organizations such as the above-mentioned Mennonite Central Committee.[38]

Another teaching advocated by many contemporaries was "assurance of salvation." It was not emphasized as much as it had been earlier in the century and was not mentioned at all in some Prairieleut GC Mennonite constitutions. Still, as one Prairieleut writer put it, "if [a] Christian is willing to abide under the rule and reign of Christ," she or he could be assured of salvation.[39] The Salem MB Church *Constitution* agreed: "We believe in the definite assurance of personal salvation."[40] Emmanuel MB's *Constitution* confirmed as well that "eternal life is [our] present possession."[41]

Growing up at Zion, Californian Phil Hofer recalled singing the appropriately named "Assurance March," with its popular chorus, "We can know that Jesus saved us."[42] A Mennonite Brethren Conference evaluation of the Zion congregation, in 1985, had elicited from some members the opinion that less emphasis on "assurance" at Zion in more recent times had in fact granted church members a "license to sin."[43] The church's *Constitution*, which had included the doctrine of assurance of salvation in 1962, had not mentioned it in a revised 1980 document.[44]

Earlier, dispensationalist Samuel J. R. Hofer had warned against assurance views that had confirmed the "eternal security" of all persons who had at one time accepted Christianity.[45] Hofer himself had purportedly said that he had not "willfully" sinned since 1918, the time of his salvation experience. That did not mean, however, that he might not be enticed to sin in the future. Grace Bible Institute President and KMB leader Joseph Schmidt had referred to the whole issue as "an unprofitable, time-wasting question."[46]

The "once saved, always saved" teaching had been popular, however, in some Prairieleut churches.[47] The Rev. Virgil Kleinsasser, for example, believed that "eternal security" was the "clear teaching of the Bible."[48] In response to concern expressed by KMB conference leader, C. F. Plett, Kleinsasser had reiterated, "We as Christians have no more to do with keeping ourselves saved than we had with becoming saved."[49] Fifty years after making that comment, Kleinsasser added that he had not meant to imply that people could simply go out and sin without consequence.[50]

Contemporary Prairieleut churches have also developed a musical tradition different from that of Hutterian ancestors and contemporaries. Gospel hymns, with their lighter melodies, as well as contemporary "scripture songs," have replaced the ancient martyr hymns. Californian David L. Hofer composed many light gospel choruses in the 1940s and 1950s, six of which were included in the compilation *Fellowship Choruses*.

Stirling members Sarah and Anna Hofer noted that they "loved the old hymns"—hymns from the *Gesangbuch*—because one "could learn the whole gospel message there."[51] Hofer's pieces had a different, though similarly important, emphasis. They did not contain in-depth discussion of Christian theology, nor did they include detailed personal narratives such as were found in the Hutterite songbook. Instead, they presented a joyful thankfulness for the inner peace God had granted to those who had been "saved." Note the lyrics to the Hofer composition, "Jesus, Jesus, Sweetest Name I Know":

> Jesus, Jesus, sweetest name I know.
> Jesus, Jesus, oh how I love him so.
> Jesus, Jesus, from sin he set me free.
> Jesus, Jesus, someday his face I'll see.[52]

Individualism

According to the theology adhered to by Hutterians historically, God's will was discerned by individual Christians through the church as the "body of Christ." In contrast to modern America's focus on self-awareness and self-fulfillment, Hutterians had traditionally emphasized the renunciation of self and submission to God through the community, the historical interpretation of gelassenheit. In this regard, Mennonite historian James Juhnke argued that Swiss Mennonites had historically stressed humility to a greater extent than had Low German Mennonites (with whom most Prairieleut had associated).[53]

Contemporary Prairie People had adopted a more individualistic view of salvation, emphasizing the importance of God's inner call. According to this perspective God's voice came to Christians not only through the church institutionally, but directly and personally, if one was authentically "saved." And so a shot of supernaturally grounded power often flowed through the bodies and souls of individuals who went forward at revival meetings. The more fundamentalist of Hutterians felt that, without this "experience," one's spiritual status was in limbo.

Prairieleut academics like Harold Gross, who on other issues might be placed in the neoconservative camp, had also supported a highly individualistic notion of the Christian faith. Gross, a professor of philosophy at Bethel College (North Newton, Kansas), had written that "the roots of religious truth lie in the free and inwardly motivated response of the individual to divine truth as he sees it for himself." Gross's way of thinking ironically duplicated fundamentalist emphases in its primary focus on the individual. Both positions represented philosophies at odds with community-oriented Hutterianism.

The Hutterites believed that a theology of humility even impacted one's daily work, as commitment to the colony economic system and one's spiritual relationship with God had become intertwined. Hutterites were hesitant to talk about personal spiritual experiences, because individuals were thought to be at different devotional levels, at dissimilar times.

Prairieleut Jules Glanzer, too, had noted that "giving of oneself and seeking the betterment of the other person is the heart of relationship."[54] Modern Prairie People often gave central attention, however, to the ability of individual Christians to tell personal stories that spoke to relationships with God. Though it was expected that such relationships would naturally precipitate social concern and action, when such concern and action were exhibited by persons who could not, or would not, articulate a personal relationship with God, their work was questioned.

Other changes in Prairieleut religious viewpoints related to specific lifestyle issues. It was significant, for example, that a number of Prairie People had become outstanding athletes, since neither competitive nor recreational activities had been acceptable endeavors earlier. In the 1930s, for example, Joe (Smokey Joe) Mendel had lost his membership at the Onida KMB Church after participating in a national track meet in Chicago.[55] (He later tied the world record for the one-hundred-yard dash.)

Joe's father, the Rev. David J. Mendel, had once offered the congregation he served a public apology for attending one of his son's track meets. Joe's mother, who had felt very uncomfortable sitting in the stands herself, told her son afterward, "I'm sure glad you didn't jump over those sticks" (referring to hurdles).[56] In the late twentieth century, however, participation and/or attendance at athletic events, even on Sundays, raised few Prairieleut eyebrows. Joe Mendel himself had eventually been accepted into membership at another Prairieleut congregation (the Ebenezer MB Church in Doland) where, as early as 1962, the church had held a "fall Kick-Off Dinner" with a sports theme.[57]

A New View of Ministry

Modern Prairie People had also adopted a non-Hutterian view of ministry. Individuals were now typically invited to the ministry by a personal "call" from God. Prospective pastors then attended seminary and sought a church that would recognize that "call."[58] This practice manifested itself early on in the Salem KMB Church when John Tschetter "announced he would follow his heart's direction" and inaugurated a home missions program.[59] This could not have happened, in the same way, in the independent Prairieleut churches, where one's "heart's direction" required congregational confirmation via a process of collective discernment. Before the 1920s, this had included the casting of lots for ministerial assignments, which had given God a central role in final determinations.

Even in Prairieleut KMB churches, ministerial candidates had been chosen from within the congregation, from a group of people who were well known by the membership, into the mid-twentieth century. In the independent churches, individuals had been tapped on the back, their spiritual gifts recognized. Then the lot was cast, or the church voted, but no essentially personal "call" was recognized. God was not thought to interact with people in such a fashion. Implied herein was the belief that the church as a whole played a significant role in "calling" someone into the ministry.

The more individualistic "call to ministry" showed its face for the first time at the Zion KMB Church in 1948, when Clarence Hofer had returned from studies at the fundamentalist Bob Jones College and was, as he described it, "self-chosen," to be a minister.[60] Hofer had received a personal call from God, which he felt required no intermediary processing. He had also been criticized for holding that perspective.

In the 1990s, ministers in Prairieleut congregations were often "outsiders," holding professional salaries, not persons who had grown up in and were thus well known by the communities they served. In this regard the Clarence Hofer case was different in that Hofer had returned to his home congregation. Fully salaried (except in smaller congregations), contemporary ministers did not generally engage in nonpastoral work similar in nature to that performed by congregants. In comparison, the Rev. John J. Kleinsasser had often worked on the side as a mailman. Many Prairieleut ministers had farmed. J. D. Hofer, as noted, had been a carpenter. Modern pastors, alternatively, coordinated virtually every aspect of the church program as the switch to salaried status had simultaneously increased professional expectations.

Contemporaries often suggested that it was better to have ministers who had not grown up in the congregations they served. According to this line of reasoning, if a church knew a pastor too well, members might have difficulty accepting his teaching and admonition. Small indiscretions from the past, family problems and youthful mistakes, might be remembered and get in the way. This was, of course, the very reason Prairie People and Hutterites had historically wanted spiritual leaders whom they really "knew," from their own communities. It kept the leadership eternally humble, nurtured empathetic relationships, and exemplified God's ability to empower anyone he had chosen for leadership assignments.

Instead a single salaried pastor now preached on most Sunday mornings. A monopoly on scriptural interpretation had thus passed from a variety of people in the traditional multiple ministry, with its different understanding of the priesthood of all believers, to a single individual. Most congregations had established this structure by the 1960s and had generally done so for practical reasons, though in effect it was an innovation with deep theological implications. Instead of attending to the interpretive gifts of a number of ministers on alternating Sunday mornings—or even on the same Sunday —Prairieleut Christians now generally listened to the same speaker each week. And ministers themselves were thus not ministered to, at least not from the pulpit.[61]

The traditional multiple ministry had in many ways been necessitated by the unsalaried condition of each pastor. It was economically driven but also represented a more communal view of ecclesiastical involvement. Ironic practical twists in the new single minister structure, however, brought forth unique opportunities for the laity.

Hutterite ministers in the 1990s, for example, were responsible for enforcing church *Ordnungen* (ordinances), the institutionalized path by which God granted his grace to individual Christians. Even though determinations of violations and appropriate punishments were discussed openly by male members at colony meetings, ministers still "had the final say," as one Hutterite put it.

Hutterite ministers were also the only persons who read the divinely inspired sermons, which interpreted "God's Word" for the gathered community. In this regard, they had become authorities on correct interpretation of the sermons' own elucidations of scripture, as the ministers counseled individuals who had questions about beliefs and practices. Prairieleut Christians, on the other hand, believed that "God's Word" could come just as authoritatively to Christian laypersons. The Word of God was given to the church community not only through ordained servants, who interpreted the Bible and sermons correctly, but from anyone who had opened his or her self to God's direction.

Hutterites believed that if you despised a minister, you despised God "who has sent his Holy Spirit in us."[62] Modern Prairie People did not accept that high view of the clergy. Modern Prairieleut ministers did not function with the same kind of authority Hutterite ministers wielded, nor with the command Paul Tschetter had once exhibited. The 1980 *Constitution* of one Prairieleut church noted that continual criticism of the pastor could lead to removal from membership.[63] But that statement was likely more indicative of reduced levels of pastoral authority than greater ones.

Another Prairieleut innovation saw church deacons no longer ordained for life. Deacons had traditionally performed services similar in nature to Hutterite colony council members, providing a forum for continuous lay input with regard to congregational issues. This had ensured a measure of ministerial accountability during those time periods when ministers, too, had been ordained for life. Contemporary deacons were elected for limited terms of office, though this practice was introduced as late as 1964 at one Prairieleut church.[64]

An interesting case of lay utilization of a traditional Hutterian practice was manifested in the early 1940s, when Zion KMB church members David L. Hofer and Walter Warkentin, along with three others, had "cast lots" in order to determine which of a discerned collection of "ministries" each had been called to pursue.[65] Areas of need were determined after a lengthy period of prayer and meditation, which included bimonthly Saturday prayer meetings, conducted from 10:00 A.M. to 4:00 P.M., with no lunch break.

One evening, at David L. Hofer's home, a select group of projects had been written on slips of paper and placed in a Bible; then the prayer group members had drawn lots. David Hofer drew "church radio ministry" and proceeded to found radio station KRDU in Dinuba, California. Warkentin drew "Christian conference ground" and established Hume Lake Christian Camps near Kings Canyon National Park. Both enterprises experienced substantial success. Leadership selection had been placed in God's hands.

A New Kind of Church Discipline

According to one sixteenth-century Hutterite chronicler, "Where [discipline] is lacking, we live as in a tumble-down house with no one repairing it."[66] Contemporary Hutterites, like the Prairie People in earlier times, believed Jesus had given the church the power of the "keys," through Peter, to "loose and bind." Enjoined to discipline members involved in immoral activities and false teaching, the church had, in a sense, determined where an individual might spend eternity. Langham KMB pastor Andreas Stahl had been so demanding with regard to correct behavior that one woman remembered "literally withering under the glance he [Stahl] threw her way from the pulpit after she had whispered or giggled with a companion."[67]

In 1943, a member at the Zion KMB church gave a public testimony "concerning his backslidden state" and asked the church for "pardon."[68] Prairieleut pastor Jacob D. Hofer had once "humbled himself" before the congregation he served, owing to a personal conflict with a fellow congregant.[69]

Contemporary Prairieleut churches no longer interpreted the power to "loose and bind" so strictly with regard to belief and practice. Excommunications, which continued to be common into the 1960s, were almost nonexistent at century's end. As excommunicated Hutterians began to feel comfortable with the non-Prairieleut society outside, the ban had ceased to serve the spiritual function of both reminding offenders of their sins and bringing them back into membership (after repentance).

Prairieleut churches had also become more tolerant of behaviors deemed unacceptable in the past. A philosophy of ecumenical toleration had become the de facto disciplinary position. Action was still taken with regard to major moral offenses. Church constitutions still suggested disciplining those who "led an unChristian life" or, in one case, persons who did not pay church dues. Members were no longer disciplined, however, just because they could not keep a marriage together; neither were they chastised for engaging in questionable business practices; or for displaying faddish styles of dress.[70] As the Rev. John J. Kleinsasser put it bluntly (in 1947): "Church discipline is not very good but some have been dropped."[71]

Already, in 1962, the Zion MB Church *Constitution* had opposed drunkenness but had not taken a position on the use of alcohol in general.[72] The 1968 *Constitution* of the Salem MB Church, as well, though it demanded abstinence from tobacco use, had only condemned "drunkenness," with regard to alcohol consumption.[73] These positions were significant considering the strong anti-alcohol stance taken earlier.

Other congregations had taken more hard-line positions. Salem's sister congregation, Ebenezer, for example, in a constitution also published in 1968, specifically forbade the use of "alcohol beverages."[74] The Emmanuel MB Church held a similar teetotaling position.[75] In the 1980s, Zion MB dissenters criticized their congregation in writing for not disciplining members who drank socially, as well as those who had gambled in Las Vegas.

Though congregations differed with regard to specific theological positions, most Prairie People had remained steadfastly committed to regular church attendance. But there was also a Prairieleut fringe group, members of which perhaps attended church occasionally, but who held beliefs and/or practiced behavior outside of services not accepted by the church itself. Those persons were rarely excommunicated. Already in 1947, the Rev. David W. Tschetter had lamented that there was "less testifying" in church than had been the case earlier.[76]

Similarly, however, petty personal dislikes were now less likely to cause congregational division. Minor infractions, nebulously defined, no longer took up much of the church's time. The end result was a less unified, less disciplined group of people, even though, in earlier times, many unacceptable practices had simply been hidden. Contemporaries were more understanding, open-minded, and less legalistic than traditional Prairieleut assemblages. This was a church that was not as sure of itself. It was humble enough not to believe, as had its Hutterian ancestors, that it might create a community of believers "without spot or wrinkle."

When practiced, church discipline was usually dealt with privately, between individual members. The church as a whole was rarely involved, not ascribing to itself that kind of authority, though ministers and deacons at times served as conflict mediators. This represented a philosophy of discipline similar to the one Hutterians had condemned in the sixteenth century. Contemporary Prairieleut churches dealt with infractions in much the same manner, therefore, as mainline Protestants and Catholics. "Sin" itself was no longer clearly defined.

As late as 1961, one Prairieleut congregation had recommended that members desist from playing cards.[77] Eight years later, another church had gone on record against "dancing, movie attendance and lustful pictures on t.v."[78] But in the 1990s, most Prairie People tolerated all of those formerly proscribed practices. "At the devil's instigation," as the Hutterite chronicler put it, "they [describing Mennonites] have brought about a real abomination by allowing all sin to be settled privately between brothers, whether fornication, theft or anything of that sort. In this way they have gathered impure hearts and spirits among themselves and so have participated in the guilt."[79] Contemporary Prairie People viewed the traditional Hutterian philosophy of church authority and discipline as legalistic and unforgiving. The only two "lifestyle" positions that continued to be forcefully condemned were homosexuality and abortion, two issues with which Prairie People themselves appeared to have had little personal experience.

The Prairie People had also come to identify very little with the martyr ideology of the Hutterites, brought about continuously, for Hutterites, by their distinctive dress and way of life and by constant emphasis in the *Gesangbuch* and *Chronicle*. Most of the Hutterite songbook, for example, consisted of martyr's tales, which provided direct admonition to be strong in the face of worldly adversity. One of the most popular Hutterite hymns, *"O Reicher Gott in Himmelsthron,"* presented stories of early Christian martyrs.[80]

A theology of suffering, central to sixteenth-century Anabaptism, was difficult to find in modern Prairieleut (as well as Mennonite) teaching and practice. The belief that God wanted all Christians to take up the cross, as Jesus did, in order to affirm loyalty and dedication, had virtually disappeared. The only Prairieleut Hutterians who had a good understanding of that perspective were voluntary service workers and international missionaries who had spent extended periods of time in American urban centers or in Third and Fourth World countries.

The movement away from a theology of suffering was common in North American sects that had found general social acceptance.[81] Young persons were still taught that Christians should be different from "non-Christians" in their commitment to Jesus and biblical teaching. Virtually every Prairieleut church constitution recommended "separation from the world."[82] But separation was no longer symbolized by distinctive dress or even a singular position on societal involvement. Televisions and video machines had brought all manner of diverse ideologies and practices into Prairieleut homes.

For many Prairie People, following the stations of the cross somewhat literally had been transformed into a simple refusal to take a drink with one's college friends, or to insist on attending church on Sunday morning when there was a football game on television or a softball game at the local ball-park. This kind of cross-bearing was quite different in nature from that preached and experienced by Hutterian ancestors.

One Hutterite sermon noted that non-Christians "hate them, rage against them, and look to being rid of them."[83] It was difficult to equate embarrass-ment about not being able to play soccer on Sunday morning with the major limitations on personal freedom experienced by Hutterians in the past. It was a different definition of suffering with a correspondingly different kind of cost. Contemporary Prairie People lived in a society that was so open-minded it only periodically "hated" or "raged against" the counter-cultural Hutterites. Instead, the colony Hutterites had become a tourist attraction.

In 1532 Hutterite leaders in Auspitz had been beaten and their clothes torn from their bodies. Then the attackers had "turned on the sisters and neither respected nor spared their womanhood."[84] Most Prairieleut and Hutterites had suffered hatred and discrimination during World War I as German-speaking pacifists. Contemporary Prairieleut have been attacked, if at all, for other reasons.

The traditional Hutterian commitment to gelassenheit, a complete yield-ing of body, soul, and property, to God, regardless of cultural trends, had been liberalized by modern Prairie People. The Prairieleut, like most Men-nonites, had accepted American individualism and had been assimilated into mainstream society, culturally and theologically. This occurred substantively during the period from 1935 to 1960 when, as Calvin Redekop noted, Ana-baptists in general had undergone a transition from an emphasis on mutual aid and collective obligation, to a focus on the individual.[85]

The Hutterites, conversely, did not place much emphasis on building self-esteem, recognizing individual uniqueness, or self-knowledge. Instead they emphasized self-abnegation and being separate, as a people, from every-one else in society. One Prairieleut described this as "the self-centeredness of an entire people." That characterization, again, showed clearly the ideo-logical and social gap between Prairieleut and Hutterite thinking.

Prairieleut Women

The contemporary position of women in the Prairieleut com-munity was a fluid one. Prairieleut congregations have not accepted women as pastors but women have served in many nonministerial positions of influence and have been given increased voice within families. In general Prairieleut women felt they had substantially more control over their personal lives, and considerably more influence in family and church, than did female colony members. The former was basically true, the latter more open to question.

The traditional Hutterian position, still adhered to in the colonies, suggested that women were morally weaker than men.[86] Hutterite women were not allowed, therefore, to be direct participants in official Hutterite colony decision-making processes and could not vote. Werner Packull, in his book *Hutterite Beginnings*, noted the general "silence" of historic Hutterite source materials with regard to female accomplishments, even though, as he put it, Hutterite women "bore children, worked alongside their husbands, and, like them, suffered persecution and martyrdom."[87] None of this belied the fact that Hutterite women often exercised considerable influence through their husbands, the common traditionalist refrain.

Recent changes, however, showed Hutterite women taking greater control of personal lives. Colony female members were increasingly selective, for example, with regard to matters of birth control and diet, leading to a decreased birth rate and the consumption of lower calorie foods.[88]

Many, too, had developed highly personalized forms of relationship with the supernatural.[89] Younger Schmiedeleut women, in particular, had begun to express religious beliefs by employing "evangelical" terminology not traditionally used by Hutterites. Some colony defectors believed that the influence of evangelical Protestantism was motivating women to demand more equal treatment in Hutterite society as a whole, as they "accepted Christ as their personal savior" and were, through that encounter, spiritually empowered as individuals, not only as members of a communal organization.

Hutterite men, correspondingly, often suggested that it was women who were pushing colonies to modernize living quarters. Lesley Masuk, who has completed the most recent (1998) study of Hutterite women, confirmed an increased emphasis on the creation of comfortable, private, living spaces. The author has always been intrigued by the extensive involvement of Hutterite women in a variety of black market home industries that bring in extra income.

Masuk, a Prairieleut descendent who was given permission to engage in a two-month-long, participant-observer study of a Manitoba Schmiedeleut colony, discovered a few other things as well. Masuk wrote that technological innovations introduced throughout the community's economic structure (from automated milking operations to furniture manufacturing) have left Hutterite women with much "unoccupied time."[90] As a result, Masuk found a good deal of residual, sometimes expressed, anger and depression among women who felt helpless to deal with (what Masuk called) the "patriarchal intrusion" of technology. This kept them separated from most nondomestic farming operations. They had been "replaced by machines."[91]

Over the past twenty years, the author has experienced the active involvement of Hutterite colony women in many social conversations, regardless of the topic under discussion. Blunt, forthright commentary has come just as commonly from Hutterite women in the room as from their husbands and other men in attendance. The women did not keep silent when they were in disagreement with the views expressed—not even in deference to Hutterite men. These interactions included the discussion of controversial issues of social and religious importance. The same could be said with regard to personal conversations with men and women of Prairieleut background.

To a considerable extent, however, Hutterite women have continued to hold positions of overt subservience to men, the Hutterites believing God had granted males authority over females. In church services, for example, women were noticeably silent except when asked to sing. In the home environment, it was the women who, in the evening, brought in freshly picked raspberries topped with ice cream. It was the women who washed the dishes and cleaned the house.

In Prairieleut churches, alternatively, one found a gradual acceptance of more liberal views on women's roles. Though a conservative mindset had kept most women publicly silent until mid-century, there were always exceptions, even in the past. As Willis Kleinsasser noted:

> In church after Scripture was read, anyone could pray aloud. Ma was the only woman I can recall ever praying—in German. She prayed a lot. In church the men sat on one side; women and children on the other. All business was done by the entire congregation. The women were silent and couldn't vote. I remember thinking very young, "Who are they kidding. If certain men voted wrong they'll hear it at home." I was never convinced the men had as much authority as they thought.[92]

Most Prairieleut Mennonites still consider senior female leadership in the church or home unbiblical. Only the neoconservative group was open to new thinking in that area. Still, Prairieleut women have experienced much greater personal freedom and public ecclesiastical influence than women in the colonies. As early as 1917, for example, the Krimmer Mennonite Brethren Conference had annointed the wives of church elders (for spiritual service) via the laying on of hands.[93]

Many Prairieleut women had served in professional positions and one, Marie Waldner (who died in 1998), taught at the college level as early as the 1930s. It is said that prominent West Coast evangelist Jacob D. Hofer relied heavily on his wife, Agnes Fast, who either "came up with ideas for [his] sermons" or at least "created well-organized outlines" for those ideas.[94] Elizabeth F. Hofer co-authored a number of books with the Rev. Samuel J. R. Hofer.

In the West, Frances Hofer Warkentin, a granddaughter of John Z. Kleinsasser, worked alongside her husband, Walter, in establishing Hume Lake Christian Camp in the Sierra Nevadas. For many years Frances directed the camp's children's programs.[95] She was also an influential lay leader at the Zion KMB Church, where she often served as choir director. A former Sunday School student recalled a dynamic personality who related well to youth and "seemed bigger than life."[96] Frances always felt a great deal of pride, as well, in her Hutterian roots.[97]

Prairieleut women had been involved in many other church activities, as well, from sewing circles *(Die Nahvereine)* to missionary societies, all typically focused on fundraising, which Hutterian women were evidently quite good at.[98] In 1940, for example, a woman's group at the Bethel KMB Church donated five hundred dollars to improve sanctuary acoustics.[99] Four years later, the Ladies Aid group at that same church had taken on the responsibility of "support[ing] the boys in service." They also paid 50 percent of the purchase price of the church parsonage.

At the Zion KMB Church the "Willing Workers of God" had furnished the church nursery and kitchen and provided money for landscaping purposes.[100] Most fundraising projects of that nature—which continued to the present—involved handsewn quilts and baked goods sometimes sold by auction. Special offerings were taken for other projects. Prairieleut women also organized and led Bible studies and had often served as songleaders, choir directors, readers of scripture, and dispensers of communion.

Religious Practice in Transition

Modern Prairie People have moved into an era of revolutionary reassessment of religious emphases, with conservatives, neoconservatives, and evangelicals all striving for ascendance within the various congregations. The extent to which Hutterian traditions were part of that re-evaluation process depended particularly on neoconservatives who felt the ancient theological traditions should be re-examined and transmediated for utilization in the present. Neoconservatives were particularly committed to the "mutual aid" philosophy of social service, which, according to Stephen Nolt, had helped American Mennonites "refashion" their ethnic identity through the development of a whole array of nongovernmental institutional aid structures.[101]

Key features of contemporary Prairieleut belief followed an evangelical Protestant theological orientation, however, particularly with regard to a generally accepted focus on personal salvation experiences and the performance of military service in just conflicts. It was also typically expected that women would play a secondary "supporting" role in church decision making.

In the 1990s, the neoconservative minority sought to recapture elements of the more community-oriented and pacifist past. Re-evaluation of Hutterian traditions was proceeding, however, only in those churches which had substantial Hutterian memberships, a phenomenon that was itself changing rapidly with intermarriage across ethnic and denominational lines. Even within ethnically unified congregations, conservatives who were interested in the Hutterian past—owing to cultural familiarity with customary beliefs and practices—generally agreed with the evangelical majority on theological issues. Most conservatives did not support movements that threatened to significantly alter the nature of contemporary Prairieleut church life.

The Hutterites insisted that it was impossible to successfully activate Anabaptist principles without full community of goods. In opposition, Prairieleut neoconservatives recognized the value of a noncommunal Anabaptism and sought to establish an authentic middle way—a *via media*—between a socio-religious Hutterite separatism, which had retained ideological commitment to sixteenth-century Anabaptist principles, and an evangelical interpretation of the Christian faith, which had accepted rather uncritically the essential suitability of the Christian's pursuit of the American dream.

II

· ·

Customs That Remained

Ver es klana nit erht is es grusa nit veht.
(If you don't appreciate the little things you are not worthy
of bigger things.)
**Traditional Prairieleut saying, in *Hutterisch*, with English
translation**

In frying pan, slowly fry until light brown 3–4 finely sliced
medium large sized onions with one quarter lb. pork sausage,
broken into bits. In sauce pan simmer the pork brains of
1 or 2 hogs in water for a few minutes.
Prairieleut recipe for preparing pork brains, 1974

The Hutterisch Dialect/Language

Religious communities develop rituals and cultural prac-
tices that best suit their unique expressions of spirituality. These carry over
into the manner in which people relate to each other. The Hutterian understanding of what it meant to be spiritual was concretized in a particular way
of living, which was gradually disappearing among the Prairie People. In
the process, the entire religious life and thought of the traditional noncommunal Hutterian community was undergoing significant change.

This chapter reviews the present status of those Hutterian folkways—
secular and religious—which have continued to impact the lives of modern
Prairieleut. Also discussed is the issue of ethnic exclusivity, an integral com-
ponent of cultural identity, which showed both the positive and negative
faces of the Prairieleut assemblage.

A variety of idiosyncratic customs continued to direct the lives of modern Prairie People. Into the early 1900s, successful salesmen in South Dakota's West Freeman community had known it was important to be able to

speak and understand some Hutterisch. Things changed significantly in later years.

Most Prairieleut born before 1950 could still speak and/or understand the Hutterisch dialect. It was fast disappearing, however, among persons born after mid-century.[1] A 1971 publication stated that "most" members of the Emmanuel Mennonite Church (Doland, South Dakota) spoke Hutterisch "often."[2] But one member questioned whether that characterization reflected the knowledge base of younger persons in the congregation.

Eighty-year-old "Smokey Joe" Mendel noted that he had tried to teach his oldest son, Don, to speak Hutterisch but had given up with the rest of his children.[3] Other Prairieleut said that, even if they had not passed on the Hutterisch dialect, they had still used it when they "didn't want the kids to know what they were talking about."[4] Walter Warkentin noted that his wife, Frances Hofer, had used Hutterisch good-naturedly whenever she wanted to keep a secret from him.[5] Fifty-five-year-old Jake Gross remembered his mother, Anna, asking him questions in Hutterisch. He had responded, however, in English.[6]

A 1980 study of the Hutterisch dialect confirms that all but forty words originated in Austria. Exceptions dealt with objects or concepts unknown prior to the last century, such as the English "desk" and "eksercais."[7] In 1997, Saskatoon Prairieleut linguist Walter Hoover published the first Hutterisch-English dictionary.[8] Hoover was also in the process of translating the Old and New Testaments into Hutterisch.

Hoover had also written a detailed introduction to the Hutterisch dialect that focused on grammar, word origins, and English adaptations.[9] In that work, Hoover insisted, additionally, that Hutterisch was not really a "dialect" but a unique "language in its own right," with roots in the Rhaeto-Romansch language of northern Italy and southern Switzerland.[10]

The only in-depth study of Prairieleut use of Hutterisch was conducted in the early 1960s. At that time 52.5 percent of those responding still used Hutterisch either "frequently" or "half" the time. Only 15 percent of respondents had "never" spoken it.[11] A similar study conducted in the 1990s would show substantially diminished use and understanding of the dialect/language.

In general, persons born after 1970 did not understand Hutterisch at all, even though they had heard parents and/or grandparents converse in it. Since Hutterisch was not a written language, and since there was no discernible effort to make it one (outside of the Hoover translation project), the dialect will most likely die out among Prairieleut Hutterians. The Hutterites will then continue that linguistic tradition alone.

Over the years, Hutterians had given the mother tongue, Hutterisch, an almost sacred character. Its use had become a public witness to a different way of life. Throughout American history, however, bilingual accommodation to English has generally led gradually but inevitably to the loss of native speech.[12] That is exactly what happened in the Prairieleut community. The

Hutterites managed to withstand that rushing current via an isolated communal form of existence.

Language is essential to the retention of ethnic identity, a difficult-to-penetrate defensive armor. According to Prairieleut descendent Delbert Wiens, "Once the mental stranglehold of our mother tongue is broken, new ways of speaking and seeing come more quickly . . . A way of speaking is a way of seeing."[13] Mennonite Brethren patriarch J. B. Toews agreed, defining language, furthermore, as "an expression of values."[14]

In addition to losing the Hutterisch dialect, the Prairie People have almost completely lost command of the standard (High) German language, the Hutterian substitute for Latin, once used in church services. German schools held in summer months were discontinued in the 1920s and 1930s. By the following decade, most Prairieleut churches had conducted some services and business meetings in English, even as some families continued to have daily devotions in standard German.

Aaron Glanzer noted that his family had always had devotions before breakfast and that they had "always been in the High German language."[15] Glanzer also said, however, that such events had often been quite "meaningless" to him since he understood little of what was being read. In the Salem KMB Church, an attempt had been made to integrate German instruction with the regular Sunday school program, but discipline problems and poor attendance caused church leaders to give it up.[16]

Bulletins from KMB Conference meetings sixty years ago (in 1938), showed a continual mix of German and English programming. Hymns, for example, had been sung in both languages, with appropriate lyrics printed in the program. Whereas morning sessions were conducted in German, the conference had used English in afternoon assemblies.[17] By the World War II era, however, most Prairieleut had come to believe that evangelistic efforts were negatively affected by the continued use of German.[18]

The switch from German to English created a serious dilemma for older generations, however. Those brought up reading the Bible, praying, singing, and worshiping God in German felt something stronger than just an emotional attachment to the ancestral tongue. Many found it almost impossible to worship God reverently in another language. The Rev. David J. Mendel told his congregation that the last Sunday he would preach would be that preceding the congregation's switch to English.[19]

It was not always possible adequately to translate words from one language into another. Age-old feelings and inner meanings of unimaginable significance were lost in the translation process. Thus older members hung onto German with clenched hands as long as they controlled the vote at church business meetings. They also held onto traditional clothing styles. A classic contrast of fashion was thus still noticeable in the 1972 50th anniversary booklet of the Emmanuel Mennonite Church, where one found photographs not only of members like Sheila Hofer, with her early 1970s "flip" hairstyle, but also of older women like Katie M. Hofer, wearing a dark dress and shawl.[20]

Food and Music

Older Prairieleut have experienced greater success in passing on the ability to prepare traditional Hutterian foods. Grandchildren assisted this process by asking parents to prepare the foods they had enjoyed eating at the homes of their grandparents. Thus one could still sample traditional foods such as *gashtel* (dumpling soup), *nukelen* (egg dumpling soup), *kartoffelknedel* (potatoes and dumplings), *fleischkrapfen* (meat dumplings), *griebenschmaltz* (goose or pork crackling spread), *geschnelznenudel* (large frying noodles), *moos* (various kinds of fruit puddings), stringbean soup, fried corn meal, and watermelon pickles.

This was not to suggest that all Prairieleut Hutterians still prepared the above-mentioned foods, but they were at least familiar with most of them. Other traditional delicacies, such as pork brains and mincemeat, were no longer popular. Non-Hutterians as well as Hutterians had taken advantage of the recent North American obsession with ethnic foods by publishing "Hutterite" cookbooks.[21] David L. Hofer noted that his wife, Sylvia Kliewer, had "learned to make the *Hutterisch* food" while they were living with his parents during the early years of their marriage.[22] Other non-Hutterian spouses had also learned to make or enjoy favorite traditional foods.

In contrast to the retention of some culinary traditions, customary Hutterian musical forms have been lost in total, except for the Prairieleut tendency to emphasize vocal more than instrumental music. Retained for almost three hundred years, the traditional Hutterian martyr hymns were now sung only in the colonies. Larry Martens' comment that excellence of individual execution was always secondary to spiritual focus in Hutterite music perhaps typified Prairieleut musical expression, as well, though considerable emphasis was now placed on the quality of musical performance.[23]

The No-Holds-Barred Persona

Many Hutterian social customs have been lost, as have most traditional ways of dress. Theological and ecclesiastical positions have undergone radical change, as noted. Yet a "folky, ethnic feeling," as one individual described it, was still experienced by persons growing up in Prairieleut communities. It was still possible to discern subtle idiosyncracies such as the strong commitment to extended family, hard work, a sense of humility, and a discomfort with those who did not share at least part of the heritage. It was also interesting to note that, as with Hutterites, laughing too much or too loudly was often viewed with disfavor. *"Shsh, holt dai maul"* (You're too noisy) was a common parental injunction. Willis Kleinsasser wrote that his father had described loud laughter as *"hadenish"* (heathenish).[24]

The Prairie People have retained some identifying characteristics and customs, and lost others. One convention held onto is a strong sense that one should be up front and honest in personal relations. The Prairieleut have a strong antagonism to hypocritical positioning. Individuals thus tend to be forthright and honest in their discussions of both contemporary issues and mundane concerns.

Detractors have accused the Prairieleut of being "rude," "loud," "discourteous," or "unsophisticated." Since Hutterians considered themselves industrious and frugal, for example, they had sometimes expressed negative opinions of persons they felt did not work as hard, or save as much, as they had. *"Venn se nit su fil dinger tatn caufn, tatn se mear gelt hobm"* (If they didn't buy so many things, they would have more money") was a typical comment. An attitude of careful stewardship had even carried over to international missions operations.

In 1948, the Rev. John J. Kleinsasser, at the time chair of the KMB Board of Foreign Missions, had responded to a missionary's request for additional funding, in the following manner, "The trip to Columbia it seems to me would more or less be useless if you feel you have no call to that place, so why go there?"[25] The evangelist who received that response had requested additional monies to cover an exploratory excursion to a country in which he did not personally expect to be placed. Kleinsasser felt the travel request was an unnecessary one and did not mince words in expressing that opinion.

The tendency toward uncalculated honesty was refreshing, in that one always knew—even if too well—where one stood. One Prairieleut referred to that collective psychological characteristic as "having a Hutter temperament." Conversations with Prairieleut Hutterians generally included a series of positive, as well as negative comments, one following after another, but opinions were never hidden and thus no doubt remained with regard to how ideas, events, or personalities had been viewed.

As one Low German Mennonite with a Prairieleut spouse put it, "You'd think they were mad at each other, but that's just the way they talk." The son of a former Low German KMB minister added, "My dad once came back from a church business meeting and told us that during the assembly he thought some members were going to come to blows. Afterwards, however, these same people were standing around talking about their farms like old friends."[26] Walter Warkentin, who had "married into" a Prairieleut family, concurred that Hutterians "let you know what they thought." He suggested that this was done "out of love" and that such forthright honesty eliminated the possibility of hidden misunderstandings.[27]

Even Sunday School discussions had often been "lengthy" and "heated."[28] According to Samuel Hofer, "The Prairieleut who attended the Krimmer

Mennonite Church [Emmanuel, near Langham, Saskatchewan] would interrupt biblical texts and hold long and sometimes heated discussions."[29]

Visits to contemporary Hutterite colonies showed a similarly forthright, no-holds-barred way of engaging in interpersonal communication. In a recent discussion with a group of people at one colony, an individual had asked with regard to this book, "Is it gonna be like the Bible?" When asked what he meant, the man responded, "Is it going to include the bad and the good?" A Hutterite minister once gave the author a fiery fifteen-minute lecture on "Mennonite hypocrisy" before spending a comfortable afternoon exchanging opinions on social and theological issues.

It was that kind of honesty which was expected, indeed demanded, by Hutterians of all stripes. A critical approach to personal behavior and ideals was thought to foster humility and self-abnegation. People were not to think so highly of themselves that they would take offense at straightforward personal comments. In 1984, a Hutterite minister insisted, for example, that a recently published book (by the author) had been "too soft" on them. "There wasn't enough salt," he had declared.[30] Thus, when outsiders—even Mennonite conference leaders—entered the playing field of the Prairieleut community, they sometimes misunderstood the "tension" they felt they had encountered. This caused problems, as well, for some Prairieleut ministers hired by non-Hutterian congregations. A classic example of that phenomenon was seen in the 1940s-era Fresno Mennonite Brethren Church, where Prairieleut pastor J. D. Hofer had been accused of "blustery" outspokenness by his non-Hutterian parishioners. Prairieleut who were interviewed, conversely, described Hofer as an amazingly "soft-spoken" man.

In response to a questionnaire from national conference offices, one Prairieleut minister had made blunt, off-the-cuff personal remarks about every previous pastor of that congregation. He noted that one predecessor, for example, had "lacked in doctrinal preaching," and the church had thus grown "lax." At the bottom of the form, the minister had also noted that, with reference to himself, personal accomplishments "remain to be seen." He also added, humorously, that the person who had sent out the survey had given him "gray hairs."

Even men of the cloth had not been immune from honest expressions of dissent. A Prairieleut congregant once responded to an opinion expressed by his minister by stating publicly, "Oh pastor, you're crazy." That statement was not intended as a personal attack. It simply expressed disagreement with a particular position. Before beginning his sermon, a former minister at another congregation had once informed the congregation that a Sunday School teacher had "missed the whole point" of a recently completed lesson.[31]

Karl Peter proposed that intense persecution throughout Hutterian history had created a remnant of persons with "a high degree of uniformity in those psychological characteristics that were indispensable for defying the authorities." These had included "courage, perseverance and obstinacy."[32]

Perhaps the "no-holds-barred" interactional structure, still evident among noncommunal Hutterians, has a psycho-historical foundation in a history of unrelenting persecution and harassment.

Unhypocritical Prairieleut honesty also influenced the way in which the religious expressed their spirituality. Prairieleut Christians worshiped God and practiced their faith with great fervor, in an attempt to combat the "great noise" of the post-modern era.[33] Prairie People also felt they had a kind of "stick-to-itiveness" not always found in other ethnic traditions. They expected to "get the job done" when called upon and often criticized people whom they thought tolerated lackadaisical procrastination.

The Prairie People have traditionally had close, tightly knit families. Detractors thus described them as "tribal" and "cliquish," as a group of people who looked out for their own and had thought of themselves as "a cut above the rest." The social-emotional attachments that accompanied a strong sense of family and community had helped ensure, however, the endurance of the Prairieleut as a separate people. Noncommunal Hutterians felt they belonged to a social entity that was doing something important. They did not care what other people thought (at least some of the time).

In that context it was interesting to note that church-going Prairieleut often refused to criticize those who did not attend church. Some believed the Hutterian ethnic heritage, in itself, provided a vital moral force that was noticeable even in the behavior of nonattenders. This view was particularly observable among Saskatchewan Prairieleut.

One person interviewed in the Langham area noted that although it did not make "biblical sense" to him, the unchurched children of "renegade" Prairie People still behaved well, even though they had never attended Sunday School. Prairieleut childrearing patterns, including disciplinary approaches, were so similar to those adhered to in the colonies that one Prairieleut descendent noted that she and her Hutterite husband had experienced almost identical parent/child interactive patterns.[34]

Ethnic solidarity did not always, however, prevent internecine conflict. In the spring of 1984, a murder involving three Prairie People occurred in South Dakota's Freeman community. On May 17, Jennis Hofer, a member of the Bethany Mennonite Church and a former school board member, shot and killed Andrew Wipf, a fellow member at Bethany and his son, Andrew Jr., a member at the Salem MB Church.

Hofer and the Wipfs had a long-standing disagreement over water drainage on adjacent properties; legal challenges and verbal exchanges had characterized relationships in the months previous to the shootings. According to Hofer, he drove past the Wipf land around noon on the seventeenth and got upset just seeing the Wipfs working in the fields. It reminded him of all the water drainage controversies of the past. That morning, Hofer had also taken a couple of drinks, for what he described as a "painful shoulder." The two parties eventually got involved in a heated verbal exchange, and Hofer

Fig. 11.1. Emmanuel Krimmer Mennonite Brethren Church, Langham, Saskatchewan. Photograph courtesy of Edna Wurtz.

shot and killed both men. On November 9, 1984, Hofer was sentenced to two life terms in the South Dakota State penitentiary.[35]

On a more hopeful note, in July 1997, 592 persons had registered for a reunion of Langham (Saskatchewan) Prairieleut descendents.[36] Those in attendance heard speakers not only review important events from the Saskatchewan Hutterian past but challenge the audience to "continue in the faith." At the reunion, Saskatoon linguist Walter Hoover presented historic first copies of his "Hutterisch-English" dictionary.[37]

Hutterian Connections

New Prairieleut openness to relationships with, or at least respect for Hutterian traditions left open the faint possibility that the communal Hutterites might influence future social and theological developments in the Prairieleut community. This could also mean that Prairie People in turn would have an impact on the direction of Hutterite life. Interpersonal contacts have a way of forcing mental restructuring when both sides involved recognize a common purpose. In the Prairieleut/Hutterite situation, such a shared resolution might be an agreed-upon vision based on the sixteenth-century Anabaptist dream.

Relationships between Prairieleut and Hutterites would, perhaps, have

234 / The Prairie People

been closer had most Hutterites not left South Dakota for Canada during the World War I era. Fourteen of fifteen South Dakota colonies were left uninhabited at that time. The Dariusleut and Lehrerleut Hutterite branches left South Dakota for Manitoba, Alberta, and Saskatchewan and never returned. The Schmiedeleut came back but colonies had been re-established at a very slow pace. As late as 1935, there were only three Hutterite communities in the entire state.

A fissure in time, a relational gap, had thus been created at a critical juncture in Prairieleut history, during a period of time when assimilationist forces were most potent. During that important era there had been no communal relatives nearby to provide a critique of the changes occurring in the Prairieleut community. In the interim, noncommunal Hutterian churches had experienced a major ideological shift toward evangelical Protestantism with a concomitant rejection of isolationism and pacifism.

According to Arnold M. Hofer, it was also significant that the Prairie People had more relatives among the Lehrerleut and Dariusleut than among the Schmiedeleut, a strange phenomenon that deserves further research. In any case, neither group—Hutters or Hutterites—had close connections with the other for a number of decades, though some Prairie People had re-established relationships with newly created colonies, and many Hutterites had subscribed over the years to Jacob J. Mendel's Freeman *Courier*.

In comparison to the Hutter/Hutterite relational situation at mid-century, contemporary interaction between Prairieleut and Hutterites had increased considerably. In the late 1980s, two older Prairieleut men entertained a Hutterite minister in their home every other week, while members of his colony went shopping. The minister preferred conversation with Prairieleut friends to bi-monthly shopping excursions in downtown Freeman. There were many examples of such contacts. Prairieleut farmers, for example, often exchanged opinions with Hutterite neighbors on agricultural issues. They discussed such things as seed quality, the effectiveness of herbicides, and marketing strategies.

In July 1993, the Prairieleut extended family reunion of the descendents of Paul Tschetter and Maria Walter included special music by a group of girls from Oak Lane Colony.[38] Other Prairieleut had revisited historic Hutterian sites in eastern Europe. On one visit to Slovakia, Arnold M. Hofer located Habaner descendents with names like "Pullman" and "Tschetter" still living in the Sabatisch (now Sobotiste) area.

Some noncommunal Hutterians, in addition, expressed a sincere hope that communal Hutterites would not give up their way of life. As Amos Kleinsasser put it, "I hope . . . that they continue with their type of life as their belief is biblically based on Acts 2: 42–47."[39] Kleinsasser felt the Hutterite way of life was biblically founded, even though he did not personally interpret the Bible that way. The Hutterites went one step further, proclaiming quite openly that colony life was "the surest way to get to heaven."[40]

A Hutterian's Return to Community

Very occasionally, an individual with Prairieleut ethnicity decides to give up private possessions and live communally. One who has done this in recent times is evangelist Gwen Shaw. In 1975, Shaw took the unusual step of establishing a communal center in the Ozark Mountains of northwestern Arkansas.[41] Shaw—sometimes known as "Sister Gwen"—is a direct descendent of early nineteenth-century Hutterite minister and chronicler Johannes Waldner. Her Prairieleut grandfather, Peter Miller, had moved to Langham, Saskatchewan, in 1901 and had donated the land upon which the Emmanuel KMB Church was eventually built.

Gwen Shaw, a self-described prophetess and missionary, directed a Christian women's organization called "End-Time Handmaidens." Prairie People who attended Shaw's evangelistic services noted a strong emphasis on charismatic gifts of the Spirit. According to her autobiography, Shaw was also the first woman to preach from the pulpit in the Moscow Baptist Church (in 1966).[42]

Shaw was also profoundly influenced by her Hutterian past. The title of Shaw's autobiography, *Unconditional Surrender*, in itself suggests the Hutterian teaching of gelassenheit. In the mid-1970s, after a time of extended prayer, Shaw and her husband, Colonel James Shaw, established a communal center, called "Engeltal" (Angel Valley), near Jasper, Arkansas.

Hearkening back to Hutterian roots, Gwen became increasingly convinced that communal life was the ideal way for Christians to live. She continued to believe, however, that since this was a difficult and unconventional manner of existence, not all Christians were called to follow her. The thirty persons who reside at Engeltal in the late 1990s share meals and work responsibilities. Each morning members of the community—including Shaw's Prairieleut mother, Bessie—gather for prayer and meditation. Shaw notes that she has come closer to God through this communal experience.[43]

Though Shaw has not focused on this teaching in her ministry, nonresistance, too, is an ideal to which she has adhered in raising her children. In her autobiography, Shaw describes how her son, Tommy, at one point "laid his toy guns on the altar because Jesus asked him to do it." She continues, "The Lord did not want him to play games of violence, such as war games and cowboys and Indians, for God said that if he did, a spirit of violence would enter into him."[44]

Though Shaw considers herself a pacifist, she does not demand that her followers accept that position, nor has she emphasized it in her preaching. Her story, however, shows the continuing impact of the communal Hutterian past, even on those Prairie People who for many years lost connection with other Hutterians.

Other Denominations, Other Commitments

The experience of other prominent Prairieleut showed little continuing commitment to Hutterian traditions. Many individuals credited Prairieleut communities, however, for nurturing character traits that helped them achieve success later on. The ironic connection between early exposure to a semi-communal value system and later personal success is a complicated, as well as fascinating phenomenon. The same ethical structure which emphasized humility and self-denial, for example, also stressed industry and continuous effort. The latter attributes brought forth social, material, and ecclesiastical success in mainstream North America.

Solomon Walter, for example, was born near Freeman and grew up speaking Hutterisch, immersed in Prairieleut traditions. As a child, he visited the colonies with his parents on numerous occasions.[45] At age nineteen, however, Walter was attracted to the "second work of grace" theology of the Missionary Church denomination and left the Prairieleut world behind. Eight years later, Walter was ordained as a minister in the United Methodist Church, where he spent the rest of his career pastoring some very large congregations. Walter's story is characteristic of the journey away from Hutterian roots taken by thousands of people.

On the West Coast, David L. Hofer exemplified a more complex interdenominational persona via a Mennonite-based, yet ecumenical, interaction with the evangelical Protestant world at-large. Hofer grew up at the Zion KMB church and continued to be an active member into the 1970s. His evangelistic interests went far beyond the boundaries of Anabaptist congregations, however.

In 1946, after the casting of lots incident that caused a major career change —and called to mind Hutterian tradition—Hofer had established Christian radio station KRDU, which provided conservative evangelical programming, popular with a variety of denominational groups. Well known as a youth leader and songwriter, Hofer also became a leading figure in both the Gideons International (which he served as President from 1974 to 1977) and the National Religious Broadcasters Association (where he held the office of President from 1979 to 1982). In the latter position, Hofer had once accompanied President Ronald Reagan in his private limousine. Hofer's father was Elmspring Colony defector David P. Hofer, who had likely never anticipated that one of his children would become so well connected. Another Prairieleut Hutterian, Ben Glanzer, had become a pastor and musician in the Seventh-Day Adventist Church.

Marrying Outside

The genetic separateness of the Prairie People was quickly disappearing in the late twentieth century, creating an assimilated multi-culture vastly different from that of the Hutterites, who continued to experience rapid inbred population growth. Victor Peters suggested that inbreeding itself had perhaps added to the Hutterite gene pool "genetic components favoring high fertility."[46] Geneticists noted that Hutterite inbreeding had produced few detrimental and many positive physical effects. According to Sandra Hartzog: "Any detrimental effects of inbreeding within a deme may be buffered by the maintenance of favorable gene complexes or genomes and the attainment of a selective peak."[47]

Geneticist Evan Eichler's research showed that the eighteenth-century Carinthian converts (the Hofers, Kleinsassers, Glanzers, etc.) had themselves come from a highly inbred Lutheran enclave in Austria. Eichler also reminded that the idea of "marrying out" of the extended family was a recent phenomenon in world history.[48] Inbreeding had always been the norm.

Inbreeding does not accurately describe contemporary Prairieleut practice, however. By the time the Baby Boom generation becomes the oldest grouping in Prairieleut churches, there will probably be as many Friesens—a traditional Mennonite name—or even Johnsons, as Hofers and Glanzers on congregation membership rolls.

In the 1990s, it has still been possible to identify non-Mennonite Hutterians, either because of last names, since older Prairie People can identify family lines, or because they themselves had sought to preserve ethnic memories. Continued intermarriage will make such endeavors exceedingly difficult in the future.

In Russia, there were no cases of Hutterian/Russian intermarriage during the entire sojourn there. For many years in North America, the Prairie People continued the practice of marrying primarily within the ethnic enclave, a tradition of exclusion that, at times, caused problems for non-Hutterians who joined Prairieleut congregations.

In 1920, for example, Julia Schrag—a young Swiss Mennonite—married Joe K. Kleinsasser of the Hutterthal Church. On the first Sunday after their marriage, Julia arrived at church wearing a hat, during a time when most women at Hutterthal wore black shawls. According to Norman Hofer, "The preacher stood up to preach, saw her hat, glared at her and said, from the pulpit, 'Lady, in this church the women wear shawls and you will do the same.'"[49] Some non-Hutterian spouses suggested there was continuing subtle discrimination in the 1980s and 1990s, even if such was unintended. One heard similar complaints, in the opposite direction, from Prairie People who married into non-Hutterian Mennonite churches.[50]

Continued intermarriage was gradually causing the disappearance of an exclusive Prairieleut population. Modern transportation, updated communication systems, and social mobility made it difficult to maintain a genetically pure culture without living a much more isolated existence. As early as 1875, Prairieleut Elias Wipf had moved to Kansas and married Low German Mennonite Agatha Cornelson, deciding not to homestead alongside relatives in the Dakotas.[51]

Other interethnic marriages followed. The first South Dakota marriage between a Prairieleut and a non-Hutterian took place in 1887, when Peter J. Glanzer married Katherina Kielbauch. The following year, Prairieleut John Gross married Lydia Jans and joined the Reformed Church. In 1891, Jacob Kleinsasser married Low German Mennonite Katherina Pankratz (at the Hutterthal Church), and in 1908 dentist J. H. Wipf married Emma Gering, finally putting a crack in the wall that divided the Prairieleut and Swiss Mennonite communities.[52]

Jacob J. Mendel's unofficial records showed substantially more marriages of Prairie People to non-Anabaptists—during the pre–World War I time period—than to non-Hutterian Mennonites. In the Freeman, South Dakota, area inter-Anabaptist marital relationships were slow to gain acceptance.

A review of church records at the more conservative Neu Hutterthaler congregation showed that, through the year 1919, there were no interethnic marriages. By the mid-1920s, however, many "outside" marriages had materialized, particularly with Low German Mennonites.[53] Note, for example, the 1925 marriage of Adina Kleinsasser to George Goossen.[54] That trend continued in the 1930s, though there was still a strong preference for Neu Hutterthalers to marry other Prairie People.

Even on the more liberal West Coast, Egon Hofer recalled that, although he had dated girls from other ethnic backgrounds while a student at the Bible Institute of Los Angeles, he never intended to marry any of them. He had always planned "to go back to [his] own people," and he did, marrying Naomi Tschetter in 1938.[55] By the late 1950s, however, one found ethnically exclusive marriages becoming a distinct minority in most Prairieleut congregations. An important reason for this was the joint attendance of Prairieleut, Low German Mennonite, and Swiss Mennonite young persons at schools like Freeman College and Academy, James Valley Christian Academy, and Immanuel Academy.

Analysis of Zion Church (Dinuba, California) records with regard to the name Hofer, for example, showed that, from 1911 to 1990, about one-third of the Hofers had married other Prairieleut. Another one-third had married Low German Mennonites. The final third married outside the Anabaptist ethnic community. It is noteworthy, however, that all of the Prairieleut/Prairieleut marriages had taken place before the year 1940. Immanuel Academy was formally established in 1944. During the next thirty years, it had become common for persons named Hofer to marry Low German Mennonites, with an increasing tendency to marry outside Anabaptist ethnic boundaries.[56]

Ethnic Exclusivity

According to Miriam Warner, "If ethnics have known each other since they were children or young adults . . . then it is more natural for them to socialize with each other."[57] Some older Prairie People continued to express personal sensitivities with regard to ethnic delineation. Though feelings of protectiveness had diminished, one older Prairieleut noted that, when he was growing up, if someone got in trouble in the community or at school, he had always "hoped it wouldn't be a Hutter." Marian Kleinsasser Towne denoted an "inferiority complex" accompanying that sentiment, similar in nature to the guilt-by-ethnic-identification mindset articulated by Michael Arlen (with reference to his Armenian heritage) in *A Passage to Ararat*.[58]

Early Prairieleut solidarity was demonstrated negatively when a Hutterian who owed money to many people was hidden from police underneath what was described as "a Hutterite church."[59] The fugitive had evidently fled to Canada to escape lenders but had returned for a brief visit to the Freeman area, where he was discovered by a local citizen who duly reported his presence to the police. Many local saloons, too, in the early years had been owned and operated by Prairie People, though this fact could be construed as positive, negative, or neutral depending on personal views of drinking establishments.[60]

Much controversy remained, as well, with regard to Lohrentz Tschetter who, along with his spiritually minded nephew, Paul, in 1873, had spied out the American plains for possible settlement.[61] Some older Prairie People remembered hearing their parents and/or grandparents say that Lohrentz had come to America at his own expense "to get away from his problems" (alcohol, for example), or that he had been selected as a representative of the Hutterian community because "no one else would go." Paul Tschetter himself had balked at the thought of international travel.

It was also said that the delegates had a difficult time keeping track of Lohrentz during their sojourn in eastern cities, that nephew Paul had often found him sitting in a bar. In his diary account, however, Paul Tschetter included very little information about his uncle. What really happened was shrouded by hundreds of slightly different, but consistently racy, stories told by older Prairie People, many of whom had never shared such tales with younger Hutterian generations, and some of whom are no longer living.

Lohrentz died in 1878 and was buried near Olivet, South Dakota, where he had homesteaded. In 1974, during the Hutterian centennial celebration in Freeman, some Hutters who felt they knew the whole story about Lohrentz —his drinking and lack of interest in institutional religion—were upset that a commemorative marker had been placed near his grave. Ultimately, however, Tschetter's historic accomplishment had been deemed more important than that which, perhaps, had characterized his life in general.

Unfortunately, after Tschetter's death, son Lohrentz Jr. had become men-

Fig. 11.2. Neu Hutterthaler Church, 1997. Photograph by the author.

tally incapacitated, presumably from inhaling too much smoke while fighting a prairie fire. Tschetter thus spent his last thirty years in a state hospital in Yankton. That whole situation had been hidden from one grandson, who noted that, when his grandfather died and the body had been shipped to their house, his dad had told him, "Go into the house and view your grandfather's body." "Can you imagine how I felt?" the grandson continued. The boy had not even known he had this grandfather.

Persons inside the Prairieleut community spoke honestly and forthrightly about the strengths and weaknesses of fellow and sister human beings. This no-holds-barred way of interacting, discussed previously, ensured that little was hidden from those engaged in serious conversations.

A spirit of ethnic pride continued to show itself, as well, in Prairieleut documents. As noted earlier, the writer of the *History of the Hutterthal Mennonite Church*, which was published in 1968, had stated—concerning ministers in the church—that, "All except the last four were of our own Hutterisch people." The use of the words "our own" or *unser Leute*—our people—denoted a proud recognition of a particular ethnic identification. The phrase "our people" was found in many Prairieleut family histories and autobiographical jottings and was a phrase employed by other Anabaptists, as well, concerning their own particular ethnic enclaves.[62]

One older Prairieleut church leader noted that "the closed community aspect" had "continued to linger" among noncommunal Hutterians. "Taking the initiative" toward non-Hutterian individuals, for example, had still been difficult for many. That same pastor, who regretted the increasing loss of Hutterian linguistic and culinary traditions, suggested that cultural changes themselves had accompanied "loss of commitment to Christ and his church due to busy lifestyle and pressures to 'make it.'" He believed there was significant connection between Hutterian cultural and religious values.

Prairieleut cultural remnants informed by historic Hutterian economic traditions included the borrowing of farm equipment and tools, collective harvesting, combining, cornpicking, windrowing and haying, and occasional joint purchases of expensive machinery. Members of the Prairieleut community told the author that these semi-communal methods of operation continued to be practiced to a greater extent by Prairie People than by non-Hutterians in neighboring locales. Community-oriented economic traditions had generally only been retained, however, by those engaged in farming.

A Candle Not Hidden

A diverse group of people have emerged from the Prairieleut community in recent years. Numerous examples of positive Prairieleut impact on church, educational, and political communities have been noted. It is important to recognize additionally the large number of Prairie People who have been involved in international missions work. This was a place where one found a significant number of women in leadership positions, as well, since Prairieleut congregations, following the ethnocentric model adhered to by most Protestant denominations historically, had allowed females to be spiritual mentors in relationships with non-European peoples. Tillie Waldner had served in that regard as a missionary in China. Lucille Wipf, who had a masters degree in religious education, served for many years in Japan, and there were many others.[63]

South Dakotans Joseph and Janette Walter, who retired in 1991, had worked for three and a half decades with native and Spanish-speaking groups in Peru, Columbia, and Mexico. Their commitment to teach people about the Christian faith had meant years of service to diverse cultural groups, as well as living in areas impacted by poverty and disease.

Early correspondence between Walter and the Mennonite Brethren Board of Missions did show an ethnocentric view of non-European peoples, but it simply reflected the spirit of those times.[64] More noteworthy was the fact that there was no suggestion in early correspondence that the peace position might inform the missions enterprise. Thirty-five years later, Walter noted that pacifism had simply not been an option for South American Christians. There were no alternative service opportunities in the countries where the Walters had worked.[65] In any case, the Walters had devoted themselves to a simple life focused on evangelism, situated about as far away from the homeland as it was possible to get. Sacrificial love had led to many life-changing commitments to the Christian faith.

On the darker side, Prairieleut descendent Alfred Tschetter had been involved in a different kind of social-religious mission. Tschetter, son of KMB minister, David W. Tschetter, and a grandson of Paul Tschetter, had achieved national recognition for his work as an x-ray technician at the Baylor University Hospitals. Alfred's first marriage had been to a noncommunal Hutterian; his final relationship was with a woman from Indiana who had been involved with Jim Jones' People's Temple from its inception.

Alfred and his spouse had eventually moved to northern California and then followed Jones to Guyana, where both consumed poisoned grape punch and died at Jones' insistent invitation. Paul G. Tschetter, Alfred's brother, who helped coordinate funeral arrangements, had insisted that the 23rd Psalm and a short prayer be included in a short memorial service held after Alfred's body was shipped back to the United States.[66]

Prairieleut Distinctives

Notwithstanding Alfred Tschetter's choices, which showed behavioral idiosyncracies transcending ethno-religious boundaries, the various Prairieleut cultural peculiarities described in this chapter helped preserve a singular identity without communal life for a long period of time. These singularities included unique interpersonal relationship patterns, Hutterisch dialect/language expressions, and noteworthy foods and culinary practices. An honest and direct style of personal interaction had continued, as well, to define the modern Prairieleut character.

Hutterian traditions had also been preserved by a general Prairieleut tendency to marry within the group, particularly during the first sixty years of settlement in North America. Geographical proximity to the Hutterites had influenced retention of Hutterian folkways, as well, as had certain historic ideological principles.

The Prairie People have often been described as "clannish," a common characteristic of people committed to a specific ethnic community. A few individuals gained new-found interest in the religious ideals of Hutterian ancestors. Others used character strengths developed within traditional Prairieleut communities to achieve success outside Hutterian boundaries.

The influence of Hutterian customs and folkways has diminished steadily, however, throughout the twentieth century. What has remained is a greatly transformed sense of peoplehood, which continues to undergo significant change. The traditions that survive have undergone consequential metamorphosis, yet they still provide a foundation, albeit a fragile one, for the retention of a unique ethno-religious identity.

12

. . . .

The Prairieleut Dilemma

He was still living in private property and therefore had not
yet truly died to himself.
The Hutterite Chronicle, **1565**

There is no creature in this world that makes such a pitiful
mockery . . . as man. This praying, swearing, and cussing
makes a poor harmony.
Hutterite sermon on Matthew 6, circa 1650

The Mennonites are free to make errors that Hutterites do
not make because they do not have the chance to make them.
Hans Decker, Wolf Creek Colony, 1983

The Present Scene

The contemporary Prairieleut population has been esti-
mated at 3,500 people.[1] Arnold M. Hofer arrived at that figure by consulting membership lists of appropriate Mennonite congregations, then adding
children. He only counted noncommunal Hutterians, therefore, who had
maintained affiliation with Anabaptist congregations. In order to complete
a demographic analysis, Hofer relied on his extensive knowledge of family
connections, cross-marriages, and basic Prairieleut trivia. Hofer's work exem-
plifies a speculative venture, virtually impossible to duplicate by a non-
Prairieleut historian.

A significant number of the 3,500 persons that Hofer named attended
Prairieleut Mennonite churches in South Dakota. The entire Prairieleut
population, however, was scattered across the United States and Canada.
Many contemporary Prairie People were difficult to locate because they mar-

Table 8.
Prairieleut/Hutterite Demographics[a]

Date	Group	Population
1880	Prairieleut	825
	Hutterites	443
1995	Prairieleut	3,500[b]
	Alberta	50
	North Dakota	50
	Saskatchewan	150
	California	250
	South Dakota	3,000
	Hutterites	40,000

[a]This table shows approximate Hutterian membership figures in the mid-1990s.
[b]Members of Mennonite churches.

ried and attended churches outside of Mennonite communities. Twenty years ago, John D. Unruh had noted that even in the Huron, South Dakota, area, nearly 30 percent of the noncommunal Hutterians were "non-Mennonites."[2]

Arnold Hofer estimated that the larger Prairieleut population "should total 20,000 or more" if one included all those people with at least one Hutterian grandparent.[3] Thirty-five hundred Prairieleut-Mennonites thus represent, perhaps, 17.5 percent of the total noncommunal Hutterian ethnic population, as most Prairie People have disappeared into the transforming socio-economic structures of modern urban and suburban life.

The Prairieleut Identity

Near the end of the twentieth century, the Hutterisch dialect, distinctive foods, folk customs, and a unique religious heritage continued to define the Prairieleut way of life on the northern plains. These were the most visible manifestations of the Hutterian past. Evidence of Hutterian heritage was most notable in South Dakota communities, where the surrounding protection of the larger Anabaptist/Mennonite social structure had helped, ironically, to preserve the Hutterian culture.[4]

Young persons raised in South Dakota's West Freeman community, for example, still called themselves "Hutters." Students at Freeman Academy claimed to know the difference between a Hutter and a "*Schweitzer*"—a Swiss Mennonite from East Freeman—and could good-naturedly and humorously describe the idiosyncrasies of each if asked to do so. All of this was made very clear to me during the first few months of my six-year sojourn at Freeman College.

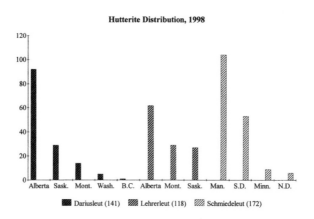

Fig. 11.3. Hutterite colony distribution, 1998. Graph by Tony Waldner.

Other sociological, psychological, and theological distinctions were difficult to grasp yet still discernible. Interpersonal relationship structures, feelings about self, interpretations of Christianity, all had a unique character in the Prairieleut community. They all emitted the faint glimmer of the Hutterian past.

A warm sense of camaraderie continued to pervade the Prairieleut commonwealth. Older Prairie People remembered Sunday afternoon visits that were "not long enough," noting "the great love amongst the people." That relational consciousness still existed in the 1990s. Guests too had experienced this love via the hospitality extended to them, even on short notice. One assumed a continuing sense of *gemutlichkeit*—hospitable congeniality —when one was almost always invited to dinner after attending Prairieleut church services. It was fascinating for this writer to watch Hutterian hosts successfully search the refrigerator and cupboards for something to serve to guests who had come to dinner as a result of spur-of-the-moment invitations.

On occasion, communal emphases emerged, as well, even if in unique forms. Barbara Kleinsasser Wiens noted, for example, that her son—California naturalist Douglas Wiens—had always insisted that the purpose of life was not "to collect things."[5] Prairieleut Hutterians also continued to give liberally to missions and social programs.

The Prairie People placed much stock, over the years, in customs that served as central forms of identity. Unique ways of thinking and living encouraged ethnic longevity, as noncommunal Hutterians developed singular ways of celebrating, eating, speaking, and expressing spirituality. Interpersonal relationships thus presupposed specific inquiry and response patterns.

Participation in customary ways of living over a long period of time, led naturally to ethnic commitment. With regard to Mennonites in general, Philosopher Delbert Wiens suggested that ethnicity "made it possible for communities to contain an astonishingly varied group of people." He proposed that what held Mennonites together had "more to do with borscht and Low German and history and genetics than with theology."[6] With regard to his Hutterian heritage, Wiens—whose mother was a Kleinsasser—might have substituted *fleischknedel* and Hutterisch. Once customs and rituals were lost, however, the commitment to groups bonded by ethnicity generally died, even if the demise was a slow one.

The Prairieleut Dilemma

At the close of the twentieth century, as ethnic groups across North America seek to regain understanding of traditional beliefs and practices, the Prairieleut find themselves confronting a supreme dilemma of self-identification, a dilemma related specifically to the way in which the noncommunal Hutterians have seen themselves as a people. What social and ideological traditions continue to characterize the Prairieleut identity? Is such a delineation essentially irrelevant, because so many have intermarried, and so many others have no interest in a social personality other than that offered by mainstream American evangelicalism?

Coming to North America in the 1870s, the Prairie People had dreams of carefully recrafting a noncommunal but community-oriented social-religious way of life, unimpeded by Tsars and Mennonites, Americans and Canadians. Tsar Alexander II had wanted Hutterians to speak the Russian language and take on military responsibilities. Mennonites wanted Hutterians to get rid of their cultural and theological distinctness. Americans and Canadians desired that the Prairieleut be assimilated into whatever their national cultures had become or were becoming.

When they arrived in Dakota Territory, the Prairie People found themselves surrounded by the same Low German Mennonites to whom they had bid farewell in Russia, and one new assemblage, as well, the Swiss Volhynians. North American societies, with their democratic and egalitarian traditions were highly attractive to third and fourth generation Prairieleut, who, after major struggles with the forces of modernity and postmodernity, gave up many customs and religious practices.

The contemporary dilemma is exacerbated by the fact that those who held on to the remnants of Hutterian culture—the conservatives—were often not the same persons who believed in traditional Hutterian theological and religious principles. In other words, those Hutterians who knew how to prepare egg dumpling soup, those who dropped by to visit on Sunday afternoons and conversed in Hutterisch, were often not the same persons who were interested in maintaining or resurrecting Hutterian theological traditions.

Those who wanted to recover the Hutterian theological past, conversely, often took little interest in the cultural practices that held a great deal of meaning for conservatives. This changed to some extent during the 1980s and 1990s, particularly as a result of the important work of the Hutterian

Fig. 12.1. Arnold M. Hofer, Prairieleut historian and Chair of the Hutterian Centennial Committee. Photograph courtesy of Olan Mills Portrait Studios.

Centennial Committee (South Dakota) and the Board of Directors of the Emmanuel Church (Saskatchewan). The Prairieleut evangelical majority, however, generally considered cultural as well as theological traditions a significant hindrance to Christian evangelism and expressed little interest in learning from the ethno-religious past.

Few contemporary Prairieleut have been interested in giving up private possessions in emulation of now distant Hutterite relatives. Only Gwen Shaw's Engeltal community and the small Stirling Mennonite group have sought to institutionalize communal forms of life. In committing themselves to a noncommunal Hutterianism, which they felt had shown some success in Europe, and which in their view more closely exemplified the teaching and practice of Jesus, the Prairie People had not believed that living on private land would cause them to lose touch with Hutterian social and theological traditions. Just the opposite would happen, thought Paul Tschetter, now that the Hutterians had freed themselves from the governmental and social oversight of Tsars and Mennonites.

Noncommunal Hutterians began life on the prairies with the definite intention of upholding ethno-religious traditions. They read the inspired sermons, sang the historic martyr hymns, conversed in the Hutterisch dialect, and maintained Hutterian cultural practices. The Prairie People also utilized a process of collective discernment with regard to the selection of ministers and church decision making. They farmed together, shared tools and implements, and married within the ethnic group. During the first decades of life in North America most intimate personal associations had been with other noncommunal Hutterians.

That way of life was not preserved for long, however. "Life on the outside" from the beginning had exposed noncommunal Hutterians, to a much greater extent than colony Hutterites, to the vicissitudes of modern social and economic life among the "English." Unable to revive a village-style social structure, the Prairieleut were quickly propelled in more individualistic directions than they had anticipated. This caused some people to develop significant insecurities, not knowing how to respond to a North American environment that was itself undergoing rapid social and religious change and that ultimately exerted strong assimilationist pressures felt by all new immigrant groups. National financial panics in the 1870s and 1890s exacerbated those personal and social anxieties.

The noncommunal Hutterian immigrants struggled to eke out an economic existence on the plains while simultaneously seeking psychological security by directing attention to spiritual matters. They did this through the avenue of traditional Hutterian ways of approaching God and doing his will. Most Prairieleut found security in the womb of the independent Hutterian churches. Others discovered a greater sense of hope among the colony Hutterites and the Krimmer Mennonite Brethren.

Communal Hutterites dealt with the question of psychological and spiritual security by stressing that residents of the colonies would receive divine protection, just as the followers of Noah did in the Book of Genesis. Hutterites described themselves as residents of a newly constructed "ark" community on the dry seas of the Great Plains. A communal way of life had indeed been attractive to many Prairieleut Hutterians during the early settlement years, causing a significant number to join the colonies.

Other dissatisfied Prairie People, not comforted by traditional Hutterian religious teachings and institutional structures, had joined ethnically homogeneous Krimmer Mennonite Brethren congregations, which provided a different kind of security through the teaching of "assurance of salvation" and an emotionally intense version of the Christian salvation experience. The KMBs had also imposed strict lifestyle requirements, many of which were more prohibitory than those adhered to by Hutterians in the independent churches or in the colonies. Prairieleut KMBs had found the security of the Hutterian "ark" in a privatized, personal encounter with Jesus, expressed within the confines of a Mennonite conference, which had imposed precise behavioral guidelines.

Eventually, the independently organized Prairieleut churches had moved in evangelical Protestant theological directions, as well. And when they did so, it was only a matter of time—a short period of twenty to thirty years—before the Hutterian congregations threw out the sermons, the *Gesangbuch*, community-oriented theological positions, the casting of lots, and even traditional folk customs and myths.

This course of events was aided by the presence of influential Mennonite neighbors nearby, persons who had similar Anabaptist roots and were moving rapidly in kindred social and theological directions. Duplicating what had previously transpired in Russia, many North American Prairieleut began to feel their own customs and traditions were somehow inferior to or less sophisticated than those esteemed by others, whether Mennonites or mainstream Americans. This was in fact the very sentiment the Rev. Paul Tschetter had so feared and abhorred in Russia. The Prairie People had often given Mennonites, in particular, the benefit of the doubt with regard to issues of culture and theology. They had even joined their denominational organizations. Mennonite churches had not, conversely, requested membership in any Hutterian religious institutions.

Mennonites had the same Anabaptist theological roots as Prairieleut Hutterians but never preached the significance of full communal life. Since community of goods was the major point of ideological demarcation between the two groups historically, and since the Prairieleut had given it up, it was extremely difficult for the Prairie People to continue to insist that the other aspects of their unique heritage—the *Lehren*, the *Gesangbuch*, the Hutterisch dialect, for example—held significant spiritual importance.

In Russia particularly, but also in the Dakotas, Mennonites implied that the traditional Prairieleut way of life was provincial and perhaps not even biblical. The *Lehren*, in particular, were referred to as outdated and inscrutable. Younger Prairieleut were often swayed by such arguments. If communal living had been found wanting, why not throw out the rest as well? There was a tremendous irony in the Prairieleut/Mennonite relationship, however, since it was that very association that had helped preserve a number of distinctive Anabaptist beliefs within the Prairieleut churches.

In North America, once the Prairieleut Hutterians gave up the communal gelassenheit, they were, in fact, tempted to give up other Hutterian distinctives, as well. The Hutterian teaching of gelassenheit required that material possessions, as well as self-will, be given up to the church, the body of Christ. The communal colony represented God's heavenly kingdom, a precursor (though an imperfect one) of what life after death might be like. Colony members were the keepers of the keys to that kingdom and God's delegates on earth.

The Prairie People envisioned the Christian faith less communally but were still committed to the notion of collective accountability and other Hutterian cultural and theological distinctives. Paul Tschetter recognized that noncommunal Hutterianism in Europe had been founded on a geographically isolated form of existence combined with a village-style organizational structure. He hoped to reproduce the results of the combination on the North American plains, but he was not successful. Tschetter found that it was extremely difficult to activate the Hutterian social/theological system when members of the Prairieleut community lived on private farms, with significant distances between homesteads, and in the midst of a society that functioned democratically and that desired all new immigrants to expiate or transform their old world beliefs and practices.

Similarly detrimental to the retention of the Hutterian traditions was the influential impact of North American evangelical Protestantism with its direct and incontrovertible answers to questions about biblical reliability, church discipline, and civic patriotism. Evangelicals caused noncommunal Hutterians to question their traditional commitment to peace, the reading of the traditional sermons, and other aspects of community-oriented religious expression. Evangelical Protestantism also promoted a worldview that was not always focused on social dimensions of faith, but on a more individualistic form of Christianity.

The Hutterian people had grown accustomed historically to dealing with governments and societies that persecuted and sometimes killed them. The remnant that stayed true to the traditions had known very well how to deal with that kind of adversity. Karl Peter suggested that the idiosyncratic Hutterian psychological and social persona had, in fact, developed in response to those pressures and had created a particular historic Hutterian ability to deal effectively with attackers. Hutterians, however, had not had much experience with societies and governments that practiced religious toleration. They did not know how to respond, therefore, to the numerous invitations from American society to "become one of us" and join the Anglicized evangelicalized mainstream. This was something totally new and it was extremely seductive.

Prairie People in the United States, in particular, had come to view their country, not only as a refuge from religious persecution elsewhere, but as the divinely chosen "city on a hill," the protector of individual freedoms throughout the world. The Prairieleut wanted to be a part of that crusade that brought "civilization" and Christianity together. They did not want to isolate themselves from the "world" any longer.

Unlike the Hutterites, who controlled access to the world outside the colony boundaries, the Prairieleut lived among "the English." Prairie People went to school with diverse types of people and were attracted, like other immigrants, to the "American dream" of democratic equality and civic obligation. KMB and non-KMB Prairie People alike tried to hold the line against non-Hutterian influences. Unlike Hutterites, however, they were not able to limit relationships between church members and "outsiders."

In the colonies, even conversations with neighbors, travel to local shopping malls, and exposure to the world of media were regulated by community leaders. The Hutterites purposely promoted dress and lifestyle requirements that ensured cultural and religious distinctiveness. Communal life provided an essential institutional glue, allowing Hutterites to retain beliefs and practices in ways the Prairie People were unable to duplicate.

Young Prairie People, particularly in the third and fourth generations, gradually left the independent Prairieleut and KMB congregations to join other Protestant and, sometimes, Catholic churches. That movement increased substantially in the post–World War II years. Younger generations could see little of value in their Hutterian roots and felt those few customs and traditions that remained were keeping their churches from growing. Younger Prairieleut found they received greater social acceptance, as well, when they disassociated from congregations known to represent a particular ethnic clan.

Another significant aspect of the Prairieleut identity struggle was the continuing physical presence of communal relatives. In South Dakota, where the great majority of Prairieleut had settled, the colonies had been a constant reminder of an alternative Hutterian tradition that was considered purer, not only by the Hutterites, but by historians, sociologists, theologians, and geneticists. Most North Americans who knew something about Hutterites knew nothing about the Prairie People, or even that they existed.

Unlike other third and fourth generation ethnic groups, the Prairieleut were continually compared, not with new immigrant populations of similar ethnic background, but with an ethno-religious group that had been in North America as long as they had, a group that had successfully resisted social and religious change within the institutional framework of a communitarian existence. Their communal kinfolk represented a living indictment of the decision made by late nineteenth-century Prairieleut ancestors to live without community of goods. This was a highly unusual social phenomenon, rarely duplicated in North American history.

It was, at times, suggested that the Prairieleut should at least have been able to retain the traditions as successfully as the Old Order Amish. The Amish too did not live communally, yet they experienced great success in maintaining religious and cultural traditions by controlling the way in which the world was allowed to affect them. The Amish had done this, furthermore, in the midst of large Mennonite communities.

There was no perfect answer to this proposition. It was true that, in the late nineteenth century when the Old Order Amish began to develop innovative and conservative responses to rapid social change, the Prairieleut population had been a very small one. Noncommunal Hutterians did not have the numerical force of the Amish. The Old Order Amish also had a longer historical presence in North America and were thus able to develop an articulate theological/cultural response over a much longer period of time, and with a significant part of the membership economically well established.

Also significant was the impact of midwestern Protestant evangelicalism, which promoted the idea that ethnically embedded theological beliefs and ecclesiastical forms subverted the Christian message. Hutterite and Amish advocates responded to such attacks by reminding their critics that evangelical beliefs and practices themselves were heavily embedded in Anglo-Saxon intellectual and political traditions. But the American Prairieleut community often accepted the evangelical critique without defending their own ethno-religious traditions.

The Old Order Amish had indeed effectively managed both evangelical theological influences and other social and ideological aspects of twentieth-century North American life. There was no easy answer to the varied experiences of Prairieleut and Amish. Another important difference, however, was related to respective points of reference with regard to alternative Anabaptist religious expressions.

The Amish, for example, had historically represented a conservative split within the Swiss Mennonite churches.[7] In North America, the Amish continued to use Mennonites as their primary reference point, viewing them as social and theological progressives. In comparison, the Amish regarded themselves as conservatives. Differences between the two groups increased correspondingly, but gradually, until the late nineteenth century, when the two groups responded differently to modern technology and other transformative societal trends.

The Prairie People, conversely, represented a progressive split in the Hutterian church. The noncommunal Prairieleut used the Hutterites as their fundamental point of reference, but saw them as social and ideological conservatives. The Prairieleut viewed themselves, alternatively, as progressives. Just as in the Amish/Mennonite case, differences between Prairieleut and Hutterites had, initially, been quite small. They were radically accentuated, however, by social and technological modernization in the early twentieth century.

These diverse doors of perception had a major impact on the social and ideological directions that propelled the two groups. Whereas the Amish were philosophically resistant to new ideas (a part of their psychological and social identity), the Prairie People were attracted to new ways of thinking and acting.

The Prairieleut came from a religious tradition that, from the early 1500s on, had emphasized community of goods, at least as an ideal. Even during those times when noncommunal interpretations of Hutterianism had prevailed, there was always controversy with regard to whether or not those sermons that outspokenly promoted communal life should be read or passed over on Sunday mornings. Even those Hutterians who decided that full community of goods was not a Christian mandate had observed many semi-communal practices.

The North American Prairieleut community maintained the Hutterian traditions successfully until the onset of World War I, but by the beginning of World War II, major assimilationist tendencies had converted Prairieleut Christianity into a tradition of faith that, from the outside, looked very much like Protestant evangelicalism. In many ways, the Prairieleut churches followed the path of other ethnic Protestant congregations on the plains during the twentieth century.[8]

When one looks at things from the inside, however, one sees a Prairieleut community that, in the late 1990s, continues to hold on to a great many cultural and theological monuments of the Hutterian past. Recapturing a vision of the importance of ethnic rootedness that began in the 1960s, many Prairieleut Hutterians sought to recenter themselves, socially and theologically, by learning more about their ancestral traditions. Even as Prairieleut communities grafted evangelical theological orientations onto an Anabaptist base in the 1930s, 1940s, and 1950s, for example, their churches had remained predominately Hutterian with regard to ethnic composition. That fact alone allowed the Prairie People to maintain many historical beliefs and practices into the present. As long as those traditions are continued, it is possible to identify a uniquely constructed ethno-religious identity.

In Europe, those Hutterians who had given up community of goods were able to retain nearly all elements of Hutterian belief and practice. In North America, the forces of assimilationism, Mennonitization, and evangelicalism combined to do battle against a five-hundred-year-old faith. There has always been a Prairieleut remnant, however, that sustained customary practices and sought to recapture elements of the religious past.

Prairieleut Hutterians in the late twentieth century thus confront a serious dilemma. On the one hand, most of what once defined them as Hutterian has been lost, including full communal life, separation from society at large, pacifism, and even genetic sameness. On the other hand, some Prairie People sense that, in throwing out old traditions, they have lost many significant understandings and ways of knowing; the baby has been thrown out with the bath water. These people talk of reviving historic traditions in new forms.

But even those who are interested in the Hutterian past come in different stripes. Some—the conservatives—have developed a symbolic interest in ethnic roots and so want to save as many old photographs, diary accounts, and sermons as possible. They visit ancestral homelands, purchase historic Habaner pottery replicas, and take an interest in genealogical research.

Others—the neoconservatives—have the sense that the churches they attend and the communities they live in might be better places if Hutterian traditions were not only studied and evaluated but selectively reintroduced in changed forms. (While these lines of demarcation are useful, they should not obscure the fact that many neoconservatives are also interested in genealogy and cultural artifacts; and conservatives, likewise, are often interested in theological issues.)

Wolf Creek Colony minister Hans Decker (who died in 1990) used to suggest that interested Prairie People start their own colonies, perhaps with slightly different modes of operation than in Hutterite communities (Decker said he could "live" with that), but colonies that were still engaged in a journey somewhere along the communal pathway. It was not a realistic possibility. Neoconservative Prairieleut might be committed to nonresistant pacifism or wish that their congregations would place greater emphasis on the social dimension of the Christian salvation experience, but they expressed little interest in community of goods.

Yet, revived curiosity about Hutterian traditions might be an initial step in the embryonic resurrection—in postmodernist renditions—of traditional-value orientations. It might, for example, provide a corrective to a mainstream culture of narcissism, with its continual denigration of the spirit of humility. In a farewell letter to his wife, early Hutterite martyr Hieronymus Kals advised, "Always esteem another more highly than yourself."[9]

Whether a people could successfully mediate historic Hutterian principles, without experiencing a traditional communal way of life, however, was extremely questionable. Delbert Wiens suggested that when one attempts to superimpose ways of thinking tied to a traditional way of life onto the structure of a modern society one engages in a struggle that can never ultimately be successful.[10]

Throughout most of human existence, however, human beings have been part of small population units: families, tribes, villages, and towns. A creative evolutionary selection process has developed human characteristics that virtually demand communal life forms, in whatever mutated way they might incarnate. Perhaps the postmodernist focus on community and decentralized institutional structures, therefore, meets the need and character of the presently evolved human condition.[11]

Toward the end of their lives, many North Americans end up in communal organizations whether they want to or not. Intellectual reflection on the communal fate might thus be an important preparatory exercise. Whether or not heaven itself is organized communally, as Hutterites and many other Christians have believed (with Hutterites serving as God's appointed mentors, as one minister suggested), most people are forced to live more communally as they get older—in nursing homes, in hospitals, even in the homes of children or other relatives. Hundreds of thousands of young men and women, furthermore, have been exposed to communal life via involvement in military, college dormitory, or voluntary service experiences.

American public school systems, as well, have communal institutional characteristics, with features that are not always as benign as one might imagine. Why, for example, were from fifty to sixty developmentally diverse thirteen-year-olds commonly asked to undress and shower together, with no concern for privacy? (The Hutterites condemned private ownership, but they did not tolerate invasions of individual space, such as those imposed on American adolescents.) Tens of thousands of Catholic and Orthodox priests, nuns, and monks also experience communal forms of existence.

The communal vision was thus perhaps not as uncommon as often pictured. It is that aspect of life which many middle-aged college-graduate veterans of dormitories look back on most fondly. But most Prairieleut Hutterians are not ready to return to a full-scale, lifelong communal life. They want, like most North Americans, to experience a few years of private property first. Nevertheless they might well end up in colony-like environments, and those places of residence might not be as warm and loving as those found on colony grounds.

It is most ironic that many noncommunal Hutterians in the late 1990s care little about the specific privileges for which their ancestors gave up house and property in the 1870s. Almost no one is bothered by the loss of the German language, the sermons, and the songbook. Only a minority are concerned about exemptions from jury duty and taking oaths. The majority do not consider nonresistance to be an essential Christian teaching.

Perhaps a new Jacob Hutter will arise in coming years, however, calling noncommunal Hutterians back to the ideals of their sixteenth-century predecessors. New leaders have sometimes caused considerable disruption. It is probable, for example, that Jacob Hutter had at one time (in 1525 and 1526) been a militant activist in the Austrian Peasant's Revolt. According to the Hutterite *Chronicle*, Hutter had indeed been "a man of military appearance."[12] Hutter later threw down his sword "for the sake of divine truth," but a combative spirit remained.

When Hutter arrived from Austria to take leadership of a group of communal Moravian Anabaptists, he noted, "They say that my coming brought division and disunity, that previously they had lived in true peace, and that I was the cause of their division."[13] Today his followers' descendents are called "Hutterians." They are not referred to as followers of Gabriel Ascherham or Simon Schutzinger, the leaders of the "peaceful" Moravian colonies whom Hutter had "shoved aside."[14]

The Prairie People are at present torn between recognition of the Hutterian legacy—preserved to some extent in still-vibrant customs—and rejection of the 450-year heritage because of a powerful sense of cultural embarrassment. A sense of loss appeared most strikingly evident as one heard Prairieleut descendents refer to the "Hutterisch community" or "our way of life" as something that was in the process of disappearing. Many Prairie People who were interviewed used the past tense "were" when speaking about distinctive Hutterian ways of thinking and living, as if to suggest that it was extremely difficult, looking at the contemporary situation, to identify that which made the Prairieleut unique.

In the 1990s, a significant minority of Prairieleut-Mennonites have struggled to sustain some semblance of their Anabaptist Hutterian heritage. But "what of the future?" asked an older Prairieleut minister. What of a future with growing numbers of Hutterians leaving the Prairieleut churches. What of a future that includes many non-Hutterians who have joined the ethnic congregations; where worship services have been multiculturalized in accordance with new theological understandings?

Can the Prairieleut heritage continue to provide guidance in this kind of milieu? Only time will tell. Prairieleut community actualities, however, provide little support for a future ethnic or religious identity. There is indeed no "Prairieleut Church of America" in the wings, nor any significant public differentiation. Without communal life, this small group of Hutterians has lost its distinctive identity, has become Americanized and evangelicalized.

The noncommunal Hutterian culture is dying a slow death with only a residual identity intact.

Most non-Anglo-Saxon ethnic groups in the United States have followed a path that shows strong correlation between economic and social success and assimilation, with an accompanying loss of traditional ways of experiencing life. One might thus wonder where the Prairie People will find themselves one hundred years from now. As young Prairieleut continue to marry outside the group, as churches become increasingly evangelical and ethnically mixed, it appears doubtful that the movement to preserve and/or transmediate traditions of the past will face anything but a hard uphill struggle in the years ahead.

Appendix A
Hutterian Family Surnames

. . . .

Fourteen family surnames continue to be found in the Hutterite colonies. These same appellations plus five additional ones are found among the Prairie People. The traditional names are listed below, categorized by ethnic derivation and accompanied by descriptions of the name's historical entry into the Hutterian world.

It should be noted, however, that three additional surnames, Baer, Randle, and Teichroeb also achieved recognition as "Hutterite names" through familial longevity within Hutterite colonies. There have been Teichroebs among the Lehrerleut since the 1920s, and Baers and Randles in the Schmiedeleut since the late 1940s. Baer and Teichroeb, furthermore, are traditional Mennonite names, one Swiss (Baer) and the other Low German (Teichroeb).

Most other twentieth-century Hutterite converts did not stay in the colonies long enough to establish their family names as recognizably Hutterian. Converts and their children rarely remained in the colonies for more than a single generation. Close connections established (temporarily) with the Bruderhof in the 1980s and early 1990s, however, presented the possibility, owing to significant intermarriage, of many additions to the family of Hutterian names.

Old Hutterite (Tyrolean, South German, and Czech)

Old Hutterite surnames are those that have been represented in Hutterite communities since the sixteenth or seventeenth century. Information was confirmed by the *Hutterite Chronicle* and by existing Hutterite birth, marriage, and death records. The *Chronicle* itself, which is the most complete Hutterite record, does not, unfortunately, include birth and death records. Therefore, if a particular family was not represented in the Hutterite leadership, or did not have members who had been involved in what were considered significant activities (positive or negative), there was no way to determine definitively the initial point at which such a family had become Hutterian.

Additional information in the appendix derives from conversations with

Prairieleut and Hutterite genealogists, as well as from a variety of church records and personal journals. It should be noted that the names listed below represent only a small fraction of the Hutterite surnames found among the thousands of communalists living in Moravian *Bruderhofe* in the sixteenth and seventeenth centuries.

1. Mendel (Maendel, Mandel, Maendelig)

In 1528, one Jacob Mandel was chosen Hutterite Servant for Temporal Affairs. He was with the original Jacob Widemann group that had initiated communal life that same year. In the 1540s and 1550s, Hans Mandel, another Hutterite leader, had frequently been imprisoned for missionary activity and was said to have baptized over 400 persons. Hans was elected Servant of the Word in 1551 and died at the stake in 1560. In 1582, another Jacob (now Maendel) had also been arrested. Still, the name has, perhaps, not been in continuous existence among the Hutterites. For over 150 years, from the late 1500s until the mid-seventeenth-century, the *Hutterite Chronicle* mentioned no Mendels.

Arnold M. Hofer, Dariusleut minister and writer Paul S. Gross, and Schmiedeleut genealogist Tony Waldner, suggested that eighteenth-century Hutterian Mendels had Jewish or Czech ethnic background, Mendel being a shortened, Germanized form of Mendelig, a traditional Jewish name. Tony Waldner noted that Hutterites had historically referred to Mendels as "Bohemians" *(Bohmen)*. The Hutterite *Kleingeschichtsbuch* concurred, as did Freeman *Courier* publisher Jacob J. Mendel. Mendel wrote that his grandmother had told him that Paul Maendel (who had joined the Hutterites in 1783, at Sabatisch) could never speak Hutterisch well, that "he always had that Bohemian sound."

There was thus some confusion with regard to the history of the Hutterian Mendel name. All authorities agreed, however, that all contemporary Hutterians were descendents of the above-mentioned Paul Maendel. The name is found today among the Lehrerleut, Schmiedeleut, and Prairieleut.

2. Pollman (Pullman, Bolman)

This name was first mentioned in the *Hutterite Chronicle* in 1761, when one Tobias Pullman was imprisoned by the Jesuit religious order in Sabatisch. Due to its South German ancestry, as well as to its association with the Sabatisch community, it was considered by most genealogists to be one of the old Hutterite names, though it could conceivably have belonged to South German immigrants who joined the Hutterites only a few years prior to 1761. By 1784, three "Pullman" families had moved from the "old Hutterite" Sabatisch Colony in Slovakia to Wischenka in Ukrainian Russia.

This name is found today only among the Prairieleut and the Slovakian Habaner. All North American "Pullman" Hutterians are most likely descended from one Andreas Pullman, a member of one of the three families that had relocated to Wischenka. In 1893, Habaner Ignatius Pullman visited Hutterite colonies in the United States but declined an invitation to join.

3. Stahl

The first mention of this name occurred in 1663, when one Johannes Stahl, at Zobelhof, Slovakia, was taken prisoner by Ottoman Empire invaders. He was never heard from again. Various Stahl families were members of the Hutterites thereafter, in Slovakia and in Romania. Three families made the trek to Wishenka. All contemporary Stahls are descended from one Johann Stahl, a ceramic potter and one of the last Hutterite "missionaries," who had been part of the three families who settled in Wishenka. The name Stahl is common among contemporary Prairieleut, as well as in all communal Hutterite Leute.

4. Walter (Walther)

Walter is probably the oldest of contemporary Hutterite names. Walters have been in continuous Hutterite membership since 1580, when one Franz Walther, a barber-surgeon from Wurttemberg, left his home and joined the Hutterian Brethren in Moravia. Nineteen years later, Franz was named Servant of the Word at Pribitz, Moravia. Contemporary Walters are descendents of one Jakob Walther, who joined the Hutterite Church at Wishenka, in 1784. Today the name Walter is found among the Dariusleut Hutterites and the Prairieleut, as well as among contemporary Habaner.

5. Wipf

This name entered the Hutterian communities sometime in the middle to late seventeenth century. In 1694, one Michael Wipf was selected as a Hutterite elder at Alwinz, Transylvania. He served in that position until his death in 1717. This name was almost eliminated from the Hutterite community as a result of intense persecution in the years that followed. By the 1760s, only Annela Wipf and her five children remained in the church. All contemporary Hutterian Wipfs are Annela's descendents. Today this is a common name among both the Prairieleut and communal Hutterites.

6. Wollman (Waleman)

In 1621, the *Hutterite Chronicle* noted that one Hans Walmann had been selected for the position of Steward in Sabatisch, Slovakia. Over one hundred years later, in 1734, the name "Wollman" reappeared in *Chronicle* accounts, when one Jacob Wollman was named *Altester* (elder). Jacob's family, and two others, made the trek to Wishenka, Ukraine, between 1774 and 1784. All contemporary North American Wollmans are descendents of Jacob Wollman. This name is found among the Dariusleut and Schmiedeleut Hutterites, as well as in Prairieleut and Habaner communities.

7. Gross
Though this was a common South German name (and thus is included with the old Hutterite grouping), it first appeared in Hutterian records in 1782, when Jerg Gross and his mother became Hutterites in Transylvania. (Jerg's father, Andreas, had lived in the colony as well but died before joining the church.) Some have suggested Mennonite background for the name, since there were Grosses among the early Swiss Anabaptists. In general, there is significant mystery about the exact historical relationship of the name to the Hutterites. All contemporary Hutterian Grosses, however, are descended from Andreas Gross. Today Grosses are found in all communal Hutterite groups and among the Prairieleut.

8. Tschetter (Czeterle)
The name Tschetter was found in records for both Sabatisch, Slovakia, and for Alwinz, Transylvania. One Abraham Tschetter was mentioned as a "Hutterite" who had converted to Catholicism in the early 1760s, after being imprisoned by the Jesuits for several years in a convent. In 1766, one Lohrenz Tschetter had been imprisoned for his beliefs. He fled with other Hutterites to Wallachia.

Since a number of Tschetters relocated to Wishenka from both Sabatisch and Alwinz, it is likely that the name had been part of the Hutterian community for a number of generations. Tschetter was, however, generally considered a Czech name because of its spelling. All Hutterian Tschetters were descendents of Lohrentz Tschetter.

Lohrentz's fourth wife, who outlived him by thirty-one years, was a Mennonite woman named Maria Isaak. It is assumed that she was part of a group of Prussian Mennonites who had joined the Hutterites at Raditchewa in 1783. Maria and Lohrentz had two sons. Today Tschetters are found in the Dariusleut and Schmiedeleut groups, as well as among the Prairieleut.

Carinthian

These former Lutheran expatriates from Carinthian Austria joined the Hutterites in Transylvania and revived communal life among them between 1755 and 1760. The Carinthian assemblage had left and/or been expelled from the Spittal district of Austria on account of heavy persecution by the Catholic Church. There had been many ethnic Carinthians, as well, among the sixteenth-century Hutterites.

Particularly interesting is the way in which this outlawed Protestant religious assemblage had historically encouraged its young people to marry within the church. Evan Eichler's research in Austrian archives brought that phenomenon to light. The Carinthian families that joined the Hutterites had thus been heavily inbred—in the interest of passing on the faith—even before they left the Spittal Region.

1. Glanzer
In 1755, four Glanzer brothers from Carinthia, accompanied by their mother and one sister; they joined the Hutterites at Alwinz, Transylvania. It is interesting to note that the oldest brother, Martin, had left his wife and one-year-old daughter behind in Carinthia (he never remarried). All contemporary Hutterian Glanzers are descended from Christian Glanzer, another of the brothers. This name is found among both the *Schmiedeleut* and the Prairieleut.

2. Hofer
Two Hofer families from Carinthia joined the Hutterites between 1755 and 1760. This name was also present among the earliest Hutterites. One Ulrich Hofer, for example, had been chosen Servant of Temporal Affairs in 1542. There has been no continuous existence of the name, however, within the Hutterite colonies. Contemporary Hofers are descended from Johann Hofer, one of the Carinthian converts.

It is of particular interest that Johann's parents, Michael Hofer and Maria Plattner, had been religious dissidents in Carinthia since at least 1719. Michael had been imprisoned at Hermannstadt in 1758 for religious heresy. At present, Hofer is the most common Hutterian surname. About one of every four communal Hutterites carries this name, which is found in all Leut groups, as well as among the Prairieleut.

3. Kleinsasser
One Johann Kleinsasser, a minister, led the expatriate group of Carinthian Lutherans to Hungary in 1755. He and his family had then joined the Hutterites, where he was ordained as a minister in 1763. Four of Kleinsasser's siblings (three brothers and a sister) had also joined the Hutterites. Five other sisters, however, had remained in Carinthia, where they converted to Catholicism and continued to occupy the historic *Kleinsasserhof* (Kleinsasser farm) near Sankt Peter, which many modern Hutterites and Prairieleut have visited. Johann's Catholic father, Hans Kleinsasser, had indeed been one of the wealthiest farmers in the Sankt Peter region. All Hutterian Kleinsassers are descended from Johann Kleinsasser. Today the surname Kleinsasser is found among Lehrerleut and Schmiedeleut Hutterites, as well as in Prairieleut communities.

4. Miller (Mueller)
This very common German name was also found among the earliest Hutterites. In 1569, one Hans Miller, for example, had been chosen Servant of the Word. Twelve years later, one Niklasch Miller was selected for that same

position. Modern Prairieleut Millers, however, are descendents of one Peter Miller, a Carinthian exile who had joined the Hutterites in Transylvania between 1755 and 1760.

Peter also had two grandsons (Mathias and Andreas) who, in 1819, joined the Chortitza Mennonite Colony. All Millers of Russian Mennonite descent are descendents of Peter Miller's third grandson, Joseph. The name is no longer found among the Hutterites.

5. Waldner (Waltner)

One Georg Waldner, a peasant farmer, and his family joined the Hutterites in Transylvania in 1756 after being exiled from Carinthia. All contemporary Waldners are descendents of Georg Waldner. Georg's son, Johannes, was a Hutterite minister who wrote the *Kleingeschictsbuch* and actively defended a communal way of life.

The Swiss Volhynian Mennonite name Waltner was a derivation of Waldner. The name emerged after a Mennonite woman named Schrag, who had married into the Hutterite community in 1797, defected with her six children upon the death of her Hutterite husband, Andreas Waldner, a son of the aforementioned Johannes Waldner. The name Waldner is today found in all Hutterite groups and among the Prairieleut. Waltner is a common name in Swiss Volhynian Mennonite communities.

6. Wurz (Wurtz)

In 1611, one Joseph Wurz was chosen Servant of the Word in Niemuhl, Moravia, a major Hutterite center. Thirty-nine years later, in 1650, one Moses Wurz was selected as Servant of the Word, in Sabatisch, Slovakia. Because of this fact, it was often thought that there had been Wurzes among the Hutterites since the seventeenth century and that some contemporary Wurzes might be their descendents. It has thus often been categorized as an "old Hutterite" name.

Geneticist Evan Eichler and genealogist Tony Waldner, however, categorized the name Wurz as Carinthian, tracing it to the years 1755–1760, when Andreas Wurz and family had accompanied the rest of the Carinthian contingent to Transylvania. Eichler's research in Carinthia has shown, however, that Andreas Wurz himself (though a Carinthian) had not originally been a resident of the Spittal district.

Arnold M. Hofer, who referred to Wurz as an "old Hutterite" name, agreed that all present Wurz descendents come from the Andreas Wurz family, something that was easy to confirm from genealogical records. Darius-leut minister Paul S. Gross, on the other hand, believed the name had Czech background. There are thus many unanswered questions about a name that today is found among all communal Hutterite groups, as well as among the Prairieleut.

Dutch/Low German Mennonite

The following names are Dutch/Low German Mennonite family names, which are actually—except in the case of Decker—far more prevalent among Mennonites than among Prairieleut or Hutterites. They represent a number of cases in which Mennonite and Hutterian intermarriage led to Hutterian church membership.

1. Decker (Dekker)
Decker is a Flemish Mennonite surname that is relatively rare among modern Mennonites. Victor Peters and Jack Thiessen did not even include it in their 1987 analysis of Mennonite names. The name entered the Hutterite world in 1783, when a Mennonite widow, Elsi Dekker (from Franztal, Prussia) and her five children (along with her sister, Maria Schmidt) joined the Hutterites at Wischenka, north of Kiev. Her son Benjamin passed on the surname to later generations. Today this name is found among Lehrerleut and Schmiedeleut Hutterites, and in Prairieleut communities.

2. Entz
In 1866, one Peter Entz married into the Hutterite church, while the communalists were living near the Ukrainian Mennonite villages. He was married to Sarah Dekker by the Rev. Michael Stahl at Hutterthal village. Five years later, his brother Johann was married to Susanna Hofer by the same Rev. Stahl. Other members of Peter's immediate family had also married Hutterite women in Russia, but they had probably done so in Mennonite churches. (The Hutterites kept no records of Mennonite marriages.)

For example, Peter Entz's father, another Peter, married a Hutterite woman named Maria Wipf in 1846. Peter's brother, Jacob, furthermore, married one Rebecca Glanzer. Neither family joined or, at least, stayed in the Mennonite church. All four cross-cultural families sailed to America on the *Pommerania* in 1877 and, at least initially, joined the Lehrerleut Elmspring Colony. In South Dakota, two other siblings married Hutterites, as well. The surname Entz is now found only among the Lehrerleut Hutterites and the Prairieleut.

3. Janzen
In 1848, Mennonite schoolteacher Jacob Janzen married Hutterite Maria Waldner, a sister of Schmiedeleut founder Michael Waldner. Twenty-two years later, in 1870, one Helena Janzen was married to a different Michael Waldner by the Rev. Michael Stahl at Hutterthal Village. This name, which is common in Mennonite communities, is now found only (with regard to Hutterians) among the Prairieleut. The last Hutterite with the surname Janzen (schoolteacher Peter) had no male heirs.

4. Knels

In 1783, Liset Knels, a Low German Mennonite widow from Pschehofka, West Prussia, joined the Hutterites (along with two sons, Johann and Abraham) when the Hutterites were living at Wischenka. Johann later married one Susanna Wurz. Abraham married Judith Wollman. This name is now found only among the Prairieleut. The last Hutterite with this name, Anna Knels, died in the late 1980s at Millerdale Colony (Miller, South Dakota).

5. Fast

This name entered the Hutterite world as a result of Mennonite A. W. Fast's marriage to a Hutterite girl, one Susanna Wurz, in Ukrainian Russia. It is possible that the two were married in the Mennonite Church. After his wife's death, however, A. W. gave up his three children for adoption to various Hutterite family members. All Fasts of Hutterian background are the descendents of John and Jacob Fast, sons of A. W. and Susanna. The name has continued among the Prairieleut but is not today found among the Hutterites.

Appendix B
Prairie People and Mennonites in the South Dakota State Legislature

. . . .

Prairie People and Mennonites in the South Dakota State Legislature, 1889–1989

Politician	Party	House	Term
D. M. Brenneman	D	House	1917–1918
W. H. Brenneman	D	House	1931–1934
John J. Gering	R	House	1937–1938
	R	Senate	1939–1940
J. C. Graber	R	Senate	1929–1930
Benny J. Gross[a]	R	House	1969–1986
Leroy J. Kaufman	R	House	1973–1976
J. G. Kleinsasser[a]	D	House	1933–1934
Leland P. Kleinsasser[a]	R	House	1979–1980
	R	Senate	1981–1988
John P. Kleinsasser[a]	R	House	1937–1938
J. J. Kleinsasser[a]	R	House	1925–1926
P. P. Kleinsasser[a]	R	House	1907–1908
H. H. Koehn	R	House	1919–1922
D. J. Mendel[a]	R	House	1909–1912
Tarrel R. Miller[c]	R-D	House	1981–1984
Herbert W. Ortman	R	House	1955–1958
Lloyd Schrag	R	Senate	1959–1972
	(President Pro Tempore of the Senate, 1967, 1968)		
Joseph K. Schrag	R	House	1921–1922
Menno Tschetter[a]	D	House	1965–1966
	D	House	1969–1976
Paul S. Tschetter[a]	D	Senate	1979–1980
A. J. Waltner[b]	R	House	1913–1916
Emil J. Waltner[b]	R	House	1927–1932
A. A. Wipf[a]	R	Senate	1913–1914
David J. Wipf[a]	R	House	1945–1956
John J. Wipf[a]	R	House	1903–1904

Continued

Politician	Party	House	Term
	R	House	1909–1912
	R	House	1925–1930
	R	Senate	1931–1932
Harvey Wollman[a]	D	Senate	1969–1974
	(Lieutenant Governor, 1975–1978; Governor, 1978)		

Notes:

[a]Denotes Prairieleut ethnicity.

[b]The name Waltner, too, is genetically connected to the Hutterians. This is discussed in chapter 8 and in appendix A.

[c]Erstwhile Republican Terry Miller joined the Democratic Party in early 1984 as a protest against the State Republican Party's support both for the death penalty and for the closing of a state university campus. From 1964 to 1967 Miller was a Hutterite novice at Forest River Colony, Fordville, North Dakota.

Notes

. . . .

Frequently cited archival sources and one journal have been identified by the following abbreviations:

CMBS   Center for Mennonite Brethren Studies. Fresno, California
CMBSH   Center for Mennonite Brethren Studies. Hillsboro, Kansas
CWS   Center for Western Studies. Sioux Falls, South Dakota
FAA   Freeman Academy Archives. Freeman, South Dakota
HCC   Hutterian Centennial Committee Collection. Freeman, South Dakota

Epigraph. Frederick Manfred, *The Chokecherry Tree* (Albuquerque: University of New Mexico Press, 1949), 198.

1. Introduction: The Prairie People (Prairieleut) (pp. 1–11)

First epigraph. Jacob Hutter, *Brotherly Faithfulness: Epistles from a Time of Persecution* (Rifton, N.Y.: Plough, 1979), 65.
Second epigraph. Hutterian Brethren, eds. *The Chronicle of the Hutterian Brethren* (Rifton, N.Y.: Plough, 1987), 301.
Third epigraph. The Rev. Hans Decker, interview with author (1988).

1. The Hutterites have been the subject of numerous genetic investigations. Examples of recent studies include E. O'Brien, P. A. Kerber, C. B. Jorde, and A. A. Rogers, "Founder Effect: An assessment of variation in genetic contributions among founders," *Human Biology* (April 1994): 185–204; and K. Nonaka, T. Miura, K. Peter, "Recent Fertility Decline in Dariusleut Hutterites," *Human Biology* (April 1994): 411–420. The latter study showed a decrease in *Dariusleut* Hutterite birthrates, from 8.13 per family in 1970, to 6.29 per family in 1985.
2. One exception is Samuel Hofer's *The Hutterites: Lives and Images of a Communal People* (Saskatoon, Sask.: Hofer Publishers, 1998).
3. Relevant volumes in this important, well-written, and carefully researched series are James Juhnke, *Vision, Doctrine, War: Mennonite Identity and Organization in America, 1890–1930* (Scottdale, Pa.: Herald Press, 1989); and Paul Toews, *Mennonites in American Society, 1930–1970* (Scottdale, Pa.: Herald Press, 1996).
4. Harry Loewen, *Why I Am a Mennonite: Essays on Mennonite Identity* (Scottdale, Pa.: Herald Press, 1988). Katie Funk Wiebe, ed., *Women Among the Brethren: Stories of Fifteen Mennonite Brethren and Krimmer Mennonite Brethren Women* (Hillsboro, Kans.: Mennonite Brethren Board of Christian Literature, 1979).

5. James Juhnke (1989). Paul Toews (1996).

6. The term "Hutter" elicited most concern historically when employed by non-Hutterians. By the 1960s and 1970s, however, the term had gained widespread acceptance in the United States. A different situation prevailed in Saskatchewan, where the term continued to have pejorative connotations.

7. Werner Packull, *Hutterite Beginnings* (Baltimore: Johns Hopkins University Press, 1995), 11.

8. Robert F. Friedmann, ed., "Andreas Ehrenpreis' An Epistle on Brotherly Community as the Highest Command of Love," in *Mennonite Quarterly Review* (October 1984), 267. "Servant of the Word" is the Hutterite designation for minister.

9. Fellowship for Intentional Community, eds., *Communities Directory* (Langley, Wash., 1995). See also Timothy Miller, *The Quest for Utopia in Twentieth Century America, Volume I* (Syracuse, N.Y.: Syracuse University Press, 1998).

10. John Bennett, *Hutterian Brethren* (Stanford, Calif.: Stanford University Press, 1967); Paul S. Gross, *The Hutterite Way* (Saskatoon, Sask.: Freeman Publishing Company, 1965); Karl Peter, *The Dynamics of Hutterite Society: An Analytical Approach* (Edmonton, Alb.: University of Alberta Press, 1987); Victor Peters, *All Things Common: The Hutterian Way of Life* (Minneapolis: University of Minnesota Press, 1965).

2. Across the Great World Ocean (pp. 12–35)

First epigraph. Andreas Ehrenpreis, *Brotherly Community* (Rifton, N.Y.: Plough, 1978), 43, 44.
Second epigraph. Joshua Hofer, ed., "The Sixth Text on Acts the Second" (Elie, Man.: James Valley Colony), 15.

1. James Stayer, "Anabaptists and Future Anabaptists in the Peasants War," *Mennonite Quarterly Review* (April 1988), 135. Stayer, in a more recent work, *The German Peasant War and Anabaptist Community of Goods* (Montreal: McGill/Queens University Press, 1991), 112, reminded that Hutterites were not the only Anabaptists interested in communal life. This was confirmed, in great detail, in Werner Packull, *Hutterite Beginnings: Communitarian Experiments during the Reformation* (Baltimore: Johns Hopkins University Press, 1995).

2. Hutterian Brethren, eds., *The Chronicle of the Hutterian Brethren, Volume I* (Rifton, N.Y.: Plough, 1987), 83, 145.

3. Hutterian Brethren, eds. (1987), 145.

4. John Voth, ed., "Peter Janzen's correspondence, dated July 27, 1880, with the *Mennonitische Rundschau,*" in Frances Janzen Voth, *The House of Jacob: The Story of Jacob Janzen, 1822–1885, and His Descendents* (Tucson: self-published, 1984).

5. "Sermon on Baptism," in John Hostetler, Leonard Gross, Elizabeth Bender, eds., *Selected Hutterian Documents in Translation* (Philadelphia: Temple University Communal Studies Center, 1975), 102.

6. Donovan Smucker, "Gelassenheit, Ehrenpreis, and Remnants: Socio-economic Models among the Mennonites," in J. R. Burkholder and Calvin Redekop, eds., *Kingdom, Cross and Community* (Scottdale, Pa.: Herald Press, 1976), 226.

7. Peter Rideman, *Account of Our Religion, Doctrine and Faith* (Rifton, N.Y.: Plough, 1970).

8. *The Chronicle of the Hutterian Brethren* provides a running account of significant events and personalities in Hutterian history, from the movement's birth to 1665. An important work that deals with Anabaptist economic theory is Peter J. Klassen's *The Economics of Anabaptism* (London: Mouton, 1964).

9. Hutterian Brethren, eds. (1987), 127, 128. See also Hans Fischer, *Jacob Huter: Leben, Froemmigkeit, Briefe* (Newton, Kans.: Mennonite Publication Office, 1956).

10. Johann Loserth, "The Anabaptists in Carinthia in the 16th Century," *Mennonite Quarterly Review* (April 1931), 241.

11. Johann Loserth (1931), 243.

12. James M. Stayer (1988), 131. James M. Stayer (1991), 147. See also Leonard Gross, *The Golden Years of the Hutterites* (Scottdale, Pa.: Herald Press, 1980).

13. A. J. F. Zieglschmid, *Das Klein-Geschichtsbuch der Hutterischen Bruder* (Philadelphia: Carl Schurz Memorial Foundation, 1947), 83–118; 129–150. Zieglschmid's work includes a brief update of Hutterite history to 1947.

14. Gary Waltner, interview with author (August 1994). Waltner is the director of the Mennonitische Buchversand, in Weierhof, Germany. See also Robert Friedmann, "Hutterite Pottery or Haban Fayences," *Mennonite Life* (October 1958), 147–151. For an excellent introduction to Habaner work—with numerous photographs—see Frantisek Kalesny, *Habani Na Slovenska* (Tatran, Czechoslovakia, 1981). Kalesny's work includes a short review in English.

15. Harold Bender, ed., "A Hutterite School Discipline of 1578 and Peter Scherer's Address of 1568 to the Schoolmasters," *Mennonite Quarterly Review* (October 1931), 231–244.

16. The Hutterian Brethren, eds., *Die Lieder der Hutterischen Bruder Gesangbuch* (Scottdale, Pa.: Herald Press, 1914), 107–115. John A. Hostetler, *Hutterite Society* (Baltimore: Johns Hopkins University Press, 1974), 32–35. This book was reissued in 1997 with a revised preface.

17. John Horsch, *Hutterian Brethren* (Scottdale, Pa.: Herald Press, 1931), 65.

18. Andreas Ehrenpreis, *Brotherly Community: The Highest Command of Love, 1650* (Rifton, N.Y.: Plough, 1978). See also Wes Harrison, *Andreas Ehrenpreis and Hutterite Faith and Practice* (Kitchener, Ont.: Herald Press, 1997).

19. H. J. C. von Grimmelshausen, *Adventures of a Simpleton* (New York: Frederick Ungar Publishing, 1962), 231.

20. The Hutterian Brethren, eds. (1987), 781, 782. This account provides a description of a raid on the Kesseldorf Colony.

21. A. J. F. Zieglschmid (1947), 201–255.

22. Erich Buchinger, *Die Geschichte der Karntner Hutterischen Bruder und in der Walachei (1755–1770) in Russland and Amerika* (Klagenfurt, 1982). A. J. F. Zieglschmid (1947), 264–297.

23. Heinrich Donner, "Report of the Anabaptist Brethren at Wishink in the Ukraine," in Arnold M. Hofer, ed., *Hutterite Roots* (Freeman, S.Dak.: HCC, 1985), 119–127. Donner was a Prussian Mennonite elder who had visited the Ukrainian Hutterites.

24. Evan Eichler, interview with author (June 1998). The document, a copy of which is in Eichler's possession, is an account of Peter Miller's interrogation. See also Evan Eichler, "Hutterite Surnames," an unpublished document (1998) based upon research in Austrian, Slovakian, Czech, Hungarian, as well as Hutterite archival collections. A copy is in the possession of the author. Eichler is a direct descendent

of Hutterite Carinthian exile Peter Miller and is a geneticist who teaches at Case Western Reserve University, Cleveland, Ohio.

25. Ibid.

26. Heinrich Donner, "Report of the Anabaptist Brethren at Wishink in the Ukraine," in Arnold M. Hofer, ed. (1985), 119–127.

27. A. J. F. Zieglschmid, ed. (1947), 411–435.

28. John A. Hostetler (1974), 101. See also John A. Hostetler and Gertrude Huntington, *The Hutterites In North America* (New York: Harcourt Brace, 1996).

29. Karl A. Peter, "The Instability of the Community of Goods in the Social History of the Hutterites" (unpublished manuscript, 1975), 13. A. J. F. Zieglschmid, ed. (1947), 418.

30. Evan Eichler (1998). A. J. F. Zieglschmid, ed. (1947), 441.

31. Emil J. Waltner, ed., *Banished for Faith* (Freeman, S.Dak.: self-published, 1968), 99–101, 110. This is a translation of the *Kleingeschichtsbuch*—the small history book —of the Hutterian Brethren, 1755–1874. This book was republished in 1989, with an epilogue written by Prairieleut descendent Gwen Shaw.

32. Arnold M. Hofer, ed. (1986), 80, 83. This book includes birth, death, baptismal, and marriage records, which have been used as the source for much analysis in this work.

33. Arnold M. Hofer, ed. (1986), 55.

34. David G. Rempel, "The Mennonite Commonwealth in Russia," *Mennonite Quarterly Review* (January, 1974), 17–22. Adam Giesinger, *From Catherine to Khruschev: The Story of Russia's Germans* (Lincoln, Nebr.: Society of Germans from Russia, 1981), 64, 65.

35. Emil J. Waltner, ed. (1968), 117–120. See also Baldo Hildebrand, *Erziehung zur Gemeinschaft* (Pfaffenweiler, Germany: Centaurus-Verlagsgesellschaft, 1993), 68.

36. Elizabeth Bender, ed., "The Last Words of Michael Waldner," in John A. Hostetler (1974), 355–357. Robert Friedmann, ed., "The Reestablishment of Communal Life Among the Hutterites in Russia (1858)," *Mennonite Quarterly Review* (April 1965), 147–152. John Voth, ed., "Peter Janzen's correspondence, dated July 27, 1880, with the *Mennonitische Rundschau*," in Frances Janzen Voth (1984), 67.

37. Joseph W. Tschetter, "A Brief Biography of Paul Tschetter 1842–1919," in Jacob M. Hofer, ed., "The Diary of Paul Tschetter," *Mennonite Quarterly Review* (July 1931), 113.

38. Karl A. Peter (1975), 5–10.

39. *Die Krimmer Mennoniten Brudergemende, Ihre Entstehung und Geschichte* (no author or date given; original galleys are in the possession of the Center for Mennonite Brethren Studies, hereafter CMBS).

40. Joseph W. Tschetter (1931), 113.

41. Arnold M. Hofer, ed., *The Diaries of Joseph "Yos" Hofer* (Freeman, S.Dak.: HCC, 1997), July, 1873 to November, 1873 entries. This recently found journal is in the possession of the Hutterian Centennial Committee (hereafter HCC).

42. Comparisons between the Rev. Paul Tschetter's diary account and former *Schmiedeleut* minister Peter Tschetter's account of a 1984 return trip to Europe showed remarkable similarities in terms of social and theological perspectives. See Peter Tschetter, *Europe 84* (Flandreau, S.Dak.: self-published, 1984).

43. Jacob M. Hofer, ed. (1931), 118.

44. Arnold M. Hofer and David P. Gross, eds., "Neu Hutterthaler Church

Records" (unpublished, 1992). These records contain much commentary from Paul Tschetter not previously made public. HCC.

45. Jacob M. Hofer, ed. (1931), 122.

46. Arnold M. Hofer and Pauline Becker, *John Hofer and Anna Wurtz Family Record* (Freeman, S.Dak.: self-published, 1991), 8.

47. Jacob M. Hofer, ed. (1931), 126–128.

48. Paul Tschetter, Lohrentz Tschetter et al., "A Card of Thanks," published in *Herald of Truth* (August 1873), in Clarence Hiebert, ed., *Brothers in Deed to Brothers in Need* (North Newton, Kans.: Faith and Life Press, 1974), 82. Hiebert's book is a "scrapbook" collection of newspaper and magazine articles, ship lists, photographs, and other accounts of Mennonite and Hutterian immigrants from Russia, 1870–1885.

49. Ernst Correll, "President Grant and the Mennonite Immigration From Russia," *Mennonite Quarterly Review* (October, 1935), 146.

50. Paul Tschetter, Lohrentz Tschetter, and Tobias Unruh, "Petition to the President of the United States" (August 8, 1873), in Clarence Hiebert, ed. (1974), 65.

51. Georg Leibbrandt, "The Emigration of the German Mennonites from Russia to the United States and Canada, 1873–1880," *Mennonite Quarterly Review* (January 1933), 10.

52. Jacob M. Hofer, ed. (1931), 122.

53. "Letter of introduction from Jay Cooke, Trustee of the Northern Pacific Railroad, introducing M. L. Hiller to President Grant," in Clarence Hiebert, ed. (1974), 64. This letter was dated July 31, 1873.

54. Jacob M. Hofer, ed. (1931), 47.

55. "Telegram from Jay Cooke to Hamilton Fish," in Ernst Correll (1935), 148. Clarence Hiebert, ed. (1974), 67. The letter was dated August 13, 1873.

56. "Telegram from Hamilton Fish to M. L. Hiller, September 5, 1873," in Ernst Correll (1935), 148, 149.

57. "A Mennonite Request," (*Dakota Territory Press and Dakotan*, December 4, 1873), in Clarence Hiebert, ed., *Brothers in Deed to Brothers in Need* (1974), 91, 92. See also Georg Leibbrandt (1933), 13. A petition was also submitted in the House of Representatives but was never debated.

58. President Ulysses S. Grant, "Annual Message to Congress," in Clarence Hiebert, ed. (1974), 92.

59. Ernst Correll, ed., "Mennonite Immigration into Manitoba: Sources and documents, 1872, 1873," *Mennonite Quarterly Review* (July, October, 1937), 196–227; 267–283.

60. Georg Leibbrandt (1933), 18.

61. Emil J. Waltner, ed. (1961), 191.

62. Ernst Correll (1935), 151.

63. George Brown Tindall, *America: A Narrative History* (New York: W. W. Norton, 1984), 700, 701.

64. Theron Schlabach, *Peace, Faith, Nation: Mennonites and Amish in 19th Century America* (Scottdale, Pa.: Herald Press, 1988), 251, 252.

65. "More About the Mennonites" (*The Saint Paul Daily Pioneer*, July 13, 1873), in Clarence Hiebert, ed. (1974), 60.

66. Ibid. See also Theron Schlabach (1988), 243.

67. Ernst Correll (1937), 200.

68. George Rath, *The Black Sea Germans in the Dakotas* (Freeman, S.Dak.: Pine

Hill Press, 1972), 104. Rath gathered this information from a pamphlet published by the State Bureau for Immigration, Pierre, South Dakota.

69. The Hutterian Brethren, eds. (1987), 1548 entry.

70. Arnold M. Hofer, ed., *A History of the Hutterite-Mennonites* (Freeman, S.Dak.: HCC, 1974), 64.

71. Peter Janzen, *"Reise Nach Amerika,"* in Frances Janzen Voth (1984), 64, 65. Peter M. Friesen, *The Mennonite Brotherhood in Russia, 1789–1910* (Fresno, Calif.: Mennonite Brethren Historical Commission, 1978), 844.

72. Arnold M. Hofer, "The Prairieleut" (unpublished presentation, Freeman College, Freeman, S.Dak., April 1984).

73. David P. Gross, ed., "Report of Why We Had to Leave Russia," in Arnold M. Hofer, ed. (1986), 100.

74. Ibid., 101. See also David P. Gross and Arnold M. Hofer, eds., "Neu Hutterthaler Church Records" (1992), 8.

75. John P. Johansen, *Immigrant Settlements and Social Organization in South Dakota* (Brookings: South Dakota State University Press, 1963), 32.

76. David P. Gross, ed. (1986), 97–100.

77. Jacob J. Mendel, *A History of the People of East Freeman, Silver Lake and West Freeman* (Freeman, S.Dak.: Pine Hill Press, 1961), 22. Elenora R. Wipf, *The Andreas and Susann Glanzer Family Record, 1842–1962* (Freeman, S.Dak.: self-published, 1962), 3, 5. Michael Hofer, "Census of Johannesruh, 1872" (unpublished document, in the possession of the Freeman Academy Archives, hereafter FAA).

78. Deloris Stahl, "The Migration of Hutterites from Russia to America," in Arnold M. Hofer, ed. (1974), 51.

79. Arnold M. Hofer and Pauline Becker (1991), 8.

80. Jacob J. Mendel (1961), 16, 17, 51–53, 86, 178.

81. Arnold M. Hofer, ed. (1997), March 1, 1877, entry.

82. Andrew J. Hofer, interview with author (July 1987). Hofer, a Prairieleut descendent, was a long-time resident of southeastern South Dakota. He had a wealth of information with regard to Hutterian folklore.

83. Robert Friedmann, ed., "Michael Waldner's *The Reestablishment of Communal Life Among the Hutterites in Russia* (1858)," *Mennonite Quarterly Review* (April 1965), 151.

3. Life on the Plains (pp. 36–61)

First epigraph. Arnold M. Hofer, ed., *A History of the Hutterite-Mennonites* (Freeman, S.Dak.: HCC, 1974), 55.

Second epigraph. Emma Mendel Hofer, ed., "The Autobiography of David J. Mendel" (self-published, n.d.), 47. A copy is in the possession of the author.

1. Arnold M. Hofer and David P. Gross, eds., "Neu Hutterthaler Church Records" (unpublished, 1992), 18. HCC.

2. J. A. Boese, *The Prussian-Polish Mennonites Settling in South Dakota, 1874 and Soon Thereafter* (Freeman, S.Dak.: self-published), 63.

3. Paul G. Tschetter, "Die Auswanderer," in Nancy M. Peterson, ed., *People of the Old Missoury* (Frederick, Col.: Renaissance House, 1989), 96. Paul G. Tschetter, "Monologue as Paul Tschetter" (videotape, 1988, in the possession of the FAA). In

order not to betray confidences I have chosen to withhold the names of many Prairie People (a few now deceased) who helped piece together the story of their people. Quotations and stories are thus not always referenced.

4. Peter G. Tschetter, interview with author (June 1998).

5. Robert F. Karolevitz, *Yankton: A Pioneer Past* (Aberdeen, S.Dak.: North Dakota State University, 1972), 134, 135. Arthur M. Huseboe, "Many Hands on the Past," in Arthur M. Huseboe, ed., *Siouxland Heritage* (Sioux Falls: South Dakota Historical Society, 1982), 6.

6. George Rath, *The Black Sea Germans in the Dakotas* (Freeman, S.Dak.: Pine Hill Press, 1972), 136. Note also Reuben Goertz, "Princes, Potentates and Plain People: The Saga of Germans from Russia," unpublished paper (1994), CWS, and John E. Pfeiffer, *The German-Russians and their Immigration to South Dakota* (Brookings: South Dakota State University Press, 1970).

7. Emma Mendel Hofer, ed., "Excerpts from the Autobiography of David J. Mendel," in Arnold M. Hofer, ed. (1974), 71.

8. Arnold M. Hofer, ed., *Hutterite Roots* (Freeman, S.Dak.: HCC, 1986), 11.

9. Robert Friedmann, ed., "Michael Waldner's The Reestablishment of Communal Life Among the Hutterites in Russia (1858)," *Mennonite Quarterly Review* (1965), 150. *"Unserer Gemeinde befindliche SeelenZahl: Anno 1875 bei April"* (n.a., n.d.; document in the possession of the Pearl Creek Colony, Iroquois, S.Dak.).

10. Arnold M. Hofer, "Former Hutterite Dorfs in Russia Visited in 1976," in Arnold M. Hofer, ed. (1986), 109.

11. C. Henry Smith, *The Story of the Mennonites* (Newton: Faith and Life Press, 1957), 49. This book was revised under the editorial direction of Cornelius Krahn in 1980.

12. John D. Unruh, *A Century of Mennonites in Dakota* (Pierre: South Dakota Historical Society, 1972), 62.

13. Paul E. Glanzer, Marilyn Wipf, and Jeannette Hofer, eds., *A Century of God's Blessing* (Freeman, S.Dak.: Pine Hill Press, 1988), 20.

14. Jerald Hiebert, ed., "Hofer Colony genealogical records" (unpublished, 1993), 1. These records are in the possession of the Stirling Mennonite Church, Stirling, Alberta.

15. Arnold M. Hofer, ed., *The Diaries of Joseph "Yos" Hofer* (Freeman, S.Dak.: HCC, 1997), September 1876 entry.

16. Kenneth J. Walter, *The Matthias M. Hofer Family Record* (Freeman, S.Dak.: self-published, 1971), 5.

17. Rolf W. Brednick, *The Bible and the Plough* (Ottawa, Ont.: National Museums of Canada, 1981).

18. Arnold M. Hofer, interview with author (July 1987). Hofer has served as President of the Hutterian Centennial Committee since it was established in 1973. A retired farmer, Hofer knows the Prairieleut story better than anyone else.

19. Ursula Liesebert, "The Martyr Songs of the Hutterian Brethren," *Mennonite Quarterly Review* (July 1993), 323.

20. Hutterian Brethren, eds., *Die Lieder der Hutterischen Bruder Gesangbuch* (Scottdale, Pa.: Herald Press, 1914).

21. Elenora Wipf, interview with author (July 1987). Wipf is a Prairieleut descendent with much knowledge about the history of noncommunal Hutterians in the Huron, South Dakota, area.

22. Arnold M. Hofer, interviews with author (May 1986 and July 1993).

23. David P. Gross and Arnold M. Hofer, eds. (1992), 19.

24. A. J. F. Zieglschmid, ed., *Das Klein-Geschichtsbuch der Hutterischen Bruder* (Philadelphia: Carl Schurz Memorial Foundation, 1947), 441.

25. *History of Zion Mennonite Church, Bridgewater, South Dakota* (n.a., n.d.). FAA.

26. John D. Unruh (1972), 101. Ruth E. Brown, "The Ethno-History of Law" (unpublished doctoral dissertation, State University of New York, Albany, 1977), 179.

27. Emma Mendel Hofer, ed., "Excerpts from the Autobiography of David J. Mendel," in Arnold M. Hofer, ed. (1974), 71.

28. Adam Giesinger, *From Catherine to Khruschchev: The Story of Russia's Germans* (Lincoln, Nebr.: Society of Germans from Russia, 1981), 55.

29. Reinhild Janzen and John M. Janzen, *Mennonite Furniture: A Migrant Tradition, 1766–1910* (Newton, Kans.: Faith and Life Press, 1991), 188–190.

30. Laverne Rippley, *The German-Americans* (New York: Gramercy Publishing, 1976), 177.

31. "Original Hutterische Settlers on Hutchinson County Land." This map is an edited copy of original county map records. HCC.

32. Jacob J. Mendel, *A History of the People of East Freeman, Silver Lake and West Freeman* (Freeman, S.Dak.: Pine Hill Press, 1961), 15.

33. "Original Hutterische Settlers on Hutchinson County Land." HCC.

34. Michael Koop and Carolyn Torma, *Folk Building of the South Dakota German-Russians* (Vermillion, S.Dak.: State Historical Preservation Center, 1984), 2.

35. Frederick Manfred, "Many Hands Make Light Work," in Arthur Huseboe, ed., *Siouxland Heritage* (Sioux Falls: South Dakota Historical Society, 1982), 16.

36. Katherina Hofer Tschetter, *My Life Story* (Chicago: self-published, 1945), 5.

37. "Hutterthal Mennonite Church Marriage Records," 435–437. FAA.

38. Jacob J. Mendel (1961), 230.

39. Arnold M. Hofer and Pauline Becker, *John Hofer and Anna Wurtz Family Record* (Freeman, S.Dak.: self-published, 1988).

40. Jacob J. Mendel (1961).

41. Paul G. Tschetter, *"Die Auswanderer"* (1989), 98.

42. Betty Bergland, "Ethnic Archeology in the Nineteenth-Century Midwest," *Journal of American Ethnic History* (Fall 1997), 79.

43. Doreen Mierau, "Prairie Peace-makers," *Saskatchewan Valley News* (June 8, 1967), 7.

44. Arnold M. Hofer, ed. (1997).

45. John P. Kleinsasser, "Memoranda," in Jacob J. Mendel (1961), 163–165.

46. Frances Janzen Voth (1984), 93.

47. Joseph A. Kleinsasser, *A History of the Bethel Mennonite Brethren Church, 1902–1979* (Freeman, S.Dak.: Pine Hill Press, 1979), 2. This is a particularly insightful social, as well as strictly congregational, history. Kleinsasser served for many years as Professor of German at Sioux Falls College, Sioux Falls, South Dakota.

48. Jacob J. Mendel (1961), 113.

49. David P. Gross and Arnold M. Hofer, eds. (1992), 824.

50. Jerald Hiebert, ed., (1993), 3.

51. Jacob J. Mendel (1961), 165.

52. O. E. Rolvaag, *Giants in the Earth* (New York: Harper, 1929). See also Willa Cather's *Oh Pioneers* (New York: Vintage, 1913).

53. Reuben Goertz, "The Legacy of the First American Tornado Ever Photographed, Dakota Territory, 1884" (unpublished paper, n.d.). This paper is in the possession of the Center for Western Studies. See also P. P. Kleinsasser, "Freeman Resident Gives Eyewitness Report of Tornado of August 28, 1884," in Jacob J. Mendel (1961), 252.

54. Katherina Hofer Tschetter (1945), 3. Katherina was a sister to Maria Hofer. John F. Funk, "On the Way," in *Herald of Truth* (September 1, 1884), in Clarence Hiebert, *Brothers in Deed to Brothers in Need* (Newton: Faith and Life Press, 1974), 427, 428. Peter P. Kleinsasser, "Centennial Recollections," Freeman *Courier* (April 6, 1961).

55. Reuben Goertz, "The Legacy of the First American Tornado Ever Photographed, Dakota Territory, 1884." CWS.

56. Martha Tschetter, *The Benjamin G. Boese Family* (Freeman, S.Dak.: self-published, 1976), xxii.

57. David P. Gross and Arnold M. Hofer, eds. (1992), 818–820.

58. Arnold M. Hofer, ed. (1997), September 1876 entry.

59. Paul Stahl, "Questionnaire About the History of Your Church," (distributed by C. F. Plett for the KMB Conference, 1947), 13. This and many other Krimmer Mennonite Brethren records are housed in the Center for Mennonite Brethren Studies. Questionnaires completed by a number of KMB Prairieleut ministers are referenced in later notes.

60. For an indepth study of how death was perceived prior to the last century, see Phillippe Aries, *The Hour of Our Death* (New York: Adolf Knopf, 1981).

61. Virgil Kleinsasser, interview with author (June 1998).

62. Arnold M. Hofer and Pauline Becker (1988), 10.

63. Arnold M. Hofer and Norman Hofer, "Taped interview with Paul L. Hofer" (1991). FAA.

64. John P. Kleinsasser, "Memoirs," in Jacob J. Mendel (1961), 164.

65. John P. Kleinsasser (1961).

66. Marian Kleinsasser Towne, ed., *Bread of Life: Diaries and Memories of a Dakota Family, 1936–1945* (Freeman, S.Dak.: Pine Hill Press, 1994), April 1938 entry.

67. Barbara Kleinsasser Wiens Entz, "Memoirs," in Walter Kleinsasser, ed., *Memoirs of the Kleinsasser Siblings* (Hillsboro, Kans.: self-published, 1990), 38.

68. Edna Kleinsasser Tschetter Olfert, "Memoirs," in Walter Kleinsasser, ed. (1990), 71.

69. Joseph A. Kleinsasser, "Memoirs," in Walter Kleinsasser, ed. (1990), 12.

70. Arnold M. Hofer, "The Prairieleut" (unpublished presentation, Freeman College, 1984).

71. Correspondence with David P. Gross (August 1987). Gross was one of the founders of the Hutterian Centennial Committee.

72. Harold Stahl, interview with author (July 1993). Stahl is a lifelong resident of the Langham area.

73. Arnold M. Hofer (1984). Also note, A. Warkentin and Melvin Gingerich, eds., *Who's Who Among the Mennonites* (Newton, Kans.: Faith and Life Press, 1943), 113, 114. For background on the Mennonite scene, 1890–1930, see James Juhnke, *Vision, Doctrine, War: Mennonite Identity and Organization in America, 1890–1930* (Scottdale, Pa.: Herald Press, 1989).

4. Communal Life or Private Property (pp. 62–78)

First epigraph. Hutterian Brethren, eds., *The Chronicle of the Hutterian Brethren*, *Volume I* (Rifton, N.Y.: Plough, 1987), 167, 168.

Second epigraph. Hutterian Brethren, eds. (1987), 180.

Third epigraph. Joshua Hofer, ed., "Sermon on Acts 2: 40–42" (Elie, Man.: James Valley Colony, 1981), 16.

1. John Voth, ed., "Peter Janzen's letter to the *Mennonitische Rundschau*" (dated July 27, 1890), in Frances Janzen Voth, *The House of Jacob* (Tucson: self-published, 1984), 67.

2. John A. Hostetler, *Hutterite Society* (Baltimore: Johns Hopkins University Press, 1974), 122.

3. These figures are based on analysis of the entire Jacob J. Mendel manuscript, *A History of the People of East Freeman, Silver Lake and West Freeman* (Freeman, S.Dak.: Pine Hill Press, 1961). For the most part, this hard-to-find book is a collection of stories that first appeared in the Freeman *Courier*, sometimes referred to as "the Hutter gossip sheet," which Mendel published and edited until 1961. Since that time, the *Courier* has continued to include news reports from various Prairieleut communities in the United States and Canada. Present publisher and editor, Tim L. Waltner, is a direct descendent of the Hutterite "Waldners."

4. Arnold M. Hofer, interviews with author (July 1987 and July 1993).

5. A. J. F. Zieglschmid, *Das Klein-Geschichtsbuch der Hutterischen Bruder* (Philadelphia: Carl Schurz Memorial Foundation, 1947).

6. John A. Hostetler (1974), 308.

7. Hutterian Brethren, eds., *Chronicle of the Hutterian Brethren, Volume I* (Rifton, N.Y.: Plough, 1987) 265–275.

8. Samuel Hofer, *The Hutterites: Lives and Images of a Communal People* (Saskatoon, Sask.: Hofer Publishers, 1998), 142.

9. Samuel Hofer (1998), 95.

10. Arnold M. Hofer, ed., *The Diaries of Joseph "Yos" Hofer* (Freeman, S.Dak.: HCC, 1997), February 1904 entry.

11. Note, for example, Larry and Edith Tschetter, *The Jacob W. Tschetter Family Record* (Freeman, S.Dak.: self-published, 1977), 5.

12. Arnold M. Hofer, ed., "The Diary of Jacob J. Hofer, 1900–1920," (unpublished, 1986), 7. HCC.

13. David W. Tschetter, "Questionnaire About the History of Your Church" (1947), 5. CMBSH. Arnold M. Hofer, ed., "The Diary of Jacob J. Hofer, 1900–1920" (1986), July 19, 1903, entry.

14. Arnold M. Hofer, ed., "The Diary of Jacob J. Hofer, 1900–1920" (1986), July 19, 1903, entry.

15. Arnold M. Hofer, "The Prairieleut" (unpublished presentation, Freeman College, 1984).

16. Marie Waldner, interview with author (July 1987).

17. Marie Waldner, interview (1987).

18. Marie Waldner, interview (1987).

19. John Voth, ed., "Peter Janzen's Correspondence, dated July 27, 1880, with the *Mennonitische Rundschau*," in Frances Janzen Voth (1984), 67.

20. Karl J. Arndt, "The Harmonists and the Hutterites," *American-German Review* (August 1944), 24–26. See also A. J. F. Zieglschmid (1947), 463.

21. A. J. F. Zieglschmid (1947), 463.

22. Karl J. R. Arndt, *George Rupp's Successors and Material Heirs 1847–1916* (Cranbury, N.J.: Associated University Presses, 1971), 129–136.

23. Newspaper article on the history of the Tidioute community (dated 1922, no author or title given). HCC. Reprinted in the *Observer* (August, 1955).

24. Arnold M. Hofer, ed. (1997), July, 1876 entry. The Stahl metamorphosis, which was influenced by dreams and visions, is more fully described in chapter nine.

25. Arnold M. Hofer, ed. (1997), March, 1877 entry.

26. Arnold M. Hofer, ed. (1997), July, 1876 entry.

27. "Hutterite Ship List Records," in Arnold M. Hofer, ed., *A History of the Hutterite-Mennonites* (Freeman, S.Dak.: HCC, 1974), 85. These records provide the basis for some of the information and analysis included in chapter four.

28. Olga Stucky and Lillian Graber, eds., *Freeman Facts and Fiction: 1879–1979* (Freeman, S.Dak.: Freeman Centennial Committee, 1979), 231.

29. Emma Hofer, trans., "Excerpts from the Autobiography of D. J. Mendel," in Arnold M. Hofer, ed. (1974), 71.

30. "Hutterite Ship List Records," in Arnold M. Hofer, ed. (1974), 75, 76. These records are the source of all of the information contained in the paragraph.

31. Arnold M. Hofer, ed. (1974), 85.

32. Jacob J. Mendel (1961), 16.

33. *Dariusleut* church records. These documents were made available by a Hutterite individual who requested anonymity.

34. Arnold M. Hofer, ed. (1997), October 1875 entry.

35. Arnold M. Hofer, ed. (1997), February 1876–September 1877 entries.

36. Arnold M. Hofer, ed. (1997), May, 1876 entry. See also A. J. F. Zieglschmid (1947), 565–568; 606–610.

37. Arnold M. Hofer, ed. (1997), September 1876 entry.

38. Arnold M. Hofer, ed. (1997), 1895 entry.

39. Arnold M. Hofer, ed. (1997), 1892 entry.

40. John A. Hostetler (1974), 89.

41. Interviews with Hutterite ministers Michael Waldner of Pearl Creek Colony, Iroquois, South Dakota, and Hans Decker of Wolf Creek Colony, Olivet, South Dakota (July 1987).

42. Mrs. Paul S. Gross, ed., *A History of the Salem Mennonite Brethren Church* (Freeman, S.Dak.: Pine Hill Press, 1986), 79.

43. "Hutterthal Mennonite Church Family Record," 154, in "Hutterthal Mennonite Church Records." These documents are housed in the FAA.

44. The California Mennonite Historical Society geneaological collection. Under the directorship of Alan Peters, the collection includes a significant amount of information on Prairieleut families. Peters' marriage to Imogene Wollman helped encourage that particular focus. The records are housed in the CMBS.

45. Arnold M. Hofer, ed. (1997), October and November 1875 entries.

46. George M. Hofer, interviews with author (July 1987, July 1993). Hofer is a long-time member of the Hutterthal Church in Freeman, South Dakota.

47. "Hutterite Marriage Records," in Arnold M. Hofer, ed., *Hutterite Roots* (Freeman, S.Dak.: HCC, 1986), 70.

48. Frances Janzen Voth (1984), 13, 14. Ruth Janzen Keck, interview with author (May, 1998). Rev. Michael Waldner, Pearl Creek Colony, Iroquois, South Dakota, interview with author (July 1987).

49. David P. Glanzer, "Report," *Mennotische Rundschau* (February 15, 1893). FAA.

50. Frances Janzen Voth (1984), 16.

51. Peter Gordon Clark, "Dynasty Formation in the Communal Society of the Hutterites" (unpublished doctoral dissertation, University of British Columbia, 1973), 147. See also Kenneth T. Morgan and Mary Holmes, untitled research note, *American Journal of Physical Anthropology* 62 (1983), 4.

52. Jacob J. Mendel (1961), 16, 107.

53. Arnold M. Hofer and Pauline Becker (1988), 5.

54. Elenora R. Wipf, *The Andreas and Susann Glanzer Family Record, 1842–1962* (Freeman, S.Dak.: self-published, 1962), 3.

55. Marie Waldner, interview with author (July 1987).

56. Jerald Hiebert, ed., "Hofer Colony Genealogical Records" (Stirling, Alb., 1993). These records are in the possession of the Stirling Mennonite Church, Stirling, Alberta. The story of the Hofer Colony is told in chapter 8.

57. Arnold M. Hofer, interview with author (July 1987). See also Jacob J. Mendel (1961), 107, 114, 148.

58. "Hutterite Ship List Records," in Arnold M. Hofer, ed. (1986), 75, 76.

59. "Hutterite Ship List Records," in Arnold M. Hofer, ed. (1974), 79.

5. Prairieleut Congregational Patterns (pp. 79–102)

First epigraph. Jacob M. Hofer, ed., "The Diary of Paul Tschetter, 1873," *Mennonite Quarterly Review* (April 1931), 123.

Second epigraph. Jacob M. Hofer, ed. (1931), 114.

Third epigraph. Paul S. Gross, *The Hutterite Way* (Saskatoon, Sask.: Freeman Publishing Company, 1965), 112.

1. LaVern J. Rippley, *The German-Americans* (New York: Gramercy, 1976), 176.

2. John P. Kleinsasser, "Memoirs," in Jacob J. Mendel, *A History of the People of East Freeman, Silver Lake and West Freeman* (Freeman, S.Dak.: Pine Hill Press, 1961), 164.

3. David L. Hofer, interview with author (June 1993). See also Rod Janzen, "Jacob D. Hofer: Evangelist, Minister and Carpenter," *California Mennonite Historical Society Newsletter* (May 1994).

4. Erwin R. Gross, ed., *History of the Hutterthal Mennonite Church, 1879–1968* (Freeman, S.Dak.: Pine Hill Press, 1968), 10.

5. Marie Waldner, interview with author (July 1987).

6. Clarence Hofer, interview with author (June 1993). Hofer, a former minister at the Zion Church, was also a well-known Reedley-area educator.

7. John D. Unruh, *A Century of Mennonites in Dakota* (Pierre: South Dakota Historical Society, 1972), 101.

8. Marie Waldner, interview with author (July 1987).

9. Arnold M. Hofer, ed., *The Diaries of Joseph "Yos" Hofer* (Freeman, S.Dak.: HCC, 1997), August 1873 entry.

10. Arnold M. Hofer, ed. (1997), August 1973 entry.

11. George M. Hofer, interviews with author (July 1987 and July 1993).

12. Erwin R. Gross, ed. (1968), 12.

13. Erwin R. Gross, ed. (1968), 3.

14. Jacob M. Hofer, ed., "The Diary of Paul Tschetter, 1873," *Mennonite Quarterly Review* (April 1931), 36.

15. Arnold J. Schilling, "An Analysis of Hutterian Hymn Melodies," (unpublished M.A. thesis, University of South Dakota, 1965).

16. Hutterian Brethren, eds., *Die Lieder der Hutterischen Bruder* (Scottdale, Pa.: Herald Press, 1914).

17. Erwin R. Gross, ed. (1968), 3.

18. *Emmanuel Mennonite Church, Doland, 50th Anniversary* (1972, n.d., n.p.). FAA.

19. *Tabernacle Hymnal #5* (Chicago: Tabernacle Publishing Company, 1945), hymn number 116.

20. *Tabernacle Hymnal #5* (1945), hymn number 218.

21. Joseph A. Kleinsasser, *A History of the Bethel Mennonite Brethren Church* (Freeman, S.Dak.: Pine Hill Press, 1979), 19.

22. Norman Hofer, correspondence with the author (August 1987); interviews with the author (July 1993 and August 1997). Norman Hofer is a member of the Hutterian Centennial Committee. He has also served as a lay leader in the General Conference Mennonite Church.

23. William Vance Trollinger, Jr., "Grace Bible Institute and the Advance of Fundamentalism among the Mennonites," *Mennonite Life* (September 1997), 4–15.

24. "Hutterthal Mennonite Church Family Records," 269. FAA.

25. *A History of the Neu-Hutterthaler Mennonite Church* (Freeman, S.Dak., n.d., n.a.). FAA.

26. Ibid.

27. The word *Vetter*—literally German for male "cousin"—was a term Hutterians used, along with *Basel* (for women) to show respect for older members.

28. Joseph W. Tschetter, "A Brief Biography of Paul Tschetter (1842–1919)," in Jacob M. Hofer, ed. (1931), *Mennonite Quarterly Review* (April 1931), 112, 113.

29. "Hutterite Baptismal Records," in Arnold M. Hofer, ed., *Hutterite Roots* (Freeman, S.Dak.: HCC, 1986), 86.

30. Centennial Book Committee, eds., *A Tale of 3 Cities: 1879–1979* (Freeman, S.Dak.: Centennial Book Committee, 1979), 112. J. A. Boese, *The Prussian-Polish Mennonites Settling in South Dakota, 1874 and Soon Thereafter* (Freeman, S.Dak.: self-published), 89. The Schartner group later threatened to "saw" the Mennonite church they were leaving in half, believing that part of it belonged to them.

31. Joseph W. Tschetter (1931), 112.

32. Paul E. Glanzer, Marilyn Wipf, and Jeanette Hofer, eds., *A Century of God's Blessing, Neu Hutterthaler Mennonite Church, 1888–1988* (Freeman, S.Dak.: Pine Hill Press, 1988), 11.

33. Paul G. Tschetter, "Monologue as Paul Tschetter" (videotape, 1988). FAA.

34. Marie Waldner, interview with author (July 1987).

35. Arnold M. Hofer, ed. (1997), May 1888–July 1892 entries.

36. Paul G. Tschetter, "Monologue as Paul Tschetter" (1988).

37. Paul E. Glanzer, Marilyn Wipf, and Jeanette Hofer, eds. (1988), 11.

38. Jacob M. Hofer, ed. (1931), 112.

39. David P. Gross and Arnold M. Hofer, ed., "Neu Hutterthaler Church Records" (1992), 19. HCC.

40. Arnold M. Hofer and Norman Hofer, "Interview with Paul L. Hofer" (video-taped, 1991). HCC.

41. David P. Gross and Arnold M. Hofer, eds. (1992), 19.

42. *A History of the Neu-Hutterthaler Church*, 16.

43. Paul E. Glanzer, Marilyn Wipf, and Jeanette Hofer, eds. (1988), 28.

44. Arnold M. Hofer, ed., "Hutterdorf Mennonite Church Record Book" (un-published, in process of being typed from handwritten manuscript). HCC. See also "History of the Hutterdorf Church" (unpublished paper, n.a., n.d.), 1. FAA.

45. Arnold M. Hofer, ed., "Hutterdorf Mennonite Church Record Book."

46. Interviews with Jake Gross (July 1993) and Kathryn Unruh (July 1987). Both Unruh and Gross were long-time members at the Hutterdorf Church.

47. John D. Unruh (1972), 63.

48. *Bethany Mennonite Church 75th Anniversary*, brochure (n.a., Freeman, S.Dak., 1980), 5. FAA

49. David P. Gross and Arnold M. Hofer, eds. (1992), 2. Early Neu Hutterthaler church records were entered by the Rev. Paul Tschetter.

50. Arnold M. Hofer, ed. (1997), July 1899 entry.

51. Arnold M. Hofer, ed. (1997), April 1900 entry.

52. Mrs. Paul S. Gross, ed., *A History of the Salem Mennonite Brethren Church* (Freeman, S.Dak.: Pine Hill Press, 1986), 75, 76.

53. Elenora R. Wipf, *The Andreas and Susann Glanzer Family Record, 1842–1962* (Freeman, S.Dak.: self-published), 19.

54. Petrea Hofer, "Old Hutterisch Weddings" (unpublished paper presented at Freeman College Mennonite History class, n.d.), 1. FAA. Interviews with various Prairie People confirmed this information.

55. Olga Stucky and Lillian Graber, eds., *Freeman Facts and Fiction* (Freeman, S.Dak.: Freeman Centennial Committee, 1979), 382.

56. Mrs. Paul S. Gross, ed. (1986), 42.

57. Interviews with the Rev. Michael Waldner and Katie Waldner, Pearl Creek Colony, Iroquois, South Dakota (June 1983 and July 1987). The Rev. Waldner died in 1991. Factual details were confirmed, with some variation, by the Prairieleut son of the photographer. The Prairieleut version did not accept the interpretation of divine intervention.

58. Jacob M. Hofer, ed. (1931), 114.

59. This often-told story may in part be apocryphal.

60. Minutes and bulletins of the "Sunday School/Christian Endeavor conventions of the Hutterite-Mennonite Churches in the Freeman, Bridgewater, Carpenter and Doland areas." FAA.

61. Malcolm Wenger, "Visitation notes—Mt. Olivet Mennonite Church," (September 3, 1970). FAA.

62. Diena Schmidt, ed., *The Northern District Conference of the General Conference Mennonite Church, 1891–1991* (Freeman, S.Dak.: Northern District Conference of the General Conference Mennonite Church, 1991), 100.

63. William Vance Trollinger, Jr. (1997), 4.

64. John D. Unruh (1972), 77.

65. Norman Hofer, interview with author (July, 1993).

6. The Attraction of the Krimmer Mennonite Brethren (pp. 103–135)

First epigraph. David V. Wiebe, *Grace Meadow: The Story of Gnadenau* (Hillsboro, Kans.: Mennonite Brethren Publishing House, 1967), 21.
Second epigraph. C. F. Plett, *The Story of the Krimmer Mennonite Brethren Church* (Hillsboro, Kans.: Kindred Press, 1985), 16.

1. In chapter 6, many sources are not identified in order to honor requests that anonymity be preserved.
2. Joshua Hofer, ed., *Hutterite Lehren on Matthew 6* (Elie, Man.: James Valley Colony, 1981).
3. Joshua Hofer, ed. (1981).
4. Robert F. Friedmann, *Hutterite Studies* (Goshen, Ind.: Mennonite Historical Society, 1961), 179, 187. Also note Robert F. Friedmann, "Hutterite Worship and Preaching," *Mennonite Quarterly Review* (1966), 10–12.
5. Hans Friedrich Kuentsche, "The Pentecost *Lehren*," in James Anderson, "The Pentecost Preaching of Acts 2: An Aspect of Hutterite Theology" (unpublished doctoral dissertation, University of Iowa, 1972), 280, 281. Anderson translated major sections of the Pentecost sermon into English.
6. Hans Friedrich Kuentsche (1972), 345.
7. Hans Friedrich Kuentsche (1972), 278.
8. C. F. Plett, *The Story of the Krimmer Mennonite Brethren Church* (Hillsboro, Kans.: Kindred Press, 1985), 16.
9. C. F. Plett (1985), 120.
10. C. F. Plett (1985), 119.
11. C. F. Plett (1985), 130.
12. Arnold M. Hofer, ed., "Diary of Katherina Wipf, 1872" (unpublished manuscript, 1987). HCC. The "spiritual battle" was also noted in Michael Hofer, "Census of Johannesruh, 1872." FAA.
13. David P. Gross and Arnold M. Hofer, eds., "The Neu Hutterthaler Church Records" (unpublished, 1992), 821. HCC.
14. Peter H. Stephenson, "Hutterite Belief in Evil Eye: Beyond Paranoia and Towards a General Theory of Invidia," *Culture, Medicine and Psychiatry* (1979), 259. This issue is discussed further in chapter 9.
15. Hutterite viewpoints were solicited via interviews with Hans Decker, Wolf Creek Colony, Olivet, S.Dak. (July 1987, June 1989), John S. Hofer, James Valley Colony, Elie, Man. (March 1987), Peter Tschetter, Pleasant Valley Colony, Flandreau, S.Dak. (July 1983, July 1987); and Jacob Waldner, Bon Homme Colony, Tabor, S.Dak. (June 1983, August 1997).
16. Mary Wipf, interview with author (July 1983). Wipf is a Hutterite defector who was featured in the film "Born Hutterite," produced in Montreal, Quebec, by the National Film Board of Canada (1997). CMBS.
17. Bert Kaplan and Thomas F. A. Plaut, *Personality and Communal Society* (Lawrence, Kans.: University of Kansas Press, 1956).
18. Karl A. Peter and Ian Whitaker, "Hutterite Perceptions of Psycho-Physiological Characteristics," *Journal of Social Biological Structures* 7 (1984), 273.
19. Hans Friedrich Kuentsche (1972), 261. Other translated sermons are included

in Caroline Hartse, "On the Colony: Social and Religious Change Among Contemporary Hutterites" (unpublished doctoral dissertation, University of New Mexico, Albuquerque), 273–299; and Vance Joseph Youmans, *The Plough and the Pen: Paul S. Gross and the Establishment of the Spokane Hutterian Brethren* (Boone, N.C.: Parkway Publishers, 1995), 121–132. Many additional translated (but unpublished) sermons are in the possession of the author.

20. C. F. Plett (1985), 25–27.

21. Egon Hofer, interview with author (February 1993). Egon, a son of Hutterite defector Dave P. Hofer, was a lay leader in the Zion Church.

22. Justina Wiebe, "Out of Darkness Into the Light," in C. F. Plett (1985), 90–98.

23. Karl A. Peter, "The Certainty of Salvation: Ritualization of Religion and Economic Rationality Among the Hutterites," *Comparative Studies in Society and History Quarterly* (April 1983), 223.

24. Jacob Hutter, "Plots and Excuses," in Walter Klaassen, ed., *Anabaptism in Outline* (Scottdale, Pa.: Herald Press, 1981), 61.

25. Karl A. Peter, *The Dynamics of Hutterite Society: An Analytical Approach* (Edmonton: University of Alberta Press, 1987), 29–32.

26. Clarence Hofer, interview with author (June 1993).

27. Conversations with the Rev. Hans Decker (1981–1989) and with numerous Hutterites, 1981–present. Caroline Hartse (1993), 209.

28. David W. Tschetter, "Questionnaire About the History of Your Church" (1945), 3. CMBSH.

29. Zion Krimmer Mennonite Brethren Church congregational meeting records. CMBS.

30. Glanzer had graciously offered copies of tape-recorded sermons.

31. David P. Gross, ed., "David W. Tschetter's The Origin and Development of the Salem KMB Church," in Mrs. Paul S. Gross, ed., *A History of the Salem Mennonite Brethren Church* (Freeman, S.Dak.: Pine Hill Press, 1986), 31.

32. *The Ebenezer Church, 1920–1960* (Huron, S.Dak., 1960, n.a.). CMBSH.

33. Arnold Hofer, ed., *History of the Hutterite-Mennonites* (Freeman, S.Dak.: HCC, 1974), 1, 2.

34. Joseph A. Kleinsasser, *A History of the Bethel Mennonite Brethren Church* (Freeman, S.Dak.: Pine Hill Press, 1979), 8.

35. Mrs. Paul S. Gross, ed. (1986), 4, 80.

36. Bethel Mennonite Brethren Church congregational records. CMBSH. Lloyd Penner, ed., *Gemeinde Chronik, Bethel KMB Church, to 1914* (unpublished, 1975), 1. CMBSH.

37. Phil Glanzer, taped interview with Mary J. Glanzer (May 1981). Tape is in the possession of Phil Glanzer.

38. David W. Tschetter, "Questionnaire on the History of Your Church" (1945), 6. CMBSH.

39. Helmut T. Huebert, *Hierschau: Example of Russian Mennonite Life* (Winnipeg: Springfield Publishers, 1986), 153–155.

40. Krimmer Mennonite Brethren Church congregational meeting records. CMBS.

41. Doreen Mierau (1991), "Prairie Peace-makers," *Saskatchewan Valley News* (June 8, 1967), 7.

42. The name recorded in the Articles of Incorporation (1904)—the *Kirche der Mennoniten Brueder*—did not, interestingly enough, include "KMB" in the title. CMBSH.

43. Mrs. Paul S. Gross, ed. (1986), 25.

44. LaVerne Hofer, "Questionnaire for Applicants to the Ministry in the KMB Conference of North America" (1945). CMBSH.

45. Zion KMB Church congregational meeting records. CMBS.

46. LaVerne Hofer (1945), 1.

47. P. M. Friesen, *The Mennonite Brotherhood in Russia, 1789–1910* (Fresno, Calif.: Center for Mennonite Brethren Studies, 1978), 591.

48. David P. Gross, "David W. Tschetter's The Origin and Development of the Salem KMB Church," in Mrs. Paul S. Gross, ed. (1986), 31. Joseph A. Kleinsasser (1979), 9.

49. *Ebenezer MB Church 50th Anniversary* (1970, n.a.), 13.

50. Rod Janzen, *Perceptions of the South Dakota Hutterites in the 1980's* (Freeman, S.Dak.: Freeman Publishing Company, 1984), 11.

51. Joseph A. Kleinsasser (1979), 20.

52. Joseph A. Kleinsasser (1979), 20.

53. Joseph A. Kleinsasser (1979), 16.

54. Arnold M. Hofer, "The Prairieleut" (unpublished presentation, Freeman College, 1984).

55. C. F. Plett (1985), 123.

56. Phil Glanzer, taped interview with Mary J. Glanzer.

57. Mrs. Paul S. Gross, ed. (1986), 2.

58. Emma Mendel Hofer, ed., in Arnold M. Hofer, ed. (1974), 71.

59. Phil Glanzer, taped interview with Mary J. Glanzer.

60. John Howard Yoder, ed., *God's Revolution* (Ramsey, N.J.: Paulist Press, 1984), 106.

61. Joseph A. Kleinsasser (1979), 120.

62. Jacob S. Mendel, "The MB Work in Chicago, Illinois" (unpublished document, n.d.). CMBSH.

63. Jacob S. Mendel, "The MB Work in Chicago, Illinois." CMBSH.

64. George Classen, "Chicago's Lakeview" (unpublished, 1978). CMBSH.

65. Lakeview MB congregational records. CMBSH.

66. John J. Kleinsasser, "Questionnaire About the History of Your Church" (1945), 3. CMBSH.

67. Alan Peters, "The Story of the Zion Church," taped presentation (1991, California Mennonite Historical Society annual meeting). Tape is in the possession of the author. C. F. Plett (1985), 202.

68. Joseph A. Kleinsasser (1979), 4.

69. Joseph A. Kleinsasser (1979), 4. John Z. Kleinsasser had been selected for the ministry at the Salem KMB Church in 1895.

70. Gary A. Nachtigall, "Mennonite Migration and Settlements of California" (unpublished M.A. thesis, California State University, Fresno, 1972), 27.

71. Ibid., 29.

72. Conversations with Clarence Hofer (June 1993), Egon Hofer (February 1993) and Walter Warkentin (June 1998). See also Gary A. Nachtigall (1972), 31. The $100,000 figure seemed reasonable when one computed Kleinsasser's South Dakota land sale profits as enumerated in various sources. Simply buying 3200 acres of land at the $85 per acre purchase price would have cost the families involved $272,000.

73. Interviews with Clarence Hofer (June 1993), Lydia Hofer (June 1998), Nancy Warkentin Neufeld (June 1998), and Walter Warkentin (June 1998).

74. Phil Glanzer, taped interview with Mary J. Glanzer (May 1981).

75. Joseph A. Kleinsasser (1979), 2.

76. For some interesting information on conditions in the early Langham settlement, the mud houses, etc., see Gwen Shaw, *Unconditional Surrender* (Jasper, Arkansas: End-Times Handmaidens, 1986), 1–35.

77. Walter Hoover, *The Hutterian Language* (Saskatoon, Sask.: self-published, 1997), 69.

78. Paul Stahl, "Questionnaire about the History of Your Church" (1945), 7. CMBSH. Doreen Mierau (1967), 7.

79. Paul Stahl (1945), 9.

80. Paul Stahl (1945), 13.

81. Catherine Masuk, interview and correspondence with author (July 1998). Lesley Masuk, correspondence with author (April 1996); interview with author (May 1998). Catherine Masuk is a member of the Board of Directors that administers the Emmanuel Church property, as well as events that take place there. She and Edna Wurtz are writing a book about the Langham-area Prairieleut. Lesley Masuk (Catherine's daughter) is conducting research with regard to Hutterian ethno-religious roots. Saskatchewan non-Hutterian KMB viewpoints were solicited from theologian Marlin Jeschke (interviews with author, October 1992 and October 1993) and novelist Margaret Epp (interview with author, July 1998).

82. Albert and Edna Wurtz, interview with the author (July 1993). The Wurtz couple are Langham-area Prairieleut descendents with a wealth of knowledge about the history of noncommunal Hutterians in Saskatchewan. See also Samuel Hofer, *The Hutterites: Lives and Images of a Communal People* (Saskatoon, Sask.: Hofer Publishers, 1998).

83. Walter Hoover (1997), 132.

84. Dinuba *Sentinel* (untitled article, February 23, 1911). See also Rod Janzen, "Jacob D. Hofer: Evangelist, Minister and Carpenter," *California Historical Society Newsletter* (1994), 1, 2, and 4–8.

85. Erwin Hofer, interview with author (July 1993).

86. Reedley Mennonite Brethren Church *Gemeinde Chronik* (unpublished document) CMBS.

87. John Goertzen, *Bethany Church 50 Years* (Fresno: Bethany Mennonite Brethren Church, 1992), 13.

88. Arnold M. Hofer, interview with author (July, 1993).

89. Mennonite Brethren Pacific District Conference Board of Reference and Counsel minutes (March–June 1947). CMBS. "Report of the 38th Pacific District Conference of the Mennonite Brethren Church of North America, held at Dinuba, California, November 22–25, 1947. CMBS. Rod Janzen, "Jacob Hofer, Evangelist, Minister and Carpenter" (1994).

90. Arnold M. Hofer, ed., "Diary of Jacob J. Hofer, 1900–1920" (unpublished, 1986), March 1902 entry. HCC.

91. Arnold M. Hofer, interview with author (July 1993).

92. Paul G. Tschetter, interview with author (June 1998).

93. Paul G. Tschetter, "Monologue as Paul Tschetter" (videotape, 1988). HCC.

94. Arnold M. Hofer, ed., "Diary of Jacob J. Hofer, 1900–1920" (1986), March 1902 entry.

95. Samuel J. R. Hofer, "Questionnaire for Applicants to the Ministry in the KMB Conference" (1947). CMBSH.

96. Joe Mendel, interview with author (July 1993).

97. Jim Hohm, interview with author (June 1998). Hohm is a former moderator of the Central District Conference of the Mennonite Brethren Church.

98. Phil Glanzer, taped interview with Mary J. Glanzer.

99. "Questionnaire for Applicants to the Ministry in the KMB Conference of North America." CMBSH.

100. Salem MB *Constitution* (1968), Article IV, section I, clause B. FAA.

101. Edna Kleinsasser Tschetter, "Memoirs," in Walter Kleinsasser, ed., *Memoirs of the Kleinsasser Siblings* (Hillsboro, Kans.: self-published, 1990), 77.

102. Dan Friesen, interview with author (February 1994). Friesen, who died in 1998, was a leader in the Mennonite Brethren Church.

103. Katherina Kleinsasser, "Memoirs," in Walter Kleinsasser, ed. (1990), 139.

104. Katherina Kleinsasser (1990).

105. Hans Friedrich Kuentsche (1972), 109.

106. John P. Kleinsasser, "Memoirs," in Jacob J. Mendel, *A History of the People of East Freeman, Silver Lake and West Freeman* (Freeman, S.Dak.: Pine Hill Press, 1961), 164.

107. Marian Kleinsasser Towne, ed., *Bread of Life: Diaries and Memories of a Dakota Family, 1936–1945* (Freeman, S.Dak.: self-published, 1994), January 1936 entry.

108. John P. Kleinsasser (1961), 164.

109. Reuben Goertz, "Drunk at First Mennonite Aid Plan Meeting" (unpublished article, 1977). CWS. The photograph is in Arnold M. Hofer, ed. (1974), 127, photograph number 13. Goertz told the author this information had been given to him by former Hutterian Centennial Committee vice-Chair Kenneth Walter, who died in 1977 in a vehicle accident. The story was confirmed by David P. Gross (interview with author, July 1987).

110. Paul G. Tschetter, "*Die Auswanderer*," in Nancy M. Peterson, ed., *People of the Old Missoury* (Frederick, Col.: Renaissance House, 1989), 99.

111. Arnold M. Hofer, ed. (1997).

112. Reuben Goertz, "Religious Life of the Volhynian Swiss Pioneers in East Freeman" (unpublished paper presented at Freeman College, April 1983), 9.

113. *Michters: America's Oldest Operating Distillery* (tourist brochure, n.d.). CWS.

114. Reuben Goertz (1977), 10. One John Gross' "bar ledger," dated July 29, 1902 to May 1903, verified Goertz's information. CWS.

115. Reuben Goertz (1977).

116. Paul Kleinsasser, "Memoirs," in Walter Kleinsasser, ed. (1990), 34.

117. W. W. Harms, *History of the Springfield KMB Church and the Community's Culture in Pioneer Years* (Hillsboro: Mennonite Brethren Publishing House, 1973).

118. Doreen Mierau (1967), 7.

119. John D. Unruh (1972), 137.

120. Catherine Albanese, *America: Religion and Religions* (Belmont, Calif.: Wadsworth, 1992), 6, 7. See also Robert Bellah and Franklin Greenspahn, *Uncivil Religion: Interreligious Hostility in America* (New York: Crossroads, 1987); Edwin Gaustad, *A Religious History of America* (New York: Harper and Row, 1974); Michael Lacey, ed., *Religion and 20th Century American Intellectual Life* (New York: Cambridge University Press, 1991); and Mark Noll, *A History of Christianity in the United States and Canada* (Grand Rapids, Mich.: Eerdmans, 1992).

121. Arnold M. Hofer, ed. (1997), addendum, 244.

7. Citizenship and the Political Order (pp. 136–157)

First epigraph. Hutterian Brethren, eds., *The Chronicle of the Hutterian Brethren*, *Volume I* (Rifton, N.Y.: Plough), 279.
Second epigraph. Senior Citizens of Freeman, South Dakota Community, *A Part of Our Lives* (Freeman, S.Dak.: Senior Citizens of Freeman, 1976), 14.

1. Jacob J. Mendel, *A History of the People of East Freeman, Silver Lake and West Freeman* (Freeman, S.Dak.: Pine Hill Press, 1961), 117.
2. Merle J. F. Funk, "Divided Loyalties: Mennonite and Hutterite Responses to the United States at War, Hutchinson County, South Dakota, 1917, 1918," *Mennonite Life* (December 1997), 28.
3. Arnold M. Hofer, "Gleanings from the Diary of Jacob J. Hofer," in Mrs. Paul S. Gross, ed. *A History of the Salem Mennonite Brethren Church* (Freeman, S.Dak.: Pine Hill Press, 1986), 78.
4. Arnold M. Hofer, "Gleanings from the Diary of Jacob J. Hofer" (1986), 78.
5. Franz Wiebe, ed., "The Martyrdom of Joseph and Michael Hofer," The *Mennonite* (August 5, 1975), 454.
6. American Industrial Committee, eds., *Crucifixions in the 20th Century* (Chicago: The American Industrial Committee, 1919).
7. Franz Wiebe, ed. (1975), 454.
8. American Industrial Committee, eds., *Crucifixions in the 20th Century.*
9. Peter H. Stephenson, *The Hutterian People: Ritual and Rebirth in the Evolution of Communal Life* (Lanham, Md.: University Press of America, 1991), 67.
10. George Tindall, *America: A Narrative History* (New York: W. W. Norton, 1990), 965. Helpful accounts and analyses of twentieth-century American history are the following: David Burner, *Firsthand America*, Vol. 2 (St. James, N.Y.: Brandywine Press, 1994); Gerald Grob and George Billias, eds., *Interpretations of American History*, Vol. 2 (New York: Free Press, 1992); and Howard Zinn, *The Twentieth Century* (New York: Harper and Row, 1984).
11. A. J. F. Zieglschmid, *Das Klein-Geschichtsbuch der Hutterischen Bruder* (Philadelphia: Carl Schurz Memorial Foundation, 1947), 478–488. This section of Zieglschmid's book is part of his personal addition to the *Kleingeschichtsbuch*, completed in consultation with leading Hutterites. It includes a brief narrative, as well as assorted documents related to the Hutterite experience during World War I.
12. Merle J. F. Funk (1997), 32.
13. Joseph A. Kleinsasser, *A History of the Bethel Mennonite Brethren Church, 1919–1979* (Freeman, S.Dak.: Pine Hill Press, 1979), 22.
14. A photograph and story are found in the *Yankton Press and Dakotan* (May 4, 1918).
15. A. J. F. Zieglschmid, ed. (1947), 487.
16. Arnold M. Hofer and Norman Hofer, "Interview with Peter J. S. Hofer" (tape, 1991). HCC.
17. Allan Teichrow, ed., "Military Surveillance of Mennonites in World War I," *Mennonite Quarterly Review* (April 1979), 96.
18. Allan Teichrow, ed. (1979), 100, 108.
19. Arnold M. Hofer, ed., "Jacob J. Hofer Diary, 1900–1920" (unpublished, 1992), August 1918 entry. FAA.

20. James Juhnke, "The Response of Churches to Conscription in United States History," in Mennonite Central Committee, eds., *Mennonites and Conscientious Objection* (Akron, Pa.: Mennonite Central Committee, 1980), 26.

21. Arnold M. Hofer and Norman Hofer, "Interview with Paul L. Hofer" (tape, 1991). FAA.

22. David P. Gross and Arnold M. Hofer, eds., "Neu Hutterthaler Church Record Book" (unpublished, 1992), 29. FAA.

23. Arnold M. Hofer and Norman Hofer, "Interview with Paul L. Hofer" (tape, 1991).

24. Ibid.

25. Arnold M. Hofer and Norman Hofer, "Interview with Peter J. S. Hofer" (tape, 1991). FAA.

26. David P. Gross and Arnold M. Hofer, eds., "Neu Hutterthaler Church Records" (unpublished, 1992), 30. Arnold M. Hofer and Norman Hofer, "Interview with Peter J. S. Hofer" (tape, 1991).

27. John A. Toews, *A History of the Mennonite Brethren Church* (Hillsboro, Kans.: Mennonite Brethren Board of Christian Literature, 1975), 351.

28. David L. Hofer, interview with author (June 1993).

29. Merle J. F. Funk (1997), 30.

30. Ibid., 31.

31. C. F. Plett, *The Story of the Krimmer Mennonite Brethren Church* (Hillsboro, Kans.: Kindred Press, 1985), 105.

32. James Juhnke, "The Response of Churches to Conscription in United States History," in Mennonite Central Committee, eds. (1980), 22.

33. Merle J. F. Funk (1997), 30.

34. Gerlof D. Homan, "Mennonites and Military Justice in World War I," *Mennonite Quarterly Review* (July 1992), 369.

35. Franz Wiebe, ed. (1975), 454.

36. Paul Stahl, "Questionnaire about the History of Your Church" (1967), 13. CMBSH.

37. Theron Schlabach, ed., "An Account of Jacob Waldner," *Mennonite Quarterly Review* (April 1974), 90.

38. Diane Larsen-Freeman and Michael H. Long, *An Introduction to Second Language Acquisition Research* (New York: Longman, 1991).

39. Arnold M. Hofer and Norman Hofer, "Interview with Peter J. S. Hofer" (tape, 1991).

40. Senior Citizens of Freeman, South Dakota Community, *A Part of Our Lives* (Freeman, S.Dak.: Senior Citizens of Freeman, 1976), 14.

41. Isaac Oberg-Quaidoo, "Hutterite Land Expansion and the Canadian Press" (unpublished doctoral dissertation, University of Minnesota, 1977), 137, 138.

42. Marian Kleinsasser Towne, ed., *Bread of Life: Diaries and Memories of a Dakota Family, 1936–1945* (Freeman, S.Dak.: self-published, 1994), November 11, 1938, entry.

43. The Hutterian Brethren, eds., *The Chronicle of the Hutterian Brethren*, Vol. 1 (Rifton, N.Y.: Plough, 1987), 754.

44. Zion KMB Church congregational records. CMBS.

45. Melvin Gingerich, *Service For Peace* (Akron, Pa.: Mennonite Central Committee, 1949), 167–169.

46. Paul Toews, "The Impact of Alternative Service on the American Mennonite World: A Critical Evaluation," *Mennonite Quarterly Review* (October 1991), 619. See also Paul Toews, *Mennonites in American Society, 1930–1970* (Scottdale, Pa.: Herald Press, 1996).

47. Abe Dueck, "North American Mennonite Brethren and Issues of War, Peace and Non-Resistance, 1940–1960," (paper presented at Mennonite Brethren symposium, Fresno, California, February 1993).

48. Rod Janzen, "Jacob D. Hofer: Evangelist, Minister and Carpenter," *California Mennonite Historical Newsletter* (1994), 1, 2, and 4–8.

49. Krimmer Mennonite Brethren Conference ledgers (1940–1950). Located in KMB Conference files, CMBS.

50. Melvin Gingerich (1949), 90–93. See also Rachel Waltner Goossen, "The 'Second Sex' and the 'second milers': Mennonite Women and CPS," *Mennonite Quarterly Review* (October 1992), 525.

51. Arnold M. Hofer, interviews with author (July 1989 and July 1993).

52. Katherina Hofer Tschetter, *My Life Story* (Chicago: self-published, 1945), 17. Marie Waldner, interview with author (July 1987).

53. Samuel J. R. Hofer "Questionnaire for Applicants to the Ministry in the KMB Conference of North America" (1947). CMBSH.

54. Mrs. F. L. Weier, ed., *Scrapbook of Activities of Weber-Hofer Unit* (undated). FAA.

55. David L. Hofer, interview with author (June 1993).

56. Marian Kleinsasser Towne, ed. (1994). Marian Kleinsasser Towne, interview with author (July 1998).

57. Marian Kleinsasser Towne, ed. (1994), 414. In this section of her book, Towne recaptured conversations from the past via semi-fictional narratives.

58. Zion KMB Church congregational meeting records (December 1943). CMBS.

59. Paul H. Glanzer, "Questionnaire for Applicants to the Ministry in the KMB Conference of North America" (1944). CMBSH.

60. Joe E. Walter, "Questionnaire for Applicants to the Ministry in the KMB Conference of North America" (1953). CMBSH.

61. Joe Walter, interview with author (June 1998).

62. Virgil Kleinsasser, "Questionnaire for Applicants to the Ministry in the KMB Conference of North America" (1948). CMBSH.

63. Melvin Gingerich (1949), 90–93. Though many women, as noted, worked in the CPS camps, one Prairieleut descendent, Susan Janzen McNichol, served alternatively as a branch commander in the Canadian Red Cross. See Frances Janzen Voth, *The House of Jacob* (Tucson, Ariz.: self-published, 1984), 84. McNichol was also said to be the first woman in the province of Saskatchewan to be issued a drivers license.

64. World War II congregational statistics come from Mennonite Central Committee Archives "Draft Census, World War II Records" (ix, 7–12). CMBS.

65. Salem KMB congregational records. CMBSH.

66. Mennonite Central Committee Archives "Draft Census, World War II Records." CMBS.

67. Willis Kleinsasser, "Memoirs," in Walter Kleinsasser, ed. (1990), 138.

68. Interviews with Clarence Hofer (June 1993) and Jake Gross (July 1993).

69. Joseph A. Kleinsasser (1979), 101.

70. Willis Kleinsasser, "Memoirs," in Walter Kleinsasser, ed. (1990), 138.

71. Walter F. Kleinsasser, "Questionnaire for Applicants to the Ministry in the KMB Conference of North America" (1956). CMBSH.

72. Clifford Walters, correspondence with author (July 1997).

73. Bethany MB Church congregational records (1942–1947). CMBS.

74. David G. Vetter, "History of Emmanuel KMB Church, 1919–1959," in Emmanuel KMB Church dedication *Bulletin* (June 26, 1960). CMBS.

75. Marian Kleinsasser Towne, ed. (1994).

76. John D. Unruh (1972), 36.

77. Walter Kleinsasser, "Memoirs" (1990), 111, 113.

78. John Redekop, "Decades of Transition: North American Mennonite Brethren in Politics," in Paul Toews, ed., *Bridging Troubled Waters: The Mennonite Brethren at Mid-Twentieth Century* (Hillsboro, Kans.: Kindred Press, 1995), 19–86.

79. Rod Janzen, *Terry Miller: The Pacifist Politician* (Freeman, S.Dak.: Pine Hill Press, 1986), 70, 71. See also the *South Dakota Legislative Manual* (Pierre, S.Dak., published each year, 1917–present); and Terry C. Anderson, *Historical Listing of South Dakota Legislators* (Pierre: State of South Dakota, 1983).

80. John Bennett, "Communes and Communitarianism," *Theory and Society* 2 (1975), 81.

81. Rod Janzen (1986).

82. Marian Kleinsasser Towne, ed. (1994).

83. Olga Stucky and Lillian Graber, eds., *Freeman Facts and Fiction, 1879–1979* (Freeman, S.Dak.: Pine Hill Press, 1979), 16, 44–46.

84. Rod Janzen (1986), 70, 90, 93, 117, 118.

85. John Redekop, *Making Political Decisions: A Christian Response* (Scottdale, Pa.: Herald Press, 1972), 40.

86. Rod Janzen (1986), 69–71. Harvey Wollman, interview with author (July 1984).

87. Zion MB Church bulletin insert (June 24, 1984). CMBS.

8. Embarrassment, Respect, and Rivalry: Prairie People, Hutterites, and Mennonites (pp. 158–188)

First epigraph. Hutterian Brethren, eds., *The Chronicle of the Hutterian Brethren, Volume I* (Rifton, N.Y.: Plough, 1987), 564.

Second epigraph. Hutterian Brethren, eds. (1987), 797.

Third epigraph. Marie Waldner, *For Half a Century* (Freeman, S.Dak.: Freeman Junior College, 1951), 63.

1. Rod Janzen, *Perceptions of the South Dakota Hutterites in the 1980's* (Freeman, S.Dak.: Freeman Publishing Company, 1984), 20.

2. Samuel Hofer, *Born Hutterite* (Saskatoon, Sask.: Hofer Publishing, 1991), 16.

3. For additional information on the Hutterite view of theft and alcohol use, see Rod Janzen (1984), 25–28. Marlene Mackie in "Outsider's Perceptions of the Hutterites," *Mennonite Quarterly Review* (January 1976) noted that only 4.3 percent of people polled in Alberta associated the Hutterites with dishonesty.

4. Karl A. Peter, "The Instability of Community of Goods in the Social History of the Hutterites" (unpublished paper, 1975), 15.

5. Miriam E. Warner, "Mennonite Brethren: The Maintenance of Continuity in a Religious Ethnic Group" (unpublished dissertation, U. C. Berkeley, 1985), 74.

6. Karl A. Peter and Ian Whitaker, "The Acquisition of Personal Property Among Hutterites and Its Social Dimension," *Anthropologica* (1981), 145–155.

7. Rod Janzen (1984), 20–31. Lesley Masuk, "Patriarchy, Technology and the Lives of Hutterite Women: A Field Study" (unpublished master's thesis, University of Saskatchewan, 1998), 83.

8. Interview with the Rev. John S. Hofer, James Valley Colony, Elie, Manitoba (March 1987).

9. Delbert Wiens, "From the Village to the City: A Grammar for the Languages We Are," *direction* (October 1973 and January 1974 issues, reprint).

10. Paul Kleinsasser, "Memoirs," in Walter Kleinsasser, ed., *Memoirs of the Kleinsasser Siblings* (Hillsboro, Kans.: self-published, 1990).

11. Phil Hofer, interview with author (March 1993).

12. Michael J. McManus, "Religion and Ethics," Fresno *Bee* (May 30, 1997).

13. Conversation with Marvin P. Riley, South Dakota State University, Brookings, South Dakota (July 1983). "87% Approve New law Restricting Hutterite Expansion," Sioux Falls *Argus-Leader* (no specific date, 1955 issue). Riley was a rural sociologist interested in Hutterite farming practices.

14. Milton Gordon, *Assimilation in American Life* (New York: Oxford University Press, 1964). See also Elliot Barkan, "Racism, Religion and Nationality in American Society: A Model of Ethnicity—From Contact to Assimilation," *Journal of American Ethnic Studies* (Winter 1995), 38–75; Oscar Handlin, *The Uprooted* (Boston: Little Brown, 1952); David Hollinger, *Postethnic America* (New York: Basic, 1995); Alan Kraut, *The Huddled Masses: The Immigrant in American Society, 1880–1921* (Arlington Heights, Ill.: Harlan Davidson, 1982); and Ronald Takaki, *A Different Mirror: A History of Multicultural America* (New York: Little Brown, 1993).

15. Milton Gordon (1964).

16. Herbert Gans, "Ethnic Invention and Acculturation, A Bumpy-Line Approach," in Richard Monk, ed., *Taking Sides* (Guilford, Conn.: Dushkin, 1994), 66–72.

17. Ronald Takaki (1993).

18. The same manifestation was evident on the West Coast in the Mexican-American community, where some third and fourth generation Hispanics were embarrassed by the continuous arrival of new immigrants from Mexico. See Ruben Navarette, Jr., *A Darker Shade of Crimson* (New York: Bantam, 1993); and Richard Rodriguez, *Hunger of Memory* (New York: Bantam, 1982).

19. Emmanuel Church congregational meeting minutes (November 12, 1969). FAA.

20. Ruth Baer Lambach, interviews with author (October 1992 and October 1996). See also Ruth Baer Lambach, "Colony Girl," in Wendy E. Chmielewski, ed., *Women in Spiritual and Communitarian Societies in the United States* (Syracuse, N.Y.: Syracuse University Press, 1993). Lambach is a former Hutterite and Bruderhof resident.

21. Caroline Hartse, "On the Colony: Social and Religious Change Among Contemporary Hutterites" (unpublished doctoral dissertation, University of New Mexico, 1993), 51.

22. Interviews with numerous Prairieleut from the Freeman and Huron areas.

23. Rod Janzen, "Five Paradigms of Ethnic Relations," *Social Education* (October

1994). See also Rod Janzen, "Multicultural Confusion," *Educational Leadership* (May 1994), and Elliot Barkan (1995).

24. Adam Giesinger, *From Catherine to Khruschchev: The Story of Russia's Germans* (Lincoln, Nebr.: Society of Germans from Russia, 1981), 292, 328, 331. According to the 1970 Soviet census, 66.8 percent of nearly 2 million German-Soviets listed German as their mother tongue.

25. Adam Giesinger (1981), 331.

26. Ben and Elsie Hofer, interviews with author (July 1983, July 1988). The Hofers are active lay leaders in the Mennonite Brethren Church.

27. Lesley Masuk (1998), 66.

28. The following quotations are from papers written by students in "Hutterite Studies" classes taught at Freeman College (Freeman, South Dakota) in 1984, 1985, and 1986.

29. Jon Wollman, "Hutterite Impressions," paper submitted for "Hutterite Studies" course (Freeman College, 1985).

30. Joe Mendel, interview with author (July 1993).

31. Hans Decker, interview with author (August 1989).

32. Catherine Albanese, *America: Religion and Religions* (Belmont, Calif.: Wadsworth, 1992).

33. J. Howard Kaufmann and Leo Driedger, *The Mennonite Mosaic* (Scottdale, Pa.: Herald Press, 1991).

34. John D. Roth, "A Fresh Breath of Life," *The Mennonite* (May 1998), 8, 9.

35. For additional information on the Bruderhof, see Samuel Hofer (1998), 131–139; Benjamin Zablocki, *The Joyful Community* (Chicago: University of Chicago Press, 1980); Ulrich Eggers, *Community for Life* (Scottdale, Pa.: Herald Press, 1988); Elizabeth Bohlken-Zumpe, *Torches Extinguished* (San Francisco: Peregrine Foundation, 1993); and the *KIT Newsletter*, a bimonthly publication written by Bruderhof defectors.

36. Leonard Pravitt, "About Hutterites," in the *KIT Newsletter* (February 1993). Pravitt included statistics that showed increasing defection, as well, among the *Lehrerleut* and *Dariusleut*. This was corroborated by interviews with Norman Hofer (August 1997 and May 1998); Nathan Hofer, a Hutterite German Teacher, Rustic Acres Colony, Madison, South Dakota (August 1997); and Jacob Waldner, Bon Homme Colony (August 1997). See also Karl A. Peter, Edward D. Boldt, Ian Whitaker, and Lance Roberts, "The Dynamics of Hutterite Defection," *Journal for the Scientific Study of Religion* (December 1982), 327–32, Mona S. Rich, "Hutterite Defectors: A Qualitative Assessment of "Ebaugh's Role-Exit Model" (M.A. thesis, University of Manitoba, 1995); and Lesley Masuk (1998), 114.

37. John A. Hostetler, "Food For Thought," the *KIT Newsletter* (1992). See also John Hostetler, "Expelled Bruderhof Members Speak Out," unpublished document (1990); and Caroline Hartse (1993), 115–120.

38. See also John F. Melland, "Changes in Hutterite House Types: The Material Expression of the Contradiction Between 'Being on the Colony' And 'Being in the World'" (unpublished doctoral dissertation, Louisiana State University, 1985); and William P. Thompson, "Hutterite Community: Artifact Ark: An Historical Study of the Architecture and Planning of a Communal Society (unpublished doctoral dissertation, Cornell University, 1977).

39. Barbara Mathieu, "The Door As Cultural Symbol: A Contrast of Hutterite

Community and Middle Class Society" (unpublished doctoral dissertation, U.C.L.A., 1985).

40. Edna Hofer, unpublished paper for "Hutterite Studies" course (Freeman College, 1980).

41. Caroline Hartse (1993).

42. Shirley Waltner, interview with author (March 1986). Waltner was a classmate of David Decker. David Decker, correspondence with author (September 1987).

43. Jerald Hiebert, interviews with author (July 1993 and July 1998). Much of the information on Stirling and its past history comes from an unpublished manuscript entitled, "History of Stirling Mennonite Church," written by Jerald Hiebert, in 1992. Hiebert had served Stirling as an ordained deacon. See also Dan and Carol Weaver, "Stirling Church History," *Directory of the Western Fellowship Mennonite Churches* (Targent, Ore.: self-published, 1997), 100–103.

44. Jerald Hiebert, ed., "Hofer Colony Genealogical Records" (1993), 4.

45. Jerald Hiebert, ed. (1993), 4.

46. Jerald Hiebert, ed. (1993), 8.

47. George Hofer, "How a Hutterian Minister Sees the Seventh Day" (Raley, Alb.: n.p., n.d.). The document is in the possession of the Stirling Mennonite Church.

48. Jerald Hiebert, correspondence with author (February 1994). Lesley Masuk, interview with author (May 1998).

49. Correspondence with Terry Miller (June 1993).

50. Jerald Hiebert (1992), 1.

51. Stirling doctrinal positions are included in the "Stirling Mennonite Church Standards" (unpublished, n.d.). A copy is in the possession of the author.

52. "Stirling Mennonite Church Standards."

53. Jerald Hiebert, ed. (1993).

54. Tony Waldner, ed., "Forest River Colony genealogical records" (unpublished documents, many handwritten), available for perusal from Tony Waldner. Waldner, the German Teacher at Forest River Colony (Fordville, North Dakota), lived outside the community with his ex-Hutterite parents for a number of years and holds a B.A. degree. See also Jacob J. Mendel (1961), 146; and Hutterian Brethren, eds., *Predigerbuch* (unpublished document, n.d.). HCC.

55. Tony Waldner, interview with author (July 1993).

56. Arnold M. Hofer, interview with author (July 1993).

57. Arnold M. Hofer, interview with author (June 1998).

58. Correspondence with Joseph P. Hofer (September 1987). Mary Waldner, interview with author (July 1993). Lesley Masuk, interview with author (May 1998).

59. Angela Steffke, correspondence with author (May 1998).

60. Lesley Masuk, interview with author (May 1998).

61. Caroline Hartse (1993), 63–68.

62. Samuel Hofer, interview with author (May 1998).

63. Caroline Hartse (1993), 362.

64. Eldon Busenitz, interview with author (July 1987).

65. Caroline Hartse, "The Emotional Acculturation of Hutterite Defectors," *Journal of Anthropological Research* (Spring 1994), 69–85. Caroline Hartse (1993), 6, 63–68, 115–120, 138, 161.

66. Arnold M. Hofer, interview with author (July 1993).

67. Max E. Stanton, "Current Status on non-Hutterite Teachers in Hutterite

Colonies" (presentation at Communal Studies Association annual meeting, October 1992), 3.

68. Conversations with a number of Prairieleut and non-Prairieleut "English Teachers," all of whom requested anonymity. See also Caroline Hartse (1993).

69. Rod Janzen, "The Hutterite High School Experiment," *Syzygy: Journal of Alternative Religion and Culture* (Summer 1993).

70. Phil Hofer, interview with author (March 1993).

71. Steve Hofer, "Videotape of Hofer family visit to Montana colonies, August 1992." Tape is in the possession of Phil Hofer, Los Angeles, California.

72. Emily Hofer, interview with author (August 1993).

73. Ernie Waldner, interview with author (June 1998).

74. "Hutterite Baptismal Records," in Arnold M. Hofer, ed., *Hutterite Roots* (Freeman, S.Dak.: HCC, 1986), 86. California Mennonite Historical Society genealogical collection. CMBS.

75. "Hutterite Marriage Records," in Arnold M. Hofer, ed. (1986), 69. California Mennonite Historical Society genealogical collection. CMBS.

76. For a rather bizarre and interesting account of a Catholic priest's attempt to convert the Hutterites, note letter from Father Emmet R. Engle to the Vatican dated December 15, 1962 (in the possession of the author).

77. "Hutterite Baptismal Records," in Arnold M. Hofer, ed. (1986), 83. California Mennonite Historical Society genealogical collection. Peter J. S. Hofer, ed., "Hutterthal Mennonite Church Family Records" (unpublished, 1990). HCC.

78. Alan Peters, "The Story of the Zion Church," taped presentation at the annual meeting of the California Mennonite Historical Society (1991).

79. The author has no known relationship to the Janzen families that became Hutterian.

80. "Hutterite Marriage Records," in Arnold M. Hofer, ed. (1986), 74.

81. Alan Peters, interview with author (September 1993).

82. Tony Waldner, interview with author (July 1993).

83. Evan Eichler, "Hutterite surnames," unpublished document (1998), 2. Document is in the possession of the author.

84. Alan Peters, "Unraveling the Origins: How Much Dutch?" *California Mennonite Historical Society Bulletin* (October 1993), 3, 4.

85. Peter J. Klassen, *A Homeland For Strangers: An Introduction to Mennonites in Poland and Prussia* (Fresno: Center for Mennonite Brethren Studies, 1989).

86. Gary J. Waltner, *The Joseph Waltner Family 1797–1960* (Freeman, S.Dak.: Pine Hill Press, 1962), 20. See also Emil J. Waltner, ed., *Banished for Faith* (Jasper, Alaska: End Time Handmaidens, 1989), 131, 132.

87. California Mennonite Historical Society genealogical collection.

88. David P. Gross, ed., "Paul Tschetter's Report of Why We Had to Leave Russia," in Arnold M. Hofer, ed. (1986), 100.

89. David P. Gross, ed. (1986).

90. Donald Kraybill (interview with author, July 1994).

91. The author was introduced to these jokes by students at Freeman College almost immediately upon arrival in the community in 1980.

92. Norman Hofer, correspondence with author (August 1993).

93. Joseph A. Kleinsasser (1979), 35.

94. David L. Hofer, interview with author (June 1993).

95. C. F. Plett (1985), 154. Mrs. Paul S. Gross, ed. (1986), 31.

96. Alan Peters (1991).

97. Clarence Hofer, interview with author (July 1993). Note also the "Pacific District Conference evaluation of the Zion MB Church summary statement." CMBS.

98. Alan Peters (1991).

99. "KMB Conference at Doland," *Mennonite Weekly Review* (October 8, 1953). "KMB Board of Missions Membership List, 1905–1960." CMBS.

100. Silas Bartsch, interview with author (April 1998). In the 1990s these towns were inhabited primarily by first and second generation Mexican-Americans.

101. Letter from two members to the Zion Mennonite Brethren Church (October 1984). CMBS.

102. Signed statement from congregational member to the Zion MB Church (January 1986), entitled "Zion Church, As I See It." CMBS.

103. Young Adult Sunday School Class statement to congregation (August 1988). Zion MB Church congregational records. CMBS.

104. Correspondence from former member to Zion MB Church (1972). Zion MB Church congregational records. CMBS.

105. Clarence Hofer, interview with author (June 1993).

106. KMB Executive Committee Meeting minutes (1960). CMBS.

107. Marlin Jeschke, interviews with author (October 1992 and February 1995). Marlin Jeschke, "Review of C. F. Plett, History of the Krimmer Mennonite Brethren Church," *Mennonite Quarterly Review* (October 1987), 424.

108. Correspondence from the Gnadenau KMB Church Council to the KMB Executive Committee (November 9, 1953). CMBS.

109. Joe Walter, interview with author (June 1998).

110. "Report of the KMB Board of Foreign Missions," (October 2, 1953). Copy is located in the "Merger Committee minutes, 1949–1960," CMBS.

111. Conversations with J. B. Toews (May 1993) and Clarence Hofer (June 1993). Theologian, historian, and seminary president, J. B. Toews, who died in 1998, had sometimes been referred to as the "MB Pope." The author recalled large numbers of people in attendance at Zion youth gatherings in the late 1960s.

112. Jacob J. Mendel (1961), 16.

113. Mrs. Paul S. Gross, ed. (1986), 65.

114. Marie Waldner, *For Half a Century* (Freeman, S.Dak., 1951), 65–73 and 81–103.

115. Information on Immanuel High School was secured from the following sources: Esther Jost, ed., *75 Years of Fellowship: Pacific District Conference of the MB Churches 1912–1987* (Fresno: Pacific District Conference of Mennonite Brethren Churches, 1987), 62; Larry Jost, "The History of Immanuel High School" (unpublished paper submitted for "Senior Seminar" course, Fresno Pacific College, 1977), 13; and interviews with former principals Clarence Hofer (June 1993), Ed Janzen (May 1992), Vernon Janzen (June 1998), Dan Neufeld (November 1990), and Arthur Wiebe (May 1992).

116. Larry Jost (1977), 52–57.

117. David L. Hofer, interview with author (June 1993).

118. Joel Wiebe, *Remembering . . . Reaching, A Vision of Service: A Fifty Year History of Fresno Pacific College* (Fresno, Calif.: Fresno Pacific College, 1994).

119. The power of the forces of assimilation is clearly shown in J. Howard Kauffman and Leo Driedger (1991).

9. Folk Beliefs, Dreams, and Visions (pp. 189–201)

First epigraph. Hans Friedrich Kuentsche, "The Great Pentecost Lehren," in James Anderson, "The Pentecost Preaching of Acts 2: An Aspect of Hutterite Theology" (unpublished doctoral dissertation, University of Iowa, 1972), 278.
Second epigraph. Phil Glanzer, interview with Mary J. Glanzer (tape, 1981).

1. Arnold M. Hofer, ed., *Hutterite Roots* (Freeman, S.Dak.: HCC, 1986), 9.
2. John J. Hofer, interview with author (July 1993).
3. Folk customs were discussed by numerous Prairieleut individuals. Particularly helpful were Andrew J. Hofer, Arnold M. Hofer, Egon Hofer, George M. Hofer, Marie Waldner, Elenora Wipf, and Albert and Edna Wurtz. Others requested anonymity.
4. Sometimes the word *"schreien"* was spelled *"schpryen."* The term "evil eye" was not commonly recognized by Prairieleut and Hutterites.
5. Lesley Masuk, interview with author (May 1998).
6. Peter H. Stephenson, "Hutterite Belief in Evil eye: Beyond Paranoia and towards a General Theory of Invidia," *Culture, Medicine and Psychiatry* (1979), 255. See also Peter H. Stephenson, *Hutterite Society: Ritual and Rebirth in the Evolution of Communal Life* (Lanham, Md.: University Press of America, 1991), 166. Interviews with Anna Hofer (July 1993), Sarah Hofer (July 1993), and Albert and Edna Wurtz (July 1993).
7. Edna Wurtz, interview with author (July 1993).
8. Peter H. Stephenson (1979), 259.
9. Peter H. Stephenson (1991), 165.
10. Levi Tschetter, interview with author (July 1983).
11. Lesley Masuk, "Patriarchy, Technology and the Lives of Hutterite Women: A Field Study" (unpublished master's thesis, University of Saskatchewan, 1998), 103. According to Masuk, thirty Manitoba Hutterites were enrolled in university courses.
12. Egon Hofer, interview with author (February 1993).
13. Evelyn Hofer, interview with author (July 1993).
14. Harold Stahl, interview with author (July 1993).
15. Tony Waldner, interview with author (July 1993).
16. Alan Dundes, *Interpreting Folklore* (Bloomington: Indiana University Press, 1980), 94, 121.
17. Peter H. Stephenson (1991), 158.
18. Arnold M. Hofer, interview with author (July 1993).
19. Edna Wurtz, interview with author (July 1993).
20. Arnold M. Hofer, interview with author (July 1993).
21. Arnold M. Hofer, ed., *A History of the Hutterite-Mennonites* (Freeman, S.Dak.: HCC, 1974), 167.
22. Erich Kaempchen, *In the Century of Progress* (Freeman, S.Dak.: self-published, 1975), 16, 32.
23. LaVern Rippley, *German-Americans* (New York: Gramercy, 1976), 177.
24. Reuben Goertz, interviews with author (July 1987 and July 1993). The full title of the work is *The 6th and 7th Books of Moses or Moses' Magical Spirit Art* (Arlington, Tex., n.d.). CWS.

25. Marie Waldner, interview with author (July 1987).

26. Arnold M. Hofer, ed. (1974), 163.

27. Walter Kleinsasser, "Memoirs," in Walter Kleinsasser, ed., *Memoirs of the Kleinsasser Siblings* (Hillsboro, Kans.: self-published, 1990), 110.

28. Jacob Janzen, letter to *Mennonitische Rundschau* (March 15, 1882), in Frances Janzen Voth, *The House of Jacob* (Tucson, Ariz.: self-published, 1984).

29. Conversations with Marie Waldner and Arnold M. Hofer (July 1987).

30. Phil Glanzer, "Taped Interview with Mary J. Glanzer" (1981). For a contemporary look at "holistic health" practices, many of which bear resemblance to folk traditions, see Elaine U. Emeth and Janet Greenhut, *The Wholeness Handbook* (New York: Continuum, 1991).

31. Egon Hofer, interview with author (February 1993).

32. Tony Waldner, interview with author (July 1993).

33. Katherina Hofer Tschetter, *My Life Story* (Chicago: self-published, 1945), 4.

34. John P. Kleinsasser, "Memoirs," in Jacob J. Mendel, *A History of the People of East Freeman, Silver Lake and West Freeman* (Freeman, S.Dak.: Pine Hill Press, 1961), 164.

35. Phil Glanzer (1981).

36. Phil Glanzer (1981).

37. Karl A. Peter and Ian Whitaker, "Hutterite Perceptions of Psycho-Physiological Characteristics," *Journal of Social Biological Structures* 7 (1984). Karl A. Peter, *The Dynamics of Hutterite Life: An Analytical Approach* (Edmonton: University of Alberta Press, 1987), 123, 132.

38. Karl A. Peter (1987), 122, 123.

39. A. J. F. Zieglschmid, ed., *Die alteste Chronik der Hutterischen Bruder: ein Sprachdenkmal aus fruhneuhochdeutscher Zeit* (Philadelphia: Carl Schurz Memorial Foundation, 1943), 1008.

40. Tony Waldner, interview with author (July 1993).

41. Peter Gordon Clark, "Leadership Succession Among the Hutterites," *Canadian Review of Sociology and Anthropology* (Summer 1977), 294–302.

42. Ibid., 298.

43. Paul S. Gross, *Pincher Creek Memories* (Pincher Creek, Alb., n.d.), 11. A copy of the document is in the author's possession.

44. Jerald Hiebert, ed., "Hofer Colony Genealogical Records" (1993), 7.

45. Peter J. S. Hofer, ed., "Huttertal Mennonite Church Family Records" (unpublished, 1990). FAA.

46. Albert and Edna Wurtz, interview with author (July 1993).

47. Stefan C. Christopher, ed., "A Description of the Beginning of True Christian Community Among the Schmiedeleut Hutterians as It Began by the Power of the Spirit" (unpublished manuscript, 1972), 2, 3. FAA.

48. Stefan C. Christopher, ed. (1972), 3.

49. Stefan C. Christopher, ed. (1972), 4.

50. Information on Fred Waldner was obtained via conversations with the Rev. Hans Decker (July 1987); Arnold M. Hofer (July 1993); the Rev. Michael Waldner (June 1983 and July 1987); Tony Waldner (July 1993); and with numerous other Prairie People and Hutterites. The following is a composite account based upon the most commonly told and reliable versions.

51. Michael Waldner (July 1987). Jacob J. Mendel always insisted that the town

of Freeman was named after Waldner, since Fred had once owned the land upon which the city of Freeman—derived from "Fritzman"—eventually stood. For alternative suggestions, see Olga Stucky and Lillian Graber, eds., *Freeman Facts and Fiction* (Freeman, S.Dak.: Pine Hill Press, 1979).

52. Tony Waldner, interview with author (July 1993).

53. Tony Waldner, interview (1993).

54. Stahl too had been ordained in Russia by Mennonite pastor Peter Wedel. The story of Stahl's decision to live communally is a composite account, taking into consideration various published and unpublished versions, all essentially similar but differing on specifics. The following sources were consulted: David P. Gross, ed., "Paul Tschetter's Report of Why We Had to Leave Russia," in Arnold M. Hofer, ed. (1986), 101; Rolf Brednick, *The Bible and the Plough* (Ottawa, Ont.: Canadian National Museum, 1981), 33–35; conversations with the Rev. Hans Decker, Wolf Creek Colony (July 1987), Arnold M. Hofer (July 1987), and the Rev. Michael Waldner, (June 1983 and July 1987). Minutes of a meeting held at the Wolf Creek Colony (dated July 18, 1876) confirmed parts of the story. That document is in the possession of the HCC. The Joseph "Yos" Hofer diary account (Arnold M. Hofer, ed., *The Diaries of Joseph "Yos" Hofer* (Freeman, S.Dak.: HCC, 1997) also substantiated part of the story.

55. Arnold M. Hofer, ed. (1997), August 1876 entry.

56. Interviews with numerous Hutterite ministers in Alberta, Manitoba, Minnesota, Montana, Saskatchewan, South Dakota, and Washington, 1981–1997.

57. Frances Janzen Voth (1984), 84, 85.

58. Melvin Gingerich, *Mennonites in Iowa* (Iowa City: Iowa Mennonite Historical Society, 1939), 134, 135.

59. Phil Glanzer (1981). Phil Glanzer (interview with author, July 1993).

60. John A. Hostetler, *Hutterite Society* (Baltimore: The Johns Hopkins University Press, 1974), 249.

61. A South Dakota Hutterite noted that the correspondence, which was in his possession, had been composed by a man from Pennsylvania.

62. Paul G. Tschetter, "Monologue on Paul Tschetter" (videotape, 1988). HCC. Paul G. Tschetter, interview with author (June 1998).

10. Contemporary Religious Beliefs (pp. 202–225)

First epigraph. Hutterian Brethren, eds., *The Chronicle of the Hutterian Brethren, Volume I* (Rifton, N.Y.: Plough, 1987), 774.

Second epigraph. Miriam E. Warner, "Mennonite Brethren: the Maintenance of Continuity in a Religious Ethnic Group" (unpublished dissertation, University of California, Berkeley, 1985), 149.

1. Catherine Albanese, *America: Religion and Religions* (Belmont, Calif.: Wadsworth, 1992). Edwin Gaustad, *A Religious History of America* (New York: Harper and Row, 1974).

2. Christian Reformed Church, eds., *Reasons II: Sects and Cults with Christian Roots* (Grand Rapids, Mich.: Christian Reformed Church, 1982).

3. C. I. Scofield, ed., *The Scofield Reference Bible* (New York: Our Hope Publica-

tions Office, 1909). See also John A. Toews, *A History of the Mennonite Brethren Church* (Hillsboro, Kans.: Mennonite Brethren Board of Christian Literature, 1975), 374, 377–379.

4. William Vance Trollinger Jr., "Grace Bible Institute and the Advance of Fundamentalism Among the Mennonites," in *Mennonite Life* (September 1997), 12.

5. William Vance Trollinger Jr. (1997), 13.

6. Elizabeth F. and Samuel J. R. Hofer, *God's Way of Salvation for the Seven Dispensations and Building God's Kingdom* (Carpenter, S.Dak., n.d.), 98–149. Note also the *Zion Mennonite Brethren Church Constitution* (1962, 1980, CMBS); and Emmanuel Mennonite Brethren Church, eds., *Our Church, Its History and Constitution* (Freeman, S.Dak., 1980), Article IV, section 6. FAA. Numerous interviews were conducted with Prairieleut Mennonites with regard to this issue.

7. C. F. Plett, *The Story of the Krimmer Mennonite Brethren* (Hillsboro, Kans.: Kindred Press, 1985), 108.

8. Elizabeth F. and Samuel J. R. Hofer, *God's Way of Salvation for the Seven Dispensations and Building God's Kingdom*, 69.

9. John J. Kleinsasser, "Questionnaire About the History of Your Church" (1945), 3. CMBSH.

10. Bethel KMB *Yearbook* (1955). Salem MB *Constitution* (1968). Hutterthal Mennonite Church *Yearbook, Directory, Constitution and Bylaws* (1990), Article III, section 2. Emmanuel Mennonite Brethren Church, eds., *Our Church, Its History and Constitution* (1980), Article IV, sections 1 and 6. Neu Hutterthaler *Constitution* (1974), Article IV, section A. FAA.

11. Jacob Hutter, "Plots and Excuses," in Walter Klaassen, ed., *Anabaptism in Outline* (Scottdale, Pa.: Herald Press, 1981), 252.

12. Zion MB Church congregational records. CMBS.

13. A variety of 1987 MB Triennial Convention reports are found in the *Christian Leader* (September 1987), 4–15.

14. Salem MB Church *Constitution* (1968), Article III, section 2e. Neu Hutterthaler *Constitution* (1974), Article IV. Ebenezer MB Church *Constitution*, Article III, section 2e. *Ebenezer MB church 50th Anniversary* (Freeman, S.Dak., 1970), 10, 13, 14. Hutterthal Mennonite Church *Constitution* (1969), 12. FAA.

15. C. F. Plett (1985), 104.

16. David W. Tschetter, "Questionnaire About the History of Your Church" (1945), 2. CMBSH.

17. Joel Wiebe, interview with author (May 1993). Wiebe was a professor and administrator at two Mennonite Brethren colleges.

18. *Constitution of the Emmanuel Mennonite Brethren Church* (Onida, S.Dak., 1968), Article III, section II. CMBSH. The *Bethel Mennonite Brethren Church Constitution* also did not incorporate the peace position. That document is included in Joseph A. Kleinsasser, *A History of the Bethel Mennonite Brethren Church, 1919–1979* (Freeman, S.Dak.: Pine Hill Press, 1979), 113.

19. Benny Gross, Leland Kleinsasser, and Harvey Wollman, interviews with author (July 1984).

20. Zion MB Church *Constitution* (1980). CMBS.

21. Harvey Wollman, interview with author (July 1984).

22. Rod Janzen, *Terry Miller: The Pacifist Politician* (Freeman, S.Dak.: Pine Hill Press, 1986), 69–71. This information was based on interviews with all known living

Prairieleut politicians in the state of South Dakota, and on John D. Unruh, *A Century of Mennonites in Dakota* (Pierre: South Dakota Historical Society, 1972), 99–101.

23. "KMB Peace and Welfare Committee Minutes and Reports," in KMB Peace and Welfare Committee ledger books (1944–1949 and 1950–1961). CMBS. Arnold M. Hofer, interview with author (August 1997).

24. "KMB Peace and Welfare Committee Minutes and Reports, 1953–1959." CMBS. The specific reference is taken from the minutes of a meeting held on May 2, 1953.

25. Arnold M. Hofer, "The Prairieleut" (unpublished presentation, Freeman College, 1984).

26. Zion MB Church *Constitution* (1980), Article 2, section 2E.

27. George M. Hofer, interview with author (July 1987).

28. Correspondence with Aaron Glanzer (September 1987).

29. Minutes of a "joint meeting" of Zion Mennonite and Neu Hutterthaler church councils (November 1969). FAA.

30. Alice Ontjes, "Among Our Churches—Neu Hutterthaler," *Northern Light* (March 1993), 4.

31. Phil Hofer, interview with author (March 1993).

32. *Constitution* of the Bethany Mennonite Church (1954), 7. CMBS.

33. Hutterthal Mennonite Church *Yearbook, Directory, Constitution and Bylaws*, 68. FAA.

34. "Questionnaire for Applicants to the Ministry in the KMB Conference of North America." CMBSH.

35. Rollo M. Entz, "The Doctrine of the Plenary Verbal Inspiration of the Scriptures" (unpublished M.A. thesis, Mennonite Brethren Biblical Seminary, 1963), 69. CMBS.

36. Jules Glanzer, "Relational Theology Expressed in the Local Church" (unpublished M.A. thesis, Mennonite Brethren Biblical Seminary, 1978), 3. CMBS.

37. "Pacific District Conference evaluation of Zion MB Church, summary statement," (July 25–28, 1985). CMBS.

38. Correspondence from Malcolm Wenger (GC Mennonite Northern District Conference Minister) to all South Dakota General Conference Mennonite churches (1970). Correspondence from Lester Janzen to Melvin Friesen, Secretary of Promotion and Stewardship for the General Conference Mennonite Church (October 1969). Correspondence from William Snyder (Executive Secretary, Mennonite Central Committee) to Melvin Friesen (December 1969). FAA.

39. Elizabeth F. and Samuel J. R. Hofer, *Most Popular Bible Questions and Answers Everybody Ought to Know*.

40. Salem MB Church *Constitution* (1968), Article III, section Ie. CMBSH.

41. Emmanuel MB Church *Constitution* (1980), Article III, number 8. CMBSH.

42. Phil Hofer, interview with author (March 1993). J. Howard Kauffman and Leo Driedger (1992), noted that 17 percent of MBs and 31 percent of GCs surveyed expressed "doubts about salvation."

43. "Pacific District Conference evaluation of the Zion MB Church, summary statement" (July 25–28, 1985). CMBS.

44. Zion MB Church *Constitution* (1962, 1980). CMBS.

45. Joseph A. Kleinsasser (1979), 27. Samuel J. R. Hofer, "Questionnaire for Applicants to the Ministry in the KMB Conference of North America" (1947), 17. CMBSH.

46. Joseph Schmidt, "Questionnaire for Applicants to the Ministry in the KMB Conference of North America" (1949). CMBSH.

47. Joseph A. Kleinsasser (1979), 101.

48. Virgil Kleinsasser, "Questionnaire for Applicants to the Ministry in the KMB Conference of North America" (1948). CMBSH.

49. Correspondence from Virgil Kleinsasser to C. F. Plett (March 3, 1950). CMBS.

50. Virgil Kleinsasser, interview with author (June 1998).

51. Sarah and Anna Hofer, interview with author (July 1993).

52. David L. Hofer, ed., *Fellowship Choruses* (Dinuba, Calif.: self-published, n.d., 48).

53. James C. Juhnke, "Mennonite History and Self-Understanding," in Calvin Redekop, ed., *Mennonite Identity* (Lanham, Md.: University Press of America, 1988), 96. Juhnke noted that this legacy of meekness led to the production of fewer successful novels "but more juvenile literature" among the Swiss, who, he suggested, had a difficult time "giving adult voice to an ethos of humility."

54. Jules Glanzer (1978), 5.

55. Tim L. Waltner, *The Times and Life of Smokey Joe Mendel* (Freeman, S.Dak.: Pine Hill Press, 1992), 25, 60. Other successful Prairieleut athletes included Elrod Glanzer, a football player who signed with the Denver Broncos; Ruth Kleinsasser, who won the 1984 Olympics trials in the 1500 meter run; and Kris Tschetter, an LPGA golfer.

56. Joe Mendel, interview with author (July 1993).

57. Ebenezer MB Church congregational records. CMBSH.

58. The KMB "Questionnaire" asked all applicants to "state briefly your call into the ministry."

59. C. F. Plett (1985), 136.

60. Clarence Hofer, interview with author (June 1993).

61. Conservative Mennonite ministers interviewed (1985–1989) universally lamented the loss of the multiple ministry concept in other Mennonite groups.

62. The Hutterian Brethren, eds., *The Chronicle of the Hutterian Brethren, Volume I* (Rifton, N.Y.: Plough, 1987), 756.

63. Emmanuel Mennonite Brethren Church, eds., *Our Church, Its History and Constitution* (1980), Article VIII, number 4. CMBSH.

64. Joseph A. Kleinsasser (1979), 75.

65. Interviews with David L. Hofer (June 1993), Walter Warkentin (June 1998), and Nancy Warkentin Neufeld (March 1993 and June 1998). The other three members of the prayer group who participated in the lot-casting were David Thiessen, John Strain, and Herman Pettit.

66. The Hutterian Brethren, eds. (1987), 423.

67. Doreen Mierau, "Prairie Peace-makers," *Saskatchewan Valley News* (June 8, 1967), 7.

68. "Suggested modifications for the Ebenezer MB Church Constitution" (1961, n.a.). Emmanuel MB Church *Constitution*, 4, 5. CMBSH.

69. Business meeting minutes of the Mennonite Brethren Church of Fresno (February 1945). CMBS. Rod Janzen, "Jacob D. Hofer: Evangelist, Minister and Carpenter," *California Mennonite Historical Newsletter* (May 1994), 1, 2, and 4–8.

70. Emmanuel MB Church, eds., *Our Church, Its History and Constitution* (1980), Article VIII, number 2. Salem MB Church *Constitution* (1970), Article IV, section i, clause h. CMBSH.

71. John J. Kleinsasser, "Questionnaire About the History of Your Church," 11. CMBSH.

72. *Zion MB Church Constitution* (1962), Article I, section 2J. CMBS.

73. Salem MB Church *Constitution* (1968), Section IIj. CMBSH.

74. Ebenezer MB Church *Constitution* (1968), 12. CMBSH.

75. Emmanuel MB Church *Constitution* (1980), Article III, number 12. CMBSH.

76. David W. Tschetter, "Questionnaire on the History of Your Church," 3. CMBSH.

77. Zion KMB Church, congregational records. CMBS.

78. Emmanuel MB Church *Constitution*, 4, 5. CMBSH.

79. The Hutterian Brethren, eds. (1987), 1543 entry.

80. Hutterian Brethren, eds., *Die Lieder der Hutterischen Bruder* (Scottdale, Pa.: Herald Press, 1914), 669.

81. Harold Bloom, *The American Religion* (New York: Simon and Schuster, 1992). Richard Quebedeaux, *The Worldly Evangelicals* (San Francisco: Harper and Row, 1978). Wade Roof, *A Generation of Seekers* (San Francisco: Harper and Collins, 1993).

82. Salem MB Church *Constitution* (1968), Section IIh. CMBSH. Neu Hutterthaler Mennonite Church *Constitution* (1974), Article IVn. FAA. Emmanuel MB Church, eds., *Our Church, Its History and Constitution* (1980). FAA.

83. Friedrich Kuentsche (1972), 251.

84. Hutterian Brethren, eds. (1987), 94.

85. Calvin Redekop, "Economic Developments in the United States, 1940–1960" (paper presented at Mennonite Brethren symposium, Fresno, California, February 1993).

86. Karl A. Peter and Ian Whitaker, "The Changing Role of Hutterite Women," In *Prairie Forum* 7 (1987), 269. Karl A. Peter, *The Dynamics of Hutterite Society* (Edmonton: University of Alberta Press, 1987), 199–204.

87. Werner Packull, *Hutterite Beginnings* (Baltimore: The Johns Hopkins University Press, 1995), 241.

88. Lesley Masuk (1998), 111, 118, 132.

89. Karl A. Peter and Ian Whitaker (1987), 270. See also Ruth Baer Lambach, "Colony Girl," in Wendy E. Chmielewski, ed., *Women in Spiritual and Communitarian Societies in the United States* (Syracuse, N.Y.: Syracuse University Press, 1993). This information was confirmed by interviews with numerous Hutterite men and women.

90. Lesley Masuk (1998), 128.

91. Lesley Masuk (1998), 79, 104.

92. Willis Kleinsasser, "Memoirs," in Walter Kleinsasser, ed., *Memoirs of the Kleinsasser Siblings* (Hillsboro, Kans.: self-published, 1990), 131.

93. C. F. Plett (1985), 114.

94. David L. Hofer, interview with author (June 1993). Hofer is a nephew of Jacob D. Hofer.

95. Walter Warkentin, interview with author (June 1998). Herman Pettit and Helen Wessel, *Jubilee: Autobiography of Herman Pettit* (Fresno, Calif.: Pathway, 1979), 105, 106.

96. Willis Kleinsasser (1990), 133.

97. Nancy Warkentin Neufeld, interview with author (March 1993).

98. "KMB Women's Missionary Society Finances, Disbursements and Reports" (1945–1961). CMBS.

99. Valerie Rempel, "She Hath Done What She Could: The Development of the Women's Missionary Services in the Mennonite Brethren Church of the United States" (paper presented at Mennonite Brethren symposium, Fresno, California, February 1993), 4.

100. Valerie Rempel (1993), 4.

101. Stephen M. Nolt, "Formal Mutual Aid Structures Among American Mennonites and Brethren: Assimilation and Reconstructed Ethnicity," *Journal of American Ethnic History* (Spring 1998), 82.

11. Customs That Remained (pp. 226–242)

First epigraph. Arnold M. Hofer, ed., *A History of the Hutterite-Mennonites* (Freeman, S.Dak.: HCC, 1974), 167.

Second epigraph. Arnold M. Hofer, ed. (1974), 162.

1. This was substantiated by Herfried Scheer, "The Hutterian-German Dialect," *Mennonite Quarterly Review* (July 1980), 243.

2. Diena Schmidt, ed., *The Northern District Conference of the General Conference Mennonite Church, 1891–1991* (Freeman, S.Dak.: Northern District Conference of the General Conference Mennonite Church, 1991), 159.

3. Joe Mendel, interview with author (July 1993).

4. Conversations with Egon Hofer (February 1993); Gloria Glanzer Thiessen (May 1998), Albert and Edna Wurtz (July 1993); and with many other Prairie People.

5. Walter Warkentin, interview with author (June 1998).

6. Jake Gross, interview with author (July 1993).

7. Herfried Scheer (1980), 229, 232.

8. Walter Hoover, *Hutterian-English Dictionary* (Saskatoon, Sask.: self-published, 1997).

9. Walter Hoover, *The Hutterian Language* (Saskatoon, Sask.: self-published, 1997).

10. Walter Hoover, *The Hutterian Language* (Saskatoon, Sask.: self-published, 1997), 24.

11. Joseph A. Wipf, "The Phonetics of the Hutterite Dialect" (unpublished M.A. thesis, University of Colorado, 1966), 243. FAA.

12. Donald Macedo, "English Only: The Tongue-Tying of America," in Richard Monk, ed., *Taking Sides* (Guilford, Conn.: Dushkin, 1994), 135–145. See also Kenneth Monteiro, *Ethnicity and Psychology* (Dubuque, Iowa: Kendall/Hunt, 1995); and William Fischer, David Gerber, Jorge Guitart, and Maxine Seller, eds., *Identity, Community and Pluralism in American Life* (New York: Oxford University Press, 1997).

13. Delbert Wiens, "From the Village to the City," *direction* (October 1973 and January 1974), 99.

14. Public statement by J. B. Toews (Mennonite Brethren Symposium, February 1993).

15. Aaron Glanzer, correspondence with author (September 1987).

16. Mrs. Paul S. Gross, ed., *A History of the Salem Mennonite Brethren Church* (Freeman, S.Dak.: Pine Hill Press, 1986), 49.

17. KMB General Conference Meeting bulletins (Dinuba, California, 1938). CMBS.

18. David Vetter, "Emmanuel MB Church, 1919–1959." FAA

19. Joe Mendel, interview with author (July 1993).

20. Emmanuel Mennonite Church, Doland, *50th Anniversary* (1972, n.a., n.p.), 21. FAA.

21. Note, for example, Joanita Kant, *The Hutterite Cookbook* (Watertown, S.Dak.: Sioux River Press, 1984), and Samuel Hofer, *The Hutterite Community Cookbook* (Saskatoon, Sask.: Hofer Publishers, 1995).

22. David L. Hofer, interview with author (June 1993).

23. Larry Martens, "Musical Thought and Practice in the Hutterite Community" (unpublished M.A. thesis, University of Kansas, 1960), 55. Also note entry in Zion KMB Church church records (July 27, 1943); and Helen Martens, "Hutterite Songs and Aural Transmission of Their Melodies from the 16th Century" (unpublished doctoral dissertation, Columbia University, 1968).

24. Willis Kleinsasser, "Memoirs," in Walter Kleinsasser, ed., *Memoirs of the Kleinsasser Siblings* (1990), 131.

25. Correspondence from John J. Kleinsasser to Sylvester Dirks (December 22, 1948). CMBS.

26. Glendon Becker, interview with author (March 1994). Becker's father had pastored a Prairieleut congregation for a number of years.

27. Walter Warkentin, interview with author (June 1998).

28. Doreen Mierau (1967), 7.

29. Samuel Hofer, *The Hutterites: Lives and Images of a Communal People* (Saskatoon, Sask.: Hofer Publishing, 1998), 143.

30. This statement was made to the author with regard to the book, *Perceptions of the South Dakota Hutterites in the 1980's* (Freeman, S.Dak.: Freeman Publishing Company, 1984).

31. Jerald Hiebert, correspondence with author (January 1994).

32. Karl A. Peter, *The Dynamics of Hutterite Society: An Analytical Approach* (Edmonton: University of Alberta Press, 1987), 130.

33. The "great noise" is Saul Bellow's term for information overload. See Saul Bellow, *The Dean's December* (New York: Pocket Books, 1982).

34. Lesley Masuk, interview with author (June 1998).

35. Tim Waltner, "Hofer Given 2 Life Sentences," Freeman *Courier* (November 1984), 1, 10.

36. Catherine Masuk, "Reunion of the Prairieleut Hutterites," Rosthern, *Valley News* (n.d., circa July 1997).

37. Ibid. Walter Hoover, "Di Hutrisha Shproch: An Introduction to the language of the Hutterian Prairie People," presentation at Langham Prairie People reunion (July 1997).

38. "Around the Town," Freeman *Courier* (July 21, 1993), 9.

39. Amos Kleinsasser, untitled reflection on visits to a number of colonies, a class assignment for "Hutterite Studies," Freeman College (January 1985).

40. Lesley Masuk, "Patriarchy, Technology and the Lives of Hutterite Women: A Field Study," (unpublished master's thesis, University of Saskatchewan, 1998), 113.

41. Gwen Shaw, interviews with author (July 1993 and June 1998). Interviews with Gloria Glanzer Thiessen (May 1998), and Ernest and Evelyn Schmidt (May 1998).

42. Gwen Shaw, *Unconditional Surrender* (Jasper, Alaska: End Times Handmaidens, 1985), 166, 288.

43. Gwen Shaw, interview with author (June 1998).

44. Gwen Shaw (1985), 127.

45. Solomon F. Walter, unpublished, untitled autobiographical account (1985). A copy is in the possession of the author.

46. Victor Peters, "Pockets of High Fertility in the United States," *Population Bulletin* (November 1968), 26–44.

47. Alice O. Martin, "The Founder Effect in a Human Isolate: Evolutionary Implications," *American Journal of Physical Anthropology* 32 (1986), 351–368. Sandra Hartzog, "Population Genetic Studies of a Human Isolate: The Hutterites of North America" (unpublished doctoral dissertation, University of Massachusetts, 1971), 5.

48. Evan Eichler, interview and correspondence with author (June 1998).

49. Norman Hofer, correspondence with author (August 1993).

50. It was customary in Prairieleut communities for a female spouse to join her husband's church.

51. Evangeline Kroeker, *Henry Kroeker, 1857–1977* (n.p., n.d.), 9. CMBSH.

52. "Hutterthal Mennonite Church Marriage Records." FAA.

53. David P. Gross and Arnold M. Hofer, eds., "Neu Hutterthaler Mennonite Church Records" (unpublished, 1992). HCC.

54. Marriage records in Jacob J. Mendel, *A History of the People of East Freeman, Silver Lake and West Freeman* (Freeman, S.Dak.: Pine Hill Press, 1961), 105–161, 238, were helpful in providing additional information for much of the following analysis.

55. Egon Hofer, interview with author (February 1993). Zion KMB Church congregational record cards. CMBS.

56. Zion KMB Church congregational records. CMBS.

57. Miriam E. Warner, "Mennonite Brethren: The Maintenance of Continuity in a Religious Ethnic Group" (unpublished doctoral dissertation, University of California, Berkeley, 1985).

58. Marian Kleinsasser Towne, interview with author (July 1998). Michael J. Arlen, *A Passage to Ararat* (New York: Ballantine, 1975). See also Mark Arax, *In My Father's Name* (New York: Simon and Schuster, 1996).

59. David P. Gross, correspondence with author (September 1987). Reuben Goertz provided context for the "hidden debtor" account. Goertz, a specialist in southeastern South Dakota history, and an active member of the Society of Germans From Russia, died in late 1993. His large collection of manuscripts was donated to the CWS.

60. Olga Stucky and Lillian Graber, eds., *Freeman Facts and Fiction* (Freeman, S.Dak.: Pine Hill Press, 1979), 88–90.

61. Information on Lohrentz Tschetter has been difficult to document. Stories included come from conversations with many prominent Prairie People, most of whom requested anonymity. These stories were told too often and by too many individuals to be ignored. They have become part of the folklore of the Prairieleut community, whether certified or not.

62. Swiss German Centennial Committee, eds., *The Swiss-Germans in South Dakota: From Volhynia to Dakota Territory* (Freeman, S.Dak.: Swiss-German Centennial Committee, 1974), 8, 12, 23.

63. Elizabeth Hofer served as a missionary in China. Rebecca Glanzer worked in India, Mary Wollman in Ethiopia, and Darlene Hofer Lomheim in Mexico and Brazil.

64. Correspondence of Joseph W. Walter to the Mennonite Brethren Board of Missions (January 1963 and September 1963). CMBS.

65. Joe Walter, interview with author (June 1998).

66. Arnold M. Hofer, correspondence with author (September 1987). Reuben Goertz, interview with author (July 1993). Paul G. Tschetter, interview with author (June 1998).

12. The Prairieleut Dilemma (pp. 243–256)

First epigraph. Hutterian Brethren, eds., *The Chronicle of the Hutterian Brethren, Volume I* (Rifton, N.Y.: Plough, 1987), 389.

Second epigraph. Joshua Hofer, ed., "Hutterite *Lehren* on Matthew 6: 1–38," (Elie, Man.: James Valley Colony), 20.

Third epigraph. Hans Decker, interview with author (July 1983).

1. Arnold M. Hofer, interviews with author (July 1993 and June 1998).

2. John D. Unruh, *A Century of Mennonites in Dakota* (Pierre: South Dakota Historical Society, 1972), 74.

3. Arnold M. Hofer, interviews with author (July 1993 and August 1997).

4. Jacob J. Mendel, *A History of the People of East Freeman, Silver Lake and West Freeman* (Freeman, S.Dak.: Pine Hill Press, 1961), 105.

5. Delbert Wiens, Marj Gerbrandt Wiens et al., "A Family Tribute," in Frances Janzen Voth, *The House of Jacob* (Tucson, Ariz.: self-published, 1984), 319. Douglas Wiens was killed in a dynamite explosion in the Sierra Nevadas in 1981.

6. Delbert Wiens, "From the Village to the City," *direction* (October 1973 and January 1974), 130.

7. Donald Kraybill, *The Amish Struggle With Modernity* (Hanover, N.H.: University Press of New England, 1994).

8. D. Aidan McQuillan, *Prevailing Over Time* (Lincoln: University of Nebraska Press, 1990). See also Robert T. Handy, *A History of the Churches in the United States and Canada* (Oxford: Oxford University Press, 1976); Martin Marty, *The Righteous Empire: The Protestant Experience in America* (New York: Harper and Row, 1970); and Thomas Wheeler, ed., *The Immigrant Experience: The Anguish of Becoming an American* (New York: Penguin, 1971).

9. Delbert Wiens, *New Wineskins for Old Wine: A Study of the Mennonite Brethren Church* (Hillsboro, Kans.: Mennonite Brethren Publishing House, 1965). Delbert Wiens (1973 and 1974), 2.

10. The Hutterian Brethren, eds., *The Chronicle of the Hutterian Brethren, Volume I* (Rifton, N.Y.: Plough, 1987), 149.

11. Cornell West, *Prophetic Thought in Postmodern Times* (Monroe, Maine: Common Courage Press, 1993).

12. The Hutterian Brethren, eds. (1987), 83.

13. The Hutterian Brethren, eds. (1987), 118.

14. James M. Stayer, *The German Peasants War and Anabaptist Community of Goods* (Montreal: McGill/Queens University Press, 1991), 143, 144. Werner Packull, *Hutterite Beginnings: Communitarian Experiments During the Reformation* (Baltimore: The Johns Hopkins University Press, 1995), 226–235.

Glossary

· ·

Anabaptists—Literally, "rebaptizers" (*ana-* being the Greek prefix meaning "re-"), the Anabaptists were radical sixteenth-century Christians who believed in the separation of church and state, pacifism, believers baptism, and a strict interpretation of church discipline. Anabaptists were disliked and heavily persecuted by both Catholics and Protestants. Hutterians and Mennonites emerged from this religious movement and have carried on the tradition.

Anfechtung—The German word for "temptation" or "contestation." Hutterians used this term to describe a deep spiritual struggle, wherein God and Satan fought for control of an individual's soul.

Basel—The South German word for female cousin or aunt. Hutterians attached the word to the first names of older female community members, to denote respect.

Bruderhof—A German word meaning "dwelling place of brothers." This term was used by Hutterians historically both as a designation for their communal villages (in North America referred to as "colonies") and as a description of the way of life preached and lived therein.

In the late 1990s, Bruderhof was also the most commonly employed designation for a communal group also known as the "Society of Brothers." Bruderhof members were followers of German theologian Eberhard Arnold, whose European commune had merged, temporarily, with the Hutterites in the 1930s.

In 1974, the Bruderhof had once again been accepted into full membership with the Hutterites. Sixteen years later, however, the *Dariusleut* and *Lehrerleut* Hutterites ended that association. A majority of the *Schmiedeleut* Hutterites followed suit one year later, causing a major division within the latter group, which had not been healed, even after the pro-Bruderhof faction itself severed relations with the Bruderhof in 1995.

In the late 1990s, the 2,500-member English-speaking Bruderhof included industry-based communal villages in such diverse locations as Pennsylvania, New York, Connecticut, and Great Britain.

Dariusleut—Literally, the "followers of Darius Walter," a late nineteenth-century Hutterite minister. They are a branch of the communal Hutterites, with colonies in Washington, Montana, Alberta, British Columbia, and Saskatchewan.

Gelassenheit—German word meaning "yieldedness." The Hutterites used the term to indicate the subordination of personal possessions and self-will to the community of faith.

Gemeinschaft—The German word for "community." Hutterites preferred the term *Gutergemeinschaft*, which they used to refer to community of goods, though in modern German, it generally referred to property jointly owned by husband and wife.

General Conference Mennonite Church (GC)—A conference established in 1860 as a result of a division in the Swiss-American Mennonite Church (MC). This was the conference that the majority of Russian Mennonites had joined upon arrival in North America in the late 1800s. The GC and Mennonite Church (MC) plan to fully "integrate" in the year 2002. The word "merge" has become outdated.

Gesangbuch—Literally, "songbook." The Hutterian hymnal, comprised of pieces written by Hutterian and other Anabaptist martyrs and church leaders.

Habaner—Those Hutterians who converted to the Catholic faith in the seventeenth and eighteenth centuries in Slovakia. They continued to live there as an identifiable ethnic group into the mid-twentieth century.

Hutter—The designation "Hutter" has been accepted by many Prairieleut descendents in South Dakota as a way to differentiate their unique ethno-religious community from that of the communal Hutterites. The term initially had negative connotations and continues to have such in some contexts. Noncommunal Hutterians are also referred to as "Prairie People," "Prairieleut," "Hutterite-Mennonites," "Hutterisch," "independent Hutterites," and "noncolony Hutterites."

Hutterian—The term "Hutterian" indicates the traditional Anabaptist beliefs and practices adhered to by communal and noncommunal "Hutterites." This word also refers to members or descendents of that ethno-religious group and is often used adjectively.

Hutterisch—The Austrian dialect/language, originating in Carinthia and the Tyrol, that is spoken by Hutterians.

Hutterite—The name most commonly used by communal Hutterians, historically and at present.

Hutterite Chronicle—A historical account of Hutterian events, beliefs, and practices, from the earliest days of the movement in the 1520s, to the present. The *Chronicle* is constantly, yet inconsistently, updated; large parts have been translated into English.

Krimmer Mennonite Brethren (KMB)—A group of Mennonites led by Jacob A. Wiebe, who separated from the Mennonite Church in the Russian Crimea in 1869. "Krimmer" is simply German for "Crimean." The KMB Conference merged with the Mennonite Brethren Conference (MB) in 1960.

Lehren—Literally, German for doctrine or precepts. They are the sermons traditionally read in Hutterian church services. Most were written in the sixteenth and seventeenth centuries. They are believed to be divinely inspired in their interpretations of the Bible.

Lehrerleut—Literally, the "followers of the Lehrer" (teacher) Jacob Wipf, a nineteenth-century Hutterian leader. The Lehrerleut are the most conservative branch of the communal Hutterites. Colonies are located in Montana, Alberta, and Saskatchewan.

Leut—Literally, German for "people." The Hutterites employ the term in conjunction with names or professions of founders of the three communal branches. It is also used to define the ethno-religious community to which colony residents (or Prairie People) belong. In Hutterisch the term used is "Leit," instead of "Leut."

Low German Mennonites—Those Mennonites who trace their ancestry to the Netherlands, Belgium, and/or northern Germany, but who eventually settled collectively in places like Prussia, Russia, Paraguay, Canada, and the United States. "Low German" is the dialect/language spoken by these people.

Mennonite—This term is used to designate various denominational groups, all of whom trace their theological and organizational roots to sixteenth-century Dutch Anabaptist leader Menno Simons.

Mennonite Brethren (MB)—The MB Conference was organized by dissenters in 1860 as an evangelical offshoot of the Mennonite Church in Russia.

Mennonite Church (MC)—The largest of the various Mennonite conferences in North America. The MC, with churches located primarily in the eastern part of the United States and Canada, is composed primarily of Mennonites of Swiss ethnicity. As noted, the MC intends to merge with the GC in the year 2002.

Prairieleut—The word "Prairieleut" means literally "people of the prairies." This term was used to describe persons of Hutterian ethnicity who decided not to live communally when they arrived in North America in the late 1800s. Most of them also had not lived communally in Russia.

Schmiedeleut—Literally, the "followers of the *Schmied*" (blacksmith) Michael Waldner, a Hutterite minister who resurrected community of goods among the Hutterians in 1859. This is the most progressive branch of the Hutterites, with colonies in Manitoba, North and South Dakota, and Minnesota. The Schmiedeleut were, in the late 1990s, experiencing major internal conflict, which had split the group in two.

Schreien—The word "schreien" is a form of the German word "Schrei," literally indicating a cry or scream. Hutterians used the word to describe a curse imposed by one individual on another, often unintentionally. The curse was sometimes thought to be activated by feelings of envy and covetousness, much akin to evil-eye belief.

Vetter—The German word for a male cousin. Hutterians added the word to the first names of older male members as a respectful appellation.

Select Bibliography

· ·

Albanese, Catherine. 1992. *America: Religion and Religions*. Belmont, Calif.: Wadsworth Publishing.

Anderson, James. 1972. "The Pentecost Preaching of Acts 2: an Aspect of Hutterite Theology." Unpublished doctoral dissertation, University of Iowa.

Barkan, Elliot. 1995. "Racism, Religion and Nationality in American Society: A Model of Ethnicity—From Contact to Assimilation. *Journal of American Ethnic Studies* (Winter): 38–75.

Bender, Harold, ed. 1931. "A Hutterite School Discipline of 1578 and Peter Scherer's Address of 1568 to the Schoolmasters." *Mennonite Quarterly Review* (October): 231–244.

Bennett, John. 1967. *Hutterian Brethren*. Stanford, Calif.: Stanford University Press.

Bergland, Betty. 1997. "Ethnic Archeology in the Nineteenth-Century Midwest." *Journal of American Ethnic History* (Fall): 76–82.

Brednick, Rolf. 1981. *The Bible and the Plough*. Ottawa, Ont.: National Museums of Canada.

Chmielewski, Wendy, ed. 1993. *Women in Spiritual and Communitarian Societies in the United States*. Syracuse: Syracuse University Press.

Christopher, Stefan C., ed. 1972. "A Description of the Beginning of True Christian Community Among the Schmiedeleut Hutterians, As It Began by the Power of the Spirit." Unpublished manuscript.

Correll, Ernst, ed. 1937. "Mennonite Immigration into Manitoba: Sources and Documents, 1872, 1873." *Mennonite Quarterly Review* (July): 196–227 and October: 267–283.

Ehrenpreis, Andreas. 1978. *Brotherly Community: The Highest Command of Love, 1650*. Rifton, N.Y.: Plough Publishing House.

Eichler, Evan. 1998. "Hutterian Surnames." Unpublished manuscript.

Emmanuel Mennonite Brethren Church, eds. 1980. *Our Church, Its History and Constitution*. Freeman, S.Dak.: Pine Hill Press.

Fischer, Hans. 1956. *Jacob Huter: Leben, Froemmigkeit, Briefe*. Newton, Kans.: Mennonite Publication Office.

Friedmann, Robert. 1961. *Hutterite Studies*. Goshen, Ind.: Mennonite Historical Society.

Friedmann, Robert, ed. 1965. "The Reestablishment of Communal Life Among the Hutterites in Russia (1858)." *Mennonite Quarterly Review* (April): 147–152.

Friesen, Peter M. 1978. *The Mennonite Brotherhood in Russia, 1789–1910*. Fresno, Calif.: Center for Mennonite Brethren Studies.

Giesinger, Adam. 1981. *From Catherine to Khruschchev: The Story of Russia's Germans*. Lincoln, Nebr.: Society of Germans from Russia.

Gingerich, Melvin. 1949. *Service for Peace*. Akron, Pa.: Mennonite Central Committee.

Glanzer, Paul E., Marilyn Wipf, Jeanette Hofer, eds. 1988. *A Century of God's Blessing, Neu Hutterthaler Mennonite Church, 1888–1988*. Freeman, S.Dak.: Pine Hill Press.

Grob, Gerald, and George Billias, eds. 1992. *Interpretations of American History, Volume II.* New York: Free Press.

Grimmelshausen, H. J. C. 1962. *Adventures of a Simpleton.* New York, N.Y.: Frederick Ungar Publishing.

Gross, Erwin R., ed. 1968. *History of the Hutterthal Mennonite Church, 1879–1968.* Freeman, S.Dak.: Pine Hill Press.

Gross, Leonard. 1980. *The Golden Years of the Hutterites.* Scottdale, Pa.: Herald Press.

Gross, Paul S. 1965. *The Hutterite Way.* Saskatoon, Sask.: Freeman Publishing Co.

Gross, Mrs. Paul S., ed. 1986. *A History of the Salem Mennonite Brethren Church.* Freeman, S.Dak.: Pine Hill Press.

Harrison, Wes. 1997. *Andreas Ehrenpreis and Hutterite Faith and Practice.* Kitchener, Ont.: Herald Press.

Hartse, Carolyn. 1993. "On the Colony: Social and Religious Change Among Contemporary Hutterites." Unpublished doctoral dissertation, University of New Mexico.

Hiebert, Clarence, ed. 1974. *Brothers in Deed to Brothers in Need.* North Newton, Kans.: Faith and Life Press.

Hiebert, Jerald. 1992. "History of Stirling Mennonite Church." Unpublished paper. Stirling, Alb.: Stirling Mennonite Church.

Hofer, Arnold M., ed., 1974. *A History of the Hutterite-Mennonites.* Freeman, S.Dak.: Hutterian Centennial Committee.

———. 1985. *Hutterite Roots.* Freeman, S.Dak.: Hutterian Centennial Committee.

———. 1997. *The Diaries of Joseph "Yos" Hofer.* Freeman, S.Dak.: Hutterian Centennial Committee.

Hofer, Arnold M., and Pauline Becker. 1991. *John Hofer and Anna Wurtz Family Record Book.* Freeman, S.Dak.: self-published.

Hofer, David M. 1924. *The Famine and Our Trip Around the World.* Hillsboro, Kans.: Mennonite Brethren Publishing House.

Hofer, Elizabeth F., and Samuel J. R. Hofer. n.d. *God's Way of Salvation for the Seven Dispensations and Building God's Kingdom.* Carpenter, S.Dak.: self-published.

———. n.d. *Most Popular Bible Questions and Answers Everybody Ought to Know.* Carpenter, S.Dak.: self-published.

Hofer, Jacob M., ed. 1931. "The Diary of Paul Tschetter." *Mennonite Quarterly Review* (July): 112–127; (October): 198–219.

Hofer, Joshua, ed. 1981. "Sermon on Acts 2: 40–42." Elie, Man.: James Valley Colony.

———. 1985. "Sermon on Matthew 6." Elie, Man.: James Valley Colony.

Hofer, Samuel. 1991. *Born Hutterite.* Saskatoon, Sask.: Hofer Publishers.

———. 1998. *The Hutterites: Lives and Images of a Communal People.* Saskatoon, Sask.: Hofer Publishers.

Hoover, Walter. 1997. *Hutterian–English Dictionary.* Saskatoon, Sask.: self-published.

———. 1997. *The Hutterian Language.* Saskatoon, Sask.: self-published.

Horsch, John. 1931. *Hutterian Brethren.* Scottdale, Pa.: Herald Press.

Hostetler, John A. 1974. *Hutterite Society.* Baltimore: The Johns Hopkins University Press (revised 1997).

Hostetler, John A., Leonard Gross, and Elizabeth Bender, eds. 1975. *Selected Hutterian Documents in Translation.* Philadelphia: Temple University Press.

Hostetler, John A., and Gertrude Huntington. 1996. *The Hutterites in North America.* New York: Harcourt Brace.

Huseboe, Arthur, ed. 1982. *Siouxland Heritage*. Sioux Falls: South Dakota Historical Society.

Hutterian Brethren, eds. 1914. *Die Lieder der Hutterischen Bruder Gesangbuch*. Scottdale, Pa.: Herald Press.

———. 1987. *The Chronicle of the Hutterian Brethren, Volume I*. Rifton, N.Y.: Plough Publishing House.

Janzen, Rod. 1984. *Perceptions of the South Dakota Hutterites in the 1980's*. Freeman, S.Dak.: Freeman Publishing Company.

———. 1986. *Terry Miller: The Pacifist Politician, From Hutterite Colony to State Legislature*. Freeman, S.Dak.: Pine Hill Press.

———. 1993. "The Hutterite High School Experiment." *Syzygy, Journal of Alternative Religion and Culture* (Summer): 339–348.

———. 1994. "Five Paradigms of Ethnic Relations." *Social Education* (October): 349–354.

———. 1994. "Jacob D. Hofer, Evangelist, Minister and Carpenter." *California Mennonite Historical Society Newsletter* (May): 1, 2, and 4–8.

———. 1994. "Multicultural Confusion." *Educational Leadership* (May): 9–12.

———. 1994. "The Prairieleut: A Forgotten Hutterite People." *Communal Societies*. Pp. 67–89.

Johansen, John P. 1963. *Immigrant Settlements and Social Organization in South Dakota*. Brookings: South Dakota State University Press.

Jost, Esther, ed. 1987. *75 Years of Fellowship. Pacific District Conference of the MB Churches 1912–1987*. Fresno, Calif.: Pacific District Conference of Mennonite Brethren Churches.

Juhnke, James. 1989. *Vision, Doctrine, War: Mennonite Identity and Organization in America, 1890–1930*. Scottdale, Pa.: Herald Press.

Kaplan, Bert, and Thomas F. A. Plaut. 1956. *Personality and Communal Society*. Lawrence: University of Kansas Press.

Karolevitz, Robert. 1972. *Yankton: A Pioneer Past*. Aberdeen, S.Dak.: North Dakota State College Press.

Kauffman, J. Howard, and Leo Driedger. 1991. *The Mennonite Mosaic*. Scottdale, Pa.: Herald Press.

Klassen, Peter J. 1964. *The Economics of Anabaptism*. London: Mouton.

Kleinsasser, Joseph A. 1979. *A History of the Bethel Mennonite Brethren Church, 1902–1979*. Freeman, S.Dak.: Pine Hill Press.

Kleinsasser, Walter, ed. 1990. *Memoirs of the Kleinsasser Siblings*. Hillsboro, Kans.: self-published.

Koop, Michael, and Carolyn Torma. 1984. *Folk Building of the South Dakota German-Russians*. Vermillion: University of South Dakota Press.

Kraybill, Donald. 1994. *The Amish Struggle with Modernity*. Hanover, N.H.: University Press of New England.

Lacey, Michael, ed. 1991. *Religion and 20th Century American Intellectual Life*. New York: Cambridge University Press.

Larsen-Freeman, Diane, and Michael H. Long. 1991. *An Introduction to Second Language Acquisition Research*. New York: Longman.

Loewen, Harry. 1988. *Why I Am a Mennonite: Essays on Mennonite Identity*. Scottdale, Pa.: Herald Press.

Martin, Alice O. 1986. "The Founder Effect in a Human Isolate: Evolutionary Implications." *American Journal of Physical Anthropology* 32: 351–368.

Masuk, Lesley. 1998. "Patriarchy, Technology and the Lives of Hutterite Women: A Field Study." Unpublished M.A. thesis, University of Saskatchewan.

McMaster, Richard K. 1985. *Land, Piety, Peoplehood: The Establishment of Mennonite Communities in America, 1683–1790*. Scottdale, Pa.: Herald Press.

Mendel, Jacob J. 1961. *A History of the People of East Freeman, Silver Lake and West Freeman*. Freeman, S.Dak.: Pine Hill Press.

Mennonite Central Committee, eds. 1980. *Mennonites and Conscientious Objection*. Akron, Pa.: Mennonite Central Committee.

Miller, Timothy. 1998. *The Quest for Utopia in Twentieth Century America, Volume I*. Syracuse, N.Y.: Syracuse University Press.

Nachtigall, Gary. 1972. "Mennonite Migration and Settlements of California." Unpublished M.A. thesis, California State University, Fresno.

Nolt, Stephen M. 1998. "Formal Mutual Aid Structures Among American Mennonites and Brethren: Assimilation and Reconstructed Ethnicity." *Journal of American Ethnic History* (Spring): 71–86.

O'Brien, E., P. A. Kerber, C. B. Jorde, and A. A. Rogers. 1994. "Founder Effect: An assessment of variation in genetic contributions among founders." *Human Biology* (April): 185–204.

Packull, Werner. 1995. *Hutterite Beginnings: Communitarian Experiments during the Reformation*. Baltimore: The Johns Hopkins University Press.

Peter, Karl A. 1987. *The Dynamics of Hutterite Society: An Analytical Approach*. Edmonton: University of Alberta Press.

Peters, Victor. 1965. *All Things Common*. Minneapolis: University of Minnesota Press.

———. 1968. "Pockets of High Fertility in the United States." *Population Bulletin* (November): 26–44.

Peterson, Nancy, ed. 1989. *People of the Old Missoury*. Frederick, Col.: Renaissance House.

Pfeiffer, John. 1970. *The German-Russians and Their Immigration to South Dakota*. Brookings: South Dakota State University Press.

Plett, C. F. 1985. *The Story of the Krimmer Mennonite Brethren Church*. Hillsboro, Kans.: Kindred Press.

Rath, George. 1972. *The Black Sea Germans in the Dakotas*. Freeman, S.Dak.: Pine Hill Press.

Redekop, Calvin. 1989. *Mennonite Society*. Baltimore: The Johns Hopkins University Press.

Redekop, John. 1972. *Making Political Decisions: A Christian Response*. Scottdale, Pa.: Herald Press.

Rich, Elaine Sommers. 1983. *Mennonite Women: A Story of God's Faithfulness, 1683–1983*. Scottdale, Pa.: Herald Press.

Rideman, Peter. 1970. *Account of Our Religion, Doctrine and Faith*. Rifton, N.Y.: Plough Publishing House.

Schlabach, Theron. 1988. *Peace, Faith, Nation: Mennonites and Amish in 19th Century America*. Scottdale, Pa.: Herald Press.

Schmidt, Diena, ed. 1991. *The Northern District Conference of the General Conference Mennonite Church, 1891–1991*. Freeman, S.Dak.: Pine Hill Press.

Shaw, Gwen Bergman. 1986. *Unconditional Surrender*. Jasper, Alaska: End-Time Handmaidens.

Stayer, James M. 1991. *The German Peasants War and Anabaptist Community of Goods*. Montreal: McGill/Queens University Press.

Stephenson, Peter H. 1991. *The Hutterian People: Ritual and Rebirth in the Evolution of Communal Life.* Lanham, Md.: University Press of America.

Stucky, Olga, and Lillian Graber, eds. 1979. *Freeman Facts and Fiction: 1879–1979.* Freeman, S.Dak.: Pine Hill Press.

Takaki, Ronald. 1993. *A History of Multicultural America.* New York: Little Brown.

Toews, John A. 1975. *A History of the Mennonite Brethren Church.* Hillsboro, Kans.: Mennonite Brethren Board of Christian Literature.

Toews, Paul. 1995. *Bridging Troubled Waters: The Mennonite Brethren at Mid-Twentieth Century.* Hillsboro, Kans.: Mennonite Brethren Historical Commission.

———. 1996. *Mennonites in American Society, 1930–1970.* Scottdale, Pa.: Herald Press.

Towne, Marian Kleinsasser, ed. 1994. *Bread of Life: Diaries and Memories of a Dakota Family, 1936–1945.* Freeman, S.Dak.: self-published.

Unruh, John D. 1972. *A Century of Mennonites in Dakota.* Pierre: South Dakota Historical Collections.

Voth, Frances Janzen. 1984. *The House of Jacob: The Story of Jacob Janzen, 1822–1885, and His Descendents.* Tucson, Ariz.: self-published.

Waldner, Marie. 1951. *For Half a Century.* Freeman, S.Dak.: Pine Hill Press.

Waltner, Emil, ed. 1968. *Banished for Faith.* Freeman, S.Dak.: Pine Hill Press (revised, 1989).

Waltner, Tim. 1992. *The Times and Life of Smokey Joe Mendel.* Freeman, S.Dak.: Pine Hill Press.

Warner, Miriam E. 1985. "Mennonite Brethren: the Maintenance of Continuity in a Religious Ethnic Group." Unpublished doctoral dissertation, University of California, Berkeley.

Wiebe, Katie Funk. 1979. *Women Among the Brethren.* Hillsboro, Kans.: Mennonite Brethren Board of Christian Literature.

Wiens, Delbert. 1965. *New Wineskins for Old Wine: A Study of the Mennonite Brethren Church.* Hillsboro, Kans.: Mennonite Brethren Publishing House.

———. 1973; 1974. "From the Village to the City." *direction* (October; January, reprint): 98–149.

Wipf, Elenora R. 1962. *The Andreas and Susann Glanzer Family Record, 1842–1962.* Freeman, S.Dak.: self-published.

Youmans, Vance Joseph. 1995. *The Plough and the Pen: Paul S. Gross and the Establishment of the Spokane Hutterian Brethren.* Boone, N.C.: Parkway Publishers.

Zieglschmid, A. J. F., ed. 1943. *Die Alteste Chronik der Hutterischen Bruder: Ein Sprachdenkmal aus Fruhneuhochdeutscher Zeit.* Philadelphia: Carl Schurz Memorial Foundation.

———. 1947. *Das Klein-Geschichtsbuch der Hutterischen Bruder.* Philadelphia: Carl Schurz Memorial Foundation.

Index

. . . .

University Press of New England publishes books under its own imprint and is the publisher for Brandeis University Press, Dartmouth College, Middlebury College Press, University of New Hampshire, Tufts University, and Wesleyan University Press.

About the Author

Rod Janzen was born in 1953, in Dinuba, California, and was raised in California's San Joaquin Valley. Janzen received his doctorate from the University of Southern California and also studied at the University of California, Santa Barbara, and at Oxford University. Janzen has published two previous books and a number of articles related to Anabaptist/Hutterian studies. He has also written a variety of pieces dealing with American ethnic history. Janzen serves as Professor of Social Sciences at Fresno Pacific University and is an active member of the Mennonite Church. He is the President of the California Mennonite Historical Society and serves as editor of *Communal Societies.*

Library of Congress Cataloging-in-Publication Data
Janzen, Rod
The prairie people :   forgotten Anabaptists   /   Rod Janzen.
 p.   cm.
Includes bibliographical references and index.
ISBN 0–87451–930–6 (cl. : alk paper).   —
ISBN 0–87451–931–4 (pbk. : alk paper)
 1. Hutterite Brethren—Great Plains—History.   I. Title.
BX8129.H8J36   1999
289.7'78—dc21   99–18711